Religion on the American Frontier

1783–1850

Vol. III

The Congregationalists

Religion on the American Frontier · 1783–1850

Vol. III
The Congregationalists

A Collection of Source Materials

By

WILLIAM WARREN SWEET

COOPER SQUARE PUBLISHERS, INC.

New York · 1964

This volume of
Congregational Source Materials
is dedicated to
The Faculty and Students, past and present, of the
Chicago Theological Seminary, founded by
frontier Congregationalists in 1855 to
train a ministry for the West

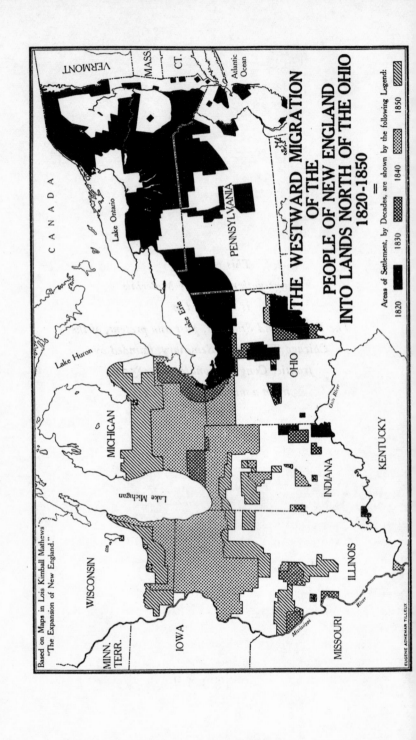

THE WESTWARD MIGRATION
OF THE
PEOPLE OF NEW ENGLAND
INTO LANDS NORTH OF THE OHIO
1820-1850
—
Areas of Settlement, by Decades, are shown by the following Legend:

1820   1830   1840   1850

Based on Maps in Lois Kimball Mathews'
"The Expansion of New England."

EUGENE ATHEMAN VILLEUX

PREFACE

THIS is the third volume in the series *Religion on the American Frontier*. This work has been in process since my coming to the University of Chicago in 1927, the original plan being to make available source materials for an understanding of all the religious forces which made any impact upon the frontier. The first volume, *The Baptists* (Henry Holt & Co., 1931), set the general pattern for the series, though it is hoped that each successive volume has profited from the experience gained as the work has proceeded.

It has been difficult to avoid duplicating some of the materials which have already appeared in the volume on *The Presbyterians* (Harper & Bros., 1936), since the Congregationalists and Presbyterians co-operated in such organizations as the American Home Missionary Society and the American Board of Commissioners for Foreign Missions, the principal agencies in carrying forward the operations of the Plan of Union. This, however, I think, has been successfully accomplished, and certain important factors in the operations of the Plan of Union have been made clear in this volume which may have been difficult to understand when approached from the Presbyterian angle.

As in both previous volumes I am indebted to several of my students who have been members of my seminars from 1935 to 1938 for rendering assistance in the editing of the manuscripts appearing in this volume. Mr. Alfred T. De-Groot, Winthrop S. Hudson, and Thomas P. Inabinett, members of my seminar in the spring quarter of 1938; Dr. Richard D. Leonard and William A. Karraker, members of my seminar in the autumn of 1935; and C. E. Buckingham and C. S. Hiltner, members of a previous seminar, deserve especial mention for their fine co-operation. Sidney E. Mead and Lewis K. Wheelock have worked with me as research assistants in various tasks connected with this volume. As in the Presbyterian volume, the maps have been prepared by Mr. Eugene A. Tilleux, a former member of my seminary, but now connected with the Statistical Review Section of the Works Progress Administration in Washington. My thanks are especially due to my colleague, Professor Matthew Spinka, former librarian of the Chicago Theological Seminary, who rendered invaluable service in putting at my disposal all the facilities of the library over which he presided and also for reading parts of the manuscript.

WILLIAM WARREN SWEET

UNIVERSITY OF CHICAGO
February 15, 1939

TABLE OF CONTENTS

PAGE

LIST OF ILLUSTRATIONS xi

PART I. GENERAL INTRODUCTION

CHAPTER

   I. CONGREGATIONALISM IN 1783 3

  II. WESTERN CONGREGATIONALISM AND THE PLAN OF UNION . 13

 III. CONGREGATIONAL HOME AND INDIAN MISSIONS 43

PART II. DOCUMENTS ILLUSTRATING THE WORK OF CONGREGATIONALISTS ON THE FRONTIER

  IV. THE MISSIONARY SOCIETY OF CONNECTICUT: LETTERS AND REPORTS FROM THE FRONTIER 67

   V. CHURCH RECORDS 106

  VI. MINUTES OF THE CONVENTION OF THE CONGREGATIONAL CHURCHES OF ILLINOIS, 1834, AND OF THE CONGREGATIONAL ASSOCIATION OF ILLINOIS, 1835–40 156

 VII. THE AUTOBIOGRAPHY OF FLAVEL BASCOM, 1833–40 . . . 231

VIII. EARLY CONGREGATIONALISM IN MICHIGAN: LETTERS AND REPORTS FROM HOME MISSIONARIES, 1825–42 285

  IX. CONGREGATIONAL INDIAN MISSIONS: LETTERS AND REPORTS FROM MISSIONARIES TO THE AMERICAN BOARD OF COMMISSIONERS FOR FOREIGN MISSIONS, 1831–38 340

   X. DOCUMENTS RELATING TO THE CONGREGATIONAL AND PRESBYTERIAN CONVENTION OF WISCONSIN, 1840–47 368

BIBLIOGRAPHY

BIBLIOGRAPHY 407

INDEX

INDEX 421

LIST OF ILLUSTRATIONS

THE WESTWARD MIGRATION OF THE PEOPLE OF NEW ENGLAND
INTO LANDS NORTH OF THE OHIO, 1820–1850 . . *Frontispiece*

PAGE

CONGREGATIONAL CHURCHES IN ILLINOIS, INCLUDING THE FIRST
CHURCHES OF THE CONGREGATIONAL ASSOCIATION OF ILLINOIS,
AND OF THE FOX RIVER UNION, AND INDEPENDENT CONGREGA-
TIONAL CHURCHES TO NOVEMBER, 1836, IN THEIR RELATION
TO THE ILLINOIS PRESBYTERIES TO OCTOBER, 1834 24

FIELD OF THE MISSIONARY LABORS OF REV. ISAAC W. RUGGLES IN
SOUTHEASTERN MICHIGAN, 1825–1835 30

PART I

General Introduction

CHAPTER I

Congregationalism in 1783

THE close of the War for Independence found the Congregationalists the most numerous as well as the most influential religious body in America. Though confined almost exclusively to New England, they were at the same time nationally important because of their educational and cultural leadership. The estimated population of New England at the close of the Revolution was 1,090,000, while the number of Congregational churches was placed at 656. This would mean 1 Congregational church to every 1,661 of the population. The number of Baptist churches was placed at 163, with a total estimated membership of 10,000; there were 40 Episcopalian parishes, with a membership of 2,500; there were 4,000 Quakers in twenty monthly meetings. All told, there were 879 religious organizations in New England, which would mean that Congregationalists were at least three times as numerous as all others combined.[1] Ezra Stiles estimated that in 1760 there were 445,000 Congregationalists in New England. This figure, however, was obtained by simply subtracting the estimated number of dissenters from the total population. Thus Stiles considered every inhabitant of New England a Congregationalist if he

[1] George Punchard, *History of Congregationalism* (5 vols.; Boston: Congregational Publishing Society, 1881), IV, 652–53. See also J. S. Clark, *A Historical Sketch of the Congregational Churches in Massachusetts from 1620 to 1858* (Boston: Congregational Board of Publication, 1858); John M. Comstock, *The Congregational Churches of Vermont and Their Ministry, 1762–1914* (St. Johnsbury, Vt., 1915); Henry A. Hazen, *The Congregational and Presbyterian Ministry and Churches of New Hampshire* (Boston, 1875); *Contributions to the Ecclesiastical History of Connecticut* (New Haven, 1861), esp. the section on "Historical Sketches of the Congregational Churches of Connecticut," pp. 340–516.

were not a dissenter, which, of course, is not at all in accord with the real facts.[2]

The large and important part played by the New England Congregational clergy in winning independence for the nation was to prove of great advantage to them in the years immediately following in maintaining their special privileges as over against the forces which were attempting to bring about separation of church and state.[3] The clergy of New England had also exercised a powerful influence in the making of the new constitutions which had become necessary with independence. In a sense the written constitution and the constitutional convention were the children of the New England pulpit. For years Congregational ministers had preached that just government originated in compacts; and now, that the old compact between the mother-country and the colonies had been abrogated, the people, they argued, through their representatives must formulate another. And in the formation of the constitutions the clergy were active and influential. In Massachusetts, for instance, thirteen ministers were members of the constitutional convention. Rev. Jonas Clark of Lexington was one of the leaders in demanding that Massachusetts form her constitution by means of a convention elected by the people. He was a member of the convention and was chosen to preach the first election sermon under the new government. A few years later, when Massachusetts was in the throes of adopting the federal Constitution, General Lincoln wrote General Washington, "It is fortunate for us, that the clergy are pretty generally with us. They have in this state a very great influence over the people."[4]

[2] Ezra Stiles, *Itineraries and Correspondence*, ed. F. B. Dexter (New Haven: Yale University Press, 1918), pp. 92–94. Stiles estimated that there were 62,420 dissenters in 1760.

[3] Alice M. Baldwin, *The New England Clergy and the American Revolution* (Durham, N.C.: Duke University Press, 1928).

[4] *Writings of Washington* (Sparks ed.), IX, 330 n. For a full discussion of the influence of the New England clergy in constitution-making see Baldwin, *op. cit.*, chap. x: "The Making of Constitutions"; see also *ibid.*, p. 172.

While the New England Congregational clergy were occupied during the Revolution and in the years immediately following with public questions and were exercising a large and no doubt beneficent influence on government and public affairs, the cause of the churches themselves and religion generally suffered. In fact, it may be accepted as a truism that, when the spiritual leaders of a people are primarily concerned with the affairs of state, with politics and war, religion as such must necessarily suffer eclipse. And such certainly was the case throughout New England in the years immediately succeeding independence.

The close of the Revolution found the New England churches generally in a "delapidated and impoverished condition." Many ministers had been in the armies, not a few had been killed or wounded, and some were broken down by sickness and unusual hardship. Congregations had been broken up as a result of the war, and not a few meetinghouses had been burned or ruined by the enemy. As a result, many congregations had to be reorganized and repairs to churches made by people, many of whom had been impoverished by the war.[5]

Much of the decline of religion and of the laxity in morals of this period is accounted for on the ground of Deistic and French influence. "The French Revolution," to quote William Ellery Channing, "diseased the imagination and unsettled the understanding of men everywhere. . . . . The tone of books and conversation was presumptuous and daring. The tendency of all classes was to skepticism."[6] Channing's testimony is supported by a contemporary, Judge White, who states: "So deeply and so generally had the French *mania* seized upon the popular mind in this country, and so susceptible of its fiery influence were the ardent spirits of

[5] Punchard, *op. cit.*

[6] *Memoir of William Ellery Channing with Extracts from His Correspondence and Manuscripts* (London, 1850), I, 43.

young men, all alive to freedom of thought, of action, and indulgence, that reason, argument and persuasion, had for a time no power against it."[7] It was the period in which Thomas Paine was the great vogue. He had published his *Age of Reason* in 1793, and his power of ridicule and his simple and direct style, together with the gratitude and fame which he had won because of the service he had rendered the cause of independence during the most critical years of the American Revolution, gave him a peculiar and powerful influence. The youth of the land were particularly susceptible to Paine's attack, and, as Lyman Beecher tells us, "boys that dressed flax in the barn, as I used to, read Tom Paine and believed him."[8] Ethan Allen, the hero of Ticonderoga, published in Vermont in 1785 his *Reason the Only Oracle of Man*, which, though the work of an amateur, displayed considerable keenness in detecting the inherent weaknesses of the established New England religion, and has been termed the "first real anti-Christian work in America."[9] While roundly denounced by New England Congregational leaders such as Ezra Stiles and Timothy Dwight, Ethan Allen exercised little influence on the religious life of the time. He does, however, more or less symbolize the rising revolt against the established order in New England.

While much of the general decline in religion of the time may be laid at the door of Deism and like influences, yet we now know that a period of warfare, such as that through which the country had just passed, is always hurtful to the

[7] Quoted in *ibid.*, pp. 44 and 45. For a fuller discussion of the relation of Deistic influence to the religious situation of the time see G. A. Koch, *Republican Religion: The American Revolution and the Cult of Reason* (New York: Henry Holt & Co., 1933), esp. chap. viii. See also W. W. Sweet, "The Churches as Moral Courts of the Frontier," *Church History*, March, 1933.

[8] *Autobiography, Correspondence, etc.*, ed. Charles Beecher (2 vols.; New York, 1864), I, 43.

[9] B. T. Schantz, "Ethan Allen's Religious Ideas," *Journal of Religion*, XVIII (1938), 183-217; see also Koch, *op. cit.*, *passim*.

cause of vital religion. Trumbull, the historian of Connecticut, wrote:

A state of war, is peculiarly unfriendly to religion. It dissipates the mind, diminishes the degree of instruction, removes great numbers almost wholly from it, connects them with the most dangerous company, and presents them with the worst examples. It hardens and emboldens men in sin; is productive of profaneness, intemperance, disregard to propriety, violence and licentious living.[10]

There is much contemporary evidence to prove that the state of religion in the average New England community at this time left much to be desired. We are told that the churches were composed almost entirely of people considerably advanced in life and that there were practically no meetings except those on the Sabbath. The period is described by Rev. Joel Hawes, of Hartford, Connecticut, as one in which the Holy Spirit appeared "to have withdrawn his gracious presence from the churches; ministers and people were extensively settled on their lees, and a moral dearth of the most portentious character had overspread the land." Timothy Dwight called attention to the "cold contemptuous indifference toward every moral and religious subject." From Lebanon, Connecticut, it was reported that "family religion was very unfashionable. The house of God was very much forsaken on the Sabbath, and when lecture was preached on another day, the preacher saw little else than empty pews." "For several years past," declared Rev. Nathan Perkins in 1801, "contempt of the holy sabbath, desecration of the public worship, omission of family religion, and disregard of divine ordinances have spread in a degree, which call for tears of grief; threatening in their progress to lay waste all the most valuable interests in society."

In a sermon preached at New Haven in 1801, in which were reviewed the events of the past century, Timothy

---

[10] Benjamin Trumbull, *A Complete History of Connecticut, Civil and Ecclesiastical, etc.* (2 vols.; New Haven, 1818), I, 377. (Later ed.; New London, 1898.)

Dwight, then president of Yale College, had much to say of infidelity, loose morals, and general irreligion, then so prevalent. "Loose opinions and loose practices," he states, "have found their place here also." The American war increased these evils, nor had peace restored the purity of life. He speaks of the increase in the profanation of the Sabbath and in the use of profane language, while "drunkenness, gambling, and lewdness, were exceedingly increased; and, what is less commonly remarked, but perhaps not less mischievous, than any of them, a light vain method of thinking, concerning sacred things." Further he notes the enormous evil which has crept in as a result of a depreciating currency, which, he states, "gave birth to a new spirit of fraud, and opened numerous temptations, and a boundless field for its operations; while a new and intimate correspondance with corrupted foreigners introduced a multitude of loose doctrines, which were greedily embraced by licentious men, as the means of palliating and justifying their sins."[11]

With such conditions prevailing throughout New England and indeed throughout the entire nation, we will not be surprised to learn that between 1790 and 1800 Massachusetts "gathered" fewer Congregational churches than during any previous ten years for ninety years. Only fifteen churches were planted in Massachusetts during the last decade of the eighteenth century.[12]

At the close of the Revolution there were two hundred and three Congregational churches in Connecticut, and from 1783 to the end of the century only eight new churches were organized. For seven years immediately following the close of the Revolution not a single new congregation was "gath-

---

[11] *A Discourse on Some Events of the Last Century, Delivered in the Brick Church in New Haven, on Wednesday, January 7, 1801* (New Haven, 1801), pp. 18 and 19; Koch, *op. cit.*, pp. 241–47.

[12] Punchard, *op. cit.*, IV, 655; Clark, *op. cit.*, p. 224.

ered" in Connecticut.[13] At the close of the Revolution there were ninety-nine Congregational churches in New Hampshire and by 1800 twenty-two new churches had been formed, making a total at the end of the century of one hundred and twenty-one.[14] By the close of the Revolution twenty-nine Congregational churches had been formed in the Green Mountain territory, which in 1791 became the state of Vermont. The rapid pushing of New England population into this region in the years following independence was responsible for the rapid increase of new church organizations, and between 1783 and 1800 sixty-one new churches had been formed, bringing the total for Vermont at the end of the eighteenth century to ninety.[15]

In Rhode Island there were not more than ten Congregational churches in 1790,[16] while Maine began the nineteenth century with sixty-five congregations and sixty-three ministers. The beginning of population movement from New England into New York dates from 1635 and continued with ever increasing volume for more than a hundred and fifty years. As a result of this immigration, Congregational churches were formed in Westchester, Dutchess, Putnam, Rensselaer, and Columbia counties east of the Hudson, during the seventeenth century, and by the end of the American Revolution

[13] *Contributions to the Ecclesiastical History of Connecticut.* The last section of this volume contains "Historical Sketches of the Congregational Churches in Connecticut," from which the foregoing figures have been compiled. Punchard (*op. cit.*, IV, 661) states that there were 207 churches in Connecticut in 1800.

[14] Samuel L. Gerould, *The Congregational and Presbyterian Churches and Ministers of New Hampshire* (Lebanon, N.H., 1900), Part I: "Churches and Ministers." There were six Presbyterian churches in New Hampshire in 1783.

[15] Comstock, *op. cit.*, pp. 27–125. Williston Walker, in his *History of the Congregational Churches in the United States* (New York, 1894), pp. 309–10, states that in 1800 there were but 74 Congregational churches in Vermont. The list compiled by Comstock, noted above, is a later authority.

[16] Punchard, *op. cit.*, IV, 664 and 665. Stiles (*op. cit.*) estimates that there were 5,100 Congregationalists in Rhode Island in 1760. Baptists outnumbered the Congregationalists three to one. See also A. W. Crandall, "Religious Sects in Rhode Island" (University of Chicago thesis [1920]).

several Congregational organizations had been established
west of the Hudson.[17] Examples of early churches west of the
Hudson are those at Gloversville, in Fulton County, which
was formed in 1752; the church at Stillwater in Saratoga
County was also organized in 1752 at Canaan, Connecticut,
as the members were setting out for their new home. The
rapid movement of population west of the Hudson, however,
did not begin until after the peace with Great Britain. The
Congregational significance of this movement will be the subject of the following chapter.

The Congregational churches in Massachusetts, Connecticut, and New Hampshire still enjoyed special privileges
granted to them by law. Forces favoring the complete separation of church and state were increasingly active, however,
and the dissenting bodies were taking advantage of every
opportunity to advance their cause. Baptists and Methodists were particularly active in opposing compulsory worship
and compulsory taxation for the support of Congregational
ministers. As a result, they were subject to constant annoy-
ance, which frequently amounted to persecution.[18] After
1790 the question of the relation of church and state became
increasingly a political issue, the Congregationalists becoming almost 100 per cent Federalist. On the other hand, the
dissenting bodies—Baptists, Methodists, and Episcopalians
—aligned themselves with the Jeffersonian party.[19] This
fact tended to alienate the rural sections and the poorer economic classes in the towns from Congregationalism and

[17] Most of these early Congregational churches in eastern and southern New
York became Presbyterian churches as a result of the working of the Plan of Union
of 1801 (Punchard, *op. cit.*, V, 1–16; see also Walker, *op. cit.*, pp. 310–11).

[18] William A. Robinson, *Jeffersonian Democracy in New England* (New Haven:
Yale University Press, 1916); J. F. Thorning, *Religious Liberty in Transition* (New
York: Benziger Bros., 1931).

[19] Jacob C. Meyer, *Church and State in Massachusetts, from 1740 to 1833* (Cleveland: Western Reserve University, 1930); see also I. D. Stewart, *The History of
the Freewill Baptists, for Half a Century* (Dover, 1862).

played into the hands of the Baptists, Free Baptists, and Methodists particularly. As a result of their political activity, the New England Congregational ministers declined in popular esteem and came to be considered "as party managers rather than spiritual teachers."[20] Even missionaries who were sent into the new communities were accused of having more concern in promoting party interests than in furthering the gospel.

The limited geographical position of the Congregationalists was to prove a serious handicap to their national expansion. If they had been as widely distributed throughout the country as were the Presbyterians and Baptists at the opening of the national period, their impact upon the nation would have been far more effective. The fact that they were confined almost exclusively to New England, where they were completely dominant, also tended to create among them a smug provincialism which led directly to a decided superiority complex, often causing their leaders to be more or less indifferent as to whether or not Congregationalism was planted west of the Hudson River. Their platform and polity were devised for a homogeneous population and for "a narrow home use" and were, therefore, not adapted to aggressive action on a national scale.[21]

Another serious handicap to the national expansion of Congregationalism, which became increasingly apparent with the years, was its lack of any centralized authority. Opposition to centralization in Congregationalism was particularly strong during the latter years of the eighteenth century under such leaders as Nathanael Emmons, who, as minister at Franklin, Massachusetts, from 1773 to 1827, had trained

[20] *Salem Gazette*, August 25, 1795, quoted in Thorning, *op. cit.*, p. 47.

[21] For a discussion of the handicaps under which Congregationalism labored in dealing with the expanding nation see William W. Patton, *The Last Century of Congregationalism; or the Influence on Church and State of the Faith and Polity of the Pilgrim Fathers* (Washington, D.C., 1878 [reprinted from the *New Englander*, October, 1876]).

more than a hundred young men for the ministry. He declared that the Congregational church was a pure democracy; that even the minister has no more authority than a private brother; that "one church has as much power as another"; and that there "is no appeal from the authority of a particular church to any higher ecclesiastical tribunal."[22] In opposing the formation of state associations in Massachusetts in 1803, similar to those which had been established in Connecticut following the adoption of the Saybrook Platform in 1708, Emmons had stated: "Association leads to Consociation; Consociation leads to Presbyterianism; Presbyterianism leads to Episcopacy; Episcopacy leads to Roman Catholicism; and Roman Catholicism is an ultimate fact." As a natural consequence of such a position, many Congregational leaders did not seem "to contemplate aggressive action; wide development, national boundaries." There was in American Congregationalism no provision for joint action; and little was done to cultivate a sense of unity. "Candor requires us to confess," says a Congregational leader of later years, "that our system, as bequeathed to us by the early fathers of New England, was poorly equipped for anything beyond parish-work in that section [New England] of the land" and that only in more recent times have they profited by the example of other denominations, under the pressure of necessity, in forming co-operative agencies "harmonious with Congregational principles."[23]

It is true that Connecticut Congregationalism had developed a certain degree of centralization as a result of the Saybrook Platform provisions, and, among all the New England Congregational groups, the Connecticut variety of Congregationalism was to prove itself the most aggressive and effective in the westward expansion.

[22] Edwards A. Park, *Memoir of Nathanael Emmons: With Sketches of His Friends and Pupils* (Boston: Congregational Board of Publication, 1861), chap. ix: "His Interest in Ecclesiastical Polity," pp. 144–47.

[23] Patton, *op. cit.*, p. 7.

CHAPTER II

Western Congregationalism and the Plan of Union

THE extent and variety of New England contributions to the other states of the Union are striking in the extreme. In the years immediately following the Revolution New England expanded not only into the newer regions on her borders, such as Vermont and Maine, but after 1781 the largest stream of New England migration was into the region beyond the Hudson River. So great was the movement of New England people into New York State that the inhabitants of New York and New England seemed to Timothy Dwight, in 1821, substantially one people, "with the same interests of every kind inseparably united."[1] In 1820 this shrewd observer estimated that from three-fifths to two-thirds of New York's increase of population from 1790 to 1820 had originated from New England. Others have estimated that from 1790 to 1820 southern New England alone sent 800,000 of its people to other sections of the country. Another student of New England population movements believed that in 1850 over a million and a half persons of New England descent were living outside the section.[2]

[1] *Travels in New England and New York* (4 vols.; New Haven, 1821), IV, 527. Lois Kimball Mathews, *The Expansion of New England: The Spread of New England Settlement and Institutions to the Mississippi River, 1620–1865* (Boston: Houghton Mifflin Co., 1909) is still the fullest and most satisfactory account of New England expansion.

[2] F. J. Turner, *The United States, 1830–1860* (New York: Henry Holt & Co. 1935), chap. iii: "New England," furnishes an excellent summary of the changes taking place in New England during the years under consideration; see esp. pp. 43–44.

All the states in the Union profited as a result of the migrating Yankee, South as well as North, but their principal contributions were to those regions lying directly west, such as central and western New York, the northern counties of Pennsylvania, Ohio, Michigan, Indiana, Illinois, Wisconsin, and Iowa. Calhoun is reported to have remarked that "he had seen the time when the natives of Connecticut, together with the graduates of Yale College, in Congress, constituted within five votes of a majority of that body."[3] Of the delegates in the constitutional convention of Wisconsin (1846), one-third were of New England birth and another third came from those counties in central and western New York which had been settled by New Englanders. The New England element was almost equally strong in the Iowa convention of the same year. There is abundant evidence to show that New England furnished to the West professional men—lawyers, doctors, ministers, politicians, and leaders in business—out of all proportion to their numbers.

If New England Congregationalism had gone West in equal proportion to the population of that region and if it had been able to have retained the allegiance of a fair proportion of her children on the frontier, the whole story of organized religion in trans-Appalachia would doubtless have been far different. In the preceding chapter some of the basic reasons for this failure have been indicated. It is the purpose of this chapter to follow in some detail the fortunes of western Congregationalism, particularly during the first third of the nineteenth century.

The story of the gradual drawing-together of Connecticut Congregationalism and Presbyterianism has been told in Volume II of this series and will not need to be repeated in detail here.[4] Suffice it to say that the closing years of the

---

[3] Horace Bushnell, *Work and Play: Literary Varieties* (New York: Charles Scribner's Sons, 1903 [Centenary ed.]), I, 220.

[4] W. W. Sweet, *Religion on the American Frontier*, Vol. II: *The Presbyterians* (New York: Harper & Bros., 1936), pp. 37–39.

eighteenth century and the opening years of the nineteenth saw the Congregational and the Presbyterian leaders increasingly anxious to come to some agreement that would enable them to co-operate in the expanding West. The outcome of this growing concern was the Plan of Union adopted by the General Assembly of the Presbyterian church in May, 1801, and by the Congregational General Association of Connecticut the following month.[5] Later the associations of Vermont,

[5] For an account of the steps leading to the adoption of the Plan of Union see *ibid.*, pp. 39–43. Since the specific provisions of the Plan of Union were not published in the volume on the Presbyterians, they are reproduced here and are as follows:

"1st. It is strictly enjoined on all missionaries to the new settlements, to endeavor by all proper means, to promote mutual forbearance and accommodation, between those inhabitants of the new settlements who hold the Presbyterians, and those who hold the Congregational form of Church government.

"2nd. If in the new settlements, any Church of the Congregational order, shall settle a minister of the Presbyterian order, according to Congregational principles, settling their difficulties among themselves, or by a council mutually agreed upon for that purpose. But if any difficulty shall exist between the minister and the Church or any member of it, it shall be referred to the Presbytery to which the minister and the Church shall belong, provided both parties agree to it; if not, to a council consisting of equal number of Presbyterians and Congregationalists, agreed upon by both parties.

"3rd. If a Presbyterian Church shall settle a minister of Congregational principles, that Church may still conduct their discipline according to Presbyterian principles; excepting that if a difficulty arise between him and his Church, or any member of it, the cause shall be tried by the Association to which the said minister shall belong, provided bothe parties agree to it: otherwise by a council, one half Congregationalists and the other half Presbyterians, mutually agreed on by the parties.

"4th. If any congregation consist partly of those who hold the Congregational form of discipline, and partly of those who hold the Presbyterian form, we recommend to both parties, that this be no obstruction to their uniting in one church and settling a minister; and that in this case, the Church choose a standing committee from the communicants of said church, whose business it shall be, to call to account every member of the church who shall conduct himself inconsistently with the laws of Christianity, and to give judgment on such conduct; and if the person condemned by their judgement be a Presbyterian, he shall have liberty to appeal to the Presbytery; if a Congregationalist, he shall have liberty to appeal to the body of the male communicants of the church; in the former case, the determination of the Presbytery shall be final unless the Church consent to a further appeal to the Synod, or to the General Assembly, and in the latter case, if the party condemned shall wish for a trial by a mutual council, the cause shall be referred to such a council. And provided the said standing committee of any church shall depute one of themselves to attend the Presbytery, he may have the same right to sit and act in the Presbytery, as a ruling elder of the Presbyterian church."

New Hampshire, Massachusetts, and Maine adopted the Plan in spirit if not in fact.[6] At the time of its adoption the Plan was undoubtedly welcomed by both parties to it. "It was," in the words of Professor R. H. Nichols, "the inevitable . . . . action of two bodies which thought they belonged together and had been talking about union for thirty-five years, which were knit together by many natural and personal ties and which were now faced with a common task."[7]

It was in central and western New York that the Plan of Union was first put into operation. Here the predominant New England character of the population led to the early predominance of Congregationalism, but, through the operations of the Plan of Union, by 1822 Congregationalism as such had largely disappeared through absorption by the Presbyterians, leaving only a few churches in the whole region which were too staunchly Congregational to submit to such absorption. We must understand that this was all done willingly.[8] If Congregationalists were absorbed, it was because they desired to be absorbed. In fact, the Connecticut Congregationalists, it must be remembered, thought of themselves at this time as Presbyterians, and Connecticut people predominated in central and western New York.[9] After 1852, when Congregationalists had developed a more aggressive denominational consciousness, they read into these operations a spirit which was not present at the time. Thus James H.

[6] At the time of the adoption of the Plan of Union (1801) none of the state associations but that of Connecticut had any relations with the Presbyterian General Assembly. The natural presumption would be that each association would adhere to the same working agreement with the Presbyterians as that outlined in the Plan of Union after such relationship had been established. The Vermont association entered into a similar relationship with the General Assembly in 1801; that of New Hampshire in 1810; Massachusetts in 1811, and Maine in 1828.

[7] "The Plan of Union in New York," *Church History*, March, 1936.

[8] This story has been told in detail in the author's volume on the Presbyterians (*op. cit.*, pp. 43-44); in James H. Hotchkin, *A History of the Purchase and Settlement of Western New York, etc.* (New York, 1848); and in Nichols, *op. cit.*

[9] Mathews, *op. cit.*, p. 157.

Dill, writing in 1859, speaks of the New York Congregational associations as being absorbed "by several feeble Presbyteries—seven lean kine swallowing the seven fat kine—and Presbyterianism suddenly bringing itself into full rounded proportions."[10] In this seeming absorption of Congregationalism into Presbyterianism in New York there was, however, a considerable amount of Congregationalism left, for, according to the Accommodation Plan, Congregational churches coming into presbyteries were permitted to retain their local Congregational usages.[11]

The Plan of Union, as it operated in the Western Reserve of Ohio, the region next to central and western New York, where its effects were most notable, has been described in some detail in the volume on the Presbyterians of this series.[12] It has been discussed also from the Presbyterian angle in Kennedy's *The Plan of Union*[13] and more recently by Charles L. Zorbaugh in *Church History*.[14] Its operations in Ohio have been characterized by a Congregational historian, writing in 1896, as a "well meant, but exceedingly ill-advised scheme." It was the insistence of only a few Presbyterians in having their form of government, in "horror of the 'irregularities' and 'looseness' of Congregationalism," he believes, accompanied by indifference on the part of the Congregationalists,

[10] "Congregationalism in Western New York," *Congregational Quarterly*, April, 1859, p. 153.

[11] Professor Nichols in his article on the Plan of Union in New York makes much of this point (*op. cit.*, pp. 37, 45–46). The so-called "Accommodation Plan," formulated in 1808, after all, had its roots in the Plan of Union agreement, since it provides that a committeeman from a Congregational church sent as a delegate to a presbytery shall have the "same right to sit and act in the Presbytery, as a ruling elder of the Presbyterian Church" (see Plan of Union, Art. IV). Zorbaugh, following Nichols, lays stress upon the fact that in the Western Reserve it was the Accommodation Plan and not the Plan of Union which operated (C. L. Zorbaugh, "The Plan of Union in Ohio," *Church History*, VI [June, 1937], 145–74).

[12] Sweet, *op. cit.*, pp. 44–47.

[13] W. S. Kennedy, *The Plan of Union: Or a History of the Presbyterian and Congregational Churches of the Western Reserve* (Hudson, Ohio, 1856).

[14] *Op. cit.*

which won the day for Presbyterianism on the Reserve.[15] He cites the example of Rev. Thomas Barr's opposition to the formation of a Congregational association in 1814 on the ground that he would thereby be isolated, and persuaded his Congregational brethren to form a presbytery instead. Another example in Ohio of the willingness of Congregationalists to give way before Presbyterian persistence was where "a minority of one, and a woman at that, with tears and prayers wrought the same phenomenal result."[16] This writer states that the New England immigrants to Ohio generally preferred the Congregational form of church government and accepted the less liberal Presbyterian form because they were told and believed it was but a makeshift for the time being and would soon have its day.[17] But undoubtedly during the period of the Plan of Union's most successful operation (1815–30) on the Reserve, to use the language of President Fairchild of Oberlin College, it "worked harmoniously and the churches constituted one denomination instead of two." But, as Zorbaugh points out, that "one denomination" was neither Presbyterian nor Congregational but a combination of the two, and was sometimes termed "Presbygational."[18]

Since the first settlers in the Reserve were largely from Connecticut, the majority of the early churches formed were Congregational. These were organized in 1805 into the Ecclesiastical Convention of New Connecticut. At this time

[15] D. L. Leonard, *A Century of Congregationalism in Ohio* (Oberlin, 1896), pp. 24, 35, 40, 42; see also Kennedy, *op. cit.*, pp. 162–66; Sweet, *op. cit.*, p. 45.

[16] Leonard, *op. cit.*, p. 43 n.

[17] *Ibid.*, p. 44.

[18] J. F. Fairchild, "The Story of Congregationalism on the Western Reserve," *Ohio Church History Society Papers*, V (Oberlin, 1894), 17–18; see also Zorbaugh, *op. cit.*, pp. 154–55, and James Wood, *Facts and Observations concerning the Organization and State of the Churches in the Three Synods of Western New York and the Synod of Western Reserve* (Philadelphia, 1837). R. B. Moore states in his *History of Huron Presbytery* (Philadelphia, 1892), p. 2, that it was "a type of Church government which was new to the world. It was not Congregationalism; it was not Presbyterianism; it was an effort at the combination of the two."

there were six churches on the Reserve, the oldest being that at Richfield, which had been formed in 1801 with sixteen members. In 1805 the total membership of the six churches was 147. In 1808 there were four missionaries commissioned by the Missionary Society of Connecticut, all of them evidently Presbyterian, the Congregational missionaries having departed in 1806.[19] From this time forward the Presbyterian influence was on the increase in the Reserve and soon became dominant. The coming of the Presbyterian missionaries resulted in a petition from the Convention of New Connecticut to the synod of Pittsburgh requesting that "they might be embraced within the bounds of a Presbytery," which led to the formation of the Hartford Presbytery in 1808.[20]

There is some disagreement as to the part played by Oberlin College in the Congregational-Presbyterian situation in the Reserve. Zorbaugh argues that the early influence at Oberlin was predominately Presbyterian, since Finney, Mahan, and Cowles had all had Presbyterian connections. He has evidently overlooked the fact that Finney had made arrangements to leave the Presbyterians just before coming to Oberlin and was dismissed from his presbytery in 1836 because he preferred the Congregational discipline.[21] Leonard states that "Oberlin had no love for the Plan of Union, and stood for Congregationalism pure and simple."[22] As a matter

[19] "Records of the Ecclesiastical Convention of New Connecticut (1805–1808)," *Papers of the Ohio Church History Society*, IX (1898), 1–31. The reasons for the departure of the Congregational missionaries were the unusual demand for ministers in the older sections of the country, the large increase of missionaries employed by other societies, and the penurious policy of the Connecticut society in reducing the meager salary of missionaries from seven to six dollars a week (Corbaugh, *op. cit.*, p. 151; Kennedy, *op. cit.*, pp. 39–45; and Sweet, *op. cit.*, pp. 44–46).

[20] S. J. M. Eaton, *History of the Presbytery of Erie, etc.* (New York, 1868), pp. 55–56.

[21] Zorbaugh, *op. cit.*, p. 156; Charles G. Finney, *Memoirs of C. G. Finney* (New York: A. D. Barnes & Co., 1876), p. 325.

[22] *Op. cit.*, p. 53: "Oberlin has from the first and all along been true to Congregational principles."

of fact, Oberlin was in bad repute with both Presbyterians and Congregationalists until the latter forties because of its radical doctrine known as "Perfectionism" which the orthodox considered both antinomian and immoral. Oberlin was also strongly antislavery from the start, received colored students, and "countenanced co-education." An illustration of this disapproval of Oberlin is furnished by the Huron Presbytery's refusal to license or even to examine James H. and F. H. Fairchild in 1840 because they refused to declare that they did not believe "in the doctrines taught at Oberlin and in their way of doing things."[23] In 1842 the synod of Western Reserve considered the question as to whether baptism administered by an Oberlinite might be accounted valid, while two years later a convention of Plan of Union churches was held at Cleveland to devise means of hedging in "this fountain of evil and protect the saints from its pestiferous malaria."

Congregationalism in other sections of Ohio was relatively weak. The First Congregational Church of Marietta, founded in 1796, is, in a sense, the mother-church of Congregationalism in the West. The special act of Congress under which the Ohio Company purchased lands at the mouth of Muskingum provided that a section of land should be set aside for the support of religion. It happened that the section (No. 29) set aside for this purpose fell within the city limits of Marietta and soon became valuable. In 1800 the territorial legislature created a board of trustees to manage the lands

---

[23] *Ibid.*, pp. 51–52; see also Albert T. Swing, *James Harris Fairchild, or Sixty-eight Years with a Christian College* (New York: Revell & Co., 1907), pp. 102–9. This rejection of the Fairchild brothers by the Huron Presbytery pushed forward the Congregational separation. J. H. Fairchild states in a letter dated September 21, 1840: "They professed the highest regard for us as individuals, but Oberlin; there was the rub. As I came away one of the clergymen came to me with tears in his eyes and said that he voted against me but he did not wish to shut me out of the ministry—he hoped I would do much good in the world, he thought I would, but he considered it his duty to vote against my admission to the Presbytery" (quoted in Swing, *op. cit.*, p. 108).

thus set aside and authorized them to use the proceeds to support such religious societies as should subsequently be formed and for the erection of houses of public worship. To take advantage of this provision, there was formed in 1801 the First Ecclesiastical Society in Marietta, which became the financial organization of the first church. The Presbyterian element were soon dissatisfied with Rev. Daniel Story, the minister, and in 1804 formed the Second Religious Society and requested the division of the funds. This seems a clear indication of the inclination of Presbyterians to assert their denominational preferences when opportunity offered.[24]

The Congregational church of Granville, Ohio, was formed in Granville, Massachusetts, on May 1, 1805, before the colony started for its new home in the West and maintained its Congregational character throughout the early years. There were churches formed in what is now West Zanesville (then called Springfield), Clinton, and Waterford, which in 1809 formed the Muskingum Association, which a few years later (1816) went out of existence when the ministers forming it joined the Lancaster Presbytery. Another Congregational church was formed in Licking County at Hartford in 1818 which seems to mark the end of Congregational activity in central Ohio until the 1830's.[25]

In 1850 there were one hundred and thirty-one Congregational churches in Ohio, the great majority located in the northern section of the state.[26] Of this number, sixty-seven were formed after 1830.

Indiana for some reason seems never to have attracted

[24] C. E. Dickinson, "A History of the First Religious Society in Marietta," *Papers of the Ohio Church History Society*, I (1890), 78–97, and his "A History of the First Congregational Church of Marietta, Ohio," *ibid.*, Vol. VII (1896).

[25] Beniamin Talbot, "Congregationalism in Central Ohio," *Papers of the Ohio Church History Society*, IV (1893) 28–43; see also Dickinson, "History of Congregationalism in Ohio before 1852," *Papers of the Ohio Church History Society*, VII (1896), 31–55.

[26] "Chronological List of the Congregational Churches of Ohio," *Papers of the Ohio Church History Society*, IX (1898), 68–70.

any large numbers of New Englanders.[27] As a consequence the Indiana territory was barren soil as far as Congregationalism was concerned. The Connecticut Missionary Society reported in 1816 that one of its veteran missionaries, Rev. Nathan B. Derrow, had extended his field of labor to "the whole of the state of Ohio and to the Indiana and Illinois territories." Two years later Derrow reported having spent sixty-five weeks in Indiana, where he had preached 261 sermons, but the "illiterate and enthusiastic preachers were numerous" and his success small. In 1818 the Connecticut Missionary Society had another missionary at work in Indiana, but whatever churches formed were of the Plan of Union type. The first distinctively Congregational church established in Indiana was at Terre Haute in 1834 by Rev. Merrick A. Jewett, from Baltimore, who seems to have had no Congregational background, nor had the original members of the church.[28] It was simply an independent church until 1850, when it was received into the fellowship of the Congregational churches, when Jewett was formally installed as its pastor. By 1845 churches had been formed at Michigan City, Orlando, Ontario, and Westchester, and that year the Evangelical Association of the Wabash Valley was organized. In 1854 there were but sixteen Congregational churches in Indiana.[29]

The Connecticut Missionary Society began work in Illinois soon after Samuel J. Mills and his associates made their well-

[27] There was nothing like a "New England town" in Indiana in the territorial period, nor was there any appreciable number of New England settlers (Mathews, *op. cit.*, pp. 197 ff.).

[28] Lyman Abbott was the second pastor of this church, having come to Terre Haute in 1860 to succeed Jewett (Lyman Abbott, *Reminiscences* [Boston and New York: Houghton Mifflin Co., 1915], pp. 190–93).

[29] George Punchard, *History of Congregationalism*, Vol. II: *Congregationalism in America* (5 vols.; Boston: Congregational Publishing Society, 1881), pp. 271–75. A General Association of Congregational Churches and Ministers of Indiana was formed in 1858, which reported in 1863 that it was the smallest state association in the Union (*Minutes of the Gen. Assoc. of Cong'l Churches and Ministers of Indiana, 1863*, p. 7). The total number of church members reported in the state in the latter year was 911.

known reports on moral and religious conditions in the West.[30] Between 1820 and 1830 this most active of the New England missionary societies sent fifteen men to Indiana, Illinois, Missouri, Kentucky, and Tennessee, but their labors resulted in the establishment of Presbyterian churches only. Here is an example, to use the words of a Congregational writer of more recent years, of the "unselfish prodigality with which New England poured her life into the West" in order to establish "a rival" ecclesiastical organization.[31] It must be remembered, however, that this writer is reading back into those earlier years a "rivalry" that was not then present.

In 1829 and 1830 came the "Yale Band" of the "Illinois Association," a group of seven Yale theological students who on February 21, 1829, had fixed their names to a formal agreement,[32] "to go to the state of Illinois for the purpose of establishing a seminary of learning such as shall be best adapted to the exigencies of that country," a part of them to be engaged as instructors in the seminary and the others as preachers in the surrounding country. The net result of the labors of these young enthusiasts, all of them New England Congregationalists, was the establishment of Illinois College in 1829 and the formation of numerous Presbyterian and Congregational churches.[33]

[30] Samuel J. Mills and Daniel Smith, *Report of a Missionary Tour through That Part of the United States Which Lies West of the Alleghany Mountains; Performed under the Direction of the Massachusetts Missionary Society* (Andover, 1815). Mills and John F. Schermerhorn had made a previous journey through the West in 1812.

[31] Joseph E. Roy, *History of Congregationalism in Illinois* (Chicago: Illinois Society of Church History, Congregational, 1895), pp. 24–66.

[32] The names signed to this agreement were Theron Baldwin, John F. Brooks, Mason Grosvenor, Elisha Jennay, William Kirby, Julian M. Sturtevant, and Asa Turner, Jr. Soon afterward the original seven were joined by five other young Yale graduates: William Carter, Albert Hale, Flavel Bascom, Romulus Barnes, and Lucian Farnham.

[33] Charles Henry Rammelkamp, *Illinois College: A Centennial History, 1829–1929* (New Haven: Yale University Press, 1928), esp. chap. ii: "The Foundations Laid: The Yale Band Finds Its Opportunity," pp. 9–37.

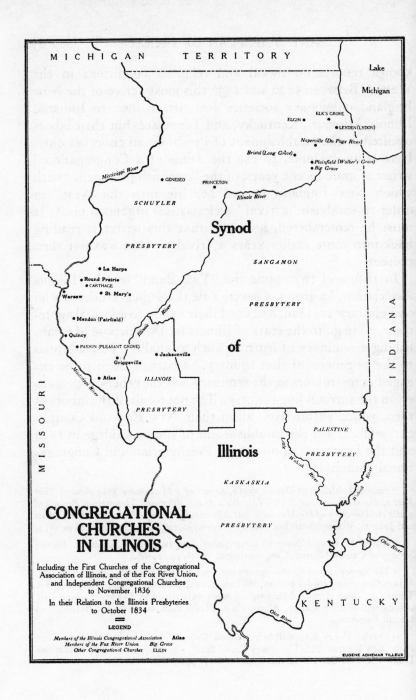

MICHIGAN TERRITORY

Lake
Michigan

ELGIN ●   ● ELK'S GROVE
                   ● LEYDEN (LYDON)
          Naperville (Du Page River) ●
    Bristol (Long Grove) ●
                   ● Plainfield (Walker's Grove)
                   ● Big Grove

● GENESEO

PRINCETON

Mississippi River

SCHUYLER

Illinois River

Synod

PRESBYTERY

SANGAMON

● La Harpe

● Round Prairie
● CARTHAGE
Warsaw   ● St. Mary's

PRESBYTERY

of

Illinois River

● Mendon (Fairfield)

● Quincy
● PAYSON (PLEASANT GROVE)
                   ● Jacksonville
    Griggsville ●

Illinois

● Atlas

ILLINOIS

PRESBYTERY

INDIANA

MISSOURI

Mississippi River

Illinois

PALESTINE

PRESBYTERY

KASKASKIA

Little Wabash River

Wabash River

Wabash River

CONGREGATIONAL
CHURCHES
IN ILLINOIS

Including the First Churches of the Congregational
Association of Illinois, and of the Fox River Union,
and Independent Congregational Churches
to November 1836

In their Relation to the Illinois Presbyteries
to October 1834
═

LEGEND

Members of the Illinois Congregational Association   **Atlas**
Members of the Fox River Union   **Big Grove**
Other Congregational Churches   ELGIN

PRESBYTERY

Ohio River

KENTUCKY

Ohio River

EUGENE ADHEMAR TILLEUX

Asa Turner, one of the Yale Band, formed a Presbyterian church at Quincy in 1830, which three years later was transformed into a Congregational church. In 1838 he crossed the Mississippi and established the first Congregational church in the territory of Iowa. Theron Baldwin, one of the first two of the Yale Band to reach Illinois and one of the founders of Illinois College, a little later established Monticello Seminary, which he served for eight years as principal; and for twenty-seven years (1843–70), as the secretary of the Society for the Promotion of Collegiate and Theological Education at the West, he performed a most significant service for higher education in the Middle West.[34] Another New England–trained missionary to Illinois was Aratus Kent, who came to the lead-mining center at Galena, Illinois, in 1828 and, after two and a half years of labor under the most discouraging conditions, succeeded in forming a Presbyterian church of six members.[35] Lemuel Foster, of Connecticut, Yale trained, organized the first Presbyterian church at Bloomington of eight members. He states that he was aware that Congregationalism would be misunderstood; that he was primarily concerned for "the cause" and cared little for the "ism."[36] Foster became conspicuous as an anti-slavery advocate and, as a result, received a severe lashing with an ox whip. Jeremiah Porter was still another New Englander of Congregational training who was one of the pioneers in establishing Presbyterian churches in Illinois. He organized the first Presbyterian church of Chicago, the first members being predominately of Congregational origin.[37]

[34] The best biographical sketch of Baldwin is that by J. M. Sturtevant in *Congregational Quarterly*, April and July, 1875.

[35] Gordon A. Riegler, "Aratus Kent, First Presbyterian Minister in Northern Illinois," *Journal of the Presbyterian Historical Society*, December, 1929, pp. 363–80.

[36] Matthew Spinka (ed.), "Journal of a Pioneer Missionary: The Rev. Lemuel Foster," *Journal of the Illinois State Historical Society*, July, 1928, pp. 183–99.

[37] Roy, *op. cit.*, pp. 31–32.

The claim of the Congregationalists that their early home missionaries were not so much interested in perpetuating their own particular "ism" in the West as they were in promoting Christianity in general is supported by the record of assistance rendered to the early Swedish Lutheran leaders in Illinois. The American Home Missionary Society made annual appropriations to assist one or more of the following Swedish Lutheran pastors during the 1850's: L. P. Esbjorn, T. N. Hasselquist, Paul Anderson, Ole Andrewson, and A. Andreen, and seemingly with no thought of proselyting. More than a hundred letters from these Swedish Lutheran ministers are to be found in the archives of the American Home Missionary Society.

The history of independent Congregationalism in Illinois begins with the 1830's, the first congregation being that at Princeton. This church was formed at Northampton, Massachusetts, in March, 1831, consisting of eighteen members. The first pastor was Lucian Farnham, of the Yale Band, who came in 1835 after several years' service at Jacksonville and Lewiston. He was succeeded in 1839 by Owen Lovejoy, the brother of Elijah P. Lovejoy, the victim of the Alton Mob (1837), which destroyed his printing press and shot him dead. As Elijah was dying, Owen knelt by his brother's side and vowed "never to forsake the cause that had been sprinkled with his brother's blood." He told his congregation, which he served for seventeen years, that he would "preach abolitionism to them until they loved it, and then continue to preach it because they loved it."[38] More than any other man he advanced the abolition cause in Illinois. He was a firm friend of Abraham Lincoln and was influential in bringing Lincoln again into active politics. Lovejoy was elected to Congress in 1856; he supported Lincoln in his campaign for the United States Senate in 1858 and defended President Lincoln against

---

[38] Joseph C. and Owen Lovejoy, *Memoir of the Rev. Elijah P. Lovejoy* (New York, 1838), pp. 246–61.

his detractors until his own death the year following the Emancipation Proclamation.[39]

The second Congregational church to be formed in Illinois was that at Mendon, north of Quincy, in February, 1833. Rev. Solomon Hardy, a graduate of Middlebury College and Andover, was its organizer. He was succeeded in 1836 by William Kirby, another of the Yale Band, who served the congregation for nine years. The transformation of the Presbyterian church at Quincy into a Congregational church in 1833 has already been noted. In a letter to the Home Missionary Society in June, 1833, Asa Turner explains the change: "My church are all Congregationalists in their feelings. One of our elders is gone; we cannot find another who will be ordained. They claim the privilege of worshipping God according to the dictates of conscience."[40] The Congregational church at Du Page, Cook County, now Naperville, was organized as a Presbyterian church in July, 1833, but was changed into a Congregational church in August, 1834.[41] The first minister was Nathaniel C. Clark, a native of Vermont and a staunch Congregationalist, who was responsible for founding numerous Congregational churches in the Fox River Valley.

A Congregational church at Jacksonville was organized on December 15, 1833. Twenty-two of its thirty-two original members came from the Presbyterian church in the town which had been formed in 1827, largely of New England people. It has been suggested that its formation was largely due to the heresy trials then in progress within the Presbyterian church, aimed largely against ministers of New England

[39] Albert J. Beveridge, *Abraham Lincoln, 1809–1858* (2 vols.; Boston: Houghton Mifflin Co., 1928), II, 265, 282, 353, 354, 356 n., 368, 390, 649, 668.

[40] G. M. Magoun, *Asa Turner, a Home Missionary Patriarch, and His Times* (Quincy, Ill., 1889); *Manual of the First Congregational Church of Quincy, Ill.* (1865).

[41] See the records of the Congregational Church of Du Page, Cook County, Illinois, in chap. vi of this volume.

origin.[42] J. M. Sturtevant, one of the Yale Band and the first instructor in Illinois College, aided in the organization of the church, though he was at that time a Presbyterian minister. William Carter, a member of the second group of Yale men to come to Illinois, became the minister of the new church. A few months previous to the formation of the Jacksonville church Edward Beecher, the president of Illinois College, and William Kirby and J. M. Sturtevant, two of the instructors, had been arraigned before the local presbytery for heresy. It does not take much stretch of the imagination to suppose that that experience caused Sturtevant to be the more inclined to assist in the formation of a Congregational church, as a possible haven, if his Presbyterian connections should become untenable.[43] Sturtevant, however, did not sever his Presbyterian connections until 1855.

The year 1835 saw the beginnings of two general Congregational organizations in Illinois: the Fox River Union, made up of the churches in the northeast section of the state with the church at Michigan City, Indiana; and the Congregational Association of Illinois, composed of the churches in the western-central section. By the end of 1836 Congregational churches in the state of Illinois numbered at least twenty, and Congregational consciousness was definitely on the increase.[44]

Perhaps nothing had more to do with the rapid separation

[42] Frank J. Heinl, "Jacksonville and Morgan County: An Historical View," *Journal of the Illinois State Historical Society*, April, 1925, p. 9.

[43] The organizing meeting of the Jacksonville Congregational Church was held in the Methodist church (*Manual of the Congregational Church* [Jacksonville, Ill., 1891], p. 4; Roy., *op. cit.*, pp. 35–38). For an account of the heresy trial and later doctrinal controversies see Charles H. Rammelkamp, "Fundamentalism and Modernism in a Pioneer College," *Journal of the Illinois State Historical Society*, October, 1928, pp. 395–408; see also *Julian M. Sturtevant: An Autobiography*, ed. J. M. Sturtevant, Jr. (New York, 1896).

[44] The minutes of the Congregational Association of Illinois, with notes, constitute chap. vi in this volume. The Constitution and Confession of Faith of the Congregational Union of Fox River appear in the records of the Du Page church in chap. v.

of the Presbyterians and Congregationalists in Illinois during the thirties and forties than the slavery issue. The Congregational people and ministers in the state were generally antislavery in their views, though few could be classed as extreme abolitionists. The growth of Illinois College was hindered in its early years because it became known as an "abolition" institution. William H. Herndon, who was Lincoln's law partner at the time of his election to the presidency, stated that his father, who was proslavery in his views, forced him to withdraw from the college because he thought it "was too strongly permeated with the virus of abolitionism."[45] Knox College, chartered in 1837, was a Presbyterian and Congregational enterprise at the start. Congregational antislavery views, however, dominated the community, especially after President Jonathan Blanchard, though a Presbyterian, identified himself with the antislavery cause, and Galesburg became the principal station on the underground railroad in Illinois.[46] Blanchard became a Congregationalist in 1842.

The first of the Congregational ministers to arrive in Michigan was Isaac W. Ruggles, who came from a pastorate of the South Bainbridge Church, one of the New York State churches which had refused to enter the Presbyterian fold. He arrived in Michigan territory in 1824. Ruggles' staunch Congregationalism and the fact that he had the field largely to himself gave the Congregationalists a start in Michigan

---

[45] W. H. Herndon and Jesse W. Weik, *Lincoln*, I, 178–79; see also Rammelkamp, *Illinois College*, chap. v: "Illinois College and the Anti-slavery Movement," pp. 101–26; also William H. Collins, "Congregationalism in Western Illinois," *Fiftieth Anniversary of the Organization of the General Congregational Association of Illinois* (Ottawa, Ill., 1894), pp. 35–37.

[46] Ernest Elmo Calkins, *They Broke the Prairie: Being Some Accounts of the Settlement of the Upper Mississippi Valley by Religious and Educational Pioneers, Told in Terms of One City, Galesburg, and of One College, Knox* (New York: Charles Scribner's Sons, 1937), pp. 172, 186 ff., 221–29. For a full discussion of the slavery issue in the Galesburg church see Hermann R. Muelder, "Congregationalists and Presbyterians in the Early History of the Galesburg Churches," *Papers in Illinois History and Transactions for the Year 1937* (Springfield: Illinois State Historical Society, 1938), pp. 53–70.

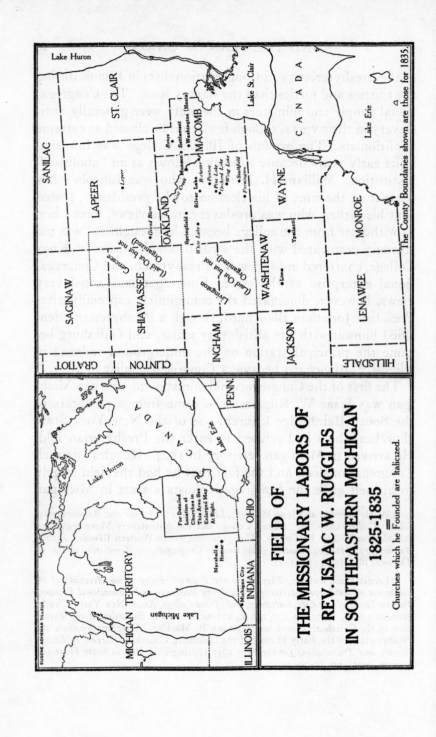

Lake Huron

ST. CLAIR

Lake St. Clair

CANADA

Lake Erie

SANILAC

LAPEER

MACOMB

Romeo

Settlement (Hosia)
Washington (Hosia)

WAYNE

MONROE

•*Lapeer*

Rochester
•*Pontiac*

•*Pine Lake*
•*Orchard Lake*
•*Silver Lake*

SouthField

•*Farmington*

Pine Creek

Grand Blanc

OAKLAND

•*Springfield*
White Lake

Genesee
(Laid Out but not Organized)

WASHTENAW

•*Lima*

•*Ypsilanti*

SAGINAW

SHIAWASSEE

Livingston
(Laid Out but not Organized)

INGHAM

LENAWEE

GRATIOT

CLINTON

JACKSON

HILLSDALE

The County Boundaries shown are those for 1835.

EUGENE ADHEMAR TILLEUX

MICHIGAN TERRITORY

Lake Huron

CANADA

Lake Erie

PENN.

For Detailed
Location of
Churches in
This Area See
Enlarged Map
At Right.

OHIO

•*Marshall*
•*Homer*

Michigan City

Lake Michigan

INDIANA

ILLINOIS

FIELD OF
THE MISSIONARY LABORS OF
REV. ISAAC W. RUGGLES
IN SOUTHEASTERN MICHIGAN
1825-1835
══
Churches which he Founded are Italicized.

which it enjoyed in few other places. Ruggles settled in Pontiac, where a Presbyterian church had been formed the previous year, but through him Congregationalism began to blossom in the surrounding territory, to the dismay of the agents of the Missionary Society in Detroit, who were committed to the formation of Presbyterian churches in the West.[47]

Ruggles' activity was indefatigable. He visited neighboring communities to preach and administer the Lord's Supper as new population arrived. He formed the Congregational church at Farmington in 1825; the Rochester church in July, 1827, and the church at Romeo in 1828. By 1833 eight Congregational churches, at least, had come into being under the fostering care of Ruggles. Congregational churches were also formed at Ypsilanti (1829) and at Lima (1830).[48]

In June, 1831, Ruggles' hands were greatly strengthened by the arrival of John D. Pierce from Sangerfield, New York, who was as stiff-backed a Congregationalist as was Ruggles himself. He had been commissioned by the American Home Missionary Society to labor either in Michigan or in Illinois. Pierce had been informed that he should join the presbytery on his arrival in the Territory and that "it would not be either wise or desirable to organize any Congregational churches." He replied that he was satisfied that the Congre-

[47] I am indebted to the research of Mr. W. S. Hudson for the facts in this account of the beginnings of Congregationalism in Michigan. Ruggles came to Michigan as a missionary of the United Domestic Missionary Society (I. W. Ruggles to M. Bruen, Pontiac, Mich., March 18, 1825 [A.H.M.S. Correspondence]). Other missionaries had been in the territory, but at the time of Ruggles' arrival only one was on the ground, a Rev. Mr. Ferry at Mackinaw (MS letter, Ruggles to Bruen, Pontiac, Mich., March 28, 1825). For the attitude of the agents in Detroit to the Congregational activities of Ruggles see MS letter, N. M. Wells and E. P. Hastings to B. H. Rice, Detroit, November 24, 1832. See chap. viii.

[48] For reports regarding the formation of these early churches see MS letters, Ruggles to Bruen, Pontiac, August 29, 1825; Ansel Bridgeman to A. Peters, Farmington, M.T., November 11, 1830; Ruggles to A. Peters, Pontiac, September 12, 1827 (Punchard, op. cit., V, 308); Bridgeman to A. Peters, Farmington, October 3, 1831, and March 27, 1832.

gational form of church polity was the scriptural mode and that, if it were adapted to primitive times and to New England in its infancy, "it would not be less so to the new settlements of the West."[49] In 1837, while laboring in Calhoun County, he had received a letter from a "leading member of the Presbytery," stating that he need expect no further support if he persisted in his intention of organizing a Congregational church in the town of Marshall. Pierce, however, was not daunted by this warning and not only formed a Congregational church at Marshall (1831) but also formed one in the town of Homer (1833) in the same county.[50]

Congregational missionaries working in Michigan began now to find difficulty in securing commissions from the American Home Missionary Society. Complaints were numerous that the agents favored Presbyterians. Pierce, writing to the American Home Missionary secretary in 1837, states that he knows no Congregational minister in the state who has not suffered from discrimination. E. P. Hastings, one of the agents, bewailed the fact that Pierce did not belong to a presbytery so it was impossible to "apply the *corrective*."[51] John P. Cleavland, another agent, urged the Marshall church to adopt Presbyterian polity; and, when it refused, he formed another church on a Presbyterian basis.[52] The controversy within Presbyterianism which eventually resulted in its bisection in 1837 served to give Congregationalists in the West increased prestige and made it easier to form churches of that order. In 1837 a Michigan association was organized, seemingly, however, only as a temporary expedient. In

[49] John D. Pierce, "Congregationalism in Michigan: A Sketch of Its Introduction, Establishment, and Progress," *Congregational Quarterly*, April, 1860, pp. 190–97.

[50] MS letter, Pierce to A.H.M.S., Marshall, May 8, 1835; *idem* to *idem*, Marshall, May 20, 1835.

[51] MS letter, Wells and Hastings to B. H. Rice, Detroit, November 24, 1832; William Page to A. Peters, Ann Arbor, August 9, 1836; Pierce to A.H.M.S., May 8, 1837; Hastings to Charles Hale, Detroit, March 5, 1835.

[52] Pierce, *op. cit.*, p. 194.

1839 and 1840, three Congregational associations were formed in Michigan: the Marshall, the Jackson, and the Eastern.[53] In 1842 a General Association for the state of Michigan was organized at Jackson. These Congregational activities in Michigan failed, however, to secure the sympathy and support of their New England brethren. The reason seems to have been that they thought the Congregationalists in the West had degenerated into a kind of Arminian perfectionism and that it was totally unworthy to be "countenanced" by them.[54]

In the year 1841 Michigan Congregationalism gained two strong recruits in Leander Smith Hobart and Marcus Harrison. Hobart was fresh from Yale Divinity School, and Harrison came over from the Presbyterian fold with his Jackson congregation. Michigan Congregationalism was now forging ahead with rapid strides. Harrison reported in 1842 that, of the nine churches in his county, five were Congregational and two others had passed resolutions to become so.[55] The Presbyterian missionary, A. P. Hoyt, at Kalamazoo, complained to the missionary office that "the evil spirit of high Congregationalism which is getting up in N. England, has got up here. There is a settled determination on the part of our Congregational ministers to cut and carve away among our churches, until they are either congregationalized or nullified."[56]

The great majority of the early Congregational churches in Michigan were made up of people of New England origin, the majority, however, having come by way of New York. Two churches, those at Vermontville and Armada, were made up of people directly from New England who migrated

---

[53] *Ibid.*, p. 194. Pierce states that between 1835 and 1840 thirteen Congregational churches were formed in Michigan (*ibid.*, p. 195).

[54] *Ibid.*, p. 196.

[55] Harrison to Badger, Jackson, March 7, 1842.

[56] Hoyt to Milton Badger, Kalamazoo, September 10, 1841.

as a colony.[57] The opening of the Erie Canal in 1825 greatly facilitated New York immigration into Michigan and beyond.

Among the earliest names that have a relationship to the beginnings of Congregationalism in Wisconsin are Cutting Marsh and Aratus Kent. The former came as a missionary to the Stockbridge Indians in 1830, working under the American Board of Commissioners for Foreign Missions; the latter we have already met at Galena, Illinois, near the mining region of southwestern Wisconsin, and in his work he crossed the line into Wisconsin territory. In 1837 came Cyrus Nichols to Racine and in the same year Moses Ordway. Two years later (January 17, 1839) the Milwaukee Presbytery was formed, made up of one Congregational and three Presbyterian churches.[58]

"The delusion that Congregational salt lost all its savor in crossing the Hudson River" had been largely exploded by the time the settlement of Wisconsin began, with the result that Congregationalists displayed more denominational independence there than in any of the other previously formed western states.[59] The division in the Presbyterian church precipitated in 1837 seemed to have caused the New School group to be all the more anxious for Congregational co-operation, while it produced a more assertive and independent attitude on the part of Congregationalists. By 1840 there had been at least thirteen Congregational churches organized in Wiscon-

[57] From county histories it has been possible to discover the communities from which the original members of a few of the churches came. Of the eleven members of the Grand Blanc church, nine were from New York, three were from Scotland, and three unknown. All ten of the original White Lake members came from New York, and, when that church became Presbyterian in 1845, eight withdrew to form a Congregational church. In the Marshall church four were from New York, five unknown; Rochester, four were from New York, six unknown. Most of the settlers from New York were second-generation New Englanders and had grown up under operation of the Plan of Union.

[58] For the facts relating to Wisconsin I have drawn largely from Richard Day Leonard, "The Presbyterian and Congregational Convention of Wisconsin, 1840–1850" (University of Chicago thesis [1938]).

[59] Punchard, *op. cit.*, V, 326.

sin.[60] The presbytery which had been formed in 1839 was a
Plan of Union affair and, at its first meeting, extended an invitation to the Congregational churches to co-operate with
them.[61] The Congregationalists, however, seem to have been
quite reluctant to enter into any union with the Presbyterians.[62] Evidently their past experience and the fact that immigration from New England was pushing into the territory in
much greater numbers than from other regions help explain
that reluctance. At the meeting of the presbytery, June 16,
1840, a call was made for a meeting to be held at Troy,
October 6 of the same year, and at the same time and place
a Congregational convention was summoned. Here in a
little one-room country schoolhouse, since there was no
church building in the place, the Presbyterian and Congregational Convention of Wisconsin was formed. This provided
something new in the relationship of the two churches, in
that a union of the two denominations was not sought but
simply a basis on which they could act harmoniously together.[63] The convention became to the Congregationalists
an association and to the Presbyterians a presbytery, while
the individual churches belonging to it were to remain fully
Congregational or Presbyterian. There were to be no mixed
congregations as provided in the Plan of Union. The convention soon was in full operation and working harmoniously.
The number of churches and ministers in the convention increased from a mere handful in 1840 to more than a hundred

[60] The first three permanent Wisconsin Congregational churches were South
Prairieville (Waukesha [1838]), Kenosha (1838), and Beloit (1838). In 1839–40
ten Congregational churches were formed (Punchard, *op. cit.*, p. 334).

[61] "Minutes (MSS) of the Regular and Special Sessions of the Presbytery of
Wisconsin, 1839–1840, and of the Presbyterian and Congregational Convention of
Wisconsin, 1840–1861," pp. 25–28, quoted in Leonard, *op. cit.*, p. 7.

[62] David A. Sherman to the A.H.M.S., December 17, 1840, states that the union
"was not accomplished without difficulty" and that "the Congregationalists, in
general seem to have come to the meeting, with their minds made up against a
Union."

[63] For a full discussion of the proceedings of the Troy meeting and the provisions
there adopted see Leonard, *op. cit.*, pp. 24–37; see also Punchard, *op. cit.*, pp. 336–37.

ten years later. This increase had been largely in Congregational churches and ministers, the growth being in the proportion of three Congregational to one Presbyterian.

The practical dissolution of the convention was begun by the withdrawal of the Presbyterian church of Milwaukee, in 1851, which united with some newly organized Presbyterian churches to form the presbytery of Milwaukee. The same year the presbytery of Fox River was organized, and in 1856 the synod of Wisconsin was formed. The Old School Presbyterians also became active in Wisconsin after 1850. This Presbyterian movement did not mean that the convention was destroyed, but the number of Presbyterian churches in the convention became less and less as time went on, and in 1874 the convention changed its name to the Congregational and Presbyterian Convention in recognition of the predominance of Congregationalism. Ten years later the convention became the Wisconsin Congregational Conference. But the original provisions of the earlier convention were never abrogated.[64]

Both Congregationalism and Presbyterianism in early Wisconsin were subsidized by the American Home Missionary Society, as was true everywhere else throughout the West. Up to 1851 the society had aided 121 ministers in Wisconsin, out of a total of 135. In that year there were but ten self-supporting churches in the state.[65] The early missionaries sent to Wisconsin were middle-aged men. In 1840 Stephen Peet, the agent for the territory, complained, "Not a single young man has come among us. All good men, but some peculiarity."[66] Later, however, young men were sent in increasing numbers, coming largely from Bangor, Yale, Auburn, and Union seminaries. Oberlin men were rigidly ex-

[64] Punchard, *op. cit.*, chap. vi, pp. 131–35.

[65] Stephen Peet, *History of the Presbyterian and Congregational Churches and Ministers in Wisconsin* (Milwaukee, 1851), pp. 52–54, 191.

[66] Peet to Badger, December 10, 1840.

cluded, for Oberlin theology found little favor among the leaders in early Wisconsin Congregationalism.

The salary for missionaries was fixed by the society at $400 a year, only part of which was to come from the society, as every church was expected to pay as much as possible toward the support of the ministry. The expenditures of a missionary, Noah Cooke, at Mineral Point in the year 1840, are shown in detail in the accompanying table. The

Firewood	$ 30
Shoes	12
Meat and salt	14
Clothing	50
Horse-keeping	30
Sugar and molasses	10
Medicine	5
Schooling	12
Flour and meal	30
Moving expenses in coming	125
House rent	100
Books	30
Postage	10

$458[67]

sacrificial spirit prevalent among the early missionaries is illustrated by the action of Calvin Warner. Warner was the minister in the prosperous town of South Prairieville (Waukesha), where he was popular and happy. The agent, Peet, however, asked him to visit the mining section of the state, where the little church at the town of Potosi extended him a call. Potosi was a run-down mining town and a cesspool of immorality. But Warner accepted the call, "at a sacrifice of friends, feeling, and money," as he stated in a letter to the agent.[68]

The outstanding man in this early period of Wisconsin

[67] Cooke to A.H.M.S., Mineral Point, April 1, 1844.

[68] Warner to Badger, South Prairieville, January 8, 1845; also Peet to A.H.M.S., November 30, 1846.

Congregational history is undoubtedly Stephen Peet. He was a native of Vermont, a graduate of Yale, and prepared for the ministry at Princeton and Auburn. After a four-year period of labor for the Seaman's Friend Society along the Erie Canal, and a pastorate at Euclid, Ohio, he came to Wisconsin in 1833 to become the minister of the church at Green Bay. After putting that semi-moribund church on its feet, Peet on his own initiative made a tour of Wisconsin for the purpose of survey and investigation.[69] As Dr. Leonard states, though Peet was not the first missionary to Wisconsin, he was the first to reveal its importance and the opportunity it presented for missionary effort. Peet gave Wisconsin most effective publicity in a revealing article in the *Home Missionary* (September, 1839), and the elaborate report he prepared of his survey, still reposing among the documents of the American Home Missionary Society, is irrefutable proof of his energy, vision, and statesmanship. Leonard thinks that this tour of Peet's might well be celebrated as a landmark in Wisconsin history, for it proved a powerful stimulus to that New England migration to the state which is basic in Wisconsin history.[70]

After this notable work Peet was the natural choice of the American Home Missionary Society for their Wisconsin agency. He began his seven-year service in that capacity on June 1, 1841. The work of these years in Wisconsin has already been summarized as far as the establishment of churches is concerned, and the relative rapid progress of the Wisconsin convention was largely due to Peet's energetic leadership. Owing to unfortunate misunderstandings, based on accusations that Congregationalists in Wisconsin were not receiving their share of support from the American Home Missionary Society, a controversy was precipitated which eventually led to Peet's resignation (March, 1848). Peet

[69] Peet to Badger, April 9, 1839; Peet to the A.H.M.S., March 29, 1839.

[70] Leonard, *op. cit.*, p. 69.

had been the prime mover in the founding of Beloit College, which opened its doors in 1847. After his resignation Peet devoted the remaining years of his life to the establishment of a theological seminary in Chicago which was chartered in 1855 as the Chicago Theological Seminary.[71]

The first settlers in the present state of Iowa were attracted to the region where stands the present city of Dubuque by the rich deposits of lead. To this section, therefore, came the first emissary, Cyrus Watson, of the American Home Missionary Society, in the year 1836. He was, however, as was generally the case in new settlements, antedated by a Methodist preacher, with whom Watson alternately shared a log schoolhouse as a preaching-place. Across the Mississippi at Galena, Illinois, was the veteran Aratus Kent, and farther south was Asa Turner at Quincy.[72] In 1831 Turner made a visit to Galena, and in 1836 he went on a missionary tour into the "Black Hawk purchase." Others came on tours of inspection, among them Julius A. Reed, but recently graduated from Yale College but not yet determined on his lifework. He came in 1833 and has left an interesting account of his Iowa Journey.[73] Later, after graduating from Yale Divinity School, Reed, with the assistance of Asa Turner and William Kirby, formed a Congregational church at Warsaw, Illinois. He crossed the river into Iowa on several occasions between 1836 and 1838. After 1840 he began work in Iowa, first as a missionary, later becoming the Iowa agent of the American Home Missionary Society, in which

[71] G. S. F. Savage, "A Chapter of the Early History of the Chicago Theological Seminary," *Illinois Society of Church History Papers* (*Congregational*), I (Chicago, 1895), pp. 11-23.

[72] The story of Congregational beginnings in Iowa is well told in Truman O. Douglas, *The Pilgrims of Iowa* (Boston and Chicago: Pilgrim Press, 1911). A shorter but quite satisfactory account is found in Punchard, *op. cit.*, V, 224-46. The letters of the American Home Missionary Society for Iowa afford the usual side lights on the early operations of the missionaries.

[73] *Iowa Newsletter* (1862), quoted in Douglas, "Builders of a Commonwealth," Vol. I: "The Patriarchs and Their Associates," pp. 124-27 (typewritten).

capacity he served, with an intermission of five years as agent of Iowa College, until the end of his active career.

The first Congregational church to be formed in Iowa, however, was that at Denmark. We have already noted Asa Turner's visit to Iowa in 1836. "Ever after," as Douglas states, "his eyes and heart were turned" that way. Denmark was a transplanted New England community located some miles west of the Mississippi in the extreme southeast corner of the territory. The people had brought their New England religion with them and, in the spring of 1838, invited Asa Turner and Julius A. Reed to visit them for the purpose of organizing a church. This was accomplished on May 5 of that year when thirty-two individuals "assented to the Articles of Faith" and signed the covenant. To use the words of Turner:

> They were the first to unfurl that banner on the west side of the Mississippi which more than two hundred years before their fathers unfurled over the Plymouth Rock. . . . . The infant church stood alone on the outskirts of civilization, farther west than any other that bore the family name, cherishing the hope that their doctrines and polity might roll west with the wave of immigration.

The building in which the organization took place was little more than a shanty, twenty by twenty-four; the floor was loose boards, the pews were slabs without backs. The church was formed; but who should be the minister? They desired Asa Turner; but would he consent? They asked him; he accepted, and in August of that year he began his ministry at Denmark which was to last for thirty years.[74]

On December 1, 1838, the Congregational forces in Iowa were increased 100 per cent by the coming of Reuben Gaylord and wife, whom he had married at Round Prairie, Illinois, on the way to Iowa. Like many of the other western missionaries, Gaylord was a graduate of Yale College and Yale Divinity School and had spent two and a half years as a tutor in Illinois College. Gaylord began his work at Dan-

[74] Douglas, "Builders of a Commonwealth," I, 13-58.

ville and New London, some miles north of Denmark, and the next June a church was formed at the former place. Presbyterian churches were formed at Dubuque and Davenport, which later became Congregational. Then in rapid succession churches were formed at Davenport, Fairfield, and Lyons. This first period of Congregational church-founding in Iowa closes with the year 1843. In 1840 the Congregational Association of Iowa had been formed at Denmark, the first state association to be formed west of New York.[75]

The year 1843 is made notable in the Congregational history of Iowa by the coming of the "Iowa band."[76] This was a group of eleven students at Andover Theological Seminary who in the fall of 1842 agreed to go to Iowa to serve as missionaries. When Asa Turner, the agent for Iowa, heard this news, he remarked, "Important if true." For twelve years he had been writing letters urging Iowa's needs upon the hearts and consciences of his coreligionists in the East with little response. Professor Emerson, at Andover, had bluntly stated that he thought it the duty of the students to seek fields of labor outside New England. In June, 1843, Asa Turner addressed a letter to one of the band, in which he stated, "I have received so many promises of the kind, that they do not now even begin to excite a hope." He assures them, however, that, if they do actually decide to come, they will find a healthful climate which "will permit men to live long enough, if they do their duty. If they do not, no matter how soon they die." He warns them that people will not address them as "the Rev. Mr. So-and-so, but will

[75] Douglas, *Pilgrims of Iowa*, pp. 41 ff.

[76] The names of this band were, with their native states, Harvey Adams, New Hampshire; Edwin B. Turner, Massachusetts; Daniel Lane, Maine; Erastus Ripley, Connecticut; James J. Hill, Maine; Ebenezer Alden, Massachusetts; Benjamin A. Spalding, Massachusetts; Ephraim Adams, New Hampshire; Alden B. Robbins, Massachusetts; Horace Hutchinson, Massachusetts; and William Salter, New York. Two of the number, for legitimate reasons, withdrew.

call you simply by your name, and your wife Peggy or Polly, or whatever her name may be." The letter closes with:

Come on, brethren, come with the spirit of your Pilgrim Fathers, and plant their principles in this rich soil. Don't be ashamed of your mother as soon as you cross the Alleghanies, as many of our good brethren are, even some on whom she has put honorary titles. . . . . Give my love to all that little band, and their intended ones, and say we hope soon to welcome them on the west side of the great Mississippi. May the Lord direct your way.[77]

On Sunday, November 5, 1843, the little town of Denmark and all the region roundabout was in a great stir. Seven young preachers, all fresh from Andover, and two others were to be ordained in the little church. And a surprising thing about the whole procedure was that everything went according to the Congregational way. When Turner was asked by one of the band which form of church government was best suited for the West, he replied, "Congregationalism, the world over!" The Congregational renaissance was now well on its way and perhaps more marked in Iowa than anywhere else.[78]

The Congregational pioneers in the territory of Minnesota were missionaries of the American Board of Commissioners for Foreign Missions to the Dakota Indians, whose labors began in 1834 with the coming of Samuel and Gideon H. Pond. But this story belongs to the following chapter. The first home missionaries did not begin their work in Minnesota until 1850.[79]

[77] For Turner's letter see Douglas, *Pilgrims of Iowa*, pp. 54-55.

[78] From 1840 to 1850 twenty-three Congregational churches were formed in Iowa. In 1847 the Iowa Congregationalists established Iowa College at Davenport, which was moved to Grinnell in 1860.

[79] D. Burt, "Congregationalism in Minnesota," *Congregational Quarterly*, II (1860), 67-72.

CHAPTER III

Congregational Home and Indian Missions

THE Congregationalists have the longest record of missionary endeavor of any of the American churches. One of the principal objects which attracted the Leyden Pilgrims to cross the ocean was that they might bring Christianity to the savage inhabitants of America, while the Massachusetts Bay Puritans declared in 1629 that "the propagating of the gospel is the thing wee doe professe above all to bee our ayme." The Congregationalists have always taken pride in the accomplishments of John Eliot and the Mayhews in bringing the gospel to the Massachusetts Indians and in the fact that out of their work came the first missionary society for the spreading of the gospel in America, the President and Society for the Propagation of the Gospell in New England, formed in 1649. From this time forward the Congregationalists were never without a missionary interest.[1]

[1] One of the factors with which we need to reckon in attempting to understand the rapid development of missionary interest among New England Congregationalists at the end of the eighteenth and the early part of the nineteenth centuries was the influence exerted by the Hopkinsian theology. Samuel Hopkins, the leader of this particular school of New England Calvinism, had been a pupil in the home of Jonathan Edwards and later, in developing the Edwardian theology, had laid principal stress upon what his great teacher had called "disinterested benevolence." Depravity, he taught, consisted in self-love, while holiness consisted in disinterested benevolence, the opposite of self-love. The real Christian, therefore, must be oblivious of his own interest and concerned about the highest good to the greatest number of creatures. This implies the need of spreading Christianity over the entire world. Hopkins also stressed a general atonement, emphasizing the universality of the atoning work of Christ. Thus Christ's death is as effective in bringing salvation to Negroes and Indians as to the most privileged among the New Englanders themselves (*The Works of Samuel Hopkins, D.D., etc., with a Memoir of His Life and Character* [3 vols.; Boston, 1854], Vol. I, chap. xii, pp. 378–99).

On June 21, 1774, the General Association of Connecticut passed the following resolution:

This association taking into consideration the state of ye Settlements now forming in the Wilderness to the Westward and Northward of us, who are mostly destitute of a preached Gospel, many of which are Brethren Emigrants from this Colony, think it advisable that an attempt should be made to send Missionaries among them, and for obtaining a Support for such Missionaries would recommend it to the Several Ministers of this Colony to promote a Subscription among their people for this purpose.[2]

The Association met sufficient encouragement in this enterprise that it was resolved to appoint two missionaries at once who were to start on a five- or six-month mission in the spring. The newspapers of the colony carried announcements of the mission, and funds were solicited for its support.[3] The minutes of the association for 1776 are lost, and there is no record of the sending of missionaries in subsequent meetings until 1780. But there is, however, a continuous record of home missionary activity from 1792 on, until the formation of the Connecticut Missionary Society in 1798.[4]

The Connecticut Missionary Society was formed in 1798 for the purpose of Christianizing "the Heathen of North America, and to support and promote Christian knowledge in the new settlements within the United States." This marks the beginning of the most aggressive missionary movement up to that time inaugurated. The formation of other voluntary Congregational societies of similar nature followed in rapid succession. In the same year (1798) a Congregational missionary society was formed in the counties of Berkshire (Mass.) and Columbia (N.Y.) which at once became active in sending missionaries to Vermont, New York, Pennsyl-

---

[2] *The Records of the General Association of ye Colony of Connecticut, from June 20th., 1738, to June 19th., 1799*, p. 76.

[3] *Ibid.*, pp. 80, 81, and 82.

[4] For the records from 1792 to 1798 see *ibid.*, pp. 120, 148, 154, 160, 162, 165–66, 171, 176–83, 186.

vania, and Ohio.[5] In May, 1799, the Massachusetts Missionary Society was established; in May, 1801, the Rhode Island Missionary Society was formed; in September of the same year a New Hampshire society was organized. A Maine society was chartered in 1809. The General Convention of Congregational and Presbyterian Ministers of Vermont resolved itself into a missionary society in 1807. Besides these state organizations, there were numerous county and local organizations.

The missionary magazines published by the several societies constituted an effective medium of early missionary propaganda. The *Connecticut Evangelical Magazine*, for instance, during its first year distributed 39,192 copies and reported profits of $1,759.60.[6] This periodical continued until 1814. The Massachusetts society published the *Massachusetts Missionary Magazine*; the Vermont society had its *Evangelical Magazine*; the New Hampshire society its *Religious Repository*. In 1805 the *Panoplist* was launched by Jedidiah Morse, and, although primarily interested at the beginning in defending Congregational orthodoxy against the rising tide of Unitarianism, it carried much missionary news, and in 1808 it merged with the *Massachusetts Missionary Magazine* to form the *Panoplist and Missionary Magazine*, which in 1819 became the *Panoplist and Missionary Herald* and since 1820 has continued as the *Missionary Herald*.[7]

In 1809 the Connecticut society was maintaining twenty-four missionaries who were working in Vermont, Ohio, Pennsylvania, and New York. In the year 1813–14 the number of missionaries employed was forty-three.[8]

[5] The best recent account of the formation of these early Congregational societies will be found in O. W. Elsbree, *The Rise of the Missionary Spirit in America, 1790–1815* (Williamsburg, Pa., 1928), pp. 59–71.

[6] *Conn. Evang. Mag.*, Aug., 1801, quoted in Elsbree, *op. cit.*, p. 59.

[7] Elsbree, *op. cit.*, pp. 64–67.

[8] *Conn. Evang. Mag. and Religious Intelligencer*, VIII (1815), 26.

A typical report of a missionary of this period is that of Joel T. Benedict, who performed a mission of sixteen weeks in Otsego, Delaware, and Chenango counties, New York, in 1814. During this mission he traveled 739 miles; preached seventy sermons; baptized thirty-five persons; administered the Lord's Supper five times; attended three church meetings and four conferences; visited forty families; organized two churches, and received five into church membership. He reports that religion is at low ebb in the western country and that conditions would be hopeless indeed but for the work of the missionary societies.[9] In 1814, $5,527.52 was appropriated for the support of thirty-eight missionaries; $359 was the largest amount appropriated to any one missionary, Joshua Beer, of the Western Reserve.[10] By 1818 the Connecticut society, since its organization, had employed 138 missionaries, and this year, in addition to the states already entered, its work had expanded into Indiana, Missouri, and Louisiana.[11]

It is not the purpose of this introductory statement to give a detailed account of the work of each of the numerous New England missionary agencies, and only brief summaries of their activities are here attempted. Ranking next in importance to the Connecticut society was that of Massachusetts. By 1824 this society had employed 224 missionaries. The length of their employment was from three to twelve months each, and the "destitute places" where they had served were in Massachusetts, Maine, Rhode Island, New Hampshire, Vermont, New York, Pennsylvania, Virginia, Tennessee, and various states west of the Allegheny Mountains.[12] To a much larger extent than the Connecticut society the Massachusetts

---

[9] *Ibid.*, p. 28. For the reports from each of the forty-three missionaries see *ibid.*, pp. 25–39, 41–43.

[10] *Ibid.*, pp. 47–48.

[11] *Panoplist*, XV (1819), 45.

[12] *Missionary Herald*, XIX (Annual Report, 1823), 257; *ibid.*, XX (1824), 193.

society confined its efforts to the outposts of New England. Its work in Maine particularly was important, the society reporting in 1824 that 120 towns and settlements in Maine with a combined population of more than 100,000 were destitute of "the stated enjoyment of the gospel."[13] Because of the New England emphasis of its work, the Massachusetts society exerted much less influence in the West than did the Connecticut society.

The Rhode Island society, which had as its first president Samuel Hopkins, confined its work principally to that state and had among its objects "to assist Africans in coming to a knowledge of the truth."[14] The New Hampshire society also confined its efforts to the destitute places in that state and to the adjoining regions in northern New York.[15] The Vermont and Maine societies were small, and their activities limited and local, as was also true of the several county societies.[16]

Much of the activity of these early societies was carried on by ministers who were already located in parishes but who were willing to give some of their time to itinerating through the new settlements during a certain part of the year. While engaged in this work, they were paid from four dollars and a half to five dollars per week by the society, their pulpits during their absence being supplied by neighboring pastors or by student supplies. The regular full-time missionary was generally assigned to a definite region and for a definite period, being engaged from year to year. In the Western Reserve of Ohio the amount allowed the missionaries of the Connecticut society was at first seven dollars per week, though later reduced to six dollars.

[13] Ibid., XX, 193–94.

[14] Panoplist, Vol. II (June, 1806).

[15] The Religious Repository, the official publication of the New Hampshire society was not a success, and its appearance was limited to the years 1807–9.

[16] Elsbree, op. cit., pp. 67–71.

After its formation in 1826 the principal home missionary activities of the Congregationalists were carried on through the American Home Missionary Society, the purely Congregational societies gradually becoming auxiliary to this interdenominational organization. In 1828 the New Hampshire, the Massachusetts, the Hampshire, and the Vermont Missionary societies all became auxiliary to the American Home Missionary Society. In 1829 the Rhode Island and Maine societies followed their example, and in 1831 the Domestic Missionary Society of Connecticut also became an auxiliary to the American Home Missionary Society. It was not until 1832 that the Connecticut Missionary Society turned over its work to the American Home Missionary Society.[17]

The steps in the formation of the American Home Missionary Society have been noted in the volume on the Presbyterians[18] and will not require a detailed account here. It was formed in the Brick Presbyterian Church in New York City on May 10, 1826, there being 126 representatives from thirteen states coming from four denominations. Of this number, 27 were Congregationalists. There has arisen some controversy between Presbyterians and Congregationalists as to their respective relationship to this voluntary interdenomination society during the years in which these two denominations were working together through that organization.[19] Dunning, the Congregational historian, states that "from the beginning . . . . Congregationalists were much the most prominent in gifts and in labors."[20] Rev. Gardiner

[17] George Punchard, *History of Congregationalism* (5 vols.; Boston: Congregational Publishing Society, 1881), V, 149.

[18] W. W. Sweet, *Religion on the American Frontier*, Vol. II: *The Presbyterians* (New York, 1936), pp. 59 n., 102 ff., 651-52.

[19] H. W. Ripley, "Sketch of the History of the American Home Missionary Society and the Controversy in Relation to its Origin" (Harlem, N.Y., 1862) (typewritten).

[20] Albert E. Dunning, *Congregationalism in America, etc.* (Chicago: Pilgrim Press, 1894), p. 346.

Spring, who was the minister of the Brick Presbyterian Church in New York, where the society was formed, states that it was largely Presbyterian in origin and management until 1833. Up to this time more than half its funds came from New York State alone, while "its officers were Presbyterians. Its Board of Directors in New York were exclusively Presbyterian."[21] Since the largest single agency co-operating in its formation was the United Domestic Missionary Society, which was largely a Presbyterian organization, with eighty-one missionaries already in the field, it was but natural to suppose that Presbyterian influence continued to dominate the management of the new organization.

The American Home Missionary Society became at once the principal agency through which the Plan of Union was put into operation in the West. This was simply continuing the policies of the Connecticut and the other Congregational home missionary agencies. This phase of its work has already been described in the previous chapter as well as in the volume on the Presbyterians.[22] Since the American Home Missionary Society has been given so much attention in other sections of this volume, as well as in the volume devoted to the Presbyterians, all that will be necessary here is to summarize its total activities during the years under consideration.

The society grew with amazing rapidity. Its receipts increased from $20,031.21 for the first year to $68,627.17 for the seventh year (1833) and $150,940 for the twenty-fifth year. The number of missionaries employed the first year was 169; in 1833 there were 606 on the societies' roll, laboring in 801 congregations and missionary districts. For the year 1836, the year previous to the Old School Presbyterians'

[21] *Personal Reminiscences of the Life and Times of Gardiner Spring* (2 vols.; New York, 1866), I, 265 ff.

[22] Sweet, *op. cit.*, chap. v: "The Operation of the Plan of Union and Frontier Controversy," pp. 99–125.

withdrawal from its support, the society reported 755 missionaries in its employ and $101,565.09 in receipts. In 1833 there were 489 auxiliary societies and associations. In 1840 the number of missionaries had declined to 680, while the income for the year was $80,812. For the year 1850–51 the society had recovered all it had lost and was employing 1,065 missionaries. Of these, 119 were working in Illinois; 93 in Ohio; 29 in Missouri; 6 each in Kentucky and Tennessee; 4 each in Minnesota and California; and 2 in Oregon. In the southern states Virginia had 11; the District of Columbia and Georgia, 1 each; and Maryland, 2. New York was still the largest recipient of American Home Missionary assistance with 170 missionaries; Pennsylvania employed 42; New Jersey, 11; and Delaware, 1. Maine led the New England states in the number of missionaries with 91; Vermont and Massachusetts had 61 each; New Hampshire, 46; Connecticut, 45; and Rhode Island, 7.[23]

The three secretaries, Milton Badger, Charles Hall, and David B. Coe, ended their report for the year 1850–51, which closed a quarter of a century of the society's existence with these words:

Our frontier has retreated from the banks of the Ohio to the shores of the Pacific. Our population has increased from 11,000,000 to 23,000,000. In wealth, in power, in all the elements of national importance, our progress has been such as has no parallel in history; and the work of this Society has increased in like proportion. To diffuse the light and blessing of the Gospel over this expanding domain—to bring these multiplying millions of our population under the influence of christian institutions, and thus train them to be a generation of God's praise—this has been the work intrusted to our hands. . . . .

. . . . In the vast central valley, which is henceforth to hold the sceptre of this continent, and on the shores of the Pacific, where a nation has been born in a day, a work is to be done for Christ—*and done by the present generation*—such as God has intrusted to no other people. To this work let us gird ourselves anew in the strength and with the spirit of our glorious leader.

[23] *Reports of the American Home Missionary Society Presented to the Executive Committee, for the Successive Years 1827–1851* (New York: 1827–51).

In 1815 the estimated number of Indians living within the boundaries of the United States was placed at 240,000, of whom 100,000 were living east of the Mississippi. Of these, the so-called civilized tribes—Creeks, Cherokees, Choctaws, and Chickasaws—made up about 70,000. From the organization of the American Board of Commissioners for Foreign Missions in 1810, it had in its thought the carrying forward of missionary work among the Indians.[24]

The first missionary to begin work among the Indians under the auspices of the A.B.C.F.M. was Cyrus Kingsbury, who arrived in the Cherokee country in south-central Tennessee in January, 1817. Two months later Messrs. Hall and Loring S. Williams with their wives arrived, and by September "four small log buildings" had been erected and other larger buildings planned, and twenty-six native children and youths had been taken into the missionary family for instruction, while considerable progress had been made in preparing for the planting of crops the next spring and in the stocking of the missionary farm.[25] This first missionary station was called Brainerd, "in affectionate remembrance of that able, devoted and successful missionary." Plans were also made this first year to establish another mission among the Choctaws, and Kingsbury and Williams were designated as the most suitable persons to undertake that work.[26]

A contemporary description of the mission at Brainerd in 1818 pictures a comfortable group of log buildings consisting of a mission-house, with a dining-hall, and a kitchen in the rear; several log cabins on each wing for the accommodation of the children and some of the missionaries; other log buildings for storerooms, cornhouses, and stables; a schoolhouse

[24] William E. Strong, *The Story of the American Board* (New York: Pilgrim Press, 1910), pp. 35 and 36.

[25] *First Ten Annual Reports of the American Board of Commissioners for Foreign Missions, etc.* (Boston, 1834), pp. 188–89.

[26] *Ibid.*, pp. 189–90.

accommodating one hundred pupils "on the Lancastrian plan" which was also used as a place of worship, and forty-five acres of cleared land in several fields. The principal expense of the buildings had been defrayed by the government.[27]

The Choctaw mission was called Eliot in "affectionate memorial of the venerable 'Apostle of the American Indians' " and was located four hundred miles southwest of Brainerd in Mississippi. It was begun on August 15, 1818, and in a relatively short time seven dwelling-houses, a mill, a stable, a storehouse, and two other buildings had been completed, and thirty-five acres were cleared ready for the plow. A school was opened on April 19, 1819. So enthusiastic were the Choctaws over the prospect of the school that not only did the chiefs turn over the $200 received by the nation annually from the federal government but a subscription was taken amounting to eighty cows and calves, and $500 to be paid annually.[28]

Interest in Indian missions was not peculiar to the Congregationalists but was shared by all the American churches.[29] The policy of the federal government, inaugurated in 1820 of distributing several thousands of dollars annually among missionary societies engaged in Indian work was doubtless partly responsible for the rapid expansion of Indian mission activities among Protestants and Catholics alike. And at no

---

[27] During the life of the Brainerd mission, from 1817 to 1837, thirty-seven missionaries were connected with the mission (see Robert Sparks Walker, *Torchlights to the Cherokees: The Brainerd Mission* [New York: Macmillan Co., 1931], chap. iv: "Missionaries Who Came to Brainerd," pp. 41–58).

[28] *Ibid.*, pp. 241–45; see also Strong, *op. cit.*, pp. 38–39.

[29] For the Indian activities of the other churches see W. W. Sweet, *Circuit-Rider Days along the Ohio* (New York: Methodist Book Concern, 1924), chap. iv: "The Wyandot Mission"; *Religion on the American Frontier*, Vol. II: *The Presbyterians*, chap. xiii; "Documents Illustrating the Work of the Presbyterian Indian Missions." For a discussion of government Indian policy see Annie H. Abel, *History of Events Resulting in Indian Consolidation West of the Mississippi River* ("Annual Reports of the American Historical Association" [Washington, 1906]), Vol. I. For the Baptists see Isaac McCoy, *History of Baptist Indian Missions* (New York, 1840).

period was more progress made toward Christianizing and civilizing the Indians than at this time.

Other missions were planned among the Cherokees, one to that portion of the tribe which had removed to Arkansas.[30] This mission was opened in 1821, the central station receiving the name of Dwight. This was a more difficult undertaking, owing to the great distance and to the fact that conditions were more primitive and the danger from disease and the hardships of pioneering more acute. The Chickasaws, whose country lay between that of the Cherokees and the Choctaws, were also asking for a mission, the board stating that intelligent opinion among the people of the United States as well as among the better-informed Indians themselves was that they must be civilized or become extinct. The board was of the opinion that the establishment of Indian missions as rapidly as possible was therefore most urgent, for they felt that, if the Indians became extinct, "their blood will be upon this nation."[31]

The work among the Choctaws was greatly aided by the invention of an alphabet by an ignorant half-breed, George Guess, who devised a symbol for every syllable in the Choctaw tongue. Very soon half the tribe were able to read their own language. Missionary influence was also immediately manifest by the change in dress, such as the wearing of hats, pantaloons, and shoes; by the enactment of wholesome laws, printed in the Choctaw tongue.[32]

In the year 1826–27 the number of Indian missions under the American Board was greatly augmented by the taking-over of the missions begun by the United Foreign Missionary Society, an organization of the Presbyterian, the Dutch Re-

[30] *First Ten Annual Reports*, pp. 245–46; see also Cephas Washburn, *Reminiscences of the Indians* (Boston, 1869), pp. 16 and 17.

[31] *First Ten Annual Reports*, p. 247.

[32] Grant Foreman, *The Five Civilized Tribes* (Norman, Okla.: University of Oklahoma Press, 1934), pp. 19 and 20.

formed, and the Associate Reformed churches. These missions were: two to the Osages in Arkansas and Missouri, a mission to various tribes at Mackinaw, Michigan territory, one to the Maumees in Ohio, and another to the remnants of the New York tribes near Buffalo. The board also assumed the control of the Stockbridge mission in Wisconsin as well as the Chickasaw mission which had been begun by the Presbyterian Synod of South Carolina and Georgia.[33] In 1830 the American Board was carrying on the following work among the American Indians. The Cherokee missions had eight stations, each station having its own church organization, there being a total membership of 219, of whom 167 were Indians; eight schools were in operation, and at least 600 Indians had been taught to read in the English language.[34] At the Chickasaw mission there were three stations, two missionaries, and four teachers. The Choctaw mission was maintaining nine stations in which there were about 360 Indian church members, and seven schools with 250 scholars, the majority of whom were full-blooded Choctaws. In the Cherokee mission in Arkansas there were three stations. The work among the Osages was carried on from four stations, while some twenty miles away there were several thousand emigrant Creeks among whom work was beginning. The well-known missionary, Cutting Marsh, was at the Green Bay mission among the Stockbridges. At Mackinaw there was a large mission family consisting of William F. Ferry, missionary and superintendent, and fifteen helpers. In this year a hopeful beginning was made among the Ojibeways near the southwest shore of Lake Superior, where two young men fresh from Andover, William T. Boutwell and Sherman Hall, had taken

[33] The transfer of these missions to the American board was with the full agreement of all parties. For the transfer of the Chickasaw mission see *Nineteenth Annual Meeting of the American Board of Commissioners for Foreign Missions* (1828), p. 73. In the transfer the continued patronage and favor of the churches of the synod was strongly recommended.

[34] *A.B.C.F.M. Annual Report* (1831), pp. 59–99.

up the work. The Maumee mission in Ohio was under Isaac Van Tassel as missionary and two assistants. In New York work was maintained among the Tuscaroras and the Senecas and at Cattaraugus and at a station known as Allegheny.

The whole missionary enterprise east of the Mississippi was thrown into confusion during the thirties by the agitation to remove the Indians to regions beyond that river. Some Indian missionaries had become convinced that the welfare of the Indians depended upon their removal away from the influence of the whites. One of the principal advocates of this plan was Isaac McCoy, who, as a Baptist missionary, had worked for many years among the Indians.[35] Added to these influences was the greed of the whites for the Indian lands. This was a particularly powerful influence in Georgia and Alabama, where both state and national governments joined to bring about the removal of the Choctaws, the Chickasaws, and the Cherokees. The Choctaws and the Chickasaws were finally persuaded to make treaties ceding their lands, while the Cherokees resisted and sent protests to Washington. Finally, however, a portion of the tribe were persuaded to sign a treaty, and their lands were divided and sold while the Indians were still living on them.[36]

About seven thousand of the Choctaws were transferred to their new homes in 1831, and the following year the remaining fifteen thousand were removed. The story of that removal, though conducted as humanely as possible, is a sad one indeed, the only bright spots being furnished by the fine behavior of the Christian Indians. The Chickasaws, with the proceeds from their lands, "gave themselves up to idleness, drunkenness, and gambling" and lost their independent existence, and in 1835 the mission among them was closed.

[35] For McCoy's plans see his *History of Baptist Indian Missions* and the *Annual Register of Indian Affairs within the Indian Territory, 1835–1838.*

[36] The story of these happenings from the standpoint of the missionaries is told in the *Annual Reports* of the American Board. The tragic story of the Cherokee removals will be found in Walker, *op. cit.*

The forceful removal of the Cherokees came in 1837 with results similar to that among the Choctaws.[37] Sixteen thousand Cherokees, divided into fourteen companies set out in October, 1838, and, averaging from six to fifteen miles a day, made their painful way through Tennessee, Kentucky, Illinois, Missouri, and Arkansas to their new homes. On the journey there was on an average of thirteen to fifteen deaths a day totaling some four thousand out of a population of about sixteen thousand.[38]

A painful episode in connection with the removal of the Cherokees was the treatment accorded Rev. S. A. Worcester, one of the principal missionaries, and Dr. Elizur Butler, physician and missionary, by the Georgia authorities. When ordered to take the oath of allegiance to the state of Georgia in accordance with a law recently passed, requiring such an oath of all white men living in the Indian country, they refused. Whereupon they were arrested, thrown in jail, and later sentenced to four years at hard labor in the penitentiary. An appeal to the president of the United States brought no relief. Brought to the Supreme Court of the United States, the action of the Georgia court was reversed and annulled; but the Georgia authorities refused to obey the injunction of the highest court, and for fifteen months these innocent and high-minded men were kept in confinement and were only released when the Georgia governor faced the possibility of a new process in the Supreme Court.[39]

The 1830's were disastrous years for the Indian work of the American Board and saw the abandonment of five of their missions. The mission to the Osages was abandoned in 1837,

[37] Strong, op. cit., pp. 43-47.

[38] In the report of the removal found in the Annual Report of the A.B.C.F.M. for 1839 it is stated: "This suffering and mortality were probably the necessary consequence of the measure itself, and could have been by no precaution avoided" (pp. 135-37).

[39] Walker (op. cit., chaps. xix and xx, pp. 256-96) gives a full account of these proceedings.

when their lands were ceded to the Cherokees. Owing to changes in population, the Maumee mission was given up in 1835, as was also the mission at Mackinaw in 1836 and for the same reason. As has been noted, the Chickasaw mission was closed in 1835, and the Creek mission in 1837. But these years also saw the opening of four new missions, those to the Pawnees in 1834, to the Oregon Indians in 1835, and in the same year to the Dakotas and to the Abenaquis. By 1836 the tribes within the states and territories of the United States had almost disappeared, and for that reason attention was turned increasingly to the Indians in the Far West.[40]

The Oregon Indians had come to the attention of Christian people throughout the country by the coming of five Indians from the far Northwest to St. Louis in 1831 asking for the white man's Book of Heaven. This dramatic appeal brought an immediate response, and in 1834 the Methodists sent out Jason Lee with a missionary party to begin work in Willamette Valley.[41] Within a short time after (1836) the Lee party had found their way to the Oregon country two missionaries with their wives were sent out by the American Board, Dr. and Mrs. Marcus Whitman and Rev. and Mrs. H. H. Spalding.[42] The Spaldings took up their work among the Nez Perces at Lapwai and the Whitmans at Waiilatpu among the Cayuses in what is now western Washington.

The *Annual Report* for 1846 lists in the Oregon mission three stations and a total of eight workers. Schools had been established, and a great interest was reported among the Indians especially in implements of husbandry. Whitman

[40] A. C. Bartlett, *Historical Sketch of the Missions of the American Board among the North American Indians* (Boston, 1880) (pamphlet). A general summary of the Indian missions will be found on pp. 22–24.

[41] The story of the appeal for the white man's Book of Heaven is well told in Cornelius J. Brosnan, *Jason Lee: Prophet of the New Oregon* (New York: Macmillan Co., 1932), chap. i.

[42] Clifford M. Drury's *Henry Harmon Spalding* (Caldwell, Idaho: Caxton Printers, 1936) and *Marcus Whitman* (Caldwell, Idaho: Caxton Printers, 1937) are the most detailed and authorative accounts of the Oregon mission.

states that a vast change had taken place among the Indians and that most of them possessed cattle and nearly all had farms of considerable extent. Spalding reported in this same year, however, that gambling among the Indians was on the increase and that the religious meetings had fallen off in interest. On the whole it would seem that the ten years of labor which the missionaries had given to the Oregon Indians had not produced the fruits hoped for. But the Oregon missions will never be forgotten because of the dramatic way in which they came to this end.[43]

The vast influx of settlers brought with them the inevitable white man's diseases, which always proved far more fatal to the Indians than to the whites. And such was the case with the Cayuses among whom the Whitmans had been carrying on their work. The emigration of 1847 had brought with it particularly virulent forms of measles and dysentery, and there was an appalling list of deaths among the Indians, the tribe losing about half its total number within a relatively short time. The rumor spread among the Indians, evidently started by a vicious half-breed who was living at the mission, that Dr. Whitman, instead of curing the Indians by his treatment, was actually trying to poison them all in order that he might secure their lands and cattle. The spreading of such lies brought its result in the Indian attack upon the mission on November 29, 1847, in which both Dr. and Mrs. Whitman were killed, together with most of the other men in the mission, fourteen all told. It was the usual story of Indian massacre, though in this case the women, except Mrs. Whitman, were spared as were also the children, though two died as a result of neglect. Though the other stations were not destroyed, the massacre was too great a blow to be overcome, and the Oregon mission was closed.[44]

The story of the mission among the Dakotas, though pass-

[43] For the most recent account of the massacre see Drury, *Marcus Whitman*, pp. 390–411; *Spalding*, p. 329.

[44] *Report of the A.B.C.F.M.* (1848), pp. 239–44.

ing through much the same sort of experience as befell the Oregon mission, was able to continue and eventually became the most successful of all the Indian work carried on by the American Board.

What is now the state of Minnesota was little more than Indian country in 1830. All told, there were then perhaps twenty to twenty-five thousand Dakota Indians roaming over the vast region west of Wisconsin territory. They had been little affected by civilizing influences and were still in the hunting and fishing stage of development, agriculture being almost unknown among them.[45] Missionary work began among the Dakotas with the arrival at Fort Snelling in 1834 of two brothers from Connecticut, Samuel and Gideon Pond. They came on their own initiative. Having been awakened by a rivival in their community, they felt and almost immediately responded to the call to undertake the bringing of the gospel to non-Christian people in the then Far West. Tall and strong and in their middle twenties the Pond brothers were possessed not only of a great idealism but also with a generous supply of common sense. The commander of Fort Snelling, Major Talliaferro, welcomed them, for he looked upon their coming as an opportunity of introducing agriculture among the Indians. Accordingly, it was not long until these New Englanders, accustomed to farm labor, were engaged in teaching the Indians near the fort to plow.[46]

The Pond brothers, however, were not satisfied to remain at the fort, for they were anxious to begin mission work among the Indians. Their first step in this direction was the erection of "peeled log" house seven miles from the fort, and

[45] For an excellent account of the Dakota Indians and the beginnings of the work of the American Board of Commissioners for Foreign Missions among them see S. R. Riggs, *Tah-Koo Wah-Kan: Or the Gospel among the Dakotas* (Boston: Congregational Sabbath School and Publishing Society, 1869).

[46] S. W. Pond, Jr., *Two Volunteer Missionaries among the Dakotas: Or the Story of the Labors of Samuel W. and Gideon H. Pond* (Boston and Chicago: Congregational Publishing Society, 1893).

within a mile of a large Indian village.[47] Here they took up
their abode and began to win the confidence of their Indian
neighbors.

The following year (1835) Dr. Thomas S. Williamson, who
had the previous year made a voyage up the Mississippi as
far as Fort Snelling, arrived with a commission from the
American Board to begin missionary work among the Dakotas. A native of South Carolina and educated at Jefferson
College and Yale Medical School, Williamson was "a man
of intense but simple piety, possessed of strong common
sense and indefatigable industry, absolutely devoted to missionary life. Discouragements and obstacles only aroused
him to new and stronger efforts."[48] With Williamson, his
wife, and her sister, came also another missionary, J. D.
Stevens, and Mr. and Mrs. Alexander Huggins to be employed as farmers. The Pond brothers welcomed these re-
inforcements, but, since the Ponds were free lances, they
were at first given slight consideration by the official missionaries. To forestall any disparagement of their work because of their unofficial position, Samuel Pond returned to
Connecticut in 1836 to study for the ministry and secure, if
possible, a commission from the American Board. In both
he was successful and within less than a year was back in
Minnesota, having carried on his studies privately.[49] About
this time Stephen R. Riggs, the outstanding personality
among the early Dakota missionaries, arrived on the scene,
and after a short stay at the fort joined Williamson at
Laqui-Parle, and soon a school and church were in successful
operation.[50] One of the principal contributions made by the Pond

[47] *Ibid.*, pp. 32–34, 39–46.

[48] W. W. Folwell, *History of Minnesota* (4 vols.; St. Paul: Minnesota Historical
Society, 1921), I, 170–212.

[49] Pond, *op. cit.*, pp. 108–12.

[50] S. R. Riggs, *Mary and I, or Forty Years among the Sioux* (Boston, 1879), pp.
23–26.

brothers was their work with the Dakota language. By 1840 they had mastered the Sioux tongue and had in preparation an Indian grammar and a small dictionary and were largely the teachers of the other missionaries.[51]

The missions nearest the fort were not so successful as were those farther away, owing to the greater ease with which liquor was secured by the Indians and the loose morals of the soldiers who were generally unscrupulous in their sexual relations with the Indian women. The missionaries found it easier to make women converts than men. This was due to the fact that an Indian woman's acceptance of Christianity entailed fewer changes, while among the males it would mean a change not only of dress but of his amusements and the giving up of many of his ceremonies. But, hardest of all, he had to go to work.[52]

For the next ten years the mission went forward slowly, and on the whole the actual accomplishments seemed relatively small. But the missionary force was augumented in 1848 and 1849, new stations were opened, and foundations were laid for future work and influence. The missionaries had learned the Indian customs, had secured a thorough knowledge of the language, and were familiar with the principal difficulties in attempting to Christianize and civilize the prairie Indian.

Although the next ten years is beyond the period covered by this collection of sources, a brief survey of this Dakota mission during that period will not be out of place. In 1851 two treaties were signed with the Dakotas by which they received $1,665,000 for their lands east of Lake Traverse, and provided for their removal to reservations. This meant that, if the missionaries were to continue their work, they must follow the Indians to their new homes.[53] The treaties

[51] Pond, *op. cit.*, pp. 68 and 216.

[52] Riggs, *Tah-Koo Wah-Kan*, pp. 165, 177, 179 ff.

[53] W. P. Shortridge, "The Transition of a Typical West: Illustrations from the Life of Henry Hastings Sibley, etc." (University of Minnesota dissertation [1919]),

of 1851 and the formation of Minnesota territory in 1849 started a movement of population into Minnesota, though it was slowed down in the early fifties by the attractions of California. By 1855, however, there were more than 40,000 people in the territory, which two years later was raised to 170,000.[54] This large influx of white population caused also a shift in missionary activity, and all the missionaries, except Williamson and the Riggs, left their Indian mission to take up work among the white settlers.[55] The Pond brothers, for instance, became pastors of white churches and continued in that capacity for more than thirty years.

In the midst of the Civil War, when the fortunes of the Union were at low ebb, the Dakotas went on the warpath against the incoming white settlers (August, 1862). For three weeks the Indians had things much their own way, and a reign of terror was spread throughout the Minnesota frontier. Folwell places the number of white victims during the war at 360 massacred and 90 killed in battle.[56] The federal troops, however, were soon reinforced, and in September, at the battle of Wood Lake, the Indians were routed, and about three hundred warriors were captured and placed within a prison camp at Mankato, while some fifteen hundred women and children were placed in a camp near Fort Snelling.[57] The few Christian Indians had exerted their influence to avert the massacres and were instrumental in the escape of numerous white settlers. John Otherday and Paul Maza-kootamane were the principal agents in this humane work.[58]

---

pp. 113-16; see also Sister Eucharista Galvin, "The Influences and Conditions in the Settlement of Minnesota, 1837-1866" (University of Chicago dissertation [1929]), p. 213.

[54] Galvin, op. cit., p. 212.

[55] Pond, op. cit., pp. 211-12, 257-67.   [56] Op. cit., Vol. II, map opp. p. 392.

[57] Riggs, Tah-Koo Wah-Kan, p. 392; Shortridge, op. cit., p. 146. The reasons for the Indian outbreak are set forth in Riggs, Tah-Koo Wah-Kan, pp. 343, 328-30.

[58] Paul Mazakootamane was the president of the Hazelwood Republic which had been formed in 1856 on the Upper Dakota reservation. A constitution was adopted,

Once the uprising was put down, Williamson took immediate advantage of the situation and started Christian work in the prison camp both at Mankato and at Fort Snelling. The Indians welcomed his efforts, and soon a real religious awakening among them was under way. It continued throughout the fall and winter of 1862 and 1863, and by spring almost the entire number at Mankato were baptised and professed Christianity; at the camp near Fort Snelling the labors of the Christian workers were equally successful.[59]

After several removals the Dakotas were finally located (1866) in northern Nebraska where there was a happy reunion of husbands and wives and also of the two native churches. From this time forward the story of the Dakota mission is one of growing native control, while the place of the missionaries became that of general supervisor. In 1871 there were nearly seven hundred members in eight Dakota churches, with five native pastors, two half-breed pastors, while J. W. Williamson was the only white pastor. Meanwhile the reunion of the Old School and New School Presbyterian churches (1869) and the formation of the Presbyterian Board of Foreign Missions made necessary a realignment of the Dakota work. Both Williamsons, father and son, went with the Presbyterian Board, while Riggs remained with the American Board. The Dakota work was divided between the two agencies and has gone on successfully until the present time, and it can be truthfully said that the Dakotas are Christianized.[60]

---

signed by seventeen Indians. They agreed to live by the word of God and to conform to the habits of white people and were to be treated by the United States government as a separate organization. The experiment was most successful (see Riggs, *Tah-Koo Wah-Kan*, pp. 394–400).

[59] *Ibid.*, p. 343; Pond, *op. cit.*, p. 222.

[60] For the account of the more recent years see Riggs, *Tah-Koo Wah-Kan*, pp. 366–67, 373, 418–29; *Mary and I*, pp. 227–28, 262–63 ff. For a summary of the present status of the Dakota mission see George W. Hinman, *The American Indian and Christian Missions* (New York: Revell & Co., 1933), pp. 91–93.

PART II

Documents Illustrating the Work of Congregationalists on the Frontier

CHAPTER IV

The Missionary Society of Connecticut
Letters and Reports from
the Frontier

INTRODUCTION

THE Missionary Society of Connecticut was the most important of the New England state missionary agencies. Not only was it the largest of the state missionary societies but its work was the most widespread, especially on the expanding frontier to which New Englanders were moving. Perhaps the reason why Connecticut Congregationalism was the most active in the West was because of its more effective organization. Since 1709 Connecticut had had a General Association, while each county had had its own council of ministers and churches since the adoption of the Saybrook Platform in 1708. Thus Connecticut Congregationalism had developed the most closely knit organization of any of the New England states, a fact which made possible a more effective missionary policy.[1]

The mere listing of the numbers of missionaries sent out by Connecticut Congregationalists through the agencies of the General Association (1774–98) and the Missionary Society of Connecticut after its organization in 1798 is most impressive. From 1774 to 1798, the period in which missionaries were appointed by the General Association, 48 were sent out to the frontiers of Vermont, New Hampshire, and New York. From 1798 to 1859 the Missionary Society of Connecticut commissioned and supported 276 missionaries. During this period the receipts of the society were $252,512.83, and it was estimated that not far from five hundred churches had been organized through its instrumentality. The documents here reproduced do not, of course, constitute a history of the Missionary Society of Connecticut. They have been selected as representative of the great body of materials to be found in the archives of the society and as illustrative of how the society functioned.

[1] *Contributions to the Ecclesiastical History of Connecticut Prepared under the Direction of the General Association, etc.* (New Haven, 1861). See particularly "Historical Discourse," by Leonard Bacon, pp. 1–72; and "Congregational Home Missions in Connecticut," by Horace Hooker, pp. 163–79.

1. An Address to the Frontier, May 29, 1799
2. A Letter to the Society Soliciting Assistance from Rev. Daniel Story and Rufus Putnam, Marietta, May 22, 1799
3. Documents Showing the Relationship of the Society to the Connecticut State Legislature
4. Letter from Joseph Badger, January 8, 1801
5. Proceedings concerning the Ordination and Commissioning of Ezekiel J. Chapman as a Missionary to New Connecticut, October 13, 1801
6. Report of the Trustees of the Missionary Society of Connecticut, June, 1802
7. Letter of John McMillan regarding the Licensing of Jonathan Leslie
8. Report of Abraham Scott, Missionary, January 22, 1808
9. Correspondence regarding the Affiliation with the American Home Missionary Society

1. An Address to the Frontier, May 29, 1799

At a meeting of the Trustees of the Missionary Society of Connecticut, at Hartford, May 29th, 1799. Present:

The Hon'ble John Treadwell, Esq., *Chairman.*
The Hon'ble Heman Swift, Esq.
The Hon'ble Roger Newberry, Esq.
The Hon'ble Jonathan Brace, Esq.
The Rev^d. Nathan Strong
The Rev^d. Cyprian Strong
The Rev^d. Charles Backus

Voted, That the following address be printed and sent to the inhabitants of the New Settlements in the Northern and Western parts of the United States.

TO THE INHABITANTS OF THE NEW SETTLEMENTS IN THE NORTHERN AND WESTERN PARTS OF THE UNITED STATES

Christian Friends and Brethren:

The General Association of the State of Connecticut, as the most of you are sensible, have for years past, been anxious for the welfare of the new settlements in the Northern and Western parts of the United States; and particularly that they might be furnished with the preaching of the Gospel and other means of salvation. At their request, several contributions have been made, by order of the Legislature of the State,[2] which has enabled them, for several years past, to send a number of missionaries to preach the gospel, gather churches, and administer ordinances among you. The favorable reception which missionaries have heretofore met with in general from you encourages them to continue their endeavors to promote the salvation of your souls and the souls of your children. In pursuance of so important an object, the General Association have formed themselves into a Missionary Society and constituted a Board of Trustees consisting of six civilians and six clergymen, and have among other measures again petitioned the Legislature for a contribution throughout the State, to procure monies for defraying the expenses of continuing missionaries to preach the gospel among you. The Legislature have been so impressed with the benevolent design as to grant a contribution for three years successively, beginning with the present. The first contrbution has been already made, which we are happy to say, has been liberal. In consequence thereof, The Trustees are enabled, the present year, to send a number of missionaries to gladden the hearts of our brethren through a large extent of country.

And now, Brethren and Friends, we beseech you not only to be ready to hear the preaching of our worthy brethren sent among you, but to influence as far as in your power, your children, and young people to receive instruction by their preaching, by catechisings [sic], and other proper exercises. Also we request you to assist our said brethren by in-

[2] See the following document.

forming them of the places around you proper to be visited by them, and as you may have it in your power by giving notice to such places of the times at which the missionaries intend to visit them.

Beloved Brethren, we entreat you to suffer this farther [*sic*] word of exhortation: Let it be your first and chief concern to become reconciled to God through Jesus Christ, and to lead lives of strict piety and virtue. To this end attend diligently on all means of grace, in secret, family and public devotion. When you cannot be favored with the preaching of the gospel, yet assemble, for public worship on the Sabbath. The blessing of God may be expected from the sincere attendance on his own institutions, and is not confined to the eloquence of public teachers. Let your gravest and most able men lead in your social prayers and praises, and let them read the best printed sermons they can obtain. In this way you will keep up your own habits of public worship and due observance of the Sabbath, and will lead your children into the same habits, as well as prevent much wickedness in a profanation of the Sabbath. Furnish yourselves and your children with Bibles and other good books according to your abilities and opportunities; they are the more necessary while you are destitute of the stated preaching. Take great care to educate your children in a religious manner, and use your utmost influence to prevent their growing up ignorant of the God of their fathers. As you become able exert yourselves to obtain an establishment of the gospel ministry, and good schools for the instruction of your children. The present assistance afforded you as to preaching of the gospel is, and must be but temporary. Under Providence it will depend on yourselves to enjoy the stated means of grace. In a word, Dear Brethren and Friends, we entreat you to "seek the Lord while he may be found and call upon him while he is near." He hath never said to [the] seed of Jacob, "Seek ye me in vain." May the Lord bless you and keep you, increase your seed sown and the fruits of your righteousness, and grant that your souls may be in health and prosper.

[*Signed*] JOHN TREADWELL, *Chairman*

By order of the Board,
ABEL FLINT, *Secretary.*

Passed by the Board of Trustees,
May 29, 1799
ABEL FLINT, *Secretary.*

2. A LETTER OF DANIEL STORY AND RUFUS PUTNAM, MAY 22, 1799

Rufus Putnam is the well-known soldier of the Revolution, cousin of Israel Putnam. After the war he and Rev. Menasseh Cutler secured a grant of land from Congress for the veterans of the war and organized the Ohio Land Company. In 1788 Putnam went to Ohio as superintendent of the first colony of veterans and long had great influence, both as an official of the company and as an individual of practical sense and fairness, in the settlement of the Northwest. In 1796 President Washington appointed him surveyor-general of the United States, and Putnam undertook the survey of the region in preparation for settlement.[3]

Rev. Daniel Story came to Marietta on March 17, 1789, soon after the first settlers, as a missionary in part supported by the Ohio Company. For seven years he worked as a licentiate, three-fifths of his time in Marietta, two-fifths among the surrounding settlements. When the Marietta church was formally organized on December 6, 1796, Story was called to be its pastor. At that time he was visiting relatives in Massachusetts, and, since an ordination council could not be called at Marietta, Dr. Cutler was commissioned the agent of the church and, with Story as pastor-elect, called a council at Hamilton, Massachusetts, in the name of the Marietta church. This council ordained and installed Story, Cutler giving the charge. Rev. Daniel Story was an uncle of Chief Justice Story.[4]

MARIETTA, May 22[d], 1799

REV[d] SIR:

Entertaining a hope that it will not be inconsistent with the original design of the Society in Connecticut, for extend-

[3] *Dictionary of American Biography*, XV, 284–85.

[4] Cornelius E. Dickinson, "History of Congregationalism in Ohio before 1852," *Ohio Church History Society Papers*, VII, 35.

ing the means of religious instruction in the interior parts of the United States, to send Missionaries to this part of the country; we have taken the liberty to request, that among the multitudes of our brethren, dispersed in the wilderness, we may share in that munificence, which the more wealthy parts of the community have generously afforded for this purpose. We have therefore enclosed a geographical description of the settlements formed in this vicinity.

The . . . . towns of Marietta, Waterford, Belleprie, Adams and Salem have entered into an Association for public worship. But most of the people, just beginning to clear their land, conceive themselves unable to spare a sufficiency from their necessary support, to pay for constant preaching.

The subscription in these towns is as follows, viz.:

	Cents
Marietta	$221.50
Belleprie	152.--
Waterford	125.50
Adams	75.12
Salem	38.83
Total	$612.95 Cents

Besides these towns there are several other settlements, which have not entered into the Association, and have no preaching excepting occasional[ly]. Among these last, Middleton on the Hockhocking [*sic*] River, requires, as we conceive, particular attention. The land[s] appropriated for the support of a university are in that settlement, and many people, who were unable to purchase, have settled upon those lands, expecting to pay the rent which shall be hereafter required. As they are poor, they must depend upon the liberality of others at present, for public, spiritual instruction.

The white people inhabiting this country are principally from new [*sic*] England and a large proportion from Connecticutt [*sic*]. We are likewise in the vicinity of the Connecticutt Reserve, which will be united with this part of the Northwestern Territory in forming its eastern state.

Should . . . . it be thought expedient to send more than one missionary into this country, they might preach alternately in these settlements and the Connecticutt Reserve, which would have a tendency to form a more intimate union between the people of the different parts of the state which is in anticipation.

Should it comport with the views of the Society that candidates, or ordained ministers, who have no particular charge, be employed on this mission it would be very acceptable to the people here; as they could probably be engaged for a longer time than those who have particular flocks under their care, and might possibly be willing to settle with us.

Permit us to hope that our Brethren and Friends in Connecticutt, viewing our situation with compassion, will grant us as much assistance in promoting the cause and kingdom of . . . . the Redeemer, as their circumstances will permit.

Earnestly wishing that the laudable exertions of the Society, who have generously contributed, that to the *Poor* the Gospel may be preached, may be successful in the promotion of pure and undefiled religion; we subscribe ourselves in behalf of the people in this wilderness,

With sentiments of Esteem and Respect,

Your Friends and Servants,

[*Signed*] DANIEL STORY

RUFUS PUTNAM

[To] REV^d NATHAN STRONG
[Hartford, Conn.]

3. DOCUMENTS SHOWING THE RELATIONSHIP TO THE CONNECTICUT STATE LEGISLATURE

At this time the complete disestablishment of the Congregational church in Connecticut had not been accomplished. It did not occur until 1818 and came then as a result of complex forces which had been at work for a long time. Dissenters, especially Baptists, Methodists, Quakers, and Episcopalians, maintained a strenuous opposition to the Standing Order, and certificate laws giving them tax exemptions had not proved satisfactory. The situation was made more complex by the rise of the Republican party, which challenged the rule of the Federalists, long the champions of the *status quo*, for the clergy of the Standing Order were Federalist almost to a man, thus encouraging a union of the dissenters with the Republicans in opposition. Largely under Episcopalian leadership, this union was accomplished at a meeting at New Haven in February, 1816, and the Toleration party there formed won a complete victory over the Federalists and the Established Church in the election of May, 1818. As a result of this triumph, a constitutional convention was called the same year, and, largely because of the insistence of the Baptists, Methodists, and Episcopalians, the Congregational church was disestablished in the new constitution.[5]

It is to be noted in the following document that the legislature did not appropriate state funds for the missionary activity but merely authorized the church to take collections for that purpose.

TO THE HON[ORA]BLE GENERAL ASSEMBLY OF THE STATE OF CONNECTICUT TO BE CONVENED AT HARTFORD WITHIN AND FOR SAID STATE, THE 14TH OF INSTANT MAY: [1801]

The Memorial of the Trustees of the Missionary Society of Connecticut humbly sheweth that the liberal contributions, which, pursuant to your Honor's permission, under your Honor's patronage, have for six years past, been made by the people of this State, for the purpose of supporting missionaries in the new settlements on the borders of the wilderness, and among the Indian Tribes, have, by the blessing of Heaven, produced essential and extensive benefits to those settlements, and have enabled the Trustees to take measures for the diffusion of the knowledge of Christianity among those tribes. The advantages already obtain[ed] in the new settlements are perceived in the extensive revival of pure religion amongst them—in the gathering and regular forma-

5 M. Louise Greene, *The Development of Religious Liberty in Connecticut* (Boston: Houghton, Mifflin & Co., 1905); Richard J. Purcell, *Connecticut in Transition, 1775–1818* (Washington: American Historical Association, 1918).

tion of numerous churches—in the prospect of a permanent settlement of the Christian ministry in those parts of the United States—in the promotion of civil order and a just subordination, and in the extension of those principles and habits, in general, which are essential to the welfare of society.

In the Settlement of a new country the first inhabitants, though enterprising, are generally poor, and unable to support the public worship of God, without assistance from others, and of course are in great danger of degenerating into that coldness and even aversion to religion which will deprive them of the will even after they may acquire the power, to support it. This consideration will have great weight with all who wish to advance the best interests of their fellowmen, as individuals and as members of Society, and must have peculiar force at the present time, and in this country, where a wilderness of immense extent is settling in a manner analogous to the first people of the earth, and where States will be formed in rapid succession, which will become component parts of the nation in which we have all a common interest.

It is confidently believed that the same measures which are calculated to promote the interests of men as immortal beings, and members of the great society of the Universe, are equally calculated to promote their interest as members of a State or Nation on Earth; and it is no small consolation that while we are training them for happiness in the former, we are forming them for usefulness and happiness in the latter.

The people of this State in addition to the motives resulting from general philanthropy, are impelled by the consideration that many of those for whose benefit they contribute, once their children, brethren and near connections, and lately their neighbors, who had been favoured with the same advantages with themselves, but of which, from local and other circumstances, they are now deprived.

From the gradual increase of the amount contributed, from year to year, it is evident the People are more and more impressed with the importance of the object, and it is to be hoped, that, if further opportunities are presented, they will manifest the same readiness of mind, in acts of equal or superior liberality, to promote it in [the] future.

The period, in which contributions may be sollicited [sic] from the ecclesiastical societies in this State pursuant to your Honor's permission, is now expired and unless a like permission shall be renewed, a principal Source of revenue, on which the Trustees have hitherto almost wholly relied, will fail them; and, of course, their sphere of usefulness will be greatly diminished.

Under these circumstances, and impressed with the considerations which have been suggested, the Trustees beg leave again to sollicit the patronage of the Honorable Assembly, and that your Honor's [sic] would be pleased to grant them permission to ask the annual contributions of the several ecclesiastical societies and congregations within this State, for such period of time, under such regulations, as your Honor's may limit and provide, for the purpose of supporting missions to the new Settlements, within the United States, and among the Indian Tribes, according to the best discretion of the s[ai]d Trustees, or in some other way grant the necessary aid, and they as in duty bound shall ever pray. Dated at Hartford [the] 13th [day of] May, A.D. 1801.

By order [of] and in behalf of the Board,

[Signed] ABEL FLINT, Secretary.

AT A GENERAL ASSEMBLY OF THE STATE OF CONNECTICUT HOLDEN AT HARTFORD ON THE SECOND THURSDAY OF MAY, A.D., 1801——

Resolved by this Assembly that there may be contributions in the several religious Societies and congregations in this State on the first Sabbath in May annually (and if that Day, on account of any disadvantageous circumstances, should be inconvenient, the contribution may be on any other Sabbath in that Month), for the term of three years; and the Ministers or Clergy of such Societies or congregations shall receive and pay over such contributions to the Treasurer of the Missionary Society of Connecticut, and the monies so paid over shall be appropriated by the Trustees of said Missionary Society to the annual expenditures of said Society (and not their permanent fund) for the support of such missionaries as they shall from time to time employ in preaching the Gospel in those Settlements in the Northern and Western parts of the United States, where the Ordinances of the Gospel are not established, and shall annually exhibit to the General Assembly, and to the Missionary Society, an account of the receipts and expenditures of such contributions. And his Excellency, the Governor, is requested annually to issue his proclamation accordingly.

A true copy of record
examined by
[*Signed*] THOMAS DAY, *Sec'y.*

4. A LETTER FROM JOSEPH BADGER, JANUARY 8, 1801

Joseph Badger was the first missionary sent by the Missionary Society of Connecticut to the Western Reserve. He was born in Wilbraham, Massachusetts, and served with some distinction for three years in the Colonial army during the Revolution. After the war he prepared himself for college and, with much hard work, graduated from Yale in 1785. Two years later he was ordained over the church at Blandford, Massachusetts, where he remained for thirteen years, going to Ohio to begin his missionary work in December, 1800. In 1802 he brought his family to the Reserve.

Having satisfied myself from actual observation, that the soil of the Western Reserve was good, and would admit of a dense population, and that the settlements should rapidly increase, and that a door was already opened for extensive ministerial labors, after consulting my family on the subject, we unitedly agreed to make our arrangements for a removal to that distant and almost unbroken wilderness; and committing ourselves and our dear children to the care of Him who worketh all things after the counsel of His own will, commenced our preparations with all diligence.[6]

Joseph Badger continued his work for the Missionary Society of Connecticut until 1806, when he resigned, largely because of the inadequacy of his salary, to accept an appointment for work among the Indians from the Presbyterian Synod of Pittsburgh.

The society seems to have been poorly managed during this period. Badger was appointed at a salary of $7.00 a week, but in 1803 this was reduced to $6.00, and the reduction dated nearly a year back. His protests were of no avail, and, after vainly trying to support his family on the reduced salary for three years, he resigned. The evidence indicates that such reductions were not necessary, for the society was closing each year with larger balances. In 1805, when restoration of his original salary would have kept Badger in their employ, the society spent only $2,517.49 for missionary work and had a balance in the treasury of $21,196.94. Further, in 1808, when the Presbyterians sent him east to raise money for the Indian mission, the society of Connecticut, which had refused him the additional fifty-two dollars a year when he was a Congregationalist, now gave him $100 for the Presbyterian cause.[7]

Badger continued with the Presbyterians until the spring of 1810, when he settled as a regular pastor at Ashtubula, but continued to make excursions into the surrounding country. He was supported during this period, partly by the local groups, and partly by the Missionary Society of Massachusetts. On appointment of General William Henry Harrison, he served as military chaplain and postmaster during the War of 1812. In 1826, at the request of the people of Gustavus, Trumbull County, Ohio, he organized a church at that place and continued as active pastor until 1835, when he was dismissed at his own request. In 1826 he had made application for, and from that time on received, a federal pension of $96 a year for his service in the Revolutionary War. He died on May 5, 1846, at the age of eighty-nine.[8]

[6] Joseph Badger, "Autobiography," *American Quarterly Register*, XIII (1841), 323. This autobiography, according to the Introduction, was written by Badger in his eighty-fourth year, at the request of a personal friend in Connecticut. It was not intended for publication and is dated June 16, 1840. His "family" at this time consisted of his wife and six children.

[7] David Bacon, who had been sent by the society on a mission to the Indians in Michigan, was greatly embarrassed, and even threatened with prison at one time, because of the peculiar financial policies of the society (T. D. Bacon, *Leonard Bacon: A Statesman in the Church*, ed. B. W. Bacon [New Haven: Yale University Press, 1931], p. 21).

[8] The chief sources for the life of Joseph Badger are the *Memoir of Joseph Badger* (New York, 1851); the *Autobiography* above; "Joseph Badger," *Ohio Archaelogical*

[LETTER FROM JOSEPH BADGER][9]

REV^d AND DEAR SIR:

After a long and tedious journey, I arived at No 2d. on the 1.——, the 30th of December. I went on foot and led my horse nearly two hundred miles [over] the worst road I ever saw, owing principally to the season of the year—had much rain, snow and cold.

After passing the mountains and ariving in Washington County, I passed through, and near, about twenty Presbyterian Congregations, where for two years past there has been in most of them a pretty general serious awakening. Being detained seven or eight days by bad weather at two places and by attending the meeting of the Presbytery, I formed considerable acquaintance with about sixteen of the ministers and many more of the pious people.

They appear sentimental. The doctrines of total depravity, of regeneration, election, sovereignty, and their kindred doctrines, are insisted on by the ministers, with great plainness. It is under the preaching of these doctrines, God has been pleased to carry on his work in convincing and hopefully converting many hundreds [of] souls in these parts. The awakening extended [n]early 80 miles from east to west. A number of

---

and Historical Quarterly, XXVI (1917), 1–42; *Connecticut Evangelical Magazine*, I, 239, 358–59; *ibid.*, II, 118; *ibid.*, III, 304–5, 317–20; *ibid.*, IV, 113–18, 331; *ibid.*, VI, 288; *ibid.* (2d ser.), II, 54–56; C. E. Dickinson, "Rev. Joseph Badger: The Pioneer Missionary of the Western Reserve," *Ohio Church History Society Papers*, XI (1900), 5–22; Franklin B. Dexter, *Biographical Sketches of the Graduates of Yale College* (New Haven: Yale University Press, 1907), IV, 380–84; William B. Sprague, *Annals of the American Pulpit* . . . . (New York: Robert Carter & Bros., 1858), III, 473–79; *Dictionary of American Biography*, I, 487–88; W. E. Barton, "Early Ecclesiastical History of the Western Reserve," *Ohio Church History Society Papers*, I (1890), 24–27.

[9] This letter, with some verbal changes and slight omissions, was published in the *Connecticut Evangelical Mazagine*, I (1801), 358.

new settlements northwest of the Ohio [River], extending nearly to the eastern bounds of New Connecticut, were visited in a special manner; and there yet remains many instances of serious awakening. By what I learn, both from ministers and people, the work has been generally free from inthusiasm but powerful in humbling the proud heart, and in bringing it to be swallowed up in God's will. God has done great things for his Church in this country. About six years past there were several young married men and others in single life, hopefully brought into Christ's kingdom. By the advice of a few pious and learned ministers, a number gave themselves to study. An Accademic School was established where the languages and the other arts and sciences are thoroughly taught. There has been sixteen or seventeen very worthy and pious ministers raised up in this school. It was thought by many when they saw such a number seting out for the ministry, there would be no places for them, but the late awakening has opened places enough. The settlements are [a]wakening with such rapidity and so many congregations forming, that they cannot be supplyed, but for a part of the time. There are now eight or ten young men who appear to be pious, preparing for the ministery.

The school I have mentioned is kept in Cannonsbourgh in Washington County, nearly 100 miles from this place [Youngstown, Ohio]. There are two instructors. The principal is a Mr. John Watson, educated at Princeton College, a very worthy pious minister.

There were ordained three ministers in and near this county [Trumble] last September, by the Ohio Presbytery. One of them, Mr. Wil[lia]m Wick, has settled [and] built in No. 2d, 1 Range, preaches in three congregations, lives 8 miles from Youngstown, preaches there one-third of his time. He appears to be a truly pious man, and in sentiments, a Hopkin-

sian.[10] I am happy in having a brother so near. From what
I can learn of the present situation of the settlements on this
reserve, it will be highly necessary to send on another missionary next spring if possible. I am confident from the best information I can get, I shall not be able to visit all the settlements without making too rappid a progress, to answer the
design of Missionary labours. This is the oppinion of several
Gentlemen I have consulted here.

I would write more, but have not time, as I have to ride
some distance today. I send with this a letter to my family.
Please put it into the post office.

I have to acknowledge the great goodness of God through
all my journey. My health is good; have had an uncommon
share of kindness and respect showed me, wherever my character was known. I was received by the ministers with great
cordiality. I was much disappointed with the little books;
one-half of them was the history of Lovezinsky [sic], I . . . .
[gave] them away fo[r] 18 Springs sermons to Children.
Please to send me, directing them to Youngstown, all the
numbers of the Magazines, next spring, if there should be
opportunity by some movers.

I feal as though I was at home, in regard to my work.
Under the Divine directions, I may be useful, but without
heavenly aid, there will be nothing done.

I earnestly beg the prayers of the Missionary Society for
me that I may be found faithful—and that God would in
this wilderness set up his banner and save his people.

From your cordial friend and humble servant,

JOSEPH BADGER.

YOUNGSTOWN, NEW CONNECTICUT.
    January 8, 1801

[To] REV[d] NATHAN STRONG.

[10] This last characterization was omitted in the published letter doubtless because of fear that it might alienate support from people opposed to Hopkinsian
views, who were numerous throughout New England at the time.

5. Proceedings concerning the Ordination and Commissioning of Ezekiel J. Chapman as a Missionary to New Connecticut, October 13, 1801[11]

AT A MEETING OF THE COMMITTEE OF MISSIONS AT HARTFORD, OCT. 13, 1801

Voted, That if the Committee of Missions, during the recess of the Board, should appoint a candidate for the ministry, a Missionary to New Connecticut, said Committee request[s] the Association where said Candidate was licensed to ordain him to the work of the gospel ministry, particularly as an Evangelist, previous to his entering on his mission; and that the Rev. Messrs. Levi Hart, D.D., and Cyprian Strong be requested to attend as a delegation from this Board, and assist in the ordination of said Candidate, if upon examination, he should be judged qualified for the work.

Voted, That application be made to the Association of Tolland County, to ordain to the work of the gospel ministry, with a particular reference to his laboring as an Evangelist in the new Settlements, Mr. Ezekiel J. Chapman, a licentiate from their body; and that for this purpose the following letter be transmitted to said Association:

To the Association of Tolland County, to be convened at Hebron, the 27th of October instant.

Whereas, The Trustees of the Missionary Society of Connecticut, at their session the second of September last, passed a vote in the words following, viz.:

(See the vote in the Book of Record [this is probably the item found above])

[11] This material in slightly different form was published in the *Connecticut Evangelical Magazine*, I (1801), 236-37. It is reproduced here because it gives the entire process by which a young man was commissioned and ordained as a missionary. Chapman, whom W. S. Kennedy (*Plan of Union* [Hudson, Ohio, 1856], pp. 23-24) wrongly calls Chapin, remained on the field until the spring of 1803, when he returned to New England (Barton, *op. cit.*, p. 27).

And WHEREAS, The Committee of Missions have appointed Mr. Ezekiel J. Chapman, a Candidate for the ministry licensed by you, to go on a mission to New Connecticut, the said Committee, in pursuance of the above vote, hereby request you to ordain the said Mr. Chapman, if upon examination you should think him qualified for the work of the ministry; and that you admit the Rev. Messrs. Levi Hart, D.D., and Cyprian Strong to sit in council with you and assist in the ordination, as a delegation from the Board of Trustees. The Committee also request that in case you should proceed to ordain Mr. Chapman, you transmit to the Trustees a certified copy of the minutes of your proceedings on the subject, that they may be lodged among their files. In the name and on the behalf of the Committee of Missions,

[*Signed*] ABEL FLINT, *Secretary.*

P.S. Messrs. Hart and Strong have been duly notified to attend with the Association, at the time and place of their meeting. Should they not attend, the Committee will not wish the ordination to be stayed on that account.

At a Meeting of the Association of Tolland County, convened, by adjournment in the first Society of Hebron, October 27th, 1801—Present: Rev. Messrs. John Willard, Amos Bassett, Royal Tyler, Nathan Gillet, Diodate Brockway, and Ephraim T. Woodruff.

The Rev. Nathan Williams, D.D., Moderator of the Association, being absent, the Rev. John Willard was chosen Moderator.

A letter from the Committee of Missions, appointed by the Trustees of the Missionary Society of Connecticut, addressed to the Association was read, in the words, following, to wit:

(See the within paper [copy of the request
is copied elsewhere])

Whereupon, *Voted*, That the Association resolve themselves into an ordination Council, for the purpose specified in the above letter from the Committee of missions; and that the Rev. Messrs. Levi Hart, D.D., and Cyprian Strong, who were present, be invited to sit in council with the Association, pursuant to the request of the Committee of Missions.

The Rev. Messrs. Abel Flint and Amasa Porter, being present, were also invited to join the Association as an ordaining Council.

The Rev. Amos Bassett, Scribe of the Association, requesting to be excused from officiating as Scribe on the present occasion, the Rev. Abel Flint was appointed Scribe of the Council.

The Council was then opened with prayer by the Moderator.

The Council proceeded to examine Mr. Chapman respecting his knowledge of the doctrines of Christianity, his belief in those doctrines,—his ability to reach them to others,—his experimental acquaintance with the truth; his views in entering on the work of the ministry,—his qualifications for a missionary, and his motives for entering into that service,—and gaining full satisfaction on these points,—

Voted unanimously to consecrate him to the work of the ministry, with peculiar reference to his laboring as a Missionary in the New Settlements in the United States of America;—and that the solemnity of his ordination be attended at the meeting house in this place tomorrow at half-past ten o'clock, A.M.

Voted, That the several parts of the ordination service be performed by the following persons: The Rev. Royal Tyler to make the introductory prayer, the Rev. Levi Hart, D.D., to preach the Sermon; the Rev. Cyprian Strong to make the consecrating prayer during which the Rev. Messrs. John Willard, Levi Hart, Cyprian Strong and Amos Bassett to lay on hands; the Rev. John Willard to give the Charge; the Rev. Amos Bassett to give the Right Hand of Fellowship; and the Rev. Amasa Porter to make the concluding prayer.

Passed in Council,
Attest
ABEL FLINT, *Scribe*

Wednesday, October 28th, 1801.—In pursuance of the above vote, the Rev'd Ezekiel J. Chapman was this day consecrated to the work of the gospel ministry.

Attest,
ABEL FLINT, *Scribe*

After the minutes of the Council were read, the following questions were put,

To Rev. Cyprian Strong: Mr. Strong, do you, Sir, in the name of the Committee of Missions, now publicly renew their appointment of Mr. Ezekiel J. Chapman, as a Missionary t[o] the New Settlements, and their request that he be consecrated to the work of the gospel ministry as an evangelist?

Answer: I do.

To Mr. Chapman: Mr. Chapman, do you now publicly accept of your appointment as a Missionary to the New Settlements, and do you consent to receive ordination with that view?

Answer: I do.

To the Moderator: Mr. Moderator, do you, Sir, in the name of this Council, approve of Mr. Ezekiel J. Chapman as quali-[fied] for the work of the gospel ministry, and for the missionary service?

Answer: I do.

Question: Shall the ordination solemnity now proceed?

Answer: Yes, Sir.

6. REPORT OF THE TRUSTEES OF THE MISSIONARY SOCIETY
OF CONNECTICUT, TO SAID SOCIETY, CONVENED AT
NORWALK, THE THIRD TUESDAY OF JUNE, 1802

. . . .

As the general concerns of the missionary institution are committed to the management of the Trustees, we esteem ourselves under a high responsibility for our conduct, to him whose kingdom they more immediately relate, and to the Missionary Society whose agents we are. . . . .

The narrative we have lately published, a copy of which is herewith transmitted to each member of the Missionary Society, contains a general statement of our proceedings, of missionary labors, and the state of our funds to the close of the year 1801.

"More Missionaries have lately been employed, and more missionary labors preformed than in any preceeding year. Fourteen missionaries are particularly named in the narrative, as having been employed in the course of the year, for a longer or a shorter term. Six of those missionaries, viz. the Rev. Mr. *Williston*, Mr. *Jerome*, Mr. *Porter*, Mr. *May*, the Rev. Mr. *Higgins*, and Mr. *Woodward*, have all been employed in preaching to the new settlements in the county of Luzern in Pennsylvania, and in the western counties in the state of New York.—Their particular tours and labors are so fully related in the narrative, that little more is necessary to be observed respecting them. Mr. *Williston* at present continues one half of his time in the service of the Society. He is very useful in the short circuits which he makes in the counties of Otsego, Onondaga, Cayuga, Chenango, Tioga, and Steuben in the state of New-York, and in the county of Luzerne in the state of Pennsylvania.

"Mr. *Bushnell*, after spending eleven months in the western counties of New-York, returned to Connecticut in January, 1801. During the whole term of his missionary tour, he preached not less than five sermons a week, attended nearly ninety public conferences, besides performing other missionary labors. Soon after his return, he was re-appointed to the missionary service. It was expected he would spend a few weeks in the vacant settlements in the state of Vermont, and that he would then visit the western counties in the State of New-York; but on the account of an uncommon attention among the people in Vermont to whom he preached, he obtained liberty to continue there, so long as there should be an extraordinary call for his labors there. He consequently spent about eleven months in the northern counties of that state, and returned to Connecticut in January last. The Trustees have since re-appointed him a missionary during pleasure [probably as long as he wished to act], and directed him to revisit all the churches and places where he hath formerly preached, to confirm the brethren, to advise the churches, and to compose difficulties where any have arisen, and to perform all those ministerial services which shall be necessary for the furtherance of the gospel in the places which he shall revisit.

"Exclusive of the labors of Mr. *Williston* and Mr. *Woodward*, the gentlemen who have been in the western counties of New-York, and in the county of Luzerne in Pennsylvania, have preached more than 600 sermons, besides attending numerous conferences, forming churches, baptizing hundreds of persons, and often administering the holy communion.

"Mr. *James W. Woodward* spent four months on a mission to Black River, and has been since re-appointed to labor in the same place. Hence it appears that our missionaries, in the states of New-York and Pennsylvania, during the term of their several missions, have performed services equal to about six years of ministerial labor.

"Exclusive of eleven months' labors of Mr. *Bushnell* in Vermont, Messrs. *Huntington*, *Hallock*, *Swift*, and *Morgan* have preached between three and four hundred sermons, during the past and present year, besides the performance of other missionary labors. It appears that more than three years of ordinary ministerial labor have been employed in that quarter since our last reports.

"The Rev. *Alexander Gillet* has lately entered on a mission to the northern part of Vermont for the term of four months.

"Mr. *Badger* and Mr. *Chapman* are performing missionary labors at New-Connecticut; but we have received no recent accounts from them. We consider the furnishing [of] the inhabitants of that territory with the best ministerial instruction as a matter of the first importance, and shall, by no means, lose sight to [of] so interesting an object.

"The last accounts from Mr. *Bacon*, our Indian missionary, are flattering. He expects to proceed soon to the river Miami, about 70 miles from Detroit,[12] where is a large body of Indians who speak the Chippeway [sic] language, and to open to them the designs and views of the Missionary Society and of their Trustees, and begin the communication of the gospel to them. It appears by a letter which we have lately received from him, that he has a prospect of obtaining a good interpreter upon reasonable terms, and that the Indians are disposed to give him a favorable reception. Some of them have expressed a strong desire to be instructed in the art of husbandry, and intimated that if Mr. *Bacon* could instruct them in that, such numbers of their Indians would collect about him as that his hand will be filled with more than he can do. The Chippeways are settled on the lakes Michigan, Huron, and Superior, and are scattered over extensive regions about those lakes. The Wyandots, Twitwees, Miamis, Ottowas [sic], and other tribes are settled within the same territory, or border upon it. They generally if not universally speak the same language. The introduction of a missionary, well versed in the Chippeway language, as we hope

[12] This is evidently the Maumee River in northwestern Ohio, where a mission was later established (T. D. Bacon, *op. cit.*, pp. 11-13).

Mr. *Bacon* soon will be, may happily lead the way to the spread of civilization and the gospel through a most extensive country. The Trustees earnestly wish to be a means in the hands of Providence of such immense good to large numbers of their perishing fellow men. While we pray for wisdom and the success of the mission, we ask the prayers of the Society, and of all the friends of Zion for us, that we may have light and prudence happily to conduct the missionary business, and that it may be crowned with distinguished success. And we pray it may be no less successful among our brethren of the American forests than among ourselves.

"The public contributions in May last, we are happy to observe, have been more liberal than any of the preceding. In addition to these, many private donations have been made to the Society, two of which amounted to 100 dollars each. This affords us an ample evidence of the approbation of our benevolent people, and presents us with a pleasing prospect, that their hearts and hands will be opened in future to the calls of Providence, whatever they shall be.

"The Trustees, at a late meeting, resolved, that for the current year, two missionaries be employed in New Connecticut:—That the Rev. *Jedidah Bushnell* itinerate as a missionary through the year, in the western counties of New-York and the northern counties of Vermont:—That the Rev. *Seth Williston* continue to labor as a missionary, such a part of the time as he shall not be employed to preach to the people at Lisle; and that he visit such places in the western counties of New-York as the Trustees, or in their recess, the committee of missions shall direct:—That Mr. *James W. Woodward* continue in the Black River country, unless otherwise directed by the Trustees or the committee of missions, for the term of four months:—That a permanent missionary be appointed to itinerate in the southern range of counties, in the western part of New-York state, and the northern counties of Pennsylvania, to enter on his mission the first of September next:—That a permanent missionary be employed to labor in the northern counties of Vermont:—That one missionary be sent for the term of six months, to labor in such places as the Trustees, or in their recess the committee of missions shall direct.

"The Trustees have also appropriated 200 dollars for the purchase of religious books, to be distributed among the inhabitants of the new settlements; 100 dollars of which to be taken up in the Connecticut Evangelical Magazine, the residue to be applied to the purchase and distribution of such books as the Committee of missions shall think best.

"The funds of the Society, through the smiles of Providence, and the liberality of good people, are so increased that the Trustees are of the opinion that application should be made to the legislature of the state to form a corporate body, with power to receive and hold money, lands, books or whatever shall be given to promote the designs of the missionary institutions; and by their vote they have referred the matter to your wise deliberation. The Rev. *Nathan Strong*, D.D. has been appointed to wait on you with said vote, to explain the views of the Trustees, and to transact whatever may be necessary relative to the business."

. . . .

In the name of the Board of Trustees,

ABEL FLINT, *Secretary*

HARTFORD, June 9th, 1802

7. LETTER OF JOHN MCMILLAN REGARDING THE LICENSING OF JONATHAN LESLIE

Rev. John McMillan was the first Presbyterian minister to be settled over a congregation west of the Allegheny Mountains,[13] and he became

[13] He accepted the pastoral supervision of the two congregations of Chartiers and Pigeon Creek in the Redstone country in 1776. For additional information consult W. W. Sweet, *Religion on the American Frontier*, Vol. II: *The Presbyterians* (New York, 1936), pp. 25–26.

the outstanding Presbyterian leader in western Pennsylvania. The following letter reveals his co-operation with the Missionary Society of Connecticut and his interest in securing recruits for the missionary work from Presbyterian ranks. Jonathan Leslie, the subject of the letter, served the society faithfully and well for twenty years (1808–28).[14]

CANONSBURG, November 2d, 1807

REVD. AND DEAR SIR:

The commission for Mr. Allen did not come to hand untill the 26th of October, a few days before it arrived the Pby [Presbytery] of Ohio met, and a call for settlement was presented to him, which he felt disposed to accept of, but knew not well how to justify his conduct to the Society, in case a commission should be sent to him. His friends however advised him that as he had received no account from you and as it was uncertain whither a commission would be sent, as there was no formal recommendation by the Pby. he had better comply with the wishes of the people; which he accordingly did, and therefore cannot now travel, as a missionary thro' New Connecticut.

There is another young man, who was licensed at the same time, who, I think, would be equally, if not more acceptable to the people of New Connecticut, who is willing to take Mr. Allen's place. But without approbation, we do not employ him. This much, however, I have ventured to do: A number of settlements in that part [of] the country sent requests by Mr. Scott to the Pby. for supplies; and Mr. Jonathan Lesley (which is the young man's name) was appointed to spend four or five Sab[bath]s among them. I have directed him to continue in the field of [the] mission untill [sic] the next meeting of our Pby., which will be on the 4th Tuesday of December next. If you approve of his continuing longer, you

---

[14] *Connecticut Evangelical Magazine and Religious Intelligencer*, II (1809), 44–46, 275; *ibid.*, III (1810), 21; Barton, *op. cit.*; Kennedy, *op. cit.*, p. 40; "The Report of Abraham Scott, January 22, 1808" (Doc. 8 below).

will let me know by letter to be left for me at Canonsburg.
If you do not approve of it, your silence on that subject shall
be sufficient for my direction.

Yours, etc.,

[Signed] JOHN McMILLAN

8. REPORT OF ABRAHAM SCOTT, MISSIONARY
JANUARY 22, 1808

This letter[15] affords us an intimate glimpse of the interests, policies,
and activities of the early missionaries. Abraham Scott was the first Presbyterian missionary appointed by the Society of Connecticut[16] and served
from 1807 to 1825. In this report of his activities from October, 1807,
to January, 1808, we note his great interest in the educational welfare of
the people, in Sabbath observance, in securing preachers and religious
services for the isolated districts, the rapid settlement of the country, and
the difficulties of travel.

The population of the Reserve was increasing very rapidly during this
period, being estimated at 9,000 in 1806 and 16,000 in 1810. The demand
for missionaries was proportionally great, and the Society of Connecticut
apparently had plenty of money[17] but found it impossible to find men in
New England to undertake the work.[18] Hence in February, 1807, it applied to the Presbyterian Synod of Pittsburgh, which undertook to supply
frontier-bred men.

. [15] Excerpts from this letter, along with excerpts from subsequent letters, were
published in the *Connecticut Evangelical Mazagine and Religious Intelligencer*, II
(1809), 45.

[16] *Above,* introd. to chap. iv, p. 67.

[17] *Above, ibid.*

[18] The society gave two reasons for the dearth of candidates—an unusual call
for ministers in the New England states and the increase in the number of men
employed by other missionary societies (*Connecticut Evangelical Magazine*, VI [1806],
281). Barton (*op. cit.,* pp. 29–31) suggests that the real reason for the dearth,
or at least an additional reason, was the unwillingness of the society to pay salaries
that the educated men demanded and could live on. We have noted the difficulties of
Joseph Badger and David Bacon in this regard. Apparently the frontier-bred
Presbyterians were accustomed to getting along on less than was demanded by the
men from the East.

January 22, 1808

Warren, Trumble [*sic*] *County, Ohio*
To the Connecticut Missionary Society.
REVD. AND HON[ORE]D GENTLEMEN:

In my last [report] I gave you an account of my proceedings from the first of August untill [*sic*] the fifteenth of October, 1807. I shall now transmit to you an account of my labours with other particulars since that time.

Saturday, October 17, I preached in Palmyra, Sabbath 18, in Deerfield. I then as I proposed went to Presbytery and presented the afforesaid [*sic*] applications for supplies.

Tuesday, 20th, from Presbytery I went home and did not return untill Saturday 7 of November.

Sabbath 8, I preached in Deerfield; Tuesday 10, in Ellsworth, Sabbath 15 in Palmyra, Tuesday 17 in Newton, Wednesday 18, I went to Braceville and preached there.

Thursday 19, Friday 20, and Sabbath 22, Wednesday 25 in Howland [*sic*], Friday 28 in Vienna, Sabbath 29 in Westfield. Monday 30 in Johnston. Wednesday 2 of December in Kinsman; Thursday 3 in Smithfield, Friday[4] and Sabbath 6, in Hartford; Friday 11 in Hubbardsville; Sabbath 13 in Liberty; Tuesday 15 in Howland; Thursday 17, in Champion; Sabbath 20 in Bristol; Monday 21 in Mesopotamia; Friday 25 in Hanshaw; Saturday 26 in Parkman; Sabbath 27 and Monday 28 in Neilson; Tuesday 29 in Hiram; Wednesday 30 in Mantua. [Other communities in this region of Ohio were visited, too numerous to be listed.]

To be particular, I would observe first that Mr. Jonathan Leslie was appointed by [the] Presbytery to supply [for] six Sabbaths in this purchase. He fulfilled all excepting one at Deerfield which he was prevented to do by reason of high waters.

He preached frequently through the week while in this purchase. His labours as far as I can learn were acceptable, and I trust in some measure profitable to the people which he visited. He was strongly solicited by the people of Mesopotamia and the adjacent towns, that if it would be consistent [*sic*] he would settle with them and give them part of his labours, as the people there did not consider themselves at present able to give him a sufficient support it was agreed, provided he could be appointed to spend part of his time on [a] mission, that he would settle there, and spend the remainder [of the time] with them, untill such times as they would be able [to pay] for all his labours, whether or no he has altered his views since he left this country I have not heard.

Mr. Jas. Boyd, a licentiate of Erie Presbytery, is now living in Newton. He is employed by the people of Warren and Newton to preach alternately in those two places untill the last of Aprill [*sic*] next. I find that Mr. Boyd and the people are well satisfied with each other. At present there appears the greatest probability that he will shortly become their stated pastor.

You have doubtless observed from the above naration [*sic*] respecting my labours that there have been some considerable intervals in which I have not preached, I would just observe that those cessations from public labours have been occasioned partly by disagreeable, and, at times, somewhat dangerous traveling by reason of hard frosts and high waters, and partly by weariness of speaking, however, such intervals I could still find opportunity to improve for my own and others benefit by visitation and conferences, particularly the visitation of schools. The education of children in this country is considered and made an object of particular attention.

In allmost [*sic*] all the towns that I have visited, the people are able and do actually obtain and employ teachers during the winter season, and many of them throughout the year. Their teachers in general, as far [as] I have made myself acquainted and am able to judge, are qualified. I am generally well pleased with their method of teaching, altho' not in every particular. In teaching children to read I find that in some schools they make use of novels and romances. This method does not appear to me calculated to answer the most valuable purpose. Rather in place of such books, I have recommended the Scriptures; several reasons have been offered for not using them. Some have said that the Scriptures, particularly the New Testament separately bound, cannot in this country be obtained. If this is considered an evil and any plan can be adopted to have it removed, perhaps the sooner the better. Others have objected against the use of the Scriptures in schools by saying that they are not calculated to draw the attention of youth, consequently retard their progress in learning. However everyone may know from reason, observation and experience the danger of filling the youthful mind with vanities, and neglecting the means of forming a tast[e] for, and improving it with useful knowledge. . . . .

By attending to the examination and instruction of youth, respecting the essential and fundamental doctrines of religion, I find that altho' these are things to which it appears some parents have attended; yet is truly to be lamented that by many they are too much neglected. Altho' in a number of towns in this country there are some whose minds are impressed in some measure with the necessity and importance of religion, and some, who I trust enjoy the life and power of it, yet it is sadly to be lamented that it is too much neglected in common by the multitude.

Altho' I have not been an eye and ear witness to much either of profanity or immorality in this country, yet from information I have reason to believe they are too common, particularly the inobservance of the Sabbath and particularly in this season of the year of hunting, and also in some instances attending to daily secular business. These and such like are not only practiced by the ignorant, but also by those (as I am informed) who . . . . have formerly been taught, both by precept and example the due observance of the Lord's day.

The due observance of the Sabbath is a subject upon which I have frequently insisted, both in public and private. In private conversation with some who altho' they have candidly confessed and were in some measure apparently sensible of their criminallity [sic] in the above mentioned respects; yet they would endeavour to extenuate them, criing [sic] from necessity, temptation, the example of others and such like. Thus it is that people have frequently give [sic] liberty to or rather encourage each other in the ways of iniquity. Altho' the above is the lamentable situation in some measure with the generality of people in this country, yet not universally. God has not left himself here altogether without witness, but there are some I trust who fear the Lord, speak often one to another, etc. [Not very clear!] In some places there are some that openly profess infidelity, some also that profess an adherence to the doctrine of universal salvation. Those of this last mentioned class generally profess a desire for, and give their attendance to the preaching of the Gospel, altho' the above may appear a hard and gloomy representation, yet a sense of duty obliges me to give according to my ideas a just statement.

Altho' the situation of numbers here are [sic] in many respects truly deplorable[,] consequently calls for lamentation, yet, blessed [be] my God, it is not desperate[,] consequently call[s] for the united prayers and endeavours of all who are in any measure intrusted with the means of their recovery.

Altho' on the one hand there are many things here truly distressing, yet on the other there are still some encouraging. I find that even among the worst there are many at times not past feeling. They appear willing to hear what may be said against them. Not only the seriously inclined but many others also profess and in many respects evidence a desire for the Gospel. I have been almost universally received and treated by all sorts since I came into this country with the greatest civility and friendship. There has generally been an unexpected attention to and in many places an apparent solemnity and feeling under preaching. I have generally been so short a time in particular places that I know not whether impressions that I trust have been made have long continued. I have been strongly solicited, by different classes in almost every place I have been, as soon as possible to return. Inquiries have frequently been made respecting the prospect of other missionaries in this country. I trust I need not mention the arrangements that have been made in almost all the churches here to have the gospel statedly amongst them, as I understand you have frequently particular intelligence in this respect.

Many places that are yet unable to support the gospel statedly have evidenced a desire to have it occasionally at their own expense. Exclusive of the places that formerly made application to Ohio Presbetry [*sic*] for supplies, I have since I came last into this country (that is since the first of November last) received writen [*sic*] applications from seven different places to send or take forward to the next meeting of Ohio Presbetry. There are many weak settlements that are yet unable to make application for supplies that express and I trust feell [*sic*] a desire for the Gospel. These I trust will not be altogether neglected by the licentiates or others that may be sent here to supply such places. Mr. Leslie and also some members of Erie Presbetry while supplying in this country, without expectation or desire of reward, particular[ly] attended [not very clear, probably means that these men gave some attention to neglected places].

Thus, Gentlemen, from a sense of duty and obligation agreeably to your resonable [*sic*] injunction, I have given you a brief account of such circumstances as appears to me most conducive to the promotion of your benevolent designs.

I would here observe that I have taken an account of the number of families and souls in the towns that I visited since I came last into this purchase, to this I shall for the future particularly attend, so that after some time I trust I shall be able to give the numbers in each particular town consequently the sume total in New Connecticut.

I expect that shortly I will be under the necessity of going to my family and likely will not return for two or three weeks. I propose after I return to visit the towns on the east part of the purchase northward untill [sic] I go to the mouth of Conneaught [sic] creek; thence westward on the north to Cleaveland [sic]. From Cleaveland I propose to return through Hudson and Warren. I expect to be in the city of Cleaveland about the midle [sic] of March. In Hudson about the last of Do. [March]. In Warren about the middle of Aprill [sic]. From Warren I propose to return home and expect to be in Cannonsburgh [sic], Washington County, Pennsylvania [sic] about the last of Aprill. I shall examine the post offices in the afforesaid [sic] places, so that if there is anything you would desire to let me know, you will please to write, and it is likely I shall receive it.

This journal as you have seen contains an account of 12 Sabbaths and 32 week days on which I preached. On the Sabbaths I generally delivered two discourses. On the whole 53.

With respect, Gentlemen, I remain in the Gospel, your obt. Svt.

ABM. SCOTT

N.B. The Ohio Presbetry will meet the last Tuesday of Aprill next so that if you have anything which you would desire to communicate by sending to the Rev. John McMillan [sic], Cannonsburgh [sic] it will be received.

The following I received and was requested to insert: [This refers to a copy of the minutes of the Ecclesiastical

Society of New Connecticut, September 29–30, 1807, conveying a vote of thanks for the missionaries sent. The complete minutes are printed in the *Ohio Church History Society Papers*, IX, 18–19.]

9. Correspondence regarding Affiliation with the American Home Missionary Society

After the formation of the American Home Missionary Society in 1826 the local home missionary agencies soon became auxiliary to it, generally without surrendering their own organization. The arguments for such affiliation are set forth in the following documents, which refer both to the Missionary Society of Connecticut and to the Domestic Missionary Society of Connecticut, both organizations of the Connecticut General Association.

Office of the A.H.M.S., 144 Nassau St.
New York, July 23, 1828

Rev. and Dear Sir:

Your letter of June 26 was put into my hand on my return from Maine, the 4th inst., since which the pressure of my engagements has prevented my giving the attention to your several inquiries, which their importance demands. I will now endeavor to answer them (very briefly of course) in detail.

I. Should the Domestic Miss. Society of Con.[19] be merged in the Con. Miss. Society, and the latter become auxiliary to the A.H.M.S. "*would the amount of funds raised, deducting all expenses, be greater than at present?*"

I do not hesitate to answer in the affirmative, and all the lessons of our short experience confirm me in this opinion. The funds raised in this state since the Society became national and could present to the churches the great national object, are double the amount raised in the same time, when it was a State Society, and acted alone. The Vermont State

---

[19] The Domestic Missionary Society of Connecticut was formed in 1815 for the purpose of giving aid to those churches and localities within the bounds of Connecticut where religion was on the decline (Hooker, *op. cit.*, pp. 175–79).

Society became auxiliary last year, and the result is, that they are now making an effort in which they will doubtless succeed to raise this season more than double the amount of the income of any former year. The income of the Hampshire Miss. Society and the Mass. Miss. Society, in which the Domestic Miss. Society, of that state merged when it became auxiliary to the A.H.M.S. as now proposed to be done in Connecticut, has doubtless been greatly benefited by this measure. The Rev. Mr. Wisner of Boston, who, with the Secretary, has been the principal executive man in that Society, stated before the Maine Miss. Society a few days since, that the union of the Dom. Miss. Society of Mass. with the Mass. Miss. Society, and the connection of the latter with the A.H.M.S. was the happiest event which had ever occurred in the history of Domestic Missions in that State. He did not hesitate to say that since the commencement of the labors of our Agent there in Oct. last, there had been double the amount pledged to the Society, which had ever been gained by the two Societies in the same time under their former organization. Now, these facts, in relation to Massachusetts, furnish, I think, the fairest example of what may be safely calculated on as the result of the measures proposed in Connecticut, should they be adopted, because they are the same which were adopted in Mass. and which have produced the results above named.

Among the reasons which would lead me to expect similar results in Connecticut are the following:

1. The measure proposed would reduce the missionary operations of your State to a simple undivided system. Now, if I understand the case, some of your churches contribute to the Con. Miss. Society and some to the Dom. Miss Society, according to the preference of each, while some contribute to both. It is desired, indeed, I suppose, that they will all contribute to both, and each of your State Societies has a right to employ an Agent to present its own object to all

𝟚𝟠𝟚𝟠𝟜

the churches in the State. But if this were done, there would
be two calls made on each of your churches for Dom. Missions, when, if the two Societies were united, there would be
but one. And in this age of benevolent action, when there
are so many objects presented to our churches, it is found important to present each in a single form, both that it may be
readily understood and distinguished from every other object, and that calls for contributions may not be necessarily
multiplied. If, for instance, you had two general Societies,
in the State, for Foreign Missions, two Bible, two tract, two
Education, two Sab[bath] School, and two Colonization Societies, (as you have two for Domestic Missions) all deriving
their income from the same congregations, so that each of
your churches must be addressed twice a year on behalf of
each of these objects, would not even your good people complain that solicitations were unnecessarily multiplied? Would
it not be wise to reduce the number [of] Societies to the number of distinct objects to be provided for, and they to reduce
the number of these solicitations just one half? But if this
would be wise to prevent so great an evil, then it is surely
incumbent on us to endeavor to correct the same evil in any
degree in which it exists.

2. Your question implies that an increase of expense might
result from the measures proposed. The reverse would no
doubt be the fact. If you leave it to each of your ministers
to take up collections in his own congregation, there would be
no difference. Our collection would cost the same as two.
But if each of your Societies, in its present form, should employ an Agent to go through the State, which is doubtless the
most efficient way of raising money for the benevolent purposes, in Connecticut as well as in other States, these two
agents on the present plan would incur double the expense
which would be required to support a single Agent, were the
two Societies united; and in that case only one Agent would
be needed. And the union of your Society with ours would

not increase that expense, for though the Agent, in case of your becoming auxiliary would be the joint agent of the auxiliary and the Parent Society, the nomination of the man, and the fixing of the amount of his salary would, in all cases, if your desired it rest with the Auxiliary, while his sole business would be to raise funds for the Auxiliary, and otherwise promote its interest, as such. Besides the proposed arrangement would not increase atall [*sic*] the expenses of the Parent Society. Its office here must be maintained whether your Society becomes Auxiliary or not. The Treasurer and members of the Committee serve gratuitously, and there are several gentlemen here whose contributions are more than sufficient to sustain the Secretary and Assistant, and who will not see these offices vacated for the want of support. The only additional expense therefore to the Parent Society would be that of an increased correspondence. These are the arguments on the side of economy in expenditure, while I have no doubt that the same Agent, acting for the national Society, in any State, will raise a large percentage more for the State Society, as an Auxiliary, than he would be able to raise for the same society acting independently. He would be able to make use of a much larger array of facts, as having a direct bearing on the object of his appeal, and it is found that liberal minded men, every where are disposed to give, in proportion to the extent of the object to be effected. I am persuaded therefore that such a connection between the Con. Miss. Society and the A.H.M.S. as should identify their objects as one and the same and enable them to act by a joint agency, would very much increase the funds of the Con. M. S. and at less expense than without such a connection.

II. Your next question is, *"Would these funds be better applied?"* In my answer to this, I am far from intimating any dissatisfaction with the manner in which the Con. Society has hithertoe [*sic*] disposed of its funds, nor have I any lack of confidence in the discretion of its Trustees, as to future appropriations. I only speak of the proposed measures, therefore, as embracing a plan which furnishes additional facilities to the best application of its funds through the national Society. Let the constitution of your Society be so modified that it may appropriate as much of its income as may be necessary to the aid of feeble congregations in your own State, with the liberty of expending the remainder, through the National Society, or otherwise, as may be judged expedient from time to time, and it would realize the following advantages.

1. With the increase of funds which it would derive from the merging of the Dom. Miss. Society in itself, and its own connection with the A.H.M.S. it would have no lack of means to supply at once all the destitute in Connecticut. This work would accordingly be done up and *finished* as fast as men could be found to occupy your vacant places.

2. In the meantime, I can not doubt that besides doing the needed work in Connecticut, a sum would be raised sufficient to carry on the full amount of your Society's present operations at the West. If there is any lack of this sum, the National Society will make it up. Then, if your Society become Auxiliary and confide to us the appropriation of such amount as they may have to expend at the West, we might enter at once into their responsibilities and engagements, and as relates to the assumption of new missions hereafter, they would always have the right to direct the appropriation, through us, of their own funds, and if at any time they whould find us indiscreet and unfaithful, they would have a right to withdraw from their connection. But, without arrogating to ourselves any superior wisdom in this business, we do possess facilities which can be enjoyed by no State Society, holding correspondence with only a small section of the territory to be aided. Our correspondence is general with the West and South, and is becoming more so every month. This enables us to estimate the comparative claims of different

portions of the country, and thus to seize upon the most important points to be occupied with more accuracy than if our correspondence were less extensive.

As to any *alteration in your plan of appropriation*, I have none to suggest. Our own method probably does not differ essentially from yours at the present time. We hold ourselves in readiness to conform in this respect to the condition and circumstances of the country, and of the particular places needing aid.

III. *"Will the missionary spirit of the country at [large] receive a greater impulse?"* I answer, this was expected, when the National Society was formed, and this has most manifestly been the result, wherever its operations have been sustained by the co-operation of State and other Societies, and we desire the co-operation of all such Societies to give to the National Institution the strength which it needs. We have now all of the State Societies of New England numbered amongst its auxiliaries except Connecticut; and Connecticut, though last, is not least in importance to the onward movement of the great work.

With the strength of New England and New York combined there is every encouragement to believe that the Society will be able to walk over the obstacles which are thrown in its way in some parts of the Presbyterian Church, and exert a powerful and lasting influence on the Western and Southern States. But without this union of effort, the influence of these states must be proportionally weakened.

Looking to God to direct both you and us to the happiest and best measures, I am

Very truly,

Your friend and Br.

ABSALOM PETERS

REV. H. HOOKER
Cor. Sec. of the
Con. Miss. Socy.

[Meeting of the General Association of Connecticut, 1830,
  Minutes, p. 8:]
  ARTICLE I.—This Society shall be known by the name of
the Missionary Society of Connecticut, Auxiliary to the
American Home Missionary Society.

. . . .

ART. III.—The object of this Society shall be to co-operate
with the American Home Missionary Society in building up
the waste places of Connecticut, and in sending the Gospel
to the destitute, and assisting feeble congregations in other
and more destitute portions of the United States, according
to the provisions of the 8th Article of the Constitution of the
Parent Society, with such stipulations as shall secure to this
Society the control of the raising and application of funds,
the selection and appointment of missionaries, and the general designation of their fields of labour; the said stipulations
to be mutually agreed upon by the Directors of this Society,
and the Executive Committee of the A.H.M.S.
[The following is taken from the *Minutes* of 1831, p. 5:]
  Voted, That the alterations in the Constitution of the Domestic Missionary Society of Connecticut, with a view to
its becoming auxiliary to the American Home Missionary
Society, proposed at the last meeting of this Body, be
adopted.

CHAPTER V

Church Records

INTRODUCTION

MADISON, OHIO, is located in the Western Reserve, forty-two miles east of the city of Cleveland. It was in this region that Congregationalism and Presbyterianism tried out most fully the Plan of Union of 1801. The Madison church was one of the few Congregational churches which retained its Congregational character throughout the period of contact and controversy between the two bodies. The records here printed are for the years 1814–17 and cover the period of establishment.

The Congregational church in Du Page, Cook County, Illinois, was one of the three first Congregational churches in that state. When the Congregationalists established their first church in Illinois, that at Princeton (1831), there were already a number of Presbyterian churches in the state, and in 1833, when the Congregational church at Du Page was formed, the Presbyterians had a synod consisting of three presbyteries, with thirty-three ministers. Established in July, 1833, as a Presbyterian church, the Du Page church was changed into a Congregational church in August, 1834. The first settlers of the Du Page region were all from New England, or of New England background, and Congregational in their sympathies. The first minister, Nathaniel C. Clark, was a native of Vermont and a staunch Congregationalist. The leading layman of the community, I. P. Blodget, was a vigorous abolitionist, and the fact that the Presbyterians at this time were straddling the fence on the slavery issue was doubtless one of the reasons for the change to Congregationalism within a year after the church had been established. The change did not mean, however, that the congregation repudiated the Plan of Union.

The records of the Du Page church here printed cover the years from 1833 to 1840 and illustrate the process by which a strongly Congregational community succeeded in establishing a Congregational church in spite of dominant Presbyterian influence.[1]

[1] Joseph E. Roy, "History of Congregationalism in Illinois," *Illinois Society of Church History, Congregational, Historical Statement and Papers* (Chicago, 1895), pp. 24–66.

RECORD OF THE FORMATION OF THE CONGREGATIONAL
CHURCH IN MADISON, OHIO, 1814–17

It being the desire of a number of Christian Bretheren from different parts of the Country, in Madison, County of Geauga and State of Ohio, to be formed and Organized into a Church of the Congregational Order—a Meeting was held on July 29th 1814—at the House of Lemuel Kimball in Said town— to take into Consideration the Expediancy of being Organized as aforesaid the Meeting was Opened by Prayer by the Rev. Mr. Jonathan Leslie[2]—who presided as Moderator— and after Consultation had on the Subject of Organizen or Incorporating a Church in Said Town Voted that the members present procede and adopt Suitable measures for forming Said Church—Voted that we will adopt the following articles of faith as the platform of the Congregational Church in the town of Madison aforesaid—and as the Church is Called the Ground and piller of the truth, and as it is made the Express-Duty of Christians to Contend Earnestly for the faith Once Delivered to the Saints; we the undersignd Members of the Church of Christ in Madison—feeling it to be our Duty to leave on Record our testamony in behalf of

[2] W. S. Kennedy (*Plan of Union* [Hudson, Ohio, 1856], p. 40) has the following concerning Jonathan Leslie: "Mr. Leslie was born in Adams County, Penn., in 1780. He was graduated at Jefferson College in 1806; studied Theology with Rev. J. McMillan, was liscensed in June 1807; came to the Reserve and was ordained . . . . in 1808. (Rev. Andrew Gwin preached the ordination sermon and Rev. J. McMillan delivered the charge.) He was installed over the church in Geneva and Harpersfield in November 1810, and continued in that connection for ten years. In 1835 Leslie settled in Batavia where he preached for the church and made missionary journies throughout the surrounding country. A few years later he removed to Centreville, New York, where he remained until his death. An old acquaintance speaks of him as a very clever man, ... who preached in a peculiarly nasal tone and was not quite as judicious in some respects as would have been desirable." Leslie was furnished as a missionary by the synod of Pittsburgh but was sustained by the Connecticut Missionary Society. For further reference see letter from John McMillan concerning Jonathan Leslie, included in this volume.

What we Consider as the Great leading Doctrings of the Gospel, have cordially Subscribed the following Confession of faith as our views on these Subjects—

A CONFESSION OF FAITH—

ARTICLE 1.—We believe that there is one only living and true God, who is a Spirit uncreated and unchangeable that he is essential love, everywhere present and perfect possessed of Infinite Knowledge, power Wisdom Justice Goodness and truth—

ART. 2.—We believe that the Scriptures of the Old and New Testament are a Divine Revelation, Given by Inspiration of God—and that they Contain a perfect and the only Rule of faith and practice—

ART. 3.—We believe that theire are in the Unity of the Godhead a Trinity of Persons, Father, Son, and Holy Ghost —that these Persons are in essence one and that the Son, and Holy Ghost—are Coequal with the father—

ART. 4.—We believe that God has made all things for him Self that he Superintends all his works—that he will so over rule all things as to Display his own Glory, and produce the Greatest Good—and that this will be effected in a way perfectly Concistent with the morral agency of his rational Creatures—

ART. 5.—We believe that Adam was Created Holy and happy—that he was Constituted the Moral root of his posterity that he apostatized from God, in Consequence of Which all his Descendants possess a nature morally depraved and totally alianated from God—

ART. 6.—We believe that Adam's being appointed federal Head and Representative of his posterity, that the Law of God—and every part of the Divine Administration is perfectly wise holy Just and Good—

ART. 7—We believe that without the renovation of their

natures, by the Eternal Spirit and the pardon of their Sins, none of the human race can be admitted to the kingdom of God—

ART. 8.—We believe that by the Obediance Sufferings and Death of the Son of God—all necessary provision is made for the redemption of men—so that he will become a Complete Savior to all who believe in him—

ART. 9.—We believe that the Gospel offers a free salvation to all, yet, that Such is the natural enmity of the heart to holiness, that none will ever accept this Salvation till moved thereto by the Spirit of God—

ART. 10.—We believe that those who receive Christ were Chosen in him before the foundation of the world, and that they are Saved not by works of righteousness which they have Done, but through Sovereign Gace Communicated by the Washing of rigeneration and the renewing of the Holy Ghost—

ART. 11.—We believe that the Lord Christ—has engaged to keep from final apostacy and preserve to his heavenly Kingdom all who have fled to him for Refuge—

ART. 12.—We believe that Christ has a visible Church in the world, and none in the Sight of Men but visible believers, and that none in the Sight of God but real believers, have a right of admission thereto—

ART. 13.—We believe that God has Instituted Baptism and the Lords Supper as Ordinances to be Observed in the Church to the end of the world—that Baptism is to be administered to visible believers and those committed to their nurture and admonition—and the Lords Supper to Such Visible Saints as are free from Scandal, able to examine themselves and to Disern the Lords Body—

ART. 14.—We believe that Christ has instituted a Discepline to be Observed in his Church, which is to be maintained according to his Direction—

ART. 15.—We believe that Christ has instituted an order

of men to preach the Gospel and administer its Ordinances to Suitable Subjects—

ART. 16.—We believe that at the end of the world Christ Will appear in Glory as the universal Judge—that the dead will then be Raised—the living Changed to an Immortal State—that all must appear at his Judgement Seat to Receive a Sentence according to their Works—and that the Reward bestowed on the Righteous, and the punishment inflicted on the Wicked will be equally eternal——

Voted to adopt the following Covenant[3]—

You viewing yourselves Subjects of Special Grace and having a right to the Seals of Gods Covenant, Do now before God, Angels and Men Avouch the Lord Jehovah to be your God—and Devote yourselves to him through Jesus Christ— you Renounce the Service of Sin and Satan, and Choose the living and true God for your Eternal portian—you Choose Christ for your Prophet Priest and King—and Receive the Holy Ghost—for your Sanctifier and Comforter—you take Gods Holy Word for your Directory—Solemnly Engaging to Comply with all Its Requirements—you promise to Observe and Keep the Christian Sabbath—to maintain and attend upon all the Instituted Ordinances of the Gospel, Specially public worship, the Sacraments of the new Testament—Private and family Releigion to present your Children for baptism and to Educate and bring them up in the nurture and admonition of the Lord—and to Walk With this Church in meekness and love—Watching over the members thereof— and Submitting your Selves to wholesome Decipline and also to walk orderly in all things, So as to Give Occasion of offence to none——voted that when the Church is Installed the Rev-

---

[3] This covenant is essentially the same as the one advocated by the Grand River Presbytery, although it paraphrases the Grand River Presbytery Covenant in several places and is, therefore, much shorter.

erend Messrs Badger—Leslie[4] and Barr[5] be Requested to attend, and that the Revd Mr. Barr be requested to preach on this ocation—the Meeting was then Concluded with Prayer—

NAMES OF THE CHURCH MEMBERS[6]

Jesse Ladd
John Cuningham
Thomas Montgomery
Jesse Ladd Jun.
Lemuel Kimbel
William Ensign
Acahel North
Foster Emerson
Jasper Brewster

Rhodes Cuningham
Rebeckah Mtgomery
Ruby Ladd
Polly Kimbli
Abigail Mixer
Dodge
North
Mary Ensign
Hariot Goodrich
Fanny Curtis
Maryann Hubbard
Melinda Lovel
Dosier Brewster
Rebecca Totcott
Mercy Cady

CHURCH RECORDS

September 16th [1814?].—Met by previous appointment Jesse Ladd, John Cuningham, Thomas Montgomery, Jesse Ladd Junr. Lemuel Kimball and Abigail Mixer. Rev. Messrs.

---

[4] Reference has already been made to Jonathan Leslie. He was not the minister of this church but seems to have been, as a missionary, acting in an advisory capacity, helping this church to become organized.

[5] Thomas Barr learned the carpenters and jointers' trade, being apprenticed to a Mr. Pollock. At one time he was heavily addicted to the use of alcohol, until he signed a pledge of total abstinence, and was later converted to Christianity under the preaching of Mr. Wick at Youngstown. At Greensburgh (Pa.) Mr. Barr attended the academy of Rev. T. E. Hughes, which was designed to prepare men for the ministry. Barr was licensed to preach by the Hartford Presbytery at their meeting in Brookfield, Trumbull County, September, 1809. He settled at Euclid, Ohio, having half-time preaching and the remainder of his time employed by the Connecticut Missionary Society. He is regarded by some as one of the principal fathers and defenders of Presbyterianism on the Reserve (see Kennedy, *op. cit.*, pp. 41–47).

[6] There are twenty-four persons listed here. The records show that ten of these members were admitted after the organization of the church.

Joseph Badger, Andrew Rawson,[7] Jonathan Leslie and Thomas Barr were present as council.[8] Meeting was opened by prayer by Jonathan Leslie. It appeared to the council that the preceeding Confession of Faith and covenant had been unanimously agreed to by the above named members wishing to form a church in this town. After due and prayerful deliberation the council were unanimously of opinion that it would be to the interest of the Redeemer's kingdom to organize a church in this place. Mr. Andrew Rawson Preached from Jer. 23.29. Mr. Joseph Badger read the Confession of Faith to which the candidates subscribed. They then solemnly entered into covenant with God and each other and were pronounced a Church of Christ. They received a suitable charge and the meeting was concluded with prayer by Mr. Thomas Barr.

Voted, That the communion be attended to next Lord's day.

May 4th 1816.—The church met by previous appointment.

[7] Andrew Rawson was a licentiate of the New Haven East Association in 1804 (*Contributions to the Ecclesiastical History of Connecticut, etc.* [New Haven, 1861] p. 325). The lists of the Connecticut Missionary Society include the names of Joseph Badger, Jonathan Leslie, William Wick, and Thomas Barr, but not the name of Andrew Rawson, and hence we conclude that he was not in the employment of the society (Rev. Horace Hooker, "Congregational Home Missions in Connecticut," in *ibid.*). In the *Congregational Year Book, 1854* (the first published), an "A. Rawson" is listed as minister of the Congregational church at New Boston, New Hampshire, in 1853. The later *Year Books* do not mention his name, so it is probable either that he died or that he left the Congregational church that year.

[8] "Councils, therefore, are the churches consulting together (by delegates for convenience's sake), either upon the special interests of the whole body of churches, or upon a particular subject of interest pertaining to an individual church, but which in some degree concerns the general welfare, or is one on which the individual church asks light. Two kinds of councils are here brought to view. First, those which are composed of the churches as a whole, called together to consider some matter of general concern; those have gradually acquired the name of Synods, although the early writers in their discussion of Congregational principles, use the term Synod and Council interchangeably. Secondly, those which relate to the affairs of an individual church; these are now called councils. . . . . As to membership; a Council cannot exclude any person who comes in accordance with the letter missive, nor add any, either an actual member or under the nonsensical title of "corresponding" (*Congregational Year Book, 1859*, p. 49).

Proceeded to examine Mr. Ensign and wife and Mr. North and wife and Mrs. Goodrich who had formerly been Church members. Also Mrs. Francis Curtis and Maryan Hubbard. Having obtained Satisfactory evidence of their piety and their soundness in the faith.

Voted, They shall be received into the communion of this Church next Lord's day. Concluded with prayer.

May 5th 1816.—Sabbath. The persons above named were received into the church agreeable to the above vote, except Mrs. Goodrich who had not received her dismission from the church to which she belonged.

Attest

JONATHAN LESLIE   *Missionary*

July 9th 1816.—After public worship the church met by previous appointment. After mature consideration the following regulations for the practice of the church, recommended by the Grand River Presbytery,[9] were adopted viz.

1. This church adopt the regulations proposed by the General Assembly of the Presbyterian Church and approved by the General Association of the State of Connecticut June 16th 1801. for the promotion of union and harmony amongst the churches in new settlements.

2. This Church shall have a standing committee, chosen

[9] "In 1818, the Region of the Western Reserve in Ohio was occupied by the three presbyteries of Hartford, formed from Erie in 1808, Grand River, formed from Hartford in 1814, and Portage formed from Grand River in 1818. . . . . the Synod of Pittsburgh granted the petition to divide the Hartford Presbytery, and appointed a meeting at Euclid, on the second Tuesday of November, 1814. The members of the Hartford Presbytery set off to constitute the new Presbytery, were Rev. Messrs. Joseph Badger, Giles H. Cowles and Thomas Barr. Mr. Badger was appointed to preach at the first meeting and preside until a Moderator should be chosen" (E. H. Gillett, *History of the Presbyterian Church in the United States of America* [Philadelphia, 1864] I, 283). The delegates proceeded to adopt regulations for the Grand River Presbytery, which included the gist of the Plan of Union of 1801 and twenty other articles. This presbytery was formed in accordance with the desires of Thomas Barr, who was in opposition to the formation of a Congregational association (see Kennedy, *op. cit.*, pp. 168–69).

from their male members, consisting of not less than two, and not more than seven, whose duty it shall be to take cognisance of the disorderly conduct of members and to labor to promote the spiritual interest of the church.

3. All persons applying for admission into this church either by letter, or otherwise, Shall be examined by the officers of the church, all the members of which shall consider it their duty to attend, and to ask such questions as they think necessary. If candidates give satisfactory evidence to the church of their christian character, they shall, in ordinary cases be publicly propounded, at least two weeks before their admission.

4. This church consider it their duty not to admit members of distant churches residing in this vicinity to occational communion, in ordinary cases for a longer period than one year.

5. This church consider it the duty of male heads of families, and when circumstances do not forbid, of those who are females, daily to read the Scriptures and to pray in their families. They also recommend it to all heads of families, that singing praises to God, be considered as a part of family worship.

6. This church consider it an important duty that heads of families instruct and govern their children and all under their care, agreeably to the word of God, endeavoring to restrain them from evil practices and from vicious company: and directing them by parental authority to attend catechetical lectures appointed by the pastor or church, whenever circumstances will permit.

7. This church consider it their duty to pay special attention to their baptized children; and that parents and others who are members of this church, having the more immediate care of such children, shall be accountable to the church for their religious instruction and government, so long as they continue members of their families; and for any evident neg-

lect of religious instruction, or government, shall be as liable to descipline as for any offence whatever.

8. This church consider the collecting of hay or grain on the Sabbath; attending to any part of the business of making sugar; the visiting of friends, except in cases of sickness; and the prosecuting of journiess on that day, without special necessity, a violation of Christian duty.

The church agreeably to the above regulations proceeded to the choice of a committee and John Cuningham, Jesse Ladd Jun. and Asahel North were chosen the standing committee of this church. concluded with prayer[10]

Attest

JONATHAN LESLIE *Missionary*

April 18th 1817.

The Church[11] met agreeably to previous appointment. Revrd Jonathan Leslie Moderator When they proceeded to Examine Jasper Brewster and Dosier his wife and Foster Emerson—who were accepted and prodused Letters of Recomndation from the Church to which they belonged—and were Received into this Church publickiely on the next Lords Day April 19th 1817

[10] These articles were recommended by the Grand River Presbytery in its meeting of 1814, at which time Thomas Barr and Joseph Badger were present, Joseph Badger acting as the moderator for the presbytery (see Kennedy, *op. cit.*, p. 176).

[11] The following is a list of the ministers of the Madison, Ohio, church under consideration from 1814 to 1835 (for complete details see table in *ibid.*, pp. 85, 135):

	Called	Dismissed
Alvin Hyde, Jr.	Aug. 31, 1819	....
Randolph Stone	Nov. 1, 1823	Nov. 1, 1824
Jonathan Winchester	Jan. 1, 1826	Jan. 1, 1828
Perry Pratt	Oct. 1, 1826	Oct. 1, 1827
Eliphalet Austin, Jr.	Aug. 1, 1828	Aug. 1, 1829
Caleb Burbank	Jan. 27, 1830	July 9, 1834
Henry T. Kelly	July 9, 1834	....

RECORDS OF THE CONGREGATIONAL CHURCH AT
DU PAGE, COOK COUNTY, ILLINOIS, 1833–40

DUPAGE,[12] COOK COUNTY, ILLINOIS.⎫
July 13th, 1833.⎭

By a request of a number of persons at Du Page to be organized into a church of Christ, the Rev. Jeremiah Porter,[13] the Rev. N. C. Clark,[14] Missionaries for this County & the Rev. C. W. Babbit[15] from Tazewell County met & after prayer, & some appropriate remarks proceeded to examine credentials of applicants. The following named persons were received by letter. Viz.

Israel P. Blodget(t)[16]	Leister Peet[17]
Advice Blodget(t)	Henry H. Goodrich

[12] The name "Du Page" was used to designate a territory at the fork of the Du Page River which is now part of the village of Naperville. The name originated from that of a Frenchman who had lived there. At the time of the organization of the church (1833), this territory was a part of Cook County, but in February, 1839, it was separated and formed into Du Page County.

[13] Jeremiah Porter, one of the pioneer missionaries to Illinois, was born in Hadley, Massachusetts, in 1804, and studied at William's College, Andover, and Princeton, graduating from the latter in 1831. In 1833 he came to Chicago, where he organized the first Presbyterian church of that city, but he remained only two years. Aratus Kent, in a letter written at Galena, Illinois, June 2, 1833, speaks of the large settlements of eastern immigrants on the streams which form the Du Page River, and comments on Jeremiah Porter's good work among these settlements.

[14] Rev. N. C. Clark was a very active Congregational minister who organized thirty-four Congregational churches in the Fox River territory. He became the first pastor of the Du Page church.

[15] Rev. C. W. Babbit was in the service of the A.H.M.S. In a letter to the society, written from Pekin, Tazewell County, Illinois, September 22, 1833, he apparently refers to the organization of the Du Page church in these words: ".... assisted brother Porter and Clerk in forming a Presbyterian Church. The church consists of about 20 members." Theron Baldwin, in a letter to the society dated December 24, 1834, indicates a lack of confidence in Babbit's ability.

[16] Israel P. Blodgett (1797–1861), whose son, Judge Blodgett, became a member of the Supreme Court, was born in Amherst, Massachusetts, and came to Illinois
[Footnote 16 continued on p. 117]

[17] The first school contract of Du Page County, dated September 14, 1831, engaged Leister Peet to teach "a regular English School" for twenty-two children of
[Footnote 17 continued on p. 117]

-Lucetta Barber   Thankful S. Goodrich
-Robert Strong   Eliza S. Goodrich
-Caroline W. Strong   Samuel Goodrich
-Constant Abbot(t)   Lydia Goodrich
 Isaac Clark   Pomroy Goodrich
 Clarissa R. Clark   Luch M. Goodrich

A brief summary of doctrines & covenant was read & adopted, as follows.

ARTICLES OF FAITH

ARTICLE 1.—You believe in the eternal existence of Jehovah, Father, Son, & Holy Ghost the Creator of all things; & that all his accountable creatures ought to render him perfect obedience forever.

ART. 2.—You believe that Jehovah is possessed of infinite moral excellence, & that he administers a perfect moral government over the universe; that he administers also a providential government which extends to all events great and small; that to him alone belonges the glory of the saved; "according as he hath chosen them in Christ before the foundation of the world, that they should be holy, and without blame before him in love; having predestinated them unto the adoption of children by Jesus Christ, according to the good pleasure of his will." (Eph. 1:4.5.) & that the impenitent in sin perish through their own voluntary perversion.

[Footnote 16 continued from p. 116]

with his family in 1831. He was a leader among his fellow-pioneers, and it was probably due to his initiative that the ministers were called together and the church organized. He was in ardent sympathy with the abolitionist party when it arose, a co-laborer with Lovejoy, and an enthusiastic operator of the Underground Railroad station of Du Page County (Rufus Blanchard, *History of Du Page County, Illinois* [Chicago: O. L. Baskin & Co., 1882], Part II, p. 80; Newton Bateman and Paul Selby [eds.], *History Encyclopedia of Illinois, and History of Du Page County* [Chicago: Munsell Publishing Co., 1913], II, 639; Du Page County, Illinois, Board of Supervisors, *History of Du Page County, Illinois*, compiled by C. W. Richmond [Aurora, Ill.: Knickerbocker & Hodder, 1877], p. 198).

[Footnote 17 continued from p. 116]

the Naper and other families. The term was to be of four months, the salary $12 a month—"and the understanding is, that said teacher is to board with the scholars" (Du Page County, Illinois, Board of Supervisors, *op. cit.*, pp. 12–13).

ART. 3.—You believe that the bible is given by inspiration of God, & that it contains the only infallible rule of faith, & practice.

ART. 4.—You believe that the gospel of Christ finds mankind in a state of sin & condemnation, utterly destitute of that holiness without which no man shall see the Lord & that consequently all must be renewed by the Holy Ghost, in the temper of their minds, before then can enter the kingdom of God.

ART. 5.—You believe in the divinity, incarnation, obedience, suffering & death, resurrection & ascension of Jesus Christ; that by his sufferings & death he hath made atonement for the sin of the world; & that he ever liveth to make intercession for believers, "who are kept by the power of God through faith unto salvation." 1. Pet. 1:5.

ART. 6.—You believe it to be the duty & privilege of Christians to make visible profession of Christianity receiving & applying the ordinances of baptism & the Lord's supper, as instituted by Christ & practiced by his apostles; that none but the cordial friends of Christ ought to partake of the Lord's supper; & that baptism is to be applied to believers & their infant seed.

ART. 7.—You believe that the first day of the week is the Christian Sabbath & is to be sanctified by an holy resting all that day; even from such worldly employments & recreations as are lawful on other days & spending the whole time in the public and private exercise of God's worship except so much as is to be taken up in the works of necessity & worship.

ART. 8.—You believe it to be the duty of Christians who are heads of families to maintain the daily worship of God in their families morning & evening; & faithfully to instruct their children & others under their care in the christian religion, & to bring them to the public worship of God on the Sabbath.

ART. 9.—You believe that Christians according to their

several ability, are under a sacred obligation to support the preaching of the gospel at home; & to contribute liberally of their substance for the spread of the gospel abroad.

ART. 10.—You believe that the present life is the only state of probation for mankind & that there will be a resurrection both of the just & of the unjust.

ART. 11.—You believe that God has appointed a day in which he will judge the world in righteousness by Jesus Christ, when all will receive according to their works: that the wicked will go away into everlasting punishment, but the righteous into life eternal.

COVENANT

You do now in the presence of the heart-searching God, before angels & men, avouch the great Jehovah Father, Son & Holy Ghost, to be your God.

Your receive the Father as your Father, the Lord Jesus Christ as your all-sufficient & only redeemer, & the Holy Ghost as your sanctifier.

Renouncing every sinful way you devote your all, unreservedly to God, & engage to walk in all his commandments & ordinances as required in his word.

You receive the brethren of Christ in this place, as your brethren, & his friends, as your friends. You also submit yourself to the government of Christ in his church, & to the regular administration of it in this church in particular. You covenant to walk in Communion with your brethren, endeavouring to posseth divine worship, & Christian love & fellowship, by all the means of Christ's appointment & within your power: & to live as a humble Christian, in a regular & faithful attendance on the worship & ordinances of Christ in this place & in the performance of all your solemn engagements to God, & this church, untill by the providence of God you are removed.

In reliance on divine grace, this you solemnly engage.

The members then proceeded to the election of elders,[18] when Isaac Clark, Pomroy Goodrich & Leister Peet were duly elected to that office.

The meeting was then adjourned to 12 o'clock tomorrow. Closed with prayer.

Sabbath, July 14, 1833

After a sermon & other religious exercises, the above named brethren, viz. *Isaac Clark, Pomroy Goodrich & Leister Peet,* were solemnly ordained with prayer & the imposition of hands, to the office of ruling elder.

The church was then declared duly organized.

During intermission, session met & constituted with prayer. Rev. N. C. Clark presided as Moderator.

The following persons, viz Sarah Peet, Eunice Peet, & Mrs. Prudence Smith were received to the church by letter.

After the intermission the Lord's supper was administered to about 40. communicants. The exercises were closed with singing & the benediction. The meetings were solemn, & the divine presence to some degree manifested.

C. W. BABBIT, *Clerk pro. tem*

August 29, 1833.

Agreeably to appointment, session met at the house of bro. Peet 11. o'clock A.M. present elders Isaac Clark, Pomroy Goodrich, Leister Peet, Rev. N. C. Clark, labouring as a Missionary on this field presided as moderator. Constituted with prayer. Consulted as to the expediency of adopting the congregational mode of church government. Proposed and considered several resolutions, by which the church should be regulated. Agreed to present the subjects under considera-

[18] The election of elders is a characteristic of Presbyterianism. Organized as a session, the ruling elders conduct the business of the church as representatives of the members. In a typical Congregational church the communicants meet as a body for business.

tion to the church for consultation, & adoption if the church should think proper.

Pomroy Goodrich was elected clerk of session.

Adjourned with prayer.[19]

August 29, 1833

Agreably to appointment the church met at the school house near bro. Samuel Goodrich's 3. o'clock P.M. Rev. N. C. Clark presided as moderator.

The subjects under consideration by the session, in the morning were brought before the church.

Rev. N. C. Clark & bro. Pomroy Goodrich were appointed a committee to consult with the church & Christians in this county & vicinity respecting the form of church government to be adopted, in this region of country; & to request a general conference of the churches & Christians for consultation on this subject, that, if possible there may be unison.

Resolved, That a church meeting for prayer & conversation be held on the last Friday of each month at the place & hour previously designated.

Resolved, That our next communion, by the leave of providence, be on the first Sabbath in October next.

Brother Isaac Clark was appointed as committee to see that the sabbath schools books were repaired numbered & registered.

Resolved, That the minister, as soon as practicable, visit every family in the settlement, & that each of the brethren in turn when called upon, accompany him; to ascertain the state of religious feeling, & to awake attention on the subject.— Especially to explain the object & plan of sabbath schools, & distribution of tracts, & to distribute tracts according to the manner of monthly distribution.

Resolved, That a contribution for the purpose of defraying

[19] As all meetings were opened and closed with prayer, that item in the minutes will hereafter be omitted.

the expenses of the church, be taken at the monthly church meeting.

Resolved, That there be a weekly prayer meeting in the neighbourhood of bro. Strong. Brothers Blodget, S. Goodrich, Strong & I. Clark pledged themselves to maintain it.[20]

Resolved, That there be a weekly prayer meeting in the neighbourhood of bro. Pomroy Goodrich.

September 27, 1833.

No meeting on account of sickness & storm.[21]

Sabbath, October 6, 1933.

The Lord's supper was not administered according to appointment in consequence of the sickness of the Rev. Mr. Clark's family.

October 25, 1833.

No meeting on account of sickness.

November 29, 1833

The church & session met agreably to appointment at the house of bro. Samuel Goodrich. Present Rev. N. C. Clark & all the elders.

[20] The church comprised five groups of people, each located about one of the leaders of the church. The central group was located near the old settlement of Captain Napers; the Goodrich or East Branch was about five miles to the Southeast; the Lisle or Downers Grove was to the East; Big Woods Neighborhood was to the west; East Du Page or Strong and Clark's Settlement was to the south; there was also a northern settlement.

[21] The prairies were swampy and damp, the summers hot and the winters bitterly cold, and epidemic disease periodically decimated the population. Jacksonville was visited by cholera early in the summer of 1833. "Most of those who could do so fled from the town, and in a few days not more than four or five hundred people remained. Of these more than one in every ten fell a victim to the disease" (Julian M. Sturtevant, *An Autobiography*, ed. J. M. Sturtevant, Jr. [New York: Fleming H. Revel Co., 1896], p. 205). In January, 1834, one-tenth of the population of Quincy died of the same disease (Donald C. Tewkesbury, *The Founding of American Colleges and Universities before the Civil War* [New York: Columbia University Press, 1932], p. 26).

The committee, appointed August 29 to consult with the churches & Christians in this vicinity, relative to the form of church government, reported.

1. That the churches already formed chose to remain as they were;—Presbyterian.

2. That probably a majority of Christians not organized into churches *would prefer the Congregational mode of government.*

3. "That a conference of the churches & Christians was agreed on to be held at Chicago during the time of the session of court in October. The court did not sit as was expected, consequently there was no conference."

The report was accepted.

Resolved, That the committee make further effort to procure a conference of the churches & Christians to deliberate on the form of church government, that there may be union.

Resolved, That the members of this church totally abstain from the manufacture, traffic & use of ardent spirits, & from furnishing them on any occasion, except for medicinal, chemical, or mechanical purposes.

Resolved, That it is the indispensable duty of church members, where not hindered by unavoidable providences, to attend all church appointments & by neglecting to do so, they subject themselves to censure & discipline of the church.

A lecture preparatory to the Lord's supper was preached by Rev. N. C. Clark. Closed with prayer.

January 31, 1834.

The session & church met at the house of Rev. N. C. Clark.

Resolved, That the monthly distribution of tracts be carried on through the year, if not prevented for want of tracts.

Resolved, That the Rev. N. C. Clark be a committee to take the tracts into his hands, & superintend their distribution.

Resolved, That the Lord's supper be administered, hereafter, once in two months, if not hindered by unavoidable providences, beginning the first Sabbath in March.

After an interesting session of prayer & conversation in which was manifested much concern for the prosperity of religion. Closed with singing & the benediction.

February 28, 1834.

The session & church met at the house of Rev. N. C. Clark. Mr. George Martin & wife presented a certificate of their good standing in the church of Scotland requested the privilege of occasional communion with us. Their request was granted. Lecture preparatory to the Lord's supper was preached. Closed with singing & the benediction.

A circular was read from the Illinois bible society requesting aid for that institution. Whereupon it was

Resolved, That we do something in aid of that society, & that a subscription paper be circulated for that purpose. Sixteen dollars were raised at the meeting.

The time principally spent in prayer and conversation.

April 25, 1834.

In consequence of the absence of the Moderator the meeting of the session & church was postponed one week.

May 2, 1834.

The session & church met agreably to appointment at the house of Rev. N. C. Clark. Being disappointed in obtaining wine the administration of the Lord's supper, which was expected to take place next sabbath, was by vote, put off two weeks. Consequently the preparatory lecture was defered.

A subscription paper was drawn up & circulated for the purpose of raising something to aid in support of the Missionary, labouring this vicinity, for the year ending July 1st, 1834.

The following persons, viz. Haskins Crocker, Betsey Crocker, Lydia Crocker, Joshua Crocker, were received as members of this church, by letter.

The subject of church government was then introduced, which occassioned some discussion, after which the following resolutions were adopted. viz.

Resolved, That we desire the name & form of government of our church to be changed from Presbyterian to Congregational.[22] One member absent. All who were present, but one, voted in favour of the resolution.

Resolved, That a copy of the above resolution be transmitted to the churches & Christians at Chicago, Hickory Creek, Meacham's Grove, Walker's Grove, & Ottawa, & that they be requested to send delegates to meet delegates from this church, at Walker's Grove, on the 2nd. Tuesday of June next, 10. o'clock A.M. to take into consideration, the expediency & propriety of adopting the Congregational mode of church government.

Resolved, That we send four delegates to the contemplated convention. The following brethren were appointed, viz. John Dudley, Dr. C. Abbott, Henry Goodrich, Isaac Clark.

After sometime spent in prayer, & religious conversation closed with singing & the benediction.

July 5, 1834.

The session & church met at the home of Rev. N. C. Clark.

Resolved, That we take up the subject of church government & decide what form we will adopt the next meeting.

After some discussion it was

Resolved, That we raise one hundred dollars to help sup-

[22] On May 2, 1834, the matter of changing from Presbyterianism to Congregationalism was voted on and passed. Since the entire church was at the meeting of the session, it appears that Congregational procedure already obtained. On August 1, 1834, the matter was once again voted on and passed, and the church then began legally as a Congregational church. The Presbyterian office of elder was dispensed with.

port preaching among us, for the year ending July 1st, 1835.

Lecture preparatory to the Lord's supper was preached. Closed with singing & the benediction.

Sabbath, July 13, 1834.

William, son of Lucetta Barber (Widow) was baptised.

July 25th, 1834.

Meeting defered one week.

August 1st, 1834.

The church met at the house of Rev. N. C. Clark according to appointment. The absentees of the last meeting who were present, gave their excuse for absence, & were sustained.

The subject of church government was brought up and discussed, After which it was,

Resolved, That the name & form of government of our church be changed from Presbyterian to Congregational.

Brothers Isaace Clark, Pomroy Goodrich, & Leister Peet, were chosen deacons.

August 29, 1834.

A few of the brethren were together, & in consequence of a protracted meeting in the Baptist church being in progress, adjourned one week.

September 5, 1834.

The church met agreably to adjournment, at the house of Rev. N. C. Clark. The absentees of the last meeting who were present, gave their excuse for absence & were sustained.

In consequence of the uncertainty of having a place near Naper's to meet, the next sabbath, it was voted that the communion be defered two weeks.

Deacon Pomroy Goodrich was elected church clerk.

Sabbath, November 23, 1834.

During the intermission a letter was read to the church from the Congregational church of Jacksonville, giving notice of a convention of Congregational churches to be held at Quincy on the 28. instant; & requesting this church to send a delegate or delegates to said convention,[23] whereupon the church—

Resolved, That we approve of the object of the convention to be held at Quincy the 28th. inst, & that the reason we do not send a delegate, is, was of sufficient time to have him arrive there.

Resolved, That the letter from the Jacksonville church be answered; & that a copy of the above resolution be forwarded, signed by the Moderator & Clerk; & also that the convention, through that church, be requested to notify us of their doings.

The Lord's supper was administered by Rev. J. Porter. Previous to which the church manifested a willingness to renew their covenant with each other & God, & as a token of their willingness, arose & stood while the covenant was read, & anew gave their public assent to it. A solemn, & interesting session. The spirit of God was manifestly present.

November 28, 1834.

The church met according to appointment at the house of Rev. N. C. Clark. The moderator being absent Deac. Isaac Clark presided. In view of the state of feeling in the church & community it was

Resolved, That the families in every part of the settlement be visited by the minister & some brother accompanying him as soon as consistent with his other duties;

[23] "In 1835 at Big Grove, in an unoccupied log cabin was convened the first Congregational Council known in the denominational history of the State as that of Fox River" (Newton Bateman and Paul Selby [eds.], Historical Encyclopedia of Illinois [Chicago: Munsell Publishing Co., 1901], I, 115-16).

A letter was read from the Congregational church at Big Grove requesting this church to send delegates to a convention of Congregational churches to be held at that place, on the 25th of June for the purpose of taking into consideration the expedience of forming an association of the Congregational churches in this part of the state. Whereupon it was;

Resolved, That we comply with their request, & send some delegates.

Deacons Isaac Clark & Pomroy Goodrich & brothers John Dudley & Samuel Goodrich were appointed delegates to attend the above named convention.

A letter was read from the moderator of the convention held at Quincy 28th. of last November,—giving information of the doings of that convention, & requesting us, if we approved of them, to adopt their confession of faith & covenant & constitution, & thus become associated with the churches then represented in an ecclesiastical body. Whereupon it was;

Resolved, That we approve of the doings of the convention at Quincy; but do not deam it expedient to comply fully with their request, till after the convention to be held at Big Grove.

A request was presented from the church at Blackstone's Grove desiring that our respective seasons for celebrating the Lord's supper, be on different days so that we may unite by our ministers & delegates in the celebration of it. Whereupon it was

Resolved, That we comply with the request of the church at Blackstone's Grove:—defer our communion till the first of June, & appoint delegates to attend, with our minister at that place the first sabbath in May.

Deacon I. Clark, Deacon L. Peet, Dr. C. Abbott & Samuel Goodrich were appointed to attend the celebration of the Lord's supper at Blackstone's Grove the first sabbath in May next.

Closed the meeting, after a season of prayer for the conversion of the world, with singing.

POMROY GOODRICH, *Church Clerk*

April 24th, 1835

The following resolutions were offered & after some discussion adopted, viz.

Resolved, That persons uniting with this church by letter be required to give a brief relation of their religious experience & answer such questions relative to their views of doctrine & duty as the Moderator & members of the church, may think proper to ask.

Resolved, That we consider the obligation of parents to give up their children in baptism as recognized in the sixth article of our confession of faith scriptural and highly important, but in some cases where persons, differ from us, on this subject, & cannot, owing to conscientious scruples, practise infant baptism, we think that they may unite with us: & that assent to that requisition in the before named article may be dispensed with.[24]

The Clerk being absent Dr. C. Abbott was appointed Clerk *pro tempore*.

A letter of dismission & recommendation was voted to Dr. Constant Abbott. Also a certificate of her Christian walk while residing with us, was voted to his wife. Adjourned to meet at Deacon I. Clark's on the first of July next.

C. ABBOTT, *Clerk protem.*

July 1, 1835.

The church met pursuant to adjournment at the house of Deacon I. Clark. Moderator absent. Dea. I. Clark presided. On motion—

[24] An allowance possible only in a Congregational church and not in a Presbyterian body, which would require sanction of higher judicatories in the ecclesiastical organization.

Resolved, That Rev. N. C. Clark be invited to labour with us the ensuing year.

Resolved, That Mr. Clark preach on the sabbath in the following places & order, viz. On the first & fifth sabbath of each month at, or near his home. On the second and fourth, in the neighbourhood of Capt. Joseph Naper, & on the third, in the neighbourhood of Luther Hatch.

Messrs George Martin, Luther Hatch, & Josiah Strong were appointed a committee to solicit funds to support preaching this year.

C. ABBOTT, *Clerk pro. tem.*

July 31, 1835.

The church met at the house of Rev. N. C. Clark.

Deacon Isaac Clark one of the delegates to the convention held at Big Grove 25. June, reported.

That articles of faith, Covenant, & Constitution were agreed to, at the convention, and ordered to be presented to the churches there represented, & all those churches which should adopt them would be considered as associated in an ecclesiastical body.

The above named articles of faith, Covenant & constitution were agreed to, at the convention, and ordered to be presented to the churches there represented, & all those churches which should adopt them would be considered as associated in an ecclesiastical body.

The above named articles of faith, Covenant & constitution were presented to the church, & after examination were adopted.

The following brethren were appointed delegates to attend the meeting of the Congregational union to be held at Plainfield on the third of September next, viz Deacon Pomroy Goodrich & Robert Strong.

A letter was read from the church at Plainfield requesting this church to send two members to attend a council to be held, at that place the third Wednesday in August next. Whereupon it was

Resolved, That we comply with the request of the church at Plainfield.

Josiah Strong & Samuel Goodrich was appointed to attend the council.

Preparatory lecture was preached by Rev. Alfred Greenwood,[25] after which the meeting was closed with singing & the benediction.

April 29, 1836.

The Church convened pursuant to appointment. Information was given that the Big tent was expected early this season, & that probably an opportunity would be given us to hold a protracted meeting in it in the course of the season. Whereupon it was

Resolved, That as soon as providence shall open the door by putting means within our reach, we will have a protracted meeting in this settlement; & punctually & constantly attend it, & provide means for our families to attend; if not prevented by providences: & also use our influence to have others attend.

Preparatory lecture preached. Adjourned to meet at this place, next Monday, the 2. of May.

Closed with singing & the benediction.

May 20, 1836.

Church met. Deac. Isaac Clark presided.

Information was given that it was the intention of Rev. N. C. Clark to leave this people after the first of July next. Whereupon it was

[25] Minister of the Congregational church of Plainfield. In a letter to A.H.M.S., dated December 16, 1835, he writes that he came to Chicago at the suggestion of Rev. J. Porter. He arrived July, 1834, and went to Walker's Grove, where in September or October he organized the Plainfield Congregational Church on the principle of entire abstinence from the use of ardent spirits or traffic in them except as medicine.

Resolved, That we view it our imperative duty to adopt measures immediately, to supply ourselves with the stated ministry.

Resolved, That we can raise the sum of three hundred dollars, toward the support of a minister, & that we will ask the A.H.M.S. to send us a man, & give us a sum sufficient to make up his support, provided one third of his labours be performed at Naperville, & such proportion in the neighbourhood of Mr. Hatch, as the people there shall subscribe for his support, & the remainder in the neighborhood of Deacon I. Clark.

Resolved, That the officers of the church be a committee to take measures to supply us with preaching.

Closed with prayer.

POMROY GOODRICH, *Ch. Clerk.*

May 27, 1836.

The church met at the house of Rev. N. C. Clark. The "rules of discipline of the Congregational Union of Fox River" were presented to the church for adoption. After examining them, it was

Resolved, That our delegates to the Fox River Union be instructed to request an amendment of the 14th article, so that it read "if either party object" instead of "unless by consent of parties" & also of the 18th article; so that it embrace the principle contained in the 18th. chap. Mat. in the provision for dealing with churches.

Resolved, That our delegates be instructed to accept the rules of the Union with the exception of the 14th & 18th articles, & those with the amendments proposed.

Resolved, That the Treasurer of the church be instructed to furnish, out of any money in the treasury not otherwise appropriated, the necessary expenses of delegates when sent abroad, on business of the church.

Deacs. Isaac Clark & Pomroy Goodrich were chosen to attend the meetings of the Congregational Union.

The officers of the church were requested to confer with the Rev. Theron Baldwin, the agent of the A.H.M.S. who is to be here in a few days, on the subject of obtaining a minister.

POMROY GOODRICH, *Ch. Clk.*

Sabbath, July 10, 1836.

After a sermon by the Rev. Isaac Foster,[26] the Lord's supper was celebrated. Congregation large, attentive & solemn.

Sab. September 11, 1836.

After a sermon by Rev. Eliphalet Strong,[27] Edward Payson son of William Smith was baptized. Mrs Daphone Ball presented a letter, gave some account of her religious experience and by vote was received to the church. Miss Daphone Ball was received on examination.

Mrs Nancy Stanley, Mrs Daphone Ball & Miss Daphone Ball publicly adopted the articles of faith & covenent of this church.

The Lord's supper was administered. Closed with singing the benediction.

N. C. CLARK *Moderator*

[26] In a letter to A.H.M.S. from Plainfield, Illinois, dated October 1, 1836, he says: ". . . . from last information I can obtain there are 60 to 70,000 persons in the northern part of the State (to say nothing about Wisconsin territory) that have not more than about a dozen efficient ministers of all the evangelical denominations and I have heard of only one of our order-Brother Clark, north of here, this side of Green Bay a distance of 2 to 300 miles." Foster also speaks of a meeting in Gladstone in which Brother Foster, from the Baptist church, and Brother Clark aided him, and in which many were converted, which suggests revivalist activity and occasional disregard of denominational lines.

[27] Rev. Eliphalet Strong had been a missionary in Hinsdale, New Hampshire, and had come west for his health (letter to the A.H.M.S., April 24, 1837). In another letter to the society he writes of aiding Brother Clark in organizing the East Du Page church.

Feb. 18, 1837.

Church met at the school house near Samuel Goodrich according to appointment. Preparatory lecture by Rev E. Strong

Rev E. Strong Col William Smith P. Goodrich were appointed a committee to prepare and forward a [note] to the Editor of the Alton Observer expressing our Gratitude to the Church at Cazanovia N.Y. for a Communion Set presented through the agency of Rev N. C. Clark.

POMEROY GOODRICH, *Clerk.*

At a stated Monthly Meeting of the Church Met at the house of Dea Isaac Clark on Wednesday the 24th day of February 1837 Jeames Towner was chosen Moderator and William Smith was chosen Secretary pro tem.

Resolved on Motion that a committee of two be appointed by the chair to prepare and circulate as subscription paper for the purpose of raising money to pay the Rev Mr Strong for his services in preaching to Sd church for three months which period expired the 19th March 1837.

Chair named Deac. I. Clark, William Smith, sd committee

POMEROY GOODRICH, *Clerk.*

At a special meeting of the DuPage Church convened pursuant to notice at the school house in the dupage school district on the 9th day of March 1837 Rev. James Towner was chosen Moderator and William Smith secretary pro tem.

A petition from George E. Parmebe and other members of this church was then read praying a letter of dismission therefrom for the purpose of organizing a church near to their respective places of abode.

Resolved on motion that the prayer of sd petition be granted.

POMEROY GOODRICH, *Clerk.*

Church met at the schoolhouse Forks Dupage for business meeting. On motion resolved that Whereas the labors of the Rev. E. Strong in preaching the gospel among us since the expiration of his service ending March remain unpaid it is therefore the duty of this church to ascertain the amount claimed by him as compensation for his labors. Deacon I. Clark was appointed to confer with Rev. Mr. Strong on the subject and report to the next meeting. Voted that the Rev. I. G. Porter[28] be installed pastor over this Church on the second Wednesday in September, 1837. Voted that the church pay to Dea. Clark such sum as they individually are disposed to be appropriated to defray the expence of frait of the tent from New York to Chicago.

Monthly church meeting at the school house Dupage. Dea. Clark, moderator. Meeting opened by Rev. E. Strong. On motion, resolved that the ordination of Mr. Porter be adjourned until presbytery shall have held its session. Resolved the committee with Rev. Mr. Porter request Presbytery to install Mr. Porter Pas. of this church. Voted to pay Rev. Eliphalet Strong for the last five sabbaths preaching here at the same rate as for his labors ending March. Appointed Hiram Standish to circulate subscription for his payment.

H. Standish, *Sec. protempore.*

December 1837.

At a meeting of the church held at the house of Henry Goodrich.

Resolved, that Pomeroy Goodrich be appointed a committee to act with those before appointed to select a site for a Meeting House.

Resolved, That Brother Robert Strong be appointed a committee to receive funds for Foreign and Domestick Missions.

[28] Apparently, Rev. I. G. Porter was a Presbyterian minister who was under the jurisdiction of the Illinois Presbytery, hence this connection is a significant instance of a Congregational church calling for a Presbyterian preacher—a procedure perfectly in order under the Plan of Union.

Also Miss Webster and Caroline B. Goodrich a committee for the same purpose.

Moved that Mr. Crocker and family have a letter of recommendation and dismission when they shall have united with some church in fellowship with us.

The Church Treasurers report read and accepted. Found in the hands of the Treasurer $o7octs.

POMEROY GOODRICH *Clerk.*

At a special Meeting of the Dupage Church held at the House of Brother Dudley the following business was transacted.

The object of Meeting was stated by the Moderator.

A Motion was presented by Br. Josiah Strong to ask of the Fox River union a delegation from that body to advise with this church. not carried.

The following motion was then presented by Mr. J. Strong seconed by Br. R. Strong.

Resolved, That in our opinion the prosperity of the church and the general interest of religion will be best promoted by drawing the bond of union as tight as possible (in union there is strength). We are therefore of opinion that the labours of our pastor had better be expanded as heretofore to preach in the south settlement every sabbath Morning every afternoon at knapersvill and that the Lord's supper be administered monthly once a month at knapersvill and once a month at in the south part of the church, the church meeting to be held in Sit. Meiner.

It was then motioned by Br. Towner & seconded by Br. Smith that subscription to be circulated by the committee be drawn for five years.

Motioned by Br. R. Strong, seconded by Deac. Clark that when the Treasurer shall have received money enough to constitute our pastor a life member of the home missionary society that the same be appropriated to that purpose.

A proposition was presented by a committee from the east dupage church to the dupage church to unite with them in the support of Mr. Porter.

Motioned by Brother J. Strong and seconded by Br. Martin that this meeting be adjourned to meet at the house of Br. Dudley on Monday next 2 o'clock p.m.

In the report of the financial committe there was found due to Mr. Porter $200
Subscription unpaid that is good   158.50
Areares to be made up—   41.50

The church met pursuant to adjournment at the house of brother Dudley.

A committee of 3 were appointed to propose a plan of action for adoption.

Br. J. Strong, Br. Dudley, & Deac. I. Clark were appointed a committee by the moderator.

The committee reported that in their opinion a religious effort should be immediately made & that it is practicable to rais the subscription to within 50 or 75 dollars and the remainder can be made out by adding to our subscriptions or by assessment or by any other plan which the church may adopt.

Motioned by Henry Goodrich and seconded by Brother Martin that Deac. Clark be added to the committee at Knapersville & J. Strong to the committee in the south part of the settlement.

Resolved, That this meeting dem it inexpedient to comply with the proposition of the east Dupage church.

POMEROY GOODRICH.

A few members of the church met at the house of Br. Dudley. The condition of the East Dupage church was brought up and a committee appointed to enquire into their affair. The Rev. Mr. Porter & Deac. I. Clark were appointed a committee for that purpose.

Monday Sept. Church met agreeably to appointment for the transaction of business. Col. Wm. Smith appointed moderator & Josiah Strong clerk of the meeting. Rev. I. G. Porter and Robert Strong were appointed a committee to propose business for the meeting. Committee reported that; "Whereas the present place of worship is far to small and otherwise inconvenienced, therefore Resolved that it is the duty of this church to devise means for the erection of a more suitable house."[29] The Dea. L. Peet, John Dudley, Wm. Smith, Josiah Strong, and Henry Goodrich were appointed a committee to select a site, recommend, a plan of the house, and the most suitable time to build, and report their decision to the next meeting. Some time spent in religious conversation.

JOSIAH STRONG, Clk. of the meeting
Attest H. STANDISH

Monthly church meeting Friday Sept. 29th. Committee reported that; "In the opinion of the committee it is indispensibly necessary to erect a house for public worship without needless delay, and in the opinion of your committee the house may be completed during the ensuing winter." Site not agreed on. On motion by Brother James Towner seconded by Brother ——— church voted to build a house for public worship the ensuing spring. James Towner, Wm. Smith, Dea. I. Clark, Josiah Strong and Samuel Goodrich were appointed a committee to make suitable arrangements, circulate subscription for building said house.

---

[29] Ten years passed before this objective was realized. "Schoolhouse, barns, and the homes of different members were used by this congregation in its public worship until January 27, 1847, when the completed structure of its first church building was dedicated. The site was donated by Captain Morris Sleight" (Bateman and Selby [eds.], *Historical Encyclopedia of Illinois, and History of Du Page County*, II, 695).

Mrs. Elizabeth Miller presented her letter, which was accepted.

The Constitution of the Fox River Union was presented and adopted by this church.

H. STANDISH (*secy. protem*)

At a meeting of the church at the school house near Samuel Goodrich's on Friday Sept. 29, 1837 the Constitution and Confession of faith of the Congregational Union of Fox River was presented and adopted by this church of which the following is a copy.

CONSTITUTION

ARTICLE 1st. This body shall be called the Congregational Union of Fox River.

2nd. This Union shall be composed of Congregational ministers and Congregational Churches. Each church shall be entitled to send to all meetings of this body their pastor (if such they have) and one delegate.

3rd. The delegates may be chosen annually, or oftener at the option of the respective churches. But each delegate shall continue to act as such until another be elected in his room.

4th. Ministers who design to join this Union may be received by vote at any regular meeting on producing satisfactory testimonials of their character and standing; and churches wishing to unite with us may be admited in like manner if their sistem of doctrine and dicipline contain nothing inconsistent with that adopted by this body—but

5th. No minister or church connected with any other ecclesiastical body can be considered a consistent member of this Union at the same time.[30]

6th. The standing officers of this body shall be a moderator, clerk, and Treasurer to be chosen annually. Should the moderator or clerk be absent from any meeting others may be appointed in their stead.—Protem.

7th. This Union shall hold two stated meetings in a year viz one on the second Wednesday in June at which the standing officers shall be elected for the year ensuing; and one on the second Wednesday in January. They may also meet on their own adjournment as often as may be necessary for the completion of unfinished business, or a special meeting may be called by the moderator in case of any emergency which in his view (with the advice of one or more ministers and one or more delegates belonging to this body) may require it—

8th. This union shall be the final judicatory of our churches.[31] They shall receive and issue all appeals and refferences which may be regularly brought before them,—When duly called upon they shall ordain, install, dismiss, try, condem and silence ministers of this body as duty may require. They shall examine and license candidates for the gospel ministry either by themselves or by committees appointed for that purpose. They shall superintend the organizing and the partition of churches and they shall settle all disputes and difficulties in our churches when submitted to their decision, agreeably to our rules.

[30] This is a direct and emphatic repudiation of the Plan of Union.
[31] The union thus assumed the function of a presbytery.

9th. This Union may adopt bylaws for the regula-
tion of their meetings in accordance with this
constitution. They may freely recommend gospel measures, and regulations to the churches;
but shall always be implicitly governed by the
laws of Christ and the obvious sense of this
constitution—and should they propose amendments they shall be communicated in writing
to the churches, at least four months previous
to the meeting of the Union, at which the
decision of the churches are to be canvassed
and declared and the concurrence of two
thirds of the united churches shall be requisite
to establish an amendment of the constitution.

PRINCIPLES OF DICIPLINE

1. The objects of Gospel dicipline are 1st to restore to the path of duty those who go out of
the way and 2nd to preserve the peace & purity
of the churches, by the excision of inclaimable
offenders.

2nd. No complaint therefore of a private or personal
injury should be received from a person who
has omited the private steps of admonition
prescribed by our Lord Mat. 18:15–16 or
manifestly appears to be actuated by a mali-
cious or vindictive spirit or is deeply interested
in the conviction of the accused; or has himself
been regularly impeached before any of our
judicatories and not acquited.

3rd. Should the common fame at any time become
injurious to the character of any church or
individual amenable to any of our judicatories,
a committee of investigation may be appointed. If from the report of such committee,

it should appear probable that the unfavorable rumors are well founded, the party accused may be cited to trial.

4. Every complaint and citation to trial shall be in writing, distinctly stating each charge, and the names of the witnes to support it; and the party accused shall be furnished with a coppy of the same, at least ten days before the time appointed for trial.

5. If the party cited to trial shall refuse, or neglect to appear at the time appointed, the judicatory after assigning some person to manage the defence may proceed to trial; but no person shall be permitted to engage in the management of a cause before any of our judicatories unless he be a member of the Union or of some one of the churches connected therewith.

6. A member of the church summoned as a witness and refusing to appear, or to give testimony may be censured according to the circumstances of the case.

7. The testimony of persons, who, although not members of the church, are credible witnesses shall be received.

8. The testimony of witnesses who are at such a distance that they cannot conveniently attend the trial, may be taken by a commission of the judicatory appointed for that purpose but it shall be taken in the presence of the parties if they choose to attend.

9th. Witnesses shall be qualified, if either party desire it, in the following or some similar form, "You solemnly promise in the presence of the heart searching God that the testimony you shall give relative to the cause now in hearing shall be the truth, the whole truth and nothing but the truth, as you shall answer it at the great day, before Him who shall judge the quick and the dead."

10. No witness afterwards to be examined ought to be present during the examination of another witness in the same case, unless by consent of parties.

11. Any person or persons feeling agrieved by any decision, or other proceedings of a church, may bring the same before the Union, by appeal or complaint as the case may be, provided, that the appellant or complainant shall present to the moderator of the church, a written notice of his intention to appeal or complain, with the reasons thereof, within two weeks from the date of the decision, or other proceedings whereby he is agrieved.

12. In all appeal causes, the church records shall be produced as evidence, and if either party have further testimony and can shew cause, it shall be admited at the decision of the Union. Should parties, or churches be labored with as offenders, they shall exhibit such records, papers or manuscripts in their possession, as may relate to the supposed offence.

13. When parties are convicted of crimes, regularly charged against them they shall be censured by the judicatory, according to the nature of the offense & the laws of Christ. If a minister persevere in essential heresy, or be found guilty of flagrant immorality, he shall be deposed. If a church be found guilty of essential heresy, or disorderly walk, & shall refuse to return; the

Union may exclude them from their body. But if the tried be found innocent, they shall be restored to the fellowship of the churches.

STANDING RULES

1. The Union shall cause a record of its proceedings to be carefully kept and each church committed with it shall keep a similar record containing especially a full account of all the evidences of trials & grounds of their official decisions.

2. The records of each church shall be presented at each anual meeting of the Union and submitted to an examination by a committee appointed for that purpose who shall suggest any alterations or improvements in the maner of keeping the same thing which they may deem needful to affect a correct & uniform system of recording the proceedings of our churches.

3. An account of the state of religion within our bounds shall be given at each annual meeting and a narative drawn up and entered on record.

CONFESSION OF FAITH

ARTICLE 1st. We believe that there is one only living and true God, the Father, Son, and Holy Ghost who is infinite, eternal and unchangable in every divine perfection.

2nd. That the scriptures of the Old and New Testament were given by inspiration of God, and are the only perfect rule of faith and practice.

3rd. That God did at first make man upright, but that our first parents sinned and fell and that in consequence of their apostacy all mankind unless renewed by the Holy Ghost do live and die devoid of the love & adverse to the service of God; and are the subjects of his righteous displeasure.

4th. That God in compassion to fallen man did send into the world his own son who took on him human nature, and by his obedience and death made a complete atonement for all mankind.

5th. That although true believers in the Lord Jesus Christ are freely justified for his sake alone yet obedience to all his commands is the only unerring test of cincere belief.

6th. That a congregation of believers joined in covenant for ordinary communion in the ordinances of the gospel is a christian church invested with authority to choose its own officers, to admit members, and to exercise government and discipline to the rules of the gospel.

7th. That Baptism and the Lords supper are ordinances to be observed in the churches of Christ until his second coming.

8th. That there will be a resurection of the dead when God will judge the world by Jesus Christ and "the wicked shall go away into everlasting punishment but the righteous into life eternal."

February 22, 1838.

Church met at the house John Dudley.

Dea. Isaak Clark and John Dudley were appointed delegates to attend the quarterly conference at Elk Grove.

Voted that the collectors or persons who hold subscriptions for benevolent purposes be requested to collect what is due and what they can and make returns at the next meeting.

Voted that a collection be taken at each communion season to defray the expenses of the Table.

Voted that church resolve to raise the sum of twenty dollars to make up the arrears of Mr. Porters sallery for the past year.

Resolved, That this meeting adjourn to meet at this place on the first thursday in March.

Thursday March 7, 1838.

Church met according to appointment.

At the previous meeting the following resolution was presented & laid over to the present time.

viz *Resolved,* That as many of the members of this church as shall be disposed to make Knapersvill the center of their opperation shall have free liberty to do so and to withdraw from this ch with a view to organize a congregational ch at that place and when said members shall have presented a certificate of such organization being completed their particular relation to this church shall cease by vote of the church.

April 17, 1839

By request of the congregational church of Dupage a counsel of ministers & delegates from the neighbouring chhs convened at the house of Henry Goodrich in dupage on Wednesday April 17, 1839. Whereupon Eliphalet Strong was called to the chair as moderator & Rev. Hiram Foot chosen clerk.

Ministers present Rev. Isack Foster, N. C. Clark, E. Strong, H. Fort.

Delegates present

From Hadley Dea. R., Beach, Joliet Josiah Beaumont, Plainfield Mr. Mewther, Elk Grove, Mark Morse, Elgin,

Mr. J. Jenny Chesterton, Robert Moody. Doct. Kenedy
N.Y. was invited to sit in council by vote of the church.

Rev. J. G. Porter pastor of the Dupage church by request
presented a written statement of the subject.

Matter of difference existing in DuPage ch.

Members of church present were invited & freely expressed
their feelings in which it appeared that the matter of difference was in regard to a place of worship.

The ch having retired the council took a recess of 10 minutes after recess council had a season of prayer and then
proceeded to express their feeling when it was found that
all were united in locating the place of pub worship at
Knapersville.

Voted that Br. Foster and Foot be a committee to draw up
a report of the council to the ch.

The following report was made by com and unanimously
adopted. Report The Council convened for the matter in
difference in regard to their location of public worship and
concentrated effort & after hearing the statement of said
church and an expression of their various feelings on the subject & taking into prayerful consideration the entrest of Zion
in relation to said location do unanimously & cordially advise
the said church to make Knapersville the common center of
their worship & effort to promote the intrest of the Redeemer
Kingdom. Remembering always the word of Holy writ that
we are not our own & that we should not liv unto ourselves
but unto him that died and rose again & thus in so doing we
follow the example of Christ & his blessed apostle & carrying
the gospel to the enemies of Christ being filled with faith &
the Holy Ghost praying always in the spirit that God would
mark his word (it being the appointed means for the salvation of sinners) effectual. And now Dear Brethren we beseech you by the mercies of God to forget all past feeling of
unkindness & jealosies & let the mind which was in Christ
be in you forgiving one another & forbearing one another as

Christ hath forgiven you striving together for the unity of the spirit in the bond of peace.

By order of council Eliphalet Strong moderator, Hiram Foot Sect. A true copy

POMEROY GOODRICH *Elder*

At a meeting of the church held at the hous of the Rev. J. Porter March 29, 1839 Robert Strong was voted clerk protem

Resolution.—*Resolved*, That in view of the present curcumstance as of the Dupage church we consider it expedient to convene a council to tak into consideration the subject matter of difference between us & such decision as the council shall make shall be final.

Resolved, That the pastor be requested to draw up a statement of the causes of the difficulty existing among us.

Voted that the council consist of seven person from the following churches, Hudley, Juliet, Plainfield, Elysian, Chewtston, Elk Grove the council to convene here on the third Wednesday in April.

Moved by Dea. Isack Clark. Seconded by Br. Henry Goodrich that we procede to organize a Society to be known by the first Congregational Society of Knapersville. Carried

Moved by br. J. Strong seconded by Mr Cushing that there be three trustees appointed to transact the business of the Society.

Moved by Br. J. Strong seconded by Br. Branch that the trustees be appointed by ballot & that they hold their office from & after the first Tuesday of June 1839 for one year.

Br. J. Strong being elected of the trustees moved to be excused.

The trustees appointed for the services of the Socity were Dea. Isaak Clark Henry Goodrich & Pomeroy Goodrich.

Moved by Br. J. Strong seconded by Br. Branch that a committee of three be appointed to prepare a code of by laws by which this Society shall be governed.

Dea. I. Clark Br. Cushing & Br. Robert Strong, were appointed committee.

Moved that Dea. Isaak Clark be appointed a delegate to attend the Fox River Union at Big Grove
Pomeroy Goodrich his alternat

Resolved, That persons coming within the limits of this church who shall apply for admission to the church by letter must do so within one year from the date of their letters. If they do not do so within that time the church will require a satisfactory reason for their neglecting to do so. Resolution by R. Strong. Carried.

Resolution by Cushing

Resolved, That when any person being a member of a church shall come to reside within the bounds of this church and shall neglect to unite with it or shall neglect to apply to the church of which he is a member shall be reported to the church of which he is a member as living in neglect of Christian duty. Carried

Moved by Br. J. Strong seconded by P. Goodrich that our delegate be instructed to manifest to the committee from presbytery[32] our intention of remaining in our present organization.

Moved by Br. J. Strong seconded by R. Strong that our delegate solicite the uneion to hold their next quarterly meeting in this place.

Ther seemed to be considerable degree of good feeling & after a season of prayer the meeting was closed.

POMEROY GOODRICH (*clerk*)

Thus far examined and approved by the union.

Attest   CALVIN BUSHNELL *Modr.*

Big Grove 14 June 1839

[32] Apparently the Presbyterian body, which the Du Page church had recently left when it adopted the Congregational form of organization, made some effort to induce the Du Page congregation to remain Presbyterian.

Quarterly meeting 3r Wednesday Sept.

At a special meeting of the Dupage church held at the school house in Knapersville July 16th 1839. Proceeded to examine the subscription for the past year and found one hundred dollars or more wanting to make up Mr. Porters salary.

Moved that the subscription for Mr. Porter salary for 1838 be made up by adding to our several subscription sums sufficient to mak out the amount.

POMEROY GOODRICH   *Clerk*

Church met at the house of Br. Rose.

The Rev. Mr. Porter proposed to the church to furnish him with hay and wood & he would deduct 76 dollars on his salary.

Church voted to accept his proposition.

BR. GOODRICH

Sacramental season at Knapersville. Very few present on account of the prevailing sickness.

Sept. 27th.—Church met at the house of Br. Rose.

Report [of] the church committee of finance was presented when it [was] found that there was forty six dollars that was not provided for Mr. Porter's salary of last year.

Moved by Deacon Clark seconded by Br. Northman that the treasurer pay to the Rev. Mr. Porter six dollars out of any money in his hands not otherwise appropriated.

POMROY GOODRICH (*clerk*)

Preparatory lecture on Saturday.

Sacrament season Sabbath Nov. 3rd at the school house in Knapersvill.

At the regular church meeting held on the 29th of Nov. 1839 at the house of William Rose moderator in the chair, on

motion resolved that Mr. James Pratt be notified that he cannot be permitted to commune with this church until he shall
have presented a certificate of his membership from the
church whence he came & also make satisfaction to this
church for unchristian conduct & further resolved that the
clerk of the church, present a copy of the above resolution to
the said James Pratt.

On motion resolved

that a committee of two be appointed
to converse with Dec. Mathew Wright in relation to his uniting with this church & that Dea. Pomeroy Goodrich & Josiah
Strong be such committee & that they report at the next
meeting.

JOSIAH STRONG—*clerk protem*
A true copy—POMEROY GOODRICH (At)

December 27th 1839.—The committee appointed at the
last church meeting to converse with Mr. Campbell of
in relation to a difficulty existing between him & Mr. Eli
Northman reported to the ch.

On motion, said report accepted & committee discharged.

By request of Br. Northman a committee of two were appointed to investigate the object in which Br. Northman
to Mr. Camp uniting with the church.

Voted that Pomeroy Goodrich and Josiah Strong with the
pastor be said committee.

The committee appointed to converse with Mather Wright
in relation to presenting his letter to the church for admission.
Report accepted & committee discharged.

On motion resolved that Dec. Mather Wright be informed
that notwithstanding any difficulty that may exist between
him & individual members of the church they view it his
duty without delay to present his letter for admission into
the church.

Resolved that if Mr. Wright cannot himself or by the aid

of individual members of the church obtain satisfaction that it is his duty to present a formal complaint to the church.

P. G. G.

Exam. & accepted except an apparent deficiency in giving christian names.

DANL ROCKWELL, *Mod.*

February 15th 1840.—At a special church meeting of the congregation church of dupage convened at the house of J. Dudley for the purpose of takeing into consideration the propriety of complying with a request from the Lockport Chh to obtain his labours half of the time for the remainder of the year.

Brother Isaac Clark was called to the chair whereupon our pastor stated beirfly his call at Lockport & the pecuniary embarassment of this church.

Voted that our pastor the Rev. J. G. Porter have liberty to preach to the Lockport chh from the present time to expiration of the present financial year.

On motion of Robert Strong resolved that notwithstanding we have consented that our pastor should be absent one half of the time for the remainder of year yet we will pay our full subscription for the present year to make up the deficiency of the past y if there shall be a ballance on hand it shall be applied to the next year.

By request of Br. Stephen received a letter of dismission & recommendation to any chh where God in his providence shall cast his lot which is in fellowship with this chh.

H. STANDISH, *Clerk protem*
POMEROY GOODRICH

May 16th 1840.—Church met by appointment. Dea. Isack Clark chosen moderator.

A communication was presented from the Rev. J. G. Porter[33] pastor of the chh formally requesting the chh to unit with him in asking presbytery to dissolve his relation as pastor to this chh.

Voted that the final decision on Mr. Porter communication be defered to adjourned meeting to be held on Monday the 25th next.

Voted that the brethren present severally express their views & feelings freely on the subject of Mr. Porter communication.

After an expression of feeling from the brethren

The committee appointed to ascertain the amount that could be subscribed for Mr. Porters salary the ensueing year presented their report so far as returns had been made.

The result shows a deficite of nearly 200 dollars for the coming year.

After some deliberation the following was adopted

Resolved, That in view of the present embarrassed state of the chh & consequent inability to rais an adequat salary in compliance with the request of Mr. Porter we deem it expedient to unite with him in requesting presbytery to dissolve the relation to us as after the expiration of the present year ——

Financial year which ends the 23rd of July 1840 & further we would be glad to retain the labors of Mr. Porter one half of the time some three or four months after the expiration of the year till we can obtain other supply.

Resolved, That a copy of the above resolution be furnished Mr. Porter signed by the moderator & clerk.

The above taken from Josiah Strongs minutes as clerk protem.

POMEROY GOODRICH, (*Clerk*)

[33] Rev. J. G. Porter, being under the jurisdiction of the presbytery, required the co-operation of his church to obtain legal and adequate dismissal from the charge. This implied no jurisdiction of the presbytery over the church itself.

July 31st 1840.—Monthly chh meeting convened at the house of Br. John Dudley by appointment.

A communication was presented from the Fox River Union proposing that the first articl of the constitution of that body amended as to read, "This body shall be styled the consociation of Fox River."

On motion Resolved that this concur in the proposed amendment. Br. Pomeroy Goodrich requested to be discharged from being Clerk of the Church.

On motion Resolved that his request be granted.

Voted Unanimously that Josiah Strong be appointed Secretary in the room of Pomeroy Goodrich

Dea. Isaac Clark presented the following propositions for consideration till thenext chh. meeting, viz.

That the article of our faith in relation to infant baptism be so amended that it shall not be considered a requisite for church membership.

Meeting closed by prayer

J. STRONG, *Clk.*

The Church & Society of Naperville would inform the Rev. J. H. Prentiss[34] that they are desirous of employing him as their minister, & do hereby pledge themselves for his support.

Resolved 1st By the Church & Society of Naperville that we raise the sum of three hundred dollars one half to be paid in produce & the balance in cash in quarterly payments, for the pur-

---

[34] Rev. J. H. Prentiss came from the Onondage Presbytery in New York, where he had been a pastor for five years. In November, 1834, he went West and began work in Joliet, which he predicted would become the greatest city in northern Illinois next to Chicago. He sought a Commission from the A.H.M.S. and requested aid to the extent of $400, which he received, the commission beginning January, 1835 (letter to the A.H.M.S., written from Joliet, Illinois, dated February 10, 1835). His case is another instance of a Congregational church calling a Presbyterian minister—an arrangement encouraged by the Plan of Union.

pose of procuring the services of Rev. J. H.
Prentiss the ensuing year.

2nd   Resolved that in view of the embarrassed
        circumstances of the Church & Society, we
        deem it expedient to solicit aid of the Home
        Missionary Society to the amount of two
        hundred dollars.[35]

3rd   Resolved that a copy of the proceedings of
        this meeting be forwarded to Rev. J. H.
        Prentiss & that we invite him to assume the
        pastoral charge of this Church & people.

4th   Resolved that Rev. Mr. Prentiss be re-
        quested to give as soon as possible a deffinite
        answer to the 3rd resolution inviting him to
        become our pastor.

Voted, That the foregoing report be accepted & adopted.

[35] The request of the committee was sent to the secretary of the A.H.M.S. on
December 1, 1840. The letter is as follows:
"The first Congregational Church of Naperville are wanting to call Rev. J. H.
Prentiss of the Ottawa Presbytery and need help from the Society for the following
reasons.

1. The difficulty of raising cash for their produce.
2. We are on government surveyed lands not yet in the market which it is expected
   will be in a few months.
3. We have lost several of our most efficient members by death or removal.
4. Naperville is the seat of justice in this county and is a strong hold of infidelity.
   Our people consist of about 60 members of whom more than $\frac{2}{3}$ are females or
   individuals from whom little can be expected. We are scattered over an extent
   of territory some seven or ten miles square. The average size of the congregation
   is 100. There is but one other Congregational church and no Presbyterian Church
   in the county and that church is supplied one half of the time by Rev. O. Lyman,
   being the only Presbyterian minister residing in the county. There is one small
   Methodist Society in this village and also a small Baptist church about four
   miles distant. The total amount of salary which we propose to make up is $500
   for the year $300 being all we can raise" (*A.H.M.S. Correspondence*).

CHAPTER VI

Minutes of the Convention of the Congregational Churches of Illinois, 1834, and of the Congregational Association of Illinois, 1835-40

INTRODUCTION

THE Congregational movement in Illinois came about as a result of the growing antagonism between the Old School and the New School parties within Presbyterianism. The New School party in Illinois was made up for the most part of a body of young New Englanders who had been brought up in Congregational institutions. They had come to Illinois as missionaries of the American Home Missionary Society, were ordained as Presbyterian ministers, and had no other intention than to establish Presbyterian churches in the new communities where they ministered. "When I came to this state in the autumn of 1833," said William Carter, "I had no other thought than that of laboring entirely in the Presbyterian church, and to build Presbyterian churches."[1] All the members of the Illinois band, to which Carter belonged, had come from Congregational churches, colleges, and seminaries and, following the advice of their "teachers and fathers in the ministry," had united with the Presbyterian church and were loyal to the Plan of Union.[2] Hardly had they begun their work in Illinois, however, before the controversy within Presbyterianism began not only to reach their ears but to affect seriously their status within that body. In 1833 two members of the faculty of Illinois College with the president, Edward Beecher, were hailed before the presbytery of Illinois for teaching the New Haven theology, while the

[1] William Carter, *A Memorial of the Congregational Ministers and Churches of the Illinois Association on Completing a Quarter of a Century of Its History* (Quincy, Ill., 1863 [pamphlet]), p. 6, quoted in George Punchard, *History of Congregationalism* (Boston: Congregational Publishing Co., 1881), pp. 283-84.

[2] Flavel Bascom, *The Beginning and Progress of Congregationalism in Illinois* (a paper read before the Congregational Club of Chicago, March 20, 1883 [pamphlet]), p. 2.

following year the ordination of the Illinois band was attacked in a memorial presented to the General Assembly.[3]

Another important influence in creating Congregational sentiment in Illinois was the slavery situation. The southern section of Illinois was peopled largely by settlers from the southern states who had little patience with the radial antislavery sentiments entertained by the young New England ministers. In Morgan County, for instance, "Down Easters" were not particularly popular. Although Jacksonville contained a considerable Yankee element, the county was overwhelmingly of southern extraction, and the New England group were almost universally antislavery in their views.[4]

With this situation in mind it is easy to understand how the New England group within the state began to react against Presbyterianism which was attempting to impose its strict standards upon them. "Recent events in the Presbyterian church," wrote Julian M. Sturtevant, "shocked the moral sense of thousands and tens of thousands of immigrants from New England," and they determined "no longer to consent to leave the church polity of their fathers behind them when they crossed the Hudson."[5] As a consequence, the number of Congregational churches in Illinois began to increase rapidly during the thirties, and by the end of 1836 there were at least twenty distinctively congregational churches within the state. In June, 1835, the Fox River Union was formed, made up of churches in the northeastern section of the state. The preceding year the congregational churches in the western section of the state had met at Quincy, at the invitation of Asa Turner (November 24–29, 1834), where steps were taken to form an Illinois association. The association held its first meeting at Jacksonville, October 25, 1835. The earlier meeting at Quincy was called a Convention of the Congregational Churches of Illinois. The minutes of the convention and of the association from its inception to 1840 are here printed for the first time.

MINUTES OF A CONVENTION OF THE CONGREGATIONAL CHURCHES OF ILLINOIS, 1834

Nov. 24.—At a meeting of delegates of the Congregational Churches of Illinois assembled at the house of Rev. Asa

---

[3] Frank J. Heinl, "Jacksonville and Morgan County: An Historical Review," *Journal of the Illinois State Historical Society*, XVIII (1925), 8; W. W. Sweet, *Religion on the American Frontier*, Vol. II: *The Presbyterians* (New York, 1936), pp. 111–25.

[4] Heinl, *op. cit.*, pp. 11–18.

[5] "Theron Baldwin," *Congregational Quarterly*, XVII (1875), 404.

Turner in Quincy Nov. 28th 1834 Brother Beckford was appointed Chairman and Brother Holmes—Clerk.

The meeting was opened by singing & prayer by the Rev. A. Turner.

The weather being inclement the following delegates only were present

From the Church in Jacksonville Revd. Wm. Carter, & Brother B. Allyn & I. Chamberlain.

From the Church in Griggsville Brother Beckford & Bates.

From the Church in Quincy Revd. Mr. Turner, Brethren Kimball, Brown, Eells, & Holmes—

From the Church in Fairfield Br. Chittenden.

It was proposed by Br. Turner that the delegates be requested to give a statement of the History, Progress, & present condition of the respective Churches which they represent.

Whereupon Brother Carter stated that the Jacksonville Church was organized 15th Dec. last. At that time embraced about 30 members, now embraces about 70 members, about one half of the addition united with the Church by profession. The Lord had blest the Church by an increased spirit of piety. The Church support their minister and are erecting a meeting house.[6]

[Marginal correction states: "wrong—the Quincy Ch. was organized 4th. Dec.—*1830* with *15* members, including Jacob Snow, admitted *same day* by Prof."]

Br. Turner stated that the Quincy Church was organized

[6] The organization of the Congregational church at Jacksonville "was one of the first results of the heresy trial [of Edward Beecher]" (Heinl, *op. cit.*, p. 10), which had aroused considerable bitterness. William Carter and J. M. Sturtevant played a prominent part in the organization (J. M. Sturtevant, "William Carter," *Congregational Quarterly*, XIII [1871], 502). In a letter from Jacksonville, dated February 10, 1834, to the A.H.M.S., Theron Baldwin mentions the reorganization of the local Presbyterian church as Congregational and says they had extended him a call. "What shall I do?" he inquires. In reply, the society said they deemed acceptance of the call inadvisable, and Baldwin (letter of June 11, 1834) states that the church reacted favorably when he declined.

the 4th Dec. *1829*, then embraced 14 members—the number of members in the fall of 1832 was about 30, a number having left the place were united with other churches & dismissed from this. In Nov. 1833, the church was reorganized on the Congregational plan.[7] Since that time about 30 members have united by profession and about the same number by Letter, making in all something more than 90 members. The Church have the last year been growing in grace. A camp meeting was held in Sept. last which was blessed by the presence of the Spirit of God.

The articles of Faith admit any to the fellowship of the Church who give Evidence of piety & agree with the doctrines of any of the Evangelical Churches.

The Church commenced supporting their minister last spring.

Brother Chittenden stated that the church at Fairfield was organized in Feby. 1833 embracing 18 members and supposed at that time there was no other Congregational Church in the state.[8] The Church now embraces 25 members & 7 are to be added next communion.

Brother Beckford stated that the Church at Griggsville was organized in the summer of 1834 embracing 12 members. Have had no stated preaching—but have held conference meeting every Sabbath.

The subject of forming some union between the Cong. Churches was now introduced for discussion by Br. Turner—and after discussion it was

Voted Unanimously,

[7] The Quincy church was organized as Presbyterian in 1831 by Rev. Asa Turner, member of the Yale Band. Flavel Bascom ("Past and Future of Congregationalism in Illinois," *Illinois Society of Church History, Congregational, Papers,* I [1895], 79) says that back of its reorganization on a Congregational basis in 1833 lay the comment of a Presbyterian minister who said that the church records would not bear the inspection of presbytery. "So the church decided to keep their records in their own way, and not trouble Presbytery to review them."

[8] The church at Fairfield (now known as Mendon) was organized by Rev. Solomon Hardy, with eighteen members (*ibid.*; Punchard, *op. cit.,* V, 285).

That an Association be formed of the Churches, upon some plan for the mutual benefit and strengthening of the Church. Voted

That Br. Turner, Chittenden, & Chamberlain be appointed a committee to draft Rules for the Association and to report to an adjourned meeting tomorrow at 10 o'clk.

Nov. 29th.—

Meeting met pursuant to adjournment.

The committee appointed to draft a Constitution and bye laws, made a report

Voted, on motion of Brother Carter

That the Report of the Committee be accepted

On motion of Br. Carter,

Resolved, That any evangelical Church may be admitted into this association . . . . [Carried unanimously].

The report of the Committee was then taken up article by article and after being amended were adopted as follows—

PREAMBLE

Several of the Congregational Churches of Illinois impressed with the importance of an association of Churches of similar views, for their mutual edification and improvement appointed delegates to meet at Quincy on the 24 Nov. 1834, for the purpose of drawing up some band of union & articles of agreement to be recommended to the several churches for their adoption. There were present from the Church at Jacksonville Brs. I. Chamberlain, & Br. B. Ally, From the Church in Quincy Br. J. I. Holmes, E. B. Kimball, R. Brown, R. Ells, A. Nichols. From the Church in Fairfield J. B. Chittenden. From the church in Griggsville Br. B. Beckford & B. Bates.

The delegates having attended to the business of their appointment beg leave respectfully to submit to their Brethren the following as the result of their deliberations—

1. This Association shall be called the Evangelical Association of Illinois [see Constitution and Articles of Faith as finally adopted, pp. 167–70].

. . . .

REGULATIONS

1. Whenever there shall be two or more Congregational ministers united with this association they may in connexion with two or more delegates Licence or Ordain any brother they may deem qualified to preach the Gospel. Provided it be done at any regular meeting of the association. Provided moreover no man shall be Licenced or Ordained without the approbation of a majority of ordained ministers present.—

2. Ministers shall be amenable in all cases of discipline to a council composed of a minister & delegate from each church in the association. Provided no minister shall be censured without the approbation of a majority of ministers present [see final action].

. . . .

On motion of Br. Chittenden seconded by Br. Eells—voted that a committee of three be appointed to submit these articles to the several Congregational Churches in this state & request a reply whether they will adopt the articles or not & that the committee be empowered to call a special meeting of the Churches if it be found necessary—at such time & place as they may designate.

Voted,

That the next annual meeting be held at Jacksonville. . . . .

1835 Oct. 22.—

The Convention of Congregational Churches of Illinois met pursuant to notice of the Committee at Jacksonville October 22—1835, in the Congregational Meeting House and was called to Order by Brother Beckford Moderator of the Quincy convention

The meeting was opened with prayer by Rev. M. Nichols of Atlas. [After this all references to formal openings of meetings will be omitted.]

On motion Brother B. Beckford was elected Moderator and Maro M. L. Reed, Clerk

The following delegates to the Convention appeared & took their seats

Brother B. Beckford of the Griggsville Church
Brother B. Baldwin and
Brother Isiah Platt of the Fairfield Church.
Rev. Alfred Greenwood from the Cong. Union of Fox River
Rev. Asa Turner and
Br. Richard Eells of the Quincy Church
Rev. Wm. Carter and
Br. Timothy Chamberlain and
Br. Josiah Seymore and
Br. M. M. L. Reed from the Jacksonville Church
Rev. Warren Nichols of the Atlas Church

Brother Greenwood then presented a report of the proceedings of the Cong. Union of Fox River which was read

Resolved

That we approve of the Constitution and articles of Faith of the Cong. Union of Fox River and cordially invite them to unite with us and send a delegation to the meetings of this association.

Delegates reported the disposition which the several Churches had made of the articles recommended by the Quincy Convention when it appeared that the Atlas and Griggsville Churches had adopted them and all others represented approved of the general principles—while they desired some minor modifications

On motion *Resolved*

That the Report of the Quincy Convention be read article by article for the purpose of free discussion.

Voted,

That Brother Turner, Carter, Ells, Greenwood—Nichols—
& Reed be a committee to revise the Constitution.

On motion Convention adjourned to meet tomorrow noon
at 9 o'clock. [After this all references to adjournment will be
omitted.]

October 23

Convention met pursuant to adjournment at the house of
Br. C. Reed. . . . .

The Committee on the Constitution reported sundry
amendments—and the report was accepted—

The Constitution was then taken up article by article and
after sundry amendments were made was laid over to be
adopted as a whole tomorrow noon.

. . . .

Voted

That Brother Asa Turner & Wm. Carter be appointed a
delegation to represent this association at the meetings of the
several Congregational Churches in N. England and New
York and That Brother Baldwin and E. Wolcott be a delegation to attend the next annual meeting of the Cong. Union of
Fox River—

On motion. . . . .

October 26th.—

Convention met pursuant to adjournment at the house of
Brother Carter. . . . .

The Constitution, Articles of Faith & Regulations were
then Read and adopted unanimously as they appear
Voted

That Brother Carter be appointed to preach a sermon on
Foreign Missions at the annual meeting

Voted

That Brother Turner be appointed to preach a sermon on the subject of Education—

Brother Nichols to preach a sermon on the subject of Sunday Schools

Brother Reed to deliver an address on Temperance

Voted

That the Clerk be instructed to procure the publication of the Constitution, Articles, of Faith & Regulations adopted by this Convention in the St. Louis Observer and the Jacksonville & Quincy papers and to send a copy thereof to the several Cong. churches—with a request that they will as soon as practicable notify the Clerk of this Convention of their decision thereon—

The minutes were then read and adopted & Convention adjourned to meet at the Meeting House at three o'clk to hear a relation of the state of the Churches. . . . .

3 o'clk P.M. . . . . Voted That Brethren Carter, Greenwood & Turner be a committee to make out a narrative of the state of the Churches—

Deac. Beckford then related the condition of the Griggsville Church⁹—

---

⁹ The busy life and varied interests of the early Illinois Congregational ministers are suggested by the letters of a later pastor of the Griggsville church, Rev. A. L. Pennoyer. Under date of January 20, 1840, he writes to the secretary of the A.H.M.S.:

"I preach twice every Sabbath, lecture also in the evening and attend a Friday night meeting. We maintain regularly the monthly and Sabbath School concerts for prayer, fraternal association and moral reform Society. The Sabbath School and Bible Class are regularly sustained. Also something is done to supply the destitute with Bibles."

Rivalry with other religious groups and general irreligiousness on the part of the population are also suggested:

"In this place there is powerful hostility to Evangelical doctrine & ministerial support. Preaching here by Mormons, Universalists, & Campbellites. The Sabbath is desecrated by manual labor, pleasure, hunting etc. Probably more than one third part of the population despise everything sacred. All the preaching by errorists only tends to vacate the restraints of religion & make wickedness abound. Occa-

Brother Baldwin reported the condition of the Fairfield Church—

Brother Greenwood Reported the Condition of the 4 churches of the Cong. Un. of Fox River—viz. Church at Du Page—Church at Walker's Grove Cook Co. & Long Grove & Big Grove of Cook Co. also of the Church at Michigan City Indiana[10]

sionally an adultry takes place among those who disregard the Sabbath & a discourse against ministers who receive 'fat salaries.' "

The frontier churches, as well as suffering from attack from without, were torn with internal dissensions. On March 14, 1840, Pennoyer wrote:

"In the church we have so many things of an unpleasant nature I hardly dare to name them in secret.

"This church has from its organization done all sorts of things—Twice they have been disbanded & a third church formed out of the same materials—Brother has been to law with brother—& some of our church meetings before I came here and since have been a 'crucifixion of Christ in the house of his friends.' We have some men of strong intellectual powers who would be leaders—& because they cannot be are constantly agitating the church. . . . . The minister who preceded me was treated without the least respect as moderator of the meeting. . . . ."

But, in spite of all, Pennoyer closed this letter, as others, with an optimistic note:

"I have preached with some success to correct the disorder. . . . . Our prospects are on the whole brightening & in a few years here will be found a large & flourishing church. . . . ."

[10] In a letter from Big Grove to the secretary of the A.H.M.S., dated April 13, 1835, Rev. Alfred Greenwood says that he came to Chicago in July, 1834, and "at the suggestion of the Rev. Mr. Porter, visited Walker's Grove for the purpose of ascertaining what the prospect was for my becoming useful to the people of that neighborhood." It was planned to make the frontier churches as self-supporting as possible, and Greenwood continues: "I spared no pain to secure a liberal subscription previously to my venturing to recommend to the church the subject of petitioning to the committee for pecuniary aid."

The two big questions then being agitated in Illinois were slavery and temperance, and the Congregationalists took the lead in both. A Congregational church was formed, Greenwood continues, at Walker's Grove, "by the name of Plainfield Congregational Church on the Principle of entire abstinence from the use of ardent spirits or traffick in them, except as medicine. . . . . The temperance cause prospers in this section of the country. A society for the promotion of temperance of 28 members was in existence at Walker's Grove when I first came into that neighborhood. A temperance society of ten members was formed in this grove on the fourth Tuesday of February last [1835]." In the same letter he reports that the Plainfield church then had twenty pupils in its Sabbath school, thirty members in its Bible class, seventy subscribers to the Temperance Society, and a library of seventy volumes.

In a letter from Plainfield of the following November 16, Greenwood reported

Brother Turner made report of the state of the Quincy Church and of the Atlas Church.[11]

---

that "the attendance of the congregations on the means of grace in this place has been good, except in the time of general sickness." Greenwood, as shepherd over the number of churches mentioned, did a great deal of itinerant work. "During my residence in this part of the country," he writes, "I have deemed it a matter of importance to visit those members of Christ's flock, who, on account of their distance at which they live from places of worship, can seldom get to the house of prayer on the Sabbath. A minister of Christ, if he would do good to such must bemuch of his time on horse-back."

[11] Rev. Warren Nichols, missionary, wrote to the secretary of the A.H.M.S. from Atlas, Illinois, under date of June 8, 1835: "My field of labor is large and becoming more interesting every month. Emigrants are moving in, some of a very interesting character. . . . . The facts in regard to infidelity and all its pollution have become trite long since. We have our share . . . . but there are some encouraging circumstances."

The paid missionaries of the society were frowned upon by the unpaid Baptist preachers of the frontier (for a full discussion of the Baptist attitude see W. W. Sweet, *Religion on the American Frontier*, Vol. I: *The Baptists, 1783–1830* [New York: Henry Holt & Co., 1931], chap. iv), and in his letter of October 1, 1835, Nichols mentions the opposition: "Prejudice . . . . is excited yet by a Baptist church in our neighborhood, [the members] . . . . are opposed to all benevolent operations of the day. They will not hear a Baptist preacher if he be sent out by the missionary Society. Their preacher says, 'Judas was the first to receive pay for preaching.'" Nichols' attitude toward the Baptists is well illustrated by what he did: "I became acquainted with him, persuaded him to pass the night with me, gave him Dr. Beecher's sermons on intemperance, an Almanack paper, and made him promise to read them; explained the object, proceedings etc. of the benevolent societies, and intend to visit him and his people, treat them kindly and give them no rest in their present course."

Three months later (January 1, 1836), Nichols addressed an enthusiastic letter to the society, telling of a revival that had visited the Atlas church:

"The Lord in mercy has visited us with his Spirit, and several have indulged hope of eternal life. . . . . Some of doubtful character are willing now to take a decided stand on the Lord's side. Our little church has doubled its number and we are expecting to receive others soon. . . . . A weekly prayer meeting is now held by the young men in Atlas. How glorious the change. One year ago it was difficult to get half a dozen of all classes of people to a prayer meeting. This is, indeed, a mere beginning of what we need, and of what we trust the Lord will yet do for us." The Bible class, he continues, has about twelve members, but "it is difficult to get people in the west to study a book." Versatility of the missionaries is indicated: "We have an interesting singing school which, for want of another person, I teach. It is a means, I think, of much good. [But] our sabbath school has not flourished and is adjourned for the season. Many of the children cannot read, and as the sabbath has always been the play day here, it is difficult to change things at once." However, Nichols was using other tactics: "I have done something in distributing Bible and tracts and have made arrangements to supply this county at least with the Bible."

Brother Carter, Seymour & Reed stated the condition of the Jacksonville Church. . . . .[12]

Oct. 26.— . . . . .

CONGREGATIONAL ASSOCIATION OF ILLINOIS

CONSTITUTION

1.—This Association shall be called the Congregational Association of Illinois.

2.—This Association is formed on the principle, that believers entering into a covenant with God and one another, to walk in the Ordinances of the Gospel, constitute a Church of Christ, and are vested with the authority by the Great Head of the Church, to choose their own officers and exercise all that discipline his word requires.

3.—All those Churches, Associations, and Ministers, who adopt this Constitution and Articles of Faith annexed, may belong to this Association

[The constitution was amended in 1839 and the following articles were added:

4. The standing officers of this Association, shall consist of a Moderator, to be chosen annually; and sstated Clerk.

5. Each Church belonging to this Association, shall be entitled to send

[12] Denominational consciousness on the frontier was usually high, as is reflected in the letter of Theron Baldwin from Pleasant Grove, Illinois, dated July 30, 1834:

"The meeting at Jacksonville was a united effort principally on the part of Presbyterians and Congregationalists. The Methodists very kindly threw open the doors of their meeting house and the preaching was mostly done there. The meeting produced very much of a sensation in that town—. . . . . Christians of different names sat together . . . . with one heart and one mind [and] with one heart and one mind wept and prayed and labored for the salvation of sinners."

The church co-operation caused some outsiders considerable apprehension. Those "who are perpetually haunted by that bug-bear *union of church and state* . . . . this union of different denominations they could not understand—there must be some deep laid plot and they inquired around with no little solicitude—*What it meant!* Their fears were allayed however, when told that it was simply the result of good feeling on the part of Christians. In fact they confessed that this was just what they always thought ought to be. What a lesson! A real union on the part of Christians of different denominations, ... so rare a thing in the 19th century, as to awaken in this way the fears of the enemies of religion!"

two or more delegates to this body—but in case of discipline, only one shall be entitled to vote.

6. This Association shall meet annually on the first Thursday in April, at 9 O'clock A.M. The object shall be to report the state of the churches, and to consult together in regard to the best modes of promoting the interests of the Redeemer's Kingdom, and by our mutual prayers and sympathies, to excite each other to greater activity, in the service of the Lord.

The changes made in the other articles are indicated by words in brackets.]

4.—A delegation from the Churches of this Association, consisting of the Pastor and one or more delegates from each Church, shall meet annually on the first Thursday of November at 2 o'clk P.M. The object shall be to report the state of the Churches, to act as an advisory council in case of difficulty, to consult together in regard to the best mode of promoting the Redeemer's Kingdom among us, and by our mutual prayers & sympathies to excite each other to greater activity in the service of the Lord. But in case of discipline only one delegate from each Church shall be considered a member of the council. [Omitted in the 1839 revision.]

5 [7].—At any regular meeting of this Association [body], when two or more [any three] Ministers are [being] present, they together with [delegates] two or more delegates from two or more [an equal number of] Churches may license or ordain any brother [candidates] they may deem [think] qualified to preach the Gospel. Provided however, that no man shall be licensed or ordained without the approbation of a majority of the ordained Ministers present.

6 [8].—Ministers in all cases of discipline shall be amenable [to this body at any of its regular meetings.] to a council composed of the Minister and delegates present, at any regular meeting of the Association. But no Minister shall be censured without the approbation of a majority of the ordained ministers present.

7 [9].—This Constitution may be altered or amended at any [regular] annual meeting of the Association by a vote of two thirds of the members present.

ARTICLES OF FAITH

1.—We believe the Scriptures of the Old and New Testaments, are the Word of God and the only infallible rule of faith & practice.

2.—There is only one living & true God, subsisting in three persons, Father, Son and Holy Ghost, who are infinite, eternal, and unchangeable in every divine perfection.

3.—That man is a sinner, and as such is justly exposed to the penalty of the Law of God. That all who repent of sin and rely on the atoning blood of our Lord and Savior, Jesus Christ, for pardon and acceptance with God, will be saved, and that those who do not will be finally lost.

4.—That the influence[s] of the Holy Spirit is [are] indispensible to make his truth effectual in the conversion of Sinners and in the sanctification of Christians [believers] and that this influence of the Spirit is perfectly consistent with the freedom of the creature

5.—That there will be a resurrection of the dead when God will judge the world by Jesus Christ, and the wicked will go away into eternal punishment, but the righteous into life everlasting. [Eternal.]

6.—That it is the purpose of God, to convert the world to himself through the agency of his people; and that it is the imperious duty of Christians, to concentrate all their energies for the promotion and extension, of the Redeemer's Kingdom. [This article is added in the revision of the articles made in 1839; other changes in the articles are indicated by words in brackets.]

REGULATIONS

I   Any evangelical Church [or minister] may unite with this Association and retain its [their] own mode of Church Government both as it regards its discipline of members and Ministers provide there is nothing in its creed inconsistent with the articles of union [faith] of this Association—

II   In our view the Providence of God demands of us constant and prayerful efforts for the conversion of souls. And we are willing to cooperate with evangelical Churches in this glorious work

III   We will consider it our duty and privilege to unite with our Pastors in holding protracted or Sacramental meetings in any place where desired, if in our view it is practicable, and there is a reasonable exputation of doing good.

IV   The standing officers of this body shall be a Moderator and Clerk to be chosen at the annual meeting.

V   The Moderator shall call a special meeting of the association, at the request of one [three] or more Minister or of one [three] or more Churches

[Each license granted by this Association, shall continue in force for 2 years. (Added in the revision of 1839; Regulations II, III, and IV are omitted in the later revision.)]

BENJAMIN BECKFORD   Moderator

MARO M. L. REED   <i>Clerk</i>

MINUTES OF THE MEETINGS OF THE CONGREGATIONAL ASSOCIATION OF ILLINOIS

1836   April 22.—

According to previous notice a "Special meeting of the Congregational Association of Illinois" was held at the Congregational Church in Quincy April 22 1836 at 9 o'clk A.M. a Quorum not being present on the 21st the day specified in the call of the Moderator.

Present Benj. Beckford Sen. Moderator & delegate from Griggsville Church, and Jos. B. Beckford delegate from the Griggsville Church. Willard Keyes and I. I. Holmes from the Quincy Church as delegates. . . . .

On motion J. I. Holmes was appointed clerk Broth Carter pastor of the Cong. Ch. in Jacksonville presented a letter of dismission from the Presby. of Schuyler & recommendation to this association and was unanimously received

On motion Br. Turner, pastor of Quincy Cong. Ch. and of Schuyler Presby. & Br. Kirby of Fairfield Cong. Ch. and of Ottawa Presbytery were invited to set us Corresponding members. On motion Br. Hubbard of the Maine Conference of Cong. Chs. was received as a member of this association.

Br. Kirby stated that the articles etc. of the Cong. Ass. of Ills. had been adopted by the Cong. Ch in Fairfield and by the Cong. Ch. in Round prairie

Br. Beckford reported that the same had been adopted by the Cong. Ch. in Griggsville.

Br. Carter—the same of the Cong. Ch. in Jacksonville

Br. Holmes—of the Cong. Ch. in Quincy and Br. Turner—of the Cong. Ch. in Atlas—

Br. Julius A. Reed presented a certified copy from the minutes of the New Haven Western Ass. Conv. of his licensure to preach the Gospel recommending him to the fellowship of the Churches. Also a certificate from Pres. Day of Yale Coll. (one of the committee appointed by the Gen. Ass. to certify the good standing of ministers traveling out of their bounds) testifying to his good standing. Br. Reed accompanied the above with a request to be taken under the care of the association and ordained by them.

On motion

Resolved, That he be received and that we proceed to the examination of the Candidate

The Examination continued in the afternoon when on motion Ass. adjourned to meet at 9 o'clk tomorrow. Closed with prayer.

April 23d.—

Ass. met . . . . Present Benj. Beckford, Jos. B. Beckford Delegates, Wm. Carter minister.

Absent J. I. Holmes, Willard Keyes, Delegates—Br. Hubbard minister

Br. Edward Hollister presented a letter of dismission from the Presby. of Orange N.B. & recommendation & on motion was unanimously received.

Br. C. L. Watson of the Presby. of Schuyler being present was invited to sit as corresponding member.

The Examination having been concluded at the previous session. Association called for a Sermon which was read from I John 4 & Heb. 12.29.

After a free expression of opinion upon the merits of the examination & sermon
On motion *Resolved*

That they be accepted & that the Ordination take place Sabbath Evening.

Parts were assigned as follows,

> Br Carter to preach the Sermon
> Br. Turner to make the Ordaining prayer
> Br. Watson to give the charge
> Br. Kirby to give the right hand of fellowship

Br. Beckford requested the advice & counsel of Ass. in reference to the difficulties in Griggsville Church Whereupon Ass. proceeded to hear statements respecting the matter, a free expression of opinion by the members and Corresponding members, Br. Turner & Kirby were appointed a committee to draw up a report expressive of the views of Association to report next Session. . . . .

Ap. 24th.—. . . . met according to adjournment [etc.].

Present, Ministers

> Wm. Carter
> Edward Hollister
> J A Reed

Delegates

Benj. Beckford, Senr.
Jos. B. Beckford
J. I. Holmes
Willard Keys

The Committee appointed to draw up a report in reference to the difficulties in the Griggsville Church reported another and their report was accepted & adopted and a copy ordered to be sent to each of the Churches. . . . .

BENJAMIN BECKFORD
Moderator

J. T. HOLMES   *Clerk*

Nov. 3 1836.—

The Illinois Congregational association commenced its first annual meeting in Fairfield Adams County Nov. 3d 1836. . . . .

Present from the Church Jacksonville
Rev. William Carter Pastor
Brethren E. Wolcott & R. Gaylord Delegates
From the Church in Quincy
Brethren Levi Welles & Rufus Brown Delegates
From the Church in Fairfield
Brethren Jno. B. Chittenden Levi Stillman & Erastus Benton Delegates
From the Church in Warsaw
Rev. Julius A. Reed Pastor[13]
From the Church in Round Prairie
Brother   Hubbard Delegate . . . .

[13] Rev. Julius A. Reed in a letter to the society, May 23, 1836, says: "I organized a small Congregational Church of ten members at Warsaw 15th inst. with the assistance of Brs. Turner and Kirby. A few more will I think unite with us. We are perfectly united. The prospect is that this little band will exert a satisfactory influence upon the village. . . . . You will observe that this report is dated at a distance from my field of labor. I have been separate from my wife the entire quarter, not being able to procure accomodation for her until now. This is the principal cause of my visit to Jacksonville."

Nov. 4th.—. . . .

On application the Congregational Church in St. Marys was admitted to the Association & Brother Greenleaf took his seat as Delegate On application the Church in Warsaw was also admitted to the association & Brother Hitchcock recognized as Delegate

The Congregational Church in La Harp was admitted to the association and Brother Brooks Delegate from that church to his seat as a member of this body.[14]

The Union Congregational Church at Griggsville was admitted to the association[15] No Delegate present. The Con-

[14] The heterogeneous character of the population and the problem it presented are suggested in the following extract from a letter of Rev. L. K. Hawley, missionary at La Harpe, Illinois, to the A.H.M.S., July 5, 1839:

"For a considerable time past my attention has been turned to the making of a survey of this portion of our Lord's vineyard. Take this village as a center, & a circle with a radius of three miles would include 100 families. Of which 14 might be called Congregationalists; 10 Methodists; 4 Cumberland Presbyterians; 5 Campbellites; 5 Unitarians . . . . 4 Mormons; a number are Universalists . . . . ; 1 Roman Cath.

"Thus it appears that a majority of the families, within the above circle, are not attached, even nominally to any sect, tho they doubtless have their prejudices. Of this majority, only about 15 families attend meeting with any considerable degree of regularity. From 30 to 40 families seldom or never attend any meetings, & make no excuse of spending the sabbath in business and amusement, which indeed is the case with some professors of religion. . . . ."

[15] Rev. A. G. Norton, in a letter to the society dated November 30, 1837, tells of the formation of the Union church:

"When I came to this place a year ago last Oct. there were two small Congregational church in existence. They both contained no more than 15 members. The need of union was deeply felt and earnest efforts were made to affect it. In Feb. last, both churches agreed unanimously to give up their separate organization and become united in one. This was happily effected. Since that time the church has gone on gradually increasing in numbers and now consists of 42 members. . . . . We have a weekly union meeting attended by members of the Congregational, Methodist and Baptist churches. . . . ."

Endeavor on the part of the missionaries to be self-supporting is indicated by Norton's further comments:

"My second year of labor in the service of your Society expired the 25 of Oct. last. . . . . I shall not at present apply for a renewal of my commission. The people seem to manifest a disposition to sustain me and I intend to give them the opportunity of trying. Our Church is nearly finished. When that is paid for, if the people do not sustain their minister *well*, the inability will be a moral one solely. . . . ." The last phrase makes clever use of the distinction prominent in New England

gregational Church at Long Grove was admitted to the association.[16] No Delegate present On motion of Brother Carter resolved that in future annual meetings of Association it be a standing rule that there be a sermon preached on

---

theology since Jonathan Edwards between "moral" and "natural" inability—the former implying merely lack of inclination.

[16] The A.H.M.S. helped to support ministers in those communities unable fully to support their own. Most of the churches were organized by the missionaries of the society, who, if the prospects seemed to warrant, would encourage the church to apply to the society for aid. The following quotations from a letter from Elisha Johnson, deacon, and Justur Bristol, James W. Gillam, and John Witherspoon, trustees, of the church in Long Grove, dated December 6, 1836, is typical:

"The Congregational church in Long Grove respectfully and ardently request aid of your benevolent society to ennable her to support the Rev. Herman S. Colton to labor statedly and constantly amongst us as a minister of the Gospel. Mr. Colton who has recently come amongst us by the invitation of this church is the man of our choice, ... Our Church was formed about 18 months ago, but has not enjoyed the stated administration of the gospel since that time. Rev. Mr. Baldwin agent of your society . . . . visited us last June and expressed his conviction to us that ours was a field of sufficient importance to demand the labors of a stated and regular ministry and told us that if we would obtain a minister that the A.H.M.S. would aid us in giving him a full support. We named to him the man who is now with us and Mr. Baldwin has since twice personally encouraged him to become our minister. Our church consists of only nine member but would probably number twenty in a very few weeks if we have a minister to labor amongst us. . . . ."

In 1839 the name of Long Grove was changed to Bristol, so the church was henceforth known as the church at Bristol.

That the local communities did not always live up to their pledges or to the expectations of the ministers is indicated by a letter from Rev. Solomon Hardy, written at Quincy, Illinois, June 18, 1834:

". . . . the church here is very worldly minded. Everyone seems anxious to see who shall be rich first. They can exert themselves that way without the example or the instructions of a minister; . . . . They have done nothing towards relieving the A.H.M.S. of any part of the burden of my support. I have heard nothing of the 100 dollars they were going to raise for my 'immediate necessities' since I saw it in print in the *Home Missionary*.

"We have a collection taken at the monthly concert which was commenced at the beginning of winter which may amount by this time to something like twelve dollars. They paid to the Agent of the Presbyterian Education Society about 7 dollars. They have formed a tract society and furnished it with tracts for the monthly distribution. These are statements of all they have done for the support of the gospel the past year and yet they are in much better circumstances than the same number of emigrants I have ever seen in any county settlement. Had I known the quantity of money there was in the settlement I never should have consented to have them apply for my whole support. . . . ."

Thursday and Friday evenings And on Saturday two or more sermons according to circumstances

Rev. William Kirby was received as a member of Association on letter of recommendation from Presbytery of Ottawa.

Rev. Messrs Lawton[17] and Turner being present were invited to sit as corresponding members

On application of Brother Edward Hollister of Griggsville Resolved that he received a certificate of his good standing in this Association accompanied with a recommendation to the Presbytery of the Western District Tennessee

On motion Resolved to call for a narrative of the state of religion in the several churches represented in this body & Brethren Gaylord Kirby & Stillman were appointed to take minutes

Before the narrative was completed On motion resolved to adjourn until 2 o'clock P.M. . . . .

2 oclock P.M.—

Calvin Brown from the Church in Fairfield took his seat as a member of this body. . . . .

Resumed and completed the narrative of the state of religion On motion resolved that Brother Asa Turner be appointed delegate to attend such ecclesiastical Bodies at the East as may be convenient and to use his influence with Ministers and Laymen of approved piety to locate in this County

Resolved, That Brethren Wolcott, Kirby and Carter be a

[17] Rev. John Lawton, missionary, wrote to the society, April 10, 1836: "Here [at Carthage] by appointment we held a 4 days meeting ending the 2nd. Sab. in March assisted by Br. Turner of Quincy Adams Co. and Fr. Reed (your missionary who is located and supplies 3 little settlements in the western part of this county. Near the close of this meeting Br. T. assisted in organizing a small chh. here consisting of 6 members from other chhs and 3 by profession. 5 or 6 more are expect to join soon—." At the time of the writing, said Lawton, "I continue, as in my first quarter, to afford a stated supply at four places, viz: Carthage, Augusta, Franklin, and Shiloh Prairie, near St. Mary's. Am occasionally at other places as strength and opportunity allow," suggesting the busy life of the missionaries.

committee to prepare resolutions on the subject of slavery for the consideration of Ass. & report this evening

Resolved, That Brethren Turner Gaylord and Brooks be a committee to prepare resolutions for the consideration of Ass. on the observance of the Sabbath. . . . .

Committee on the subject of slavery reported sundry resolutions which were accepted and after full discussion and some amendments were adopted in the following order

Inasmuch as slavery is a subject of deep and constantly increasing interest and from its very nature, must vitally affect not only the prosperity and future destiny of our country but the welfare of the human race—we feel it to be our duty both as Christians and Philanthropists publicly to bear our testimony against it

Therefore

Resolved I That Slavery as it exists in our country is a heinous sin and calls for the united efforts of the Church and every Patriot for its immediate removal—

II That as a Nation we owe the oppressed among us every possible reparation for the wrongs heaped upon them and that we can make this in no way so effectually as by furnishing them along with their emancipation every possible facility for moral and intellectual improvement

III That it is the duty of the several state Governments within whose jurisdiction slavery exists in our country to abolish it within their respective limits by speedy legislation

IV That the opposition of the laws of any community to emancipation does not justify the holding of human beings in bondage & that every slaveholder is implicated in the guilt of upholding and perpetuating such laws

V That no individual who is disaffected with slavery and about to leave a slaveholding state is justified under any circumstances in Selling his slaves.

VI That Slaveholders ought not to be admitted to our Pulpits and communion tables

VII That we highly appreciate the philanthropy and benevolence of those men who have devoted their entire energies to the cause of emancipation and deeply sympathise with them in the persecution and obloquy which they have so undeservedly experienced

VIII That we approve the course the *Alton Observer*[18] has taken on the subject of slavery & commend it to the patronage and liberality of the Churches. . . . .

1836

Nov. 5th.—. . . .

Present Brethren Wolcott Carter Kirby Reed Gaylord, Stillman, Hitchcock & Chittenden

Absent Brethren Hubbard, Willes, R. Brown Benton, C. Brown, Brooks & Greenleaf

Committee on the observance of the Sabbath made a report which was accepted and after some amendments was adopted as follows

viz.

Whereas the Sabbath is a divine institution and the command "remember the Sabbath Day to keep it holy" is of universal obligation and whereas this command is violated to an alarming degree by many professing to be Christians

THEREFORE RESOLVED I That it is the duty of all man and especially of all the friends of the Redeemer to refrain from travelling and all unnecessary business on that day and

---

[18] Elijah P. Lovejoy came to Alton in 1836 to edit the *Alton Observer*. Although he had promised to edit the paper in the interest of the church only, his antislavery views and sympathies crept into its columns. His press was destroyed again and again by the outraged citizens of Alton. The leading citizens of the town implored him to leave, but Lovejoy stated that he was ready for martyrdom. This he achieved on November 7, 1837, when in attempting to defend another press which had just arrived he was shot by a mob which had surrounded the warehouse where it was stored (G. H. Barnes, *Dictionary of American Biography*, XI, 434–35).

in all respects to abstain from the heinous sin of Sabbath breaking.

II   That is is the duty of christian Churches to discipline and if possible reclaim any member who is guilty of a violation of the fourth Commandment

III   That it is the duty of Ministers to lift the warning voice, and of all Christians to use all proper means to enlighten and correct the public mind on this subject

IV   That capitalists holding property in Rail Roads, Stages and Steam Boats by which the Sabbath is desecrated are in our view guilty of violating the spirit of this command.[19]

Committee appointed to take minutes from the narrative of the state of Religion made report which after some amendments was adopted   On motion resolved that in view of the wants of our country and the world and the universal demand for ministerial labour that it is the duty of Christians to use special efforts to induce young men of devoted piety to consecrate themselves to the ministry and to aid the needy in preparation for the work

WHEREAS on account of the pecuniary embarrassment of our benevolent societies their labours are contracted and their usefulness diminished at a time when increased exertion is demanded

. . . .

RESOLVED

That it is the duty of the Church to sustain our Domestic & Foreign Missionary Boards and enable them to employ all

---

[19] The early missionaries were greatly stirred by the lawlessness and Sabbath desecration of the frontier. Typical of their descriptions of frontier conditions is the following extract from a letter of Rev. Lucien Farnam, written to the society from Princeton, Illinois, July 1, 1836:

"My 'spirit was stirred' within me when I saw the wickedness [that] reigns on the Erie Canal. That may be called the great thoroughfare—the grand highway of corruption. How long God will bear with such wickedness I know not. Truly 'iniquity especially that of profaneness, and Sabbath breaking' abounds and the love of money, even of professors of religion seems to wax cold."

the men of suitable qualifications that shall offer themselves
for the Foreign or Domestic field

On Motion *Resolved*, That we earnestly recommend to the
Churches connected with this Association special efforts to
increase the funds of the American Home Missionary Society

On Motion *Resolved*, That Brethren Kirby & Chittenden be a
committee to prepare an abstract of the doings of this meeting to be published in the Alton Observer & such other
papers as they may think expedient

On Motion *Resolved*, That the next annual meeting of Association be holden at Round Prairie and that this meeting
be adjourned Sine Die

Closed with prayer

E. Wolcott   *Moderator*

Jn. B. Chittenden *Clerk*

1837

Nov. 2.—The second annual meeting of the Congregational
Association was holden at Round Prairie Hancock County
commencing Nov. 2, 1837. . . . .

Dr. Ero Chandler   *Moderator*

Jno B. Chittenden   *Clerk*

. . . .

From the Church in Jacksonville Rev. William Carter Pastor
Brethren Ebenezer Carter and R. M. Pierson Delegates

From the Church in Warsaw Rev. Julius A. Reed Pastor &
Brother Ero Chandler Delegate

From the Church in Fairfield Brethren Miron Gaylord and
Jno. B. Chittenden Delegates

From the Church in Round Prairie Brother Sullivan Searls
Delegate

. . . .

Nov. 3.—

Met according to adjournment. . . . . Brethren Phineas Chapman & E. A. Pease took their seats as delegates from St. Marys Church

Brother William Whittlesey presented a certified copy of his Licence to preach the Gospel from the Hartford south Association Connecticut (Also a certificate of his good standing by the committee of the general association of Connecticut recommending him to the fellowship of the Churches). Brother Whittlesey accompanied the above with a request to be taken under the care of the Association and to be ordained by them

On Motion

Resolved, That in future all Delegates to the Association are expected to show satisfactory credentials of their appointment

On Motion Rev. G. C. Sampson was received as a member of Ass. on letter of recommendation from the general Association of Connecticut on condition that he subscribe the constitution of their Ass.

On motion *Resolved*, That a narrative of the state of Religion in the several Churches represented in this body be now given and that Brethren Carter and Reed be a committee to take minutes

After hearing a part of the narrative Ass. adjourned until two oclock P.M. . . . .

2 oclock P.M.—. . . .

Brother Alanson Work being present took his seat as Delegate from the church in Round Prairie

Finished the narrative of the state of Religion

In compliance with a request presented by the Delegates from the St. Marys Church for advice in the case of a member who has requested to be dismissed from said Church *Resolved*,

That a committee be appointed to labour with the said member and in case they fail to accomplish the object of their appointment, the Church be advised to comply with his request.

Resolved, That Brethren Chandler Reed Sampson and Searls be appointed on the committee named in the above resolution

On Motion *Resolved*, That a committee be appointed to prepare and present resolutions to Ass. respecting the benevolent operations of the day & that Brethren Sampson and Reed constitute said committee

. . . . On Motion *Resolved*, That a committee be appointed to draft resolutions on the subject of insubordination to Law and that Brethren William Carter & Jno. B. Chittenden constitute said Committee

On motion *Resolved* to adjourn until tomorrow 9 oclock A.M. . . . .

1837

Nov. 4.—. . . .

Committe on the subject of insubordination to Law presented a report which was accepted

After a full discussion the report was adopted

The following is a true copy of said report

Resolved, That the spirit of insubordination to the restraints of Law so common among us at the present day affords just cause of alarm to every lover of his country. And if not speedily checked will result in the entire prostration of all civil authority in the universal prevalence of anarchy and the destruction of our civil and religious privileges, and those free institutions for which our Fathers bled and died.

II   That nothing can save us from the cricis which we are fast approaching but a general rallying of the friends of good order to the support of the Law and that we feel it incumben on every man who prefers the continuance of our happy form of government to the reign of anarchy or despotism to come up at once to the rescue, with a firm determination to encourage & sustain the Civil Magistrate in suppressing the spirit of riot and maintaining the authority of Law in that mode which the Law itself prescribes at whatever sacrifice and at all hazards

On Motion *Resolved* to adjourn till after religious services this afternoon. . . . .

On motion Rev. Asa Turner was received as a member of Ass. on letter of recommendation from Schuyler Presbytery

. . . .

On Motion *Resolved* to reconsider the resolutions adopted this morning in relation to insubordination to Law

After a second discussion the report was again adopted as before

After a recess of one hour Ass. resumed business Report of committee on the Benevolent operations of the day (abridged) was again considered and adopted   Report has been mislaid & cannot be found

On Motion *Resolved*, That Brethren Turner and Kirby be a committee to correspond with the Domestic Missionary Society of Connecticut and to represent to that body that the congregational churches of Ill. need a supply of ministers[20]

[20] The missionaries and ministers already on the frontier felt the urgent need for more workers, and many of their letters to the society emphasize this need. Under date of October 11, 1836, Rev. Isaac Foster wrote from Plainfield, Illinois:

"I suppose from the information I can obtain there are 60 or 70,000 souls in the northern part of this state that have not more than about a dozen efficient ministers of all the evangelical denominations, and I have heard of only one (Br. Clark) of our order north of here and this side of Green Bay, a distance of from 2 to 300 miles of rich fertile country filling up most rapidly. The tide of emigration is without a parallel. Who will take possession of this fairest richest portion of our continent for Christ before the enemy shall have entrenched himself in his strong holds. . . . ." He laments the "many professors of Religion who came out to this western world, professing Christ and probably intending to do much for the cause of the Redeemer, who when they get on the ground find the cares of the world so great, the necessity of providing a home so urgent and more particularly the beautiful and fertile county of cheap land so inviting, that they fall into temptation—and lose their spirituality,

On Motion *Resolved*, That a special meeting of Ass. be holden at Quincy on the last Thursday in April next—

On Motion *Resolved*, That Brethren Kirby and Chittenden be a committee to correspond with or visit the Congregational Churches in this State not here represented

On Motion *Resolved*, That the Constitution be so altered that the Clerk shall be a permanent Officer and that Jno. B. Chittenden be appointed Stated Clerk. . . . .

Met according to adjournment . . . . Committee appointed to take minutes from the narrative of the state of religion exhibited their report which was adopted   *Resolved*, That Brethren Kirby and Chittenden be a committee to publish an abstract of the minutes of this meeting and also the constitution of the Association. . . . .

Nov. 6.—. . . .

Resolvd to proceed to the examination of Brother Whittlesey in relation to his ordination

Resolved, That the examination be sustaind and that Brother Whittlesey be ordaind at 2 oclock P.M.

---

and having no shepherd to watch over them and bring them back to the fold from whence they stray, they are buried up in the world. . . . ."

That even some of the ministers succumbed to the lure of cheap land and possible monetary gain on the frontier is indicated by the letter of Rev. Albert Hale, written to the society from Jacksonville, Illinois, under date of February, 1837:

"A minister is much needed for the Carthage church, county seat of Hancock Co. The brother who resides there having been so much engaged in the business of setting up wind mills that his religious influence is utterly blown away. The most judicious friends of the Cause in that part have become anxious for a preacher who will 'know nothing but Jesus Christ and him crucified.' . . . ."

That the poorer sections of the state, or those sections making less rapid advance, were likely to suffer because of the greater attractiveness of other sections, is indicated by the letter of Rev. Albert Hale to the society, written from Alton, Illinois, May 23, 1837:

"There is a considerable number of feeble churches destitute and going to decay in those parts southern Illinois for want of laborers, & we cannot obtain men to go there. This is owing chiefly to the fact that the middle northern sections of the state have advance in wealth, enterprize & population for the few past years with vastly greater rapidity than the southern sections."

Parts were assigned as follows

> Brother Turner to preach the Sermon
> Bro. Carter to make the ordaining prayer
> Bro. Sampson to give the charge
> Bro. Reed the righ hand of fellowship

After a recess of one hour the ordination services were attended

Resolved, That Brethren Turner and Carter be a stated committee to give the necssary certificate to candidates licensed or ordained by this body

On Motion adjournd to meet at Quincy on the last Thursday in April next at 6 oclock. . . . .

BRO. CHANDLER   *Moderator*

JNO. B. CHITTENDEN   *Clerk*

1838

April 26th.—An adjourned meeting of the congregational association of Illinois was holden at Quincy commencing April 26th 1938

The Moderator appointed at the annual meeting being absent Rev. William Carter was calld to the Chair. . . . .
Present from the Church in Jacksonville
Rev. William Carter Pastor Brethren Martin Hart and R. M. Pierson Delegates
From Columbus Presbyterian Church Rev. William Whittlesey From Church in Quincy Rev. Asa Turner Pastor Brethren J. T. Holmes and Rufus Brown Delegates
From the Church in Fairfield Rev. William Kirby Pastor Brother Levi Stillman Delegate
From the Church in Round Prairie Brethren Nathan Burton and Asahel Hubbard Delegates
From the Church in St. Marys Brother E. A. Pease Delegate

An application *Resolved*, That the Congregational Church at Griggsville (the union ch. having been dissolved) be admitted to the association and that Brethren Aaron Tyler and Geo W. Johnson take their seats as Delegates from said Church

On application the Cong. Church at Woodville was received a member of the Association and Brother Simeon Curtis took his seat as Delegate

On application *Resolved*, That the Church at Mission Institute No. 1 be received as a member of Association and that Brother N. Shapley take his seat as Delegate from said church

On application the Cong. Church in Payson was received as a member of Association & Brethren Jno. Burns and Wm. Curtis Delegates from . Church took their seats as members of this Body.

Rev. Mr. Coles of Payson being present and the Rev. D. Kohler missionary of the evangelical Lutheran Synod of Pennsylvania they were invited to sit as corresponding members

Adjournd till 8 oclock tomorrow. . . . .

April 27th.—. . . . Minutes of last meeting read

.   .   .   .

On Motion *Resolved*, That the Cong. Church in Carthage be received into the Association and that Benjamin F. Morris and Homer Brown Delegates from said Church take their seats as Members of Association

On Motion *Resolved*, That the Church in Monmouth Warren Co. be receivd. into association

1838

April 27.—On motion *Resolved*, That a copy of the Constitution be furnished to the Churches admitted into the association at this meeting for their adoption

Rev. Thomas Cole of Payson[21] presented a written request to be received as a member of Association provided it should not be considered a relinquishment on his part of his preference for the discipline of the Presbyterian Church & was by vote of Ass. received accordingly.

Brethren Ero Chandler and C. A. Warren from the Church in Warsaw appeared and took their seats as members of Ass.

On Motion *Resolved*, That at the next meeting of Ass. a certified copy of the Articles of Faith of the several Churches connected with this Body be presented & be filed by the Clerk & that in future all churches wishing to unite with us exhibit their articles of Faith and satisfactory evidence of their adoption of the constitution of Association

[21] The progress of the church at Payson, Illinois, under the ministrations of Rev. Thomas Cole, is indicated by his letter to the society dated January 30, 1840:

"You will rejoice to hear that this church, organized by one of your missionaries has been blessed. . . . . The original number was nineteen. Since that time about twenty five have been dismissed in entire harmony to form a church five miles from us at Newton. We have now about eighty members in this branch of the church and our sister church . . . . near fifty. For the last two months sinners have been pressing into the Kingdom. . . . . About forty five persons, mostly between twenty and thirty years of age are the subjects of this good work. One year ago we enjoyed a gracious refreshing from the Lord, in the Newton church, principally among the children. . . . .

"In this part of the Military District, our churches are on the advance. Griggsville, Atlas, Fairfield, Clayton, Payson & Newtown have enjoyed refreshing seasons during the past year, and now the general attentions is more encouraging than I have ever seen ithere. There is new interest at Columbus, Br. Nichols place, but I do not know how extensive."

The financial policies of the eastern leaders of the society long continued to be a point of disagreement between them and the missionaries on the frontier, and Cole's further comments in this letter register a typical missionary protest:

"Do not let him   Nichols   leave that post, and may I say do not break him down by curtailments, or force him to seculars, or back to New England. I do not beg for myself: but I may beg for others. I say to you then and through you to the rich eastern churches, do not take the bread from the faithful and devoted men, that you have sent into this field of privation and arduous labour. They are worthy of your confidence and support, and the Lord has need of them here. . . . . Give them a place on which to stand, and they will move this people onward and upward. . . . .

"If a missionary *needs* 200$ from your Society, it is not economy to allow him but 150. If 400$ is *necessary* for his support, it is a greater waste of money to reduce his salary to 300$ than to raise it to $500. In the one case you give a good man 100$ above his current expenses, In the other you injure his usefulness, & waste his energies that are above the price of dollars & cents. . . . ."

Application was made for advice in a case of discipline in the Griggsville Church which was referd to a committee of three viz. Brethren Cole, Chandler & Burton

Committee appointed at the last meeting to correspond with Congregational Churches not represented in this Body presented a report which was accepted

On Motion *Resolved*, That Brethren Carter Whittlesey & Chittenden be appointed Delegates to attend the meeting of Rock River Association in Sept next

Committee appointed to correspond with the Domestic Missionary Society of Connecticut presented a report of their doings which was accepted

Brother Andrew L. Pennoyer presented a certified copy of his licence to preach the Gospel from the Presbytery of Cincinnati. Also a recommendation from that Body, accompanied by a request to be taken under the care of Association and to be ordained by them At the same time Brethren Benjamin F. Morris and Charles Burnham made application to Association for licence to preach the Gospel.

Wherefore *Resolved*, That said Brethern be examined as to their respective qualifications

On application of the Church at Mission Institute No 1 Resolved to attend the Installation of Rev. David Nelson at the Institution at 10 oclock tomorrow morning

On Motion *Resolved*, That Brethren Turner Kirby and Whittlesey be a committee to assign the parts to be performed at the Installation and also to appoint a committee to conduct the examination of candidates for ordination & Licensure committee retired & after a short interval submitted their report which was accepted

Resolved, That the examination commence at 3 oclock P.M.

The committee to whom was referred the case of discipline from Griggsville submitted the following report which was adopted by the Association

1838

April 27.—*Resolved*, That while the Association earnestly recommend the exercise of christian love kindness and forbearance on the part of the complainant they advise the Church of Griggsville affectionately to urge Brother to comply in letter and spirit with his confession made to the church as the only proper mode of shewing the sincerity of his repentance And that in the event of his refusal the Church should consider his confession null and void

On application of Brother Coles he was excused from further attendance during the remainder of the session

After a recess of 2 hours the Ass. resumed business

On Motion *Resolved*, That Rev. J. M. Gumble of the presbytery of Buffalo be invited to sit as a corresponding member

Proceeded to the examination of candidates for ordination and Licensure

Voted a recess till after religious services this evening.

After religious services resumed the examination of Candidates. Adjourned to meet at Mission Institute No 1 at 9 oclock tomorrow A.M. . . . .

April 28.—Met at Mission Institute . . . .

Proceeded to the examination of Dr. Nelson in relation to his installation over the Church in this Institution

On motion *Resolved*, That the examination be sustained and that association proceed to instal Dr. Nelson immediately

Parts of the installing services were performed as follows VIZ [similar to installation services noted above]

. . . .

On motion *Resolved* to excuse Brother Shapley from further attendance during the present session of association

On motion *Resolved* to adjourn to meet at Quincy at half past one oclock P.M.

Met at Quincy according to adjournment. . . . .

On motion *Resolved*, That association will now hear the delegates report the state of religion in their respective churches & that Brethren Kirby and Whittlesey be a committee to take minutes from said reports.[22] . . . .

[22] The tremendous odds against which the missionaries and ministers on the frontier worked are reflected in many of their letters to the society. In order to understand the seeming want of spirituality in the Illinois churches, wrote David Smith, minister at Big Grove, on November 25, 1839, one must consider "the circumstances in which the church is placed." The people, he continues, "have planted themselves in this new country, most obviously to *improve their temporal conditions.* It may be seriously doubted whether any have come solely and exclusively to promote the glory of God—to labor to promote the moral and spiritual good of their fellowmen. Whatever may be their desire to do good . . . . their wishes to benefit themselves in *temporal things* seems to be far greater. . . . . Bread to eat and clothes to wear they must have. There seems to be an absolute necessity to tax their industry to the very utmost to obtain what is needful for the body. Under these circumstances, how difficult to maintain the warmth and glow of heavenly affections which they were wont to manifest at the East . . . . further, they find themselves in a great measure separated from each other, and they cannot run together and spend an hour in religious worship with the same facility that they did in their native villages at the East. They are at hand now a variety of excuses for neglecting a weekly prayer meeting or lecture. Every month now proves to be 'a busy time,' and there are a thousand calls . . . . to interrupt anything like regular attendance at such meetings. . . . ."

The woes of the missionaries, however they might be explained, were nevertheless very real, and the treatment they received at the hands of the frontier people they were trying to serve sometimes called forth protests such as the letter of Rev. Warren Nichols of Atlas, Illinois, written February 26, 1836:

"It is impossible for people who have never lived where christian ideas of honorable character have no place, to conceive of the workings of the wicked. If I can show them some favor they will be very courteous and express many thanks, and go around the neighborhood, perhaps the same day, telling hundreds of lies about me. They want the use of my horse and waggon, or to ride with me when it suits their convenience, and do not pay . . . . or do anything for me. One man to whom I had repeatedly loaned my horse without pay, charge me three dollars for the use of a chaise 20 miles. A physician worth several thousand dollars has sent a child regularly to my singing school this winter and refused to do the least thing for us. Young ladies get Mrs. Nichols to assist in preparing dresses and bonnets (for they know little about work) and repay her by the basest of slanders. . . . . Such are the difficulties that all our missionaries contend with."

Added to the difficulties of dealing with an irreligious people was the difficulty of meeting with the infiltration of "false doctrine," for which the minister at Carthage, Illinois, writing to the society under date of August 2, 1839, shows some concern:

". . . . during the few last weeks the minds of the people have been much excited about Mormonism. The departure of the Mormons from Missouri has resulted in flooding this region with the deluded followers of that imposter Joe Smith; and their apostles and Elders are trying to enlighten the good people in regard to their religious

Brother Reed from Warsaw now appeared and took his seat as a member of association

On motion *Resolved*, That the examination in Literature and science be dispensed with

On Motion *Resolved*, That the examination of Brother Pennoyer be sustained

On Motion *Resolved*, That the examination of Brother Morris for license be sustained.[23]

---

system." The ministers fought Mormonism at its every appearance, and he continues with some elation: "They have been pretty thoroughly exposed. The history of this deluded people teaches one very instructive lesson, ... the vast importance of thorough Biblical instruction . . . . if the Ministers of the Gospel desire to save a community from error and fantacies, let them give instruction in the Bible. . . . ."

Epidemics of disease were added to the difficulties of the human relationships to make the lot of the missionary a hard one. On October 24, 1837, Rev. Julius A. Reed, suffering from ill-health and weakness, wrote the society from Warsaw, Illinois:

". . . . Of the religious prospects of this vicinity I can say nothing particularly favorable—Our meetings have thinned by the almost unprecedented prevalence of ague and fever and the dampness of the weather. The principle proprietors of the place with two or three exception are at least indifferent to religion and their influence is unfavorable. Not a few of our residents are infidels or universalists—There are of course great obstacles . . . . which require efforts more vigorous and unceasing than I with my frail constitution am capable of making."

On top of all this was the ever present difficulty of obtaining adequate meeting-places, and the propsect of losing those they already had: "Carthage, as to the state of society, is similar to Warsaw—infidelity etc. abounding. We are in danger of being deprived of the use of the log court house and possibly shall be obliged to suspend preaching, which would be a great calamity. I trust that the Lord will provide. . . . ."

[23] That B. F. Morris did good work for the society after being licensed is indicated by his letter dated just a year later (April 2, 1839), written at Carthage, Illinois:

". . . . I have labored here seven months as a minister of the Gospel—though I have resided in Carthage two years. The number of hopeful conversions during the last year is 5 or 6, of the most influential persons in the place. . . . .

"We have an interesting Sabbath School, well sustained during the whole year. Our average number has been about 55 scholars in a population of 300 souls. The volumes in the library are about 15. We are making an effort to obtain more.

"Our Bible class has been suspended during the winter for 8 or 9 months. The number ranges from 12 to 20 persons, all grown.

"We have a temperance society in the place though it is weak and inefficient, as a *society*. We had, during the winter, several discussions publicly on the license system. It resulted in bringing facts out, and the subject before the minds of those who keep the groceries in our village, and all who were not friendly to the cause of

On motion *Resolved*, That the examination of Brother Burnham for licensure be sustained

On Motion *Resolved*, That the ordination of Brother Pennoyer be performed tomorrow evening [see ordination service above]

. . . .

On Motion *Resolved*, That the clerk be authorized to cause 200 copies of the constitution to be printed

On Motion *Resolved*, That Brethren Kirby Whittlesey and Carter be a committee to examine the constitution make such corrections as they shall deem important and report at the next annual meeting

On Motion Brethren Kirby and Whittlesey were appointed a committee to prepare for publication an abstract of the doings of Association

On Motion *Resolved*, That Brethren Morris Whittlesey and Turner be a committee to report tomorrow morning as to the expediency of establishing a religious newspaper in this state

On Motion *Resolved*, That the next annual meeting of Association be holden at Griggsville. . . . .

April 29th.—. . . .

Committee on the subject of a religious newspaper reported as follows

The committee appointed to inquire as to the expediency of establishing a religious paper beg leave to report that they are unanimously of opinion that a religious periodical should be established as soon as practicable in the state and that the paper should be strictly and decidedly religious, perfectly free and untramelled in the expression of opinion on any and

---

Temperance. One thing is certain in this place there has been during the last year a great advance in the cause of temperance. The people do not seem desirous of joining a society yet they throw their influence many of them on the right side. . . . ."

every subject involving the interests of religion or the welfare of the Church of Christ

On Motion *Resolved*, That Brethren Kirby Turner Holmes and Brown be a committee to open a correspondence with individuals in Alton friendly to the establishment of a religious periodical & communicate to them the action of Association on that subject

On Motion it was recommended that a convention be calld in the several counties within the state on the 4th of July next consisting of Delegates from Temperance societies and other individuals friendly to the cause of temperance for the purpose of adopting systematic measures to carry into effect the temperance reformation so auspiciously begun. . . . .

WILLIAM CARTER *Moderator*

JNO. B. CHITTENDEN *Clerk*

1838

June 27th.—At a special meeting of the Congregational association of Illinois held at the congregational Church in Quincy for the purpose of taking into consideration the propriety of Installing the Revd. Asa Turner over the congregational Church in Quincy In the absence of the Moderator Revd. Wm. Carter was called to the chair

. . . . The following persons were received as delegates from the Congregational churches after presenting certificates of election (to wit) Fairfield D. F. Bartholomew Mission Institute N. Shapley Quincy Church Richard Ellis Rufus Brown W. Keyes

The following persons were invited to sit as corresponding members from their several ecclesiastical bodies To Wit Revd. David Nelson from the Presbytery of Missouri Rev Moses Hunter from the Presbytery of Angelica N. York Rev. Mr. Renshaw from the Congregational Association of N. York. While the Brethren were coming in a season of prayer was held by the Association after which the meeting was adjourned to one oclock P.M.

. . . .

Brother Atkins presented his certificate from the Church in Round Prairie and took his seat as member of the Association

Association proceeded to hear the statements of the parties for and against Mr. Turner

Brother John Burns from the Church in Payson presented his certificate of membership & took seat accordingly

Brother Warren from Warsaw appeared and took his seat with the Association

The following resolution after discussion was adopted by the Association

Resolved, That this association having taken into prayerful consideration the subject submitted to them are fully of the opinion that the Minority this Church in opposing the settlement of Brother Turner have shown no reasons why he should not become the Pastor of this church but have on the contrary by their admissions in favour of his piety and usefulness shown his fitness for his present field of labour

But inasmuch as a strong and decided though unreasonable opposition to his settlement does exist which in the judgment of this Association must greatly injure his usefulness— They are therefore of the opinion that they are not called upon to recommend that Brother Turner shoud be installed Pastor of this Church

WILLIAM CARTER   *Mod. P. Tem*
RICHD. ELLIS   *Clerk P. Tem*

Faithfully enterd   Attest

JNO. B. CHITTENDEN   *Stated Clerk*

1838

Nov. 1st.—The Congregation Association of Ill. held its third annual meeting Thursday Nov. 1st 1838 at 2 oclock P.M. at the Congregational Meetinghouse in Griggsville and was organisd by the appointment of

REVD. JULIUS A. REED *Mod.*

&

BR. JOHN BURNS *Clerk P.T.*

[The following churches were represented—Warsaw, Payson, Griggsville, Quincy, Winchester.]

．　．　．　．　．　．　．　．　．　．　．　．　．　．　．　．　．

After religious exercises Association proceeded to business Revd. Robert Blake Pastor of the Congregational Church in Woodburne Macoupin County presented his dismission and recommendation from Orange Association
And requested admission to this body On the presentation of such testomonials respecting his ministerial character as were highly satisfactory and his adopting our constitution and articles of faith voted that he be received into this association

Rev. Reuben Gaylord presented a certificate of his regular ordination by an ecclesiastical council held at Terrysville, August 8th 1838 and on adopting our constitution and articles of faith he was by vote received into this Association

Rev. William Kirby Pastor of the Church in Fairfield appeared and Brother Henry E. Fowler presented his certificate as delegate from said Church were excused for late attendance & took their seats.

Brother Nathan Burton and Myron Gaylord presented their certificates as delegates from the Church in Round Prairie gave their excuses for late attendance and took their Seats

Voted that the Congregational Church in Woodburne be admitted to this association provided they approve of the

Constitution and signify the same to the stated Clerk of this body

. . . .

Committee on business reported in
a request from Brother E. G. Murdock for examination with reference to ordination

Report accepted

Testimonials being called for Brother Murdock presented a certificate of his licensure by the Association of the western district of New Haven Co. Conn—see document No 2 1838 Wherefore voted that association proceed to his examination at 2 oclock P.M.

Brethren Cole and Whittlesey were appointed a committee to assign the subjects for examination

Committee on business Report

Reports of the Churches on the state of religion voted to commence the reports after religious service in the evening and pursue the same at 2 oclock tomorrow

The articles of faith of the several Churches of the Association being called for in pursuance to a vote passed at a former meeting of Association

Copies were received from the Churches at Warsaw Fairfield and Griggsville and put on file (see documents No 3 & 4 & 8½ 1838)

Report of the delegation to the Rock River Ass. being called for Brother Carter responded to the call   report accepted

Brother Brown from the committee appointed to correspond with friends at Alton with reference to the publication of a religious newspaper in this state reported   report accepted

Brethren Cole Brown and Hoyt were appointed a committee on the subject of Slavery

Voted to consider the subject of changing the time of holding the monthly concert but the consideration was suspended to give room for the committee on the assignment of parts of the examination to report and the report of said Committee as accepted is as follows: That Br. Blake examine on Christian experience and views of the ministry   Br. Kirby on Sacred Literature   Br. Whittlesey on Nat. Theology Brother Reed on the evidences of Christianity   Brother Carter on Didactic Theology   Br. Gaylord on Church History & Government   Br. Cole on ordinances . . . .

Met at 2 oclock P.M. voted to defer the order of the day and continue the suspended business

The subject of changing the time of holding the monthly concert having been thoroughly discussed it was finally disposed of by the adoption of the following resolutions

Resolved, That the members of this Association will endeavor to excite the Churches connected with us to increased effort in the cause of Foreign Missions

Resolved 2d, That we will endeavour to extend the circulation of the Missionary Herald [the official organ of the A.H.M.S.] to each family connected with our churches

The Association then proceeded to the order of the day by the examination of Brother Murdock with reference to ordination

Voted to suspend the examination till tomorrow morning

Voted that Brethren Kirby Burton and Tyler be a committee on the subject of temperance

Voted that Brethren Blake Pennoyer and Burns be a committee on the subject of Sabbath Schools

. . . .

1838

Nov. 3d.—. . . .

Voted to excuse Brother Cole to leave at his discretion

Voted liberty to Br. Burns to leave at his discretion

Voted to suspend the order of the day to hear the report

from Payson Chh. at this time as the representation from that Church will soon leave

Resolved, That it is earnestly desired by this association that all ministers and Delegates to this body should attend punctually and make arrangements to remain till the body adjourn

Committee on the subject of Slavery reported sundry resolutions   Report accepted

A minority of the committee on slavery presented an additional report which was also accepted

Committee on the subject of Sabbath Schools reported Report accepted

The Association then proceeded to the order of the day To wit the examination of Br. Murdock[24]

Voted that Br. Pennoyer examine on ordinances in place of Br. Cole who has left

After examination voted unanimously that the examination be sustained

Voted that Brethren Whittlesey and Hoyt be a committee to assign the parts of ordination services. . . . .

[24] The work of Rev. C. E. Murdock is outlined in his letter written to the society from Round Prairie, Illinois, about a year after his ordination (December 8, 1839):

"This day concludes the first year of my pastoral labors under the patronage of your society. The year has been an eventful one to me. It was begun near seventeen months ago, ... Since that time I have made three toilsome journeys from the Connecticut to the Mississippi rivers, besides shorter journeys connected with my mission, embracing in all more than 7000 miles travel. During the former part of the year my labors were principally confined to the Congregational church in Round Prairie, and the outskirts of the settlement, but for the last six months, I have preached about one third of the Sabbaths in St. Mary's, six miles from R. P. where there is a Congregational church of 15 members. I have during the year attended two stated prayer meetings each week besides other occasional meetings. . . . . The church at R. P. has 49 members. . . . .

"In my field of labor four Sabbath schools have been sustained during the summer and one throughout the year. . . . .

"The church in Round Prairie have unanimously and cordially invited me to be installed over them as their pastor, which invitation I may hereafter accept. At present the demands of labor in adjacent places and the destitution of ministers there, render it in my own judgement inexpedient. . . . . Could you help me for a year or two longer, there is a probability of my receiving my entire support by the expiration of that time without your aid. . . . ."

1838

Nov 3d.—Committee on assignment of parts to be performed in the ordination services reported as follows [see ordination services above].

. . . .

Committee on temperance submitted the following report which was adopted

ARTICLE I Entire abstinance from all that can intoxicate is the only principal on which the cause of temperance can triumph

II We will use our influence to sustain by pecuniary aid the operations of the State Temperance Society

III We earnestly recommend the circulation of the Temprance Herald and other information on the Subject of Temperance

IV We concur in the resolution passed by the State convention to petition the Legislature to repeal the existing license Laws and to enact prohibitory laws against the traffic in ardent spirits

V That we will unite with the friends of temperance in petitioning that it be made a penal offence in Candidates for office to treat in order to secure their election

VI That we recommend frequent meetings for discussing the subject of temperance in the communities where members of Association reside

Committee on the alteration of the Constitution reported Report accepted

The Constitution is amended after some discussion was adopted unanimously. . . . .

[The changes in the constitution, Articles of Faith and Regulations made at this meeting of the association have been indicated in the original made in 1836.]

JNO. B. CHITTENDEN, *Clerk.*

Names of Ministers and Churches, belonging to the
"Congregational Association of Illinois"

Ministers			Churches
Julius A. Reed Bhp.[25]	Con. ch.		Warsaw Hanc'k co.
B. F. Morris Licentiate	"	"	Carthage, "
Guy Sampson, Bhp.	"	"	St Mary's, "
E. E. Murdock, "	"	"	Round Prairie Sch'yl co.
———— ————, "	"	"	Woodville, Adams co.
William Kirby, "	"	"	Fairfield " "
———— ————, "	"	"	Quincy, " "
Thomas Cole, "	"	"	Payson, " "
William Carter, Pres'n. ch. Pittsfield, Pike co.			
William Whittlesey, Bhp. witout charge.			
A. L. Pennoyer, "	Un ch Westchester	Mary co	
Robert Blake "	Con ch Woodburn Macoupin "		
———— ———— "	" " " Jacksonville Morg. co.		
Reuben Gaylord "		Iowa Territory.	
Asa Turner "		Denmark " "	
———— ———— " Con ch Long Grove Lasalle co.			
Charles Burnam Licentiate,		Adams co.	
———— ———— Con. ch. Mis. Institute No. 1 "			

Met at 6 oclock according to adjournment Voted to
adopt the report of Committee on Sabbath schools

I   The Committee on S. Schools beg leave to report that
in their own Sabbath Schools lie at the foundation of the
best interests of society and of the christian Church

II   That since the Agents of S. Schools have been removed from their offices by the pecuniary embarrassment of
the times their places should as much as possible be supplied
by the extra exertions of Ministers and other friends of the
institution.

III   That more efficient means should be resorted to, to

[25] The Congregationalists used the term "bishop" in the early New Testament
sense as identical with "elder" (see A. Hastings Ross, *The Church-Kingdom: Lectures on Congregationalism* . . . . [Boston: Cong. S.S. and Pub. Soc., 1887], pp. 60,
61, 124, 145). The following question and answer from the *Congregational Catechism*
. . . . (New Haven, 1844) clearly indicates the Congregational usage of the term:
"*Q. 87.* Are Congregational ministers known by any other titles? *A.* Yes. They are
called the *pastors* and *bishops* of their respective churches" (p. 87).

impress the minds of Parents with the importance of S. Schools and to secure more regular attendance of Teachers

Voted to proceed to the ordination services tomorrow evening at 6 oclock

Voted to take up the report of the minority of Committee on Slavery

After discussion voted to lay the report on the table and take up the report of the Majority

The report was then taken up resolution by resolution and the following adopted

The Committee on the subject of Slavery would respectfully recommend the adoption of the following resolution viz.

I   Resolved that this Association earnestly & solemnly renew their purpose by all proper means to effect the total overthrow of the system of Slavery as it prevails in the United States

II   That the existence of Slavery in the Church of Christ and its advocacy by Christians and especially by Ministers of the Gospel calls for deep humiliation and divided condemnation

Resolved 3rd, That we will endeavour to cherish feelings of kindness towards all who may be implicated in the sin of Slavery whether as Masters or Apologists

IV   That we will bear our testimony against the sin of Slavery in public and private on all suitable occasions and lend our aid in the circulation of information through the medium of the press.

V   That we will ever maintain the right of free description and of petition and that we recommend to the community to withhold their support from all candidates for office who deny these rights

VI   That we will remember the cause of the oppressed slave in our public prayers in the sanctuary and will not knowingly admit slaveholders into our pulpits

Voted to adopt the foregoing resolution as a whole. . . . .

Voted that Brethren R. Gaylord & B. F. Morris be appointed delegates to attend the Rock River association in September next

Voted that any minister connected with this association who may be in New England during the current year shall be an accredited delegate from this body to any ecclesiastical body in fellowship with us then in session

Resolved, That it be recommended to the Churches connected with this body to secure as soon as in the Providence of God it shall be consistent the labours of settled Pastors

Voted that the Stated Clerk be directed to forward a copy of the above resolution to the Churches in connexion with us

Voted that the State Clerk & Br Kirby be a committee for the publication of the minutes

Voted that Brother Kirby be requested to preach on the subject of Slavery at the next meeting of Association

Voted the Semi Annual meeting be held at Warsaw. . . . .

JULIUS A. REED   *Mod.*

REUBEN GAYLORD *Clerk Pro. Tem.*

Faithfully enterd

Attest

JNO. B. CHITTENDEN   *Stated Clerk*

1839

April 18.—The congregational association of Ill. commenced its Semi Annual session in Warsaw Hancock County April 18th 1839 at the house of Mr Newbury . . . . [the following churches were represented—Round Prairie, Carthage, La Harp, Warsaw, Fairfield, Quincy]

On Motion *Resolvd*, That Brother M. L. Boothe be invited to sit as a corresponding member

Rev.   H. Hawley from La Harp requested admission

to Association[26]   After presenting satisfactory evidence of his ordination by the Harmony association of New Hampshire & such testimonials of his ministerial character as were highly satisfactory, his adoption of our Constitution and articles of faith he was by vote received as a member of this Body

Brother B. F. Morris was appointed a committee to wait on Mr. Montague of this place and ask liberty to occupy the meeting house owned by him during the present session of Association

On Motion Brethren Morris & Ellis were appointed a committee to prepare business for the action of Association

Having obtained liberty to occupy the meeting house & on motion voted a recess till 2 oclock P.M. to assemble at the Meetinghouse

At 2 oclock met according to adjournment

Rev. Dr. Perry of the Baptist Church being present was invited to act as a corresponding member

Brethren Griggs & Dudley were also requested to take seats as corresponding members

A communication from the citizens of Warsaw & vicinity was here presented by the committee on business No 1 of which the following [see p. 204] is a true copy

---

[26] In a letter to the society from La Harp, Illinois, January 5, 1839, Rev. L. K. Hawley tells of his coming to that town:

"The latter part of Oct. I visited this place .... & preached on the Sabbath. The next day a subscription was circulated for the purposes of securing my services. About $130 for a year were subscribed, & $200, were pledged, on condition that I would take up my residence here, & preach one half of the time.

"After satisfying myself with regard to the circumstances of this people, & of the surrounding population, I concluded to accept the invitation, making it optional with myself whether to remain more than 6 mo. I moved here with my family on the 9th of Nov. last.

"The population of the village is about 160. The country for several miles around is one of the thickest settled in the tract. .... The church with which I am connected is Congregational, & comprises 17 members. ..... We have a Temperance Soc. with about 100 members. Both of our taverns are temperance houses, but there is a grocery occasionally open, which exerts a bad influence. ....."

*To the Moderator and members of the Congregational associa-
tion of Illinois*

GENTLEMEN

The undersigned Citizens of Warsaw and vicinity having
understood from the published proceedings of your late meeting that the Revd. William Kirby was invited to preach an
anti Slavery Sermon in Warsaw on the day of April next and
waving the subject of abstract rights respectfully state that
we believe such proceeding would be against the expressed
and almost unanimous wishes of the citizens of this Community

We therefore request that you would abstain from the
preaching or discussion of Anti Slavery doctrines on the occasion of your adjourned meeting at this place

With sentiments of esteem and respect we remain yours etc

Signed By 56 names

Dated WARSAW March 20th 1839

Whereupon Brethren Kirby Eelles & Chittenden were appointed a committee to prepare resolutions for the action of
association in relation to the foregoing communication

The committee retired & Brother Morris was chosen Clerk
pro. tem   On motion the Church at Denmark was received in
fellowship with the association on condition they assent to
the Constitution and articles of faith by notifying the Clerk
Clk. notified April 15, 1840   Rev. Asa Turner Pastor and
Oliver Brooks as Delegate appeared and took their seats
from the Church in Denmark Iowa Territory. The Committee on business next presented a communication from
Rev. Guy C. Sampson which was taken up and read and
referred to a committee of three viz. Brethren Turner Hau-
ley & Hitchcock

B. F. MORRIS   *Clerk pro tem*

The Committee on the communication of the Citizens of Warsaw now returned and submitted their report which was accepted and after discussion & amendment was adopted as follows.

WHEREAS at a meeting of the congregational association held at Griggsville Nov. 3rd 1838
It was voted that Rev. Mr. Kirby of Fairfield be requested to preach on the subject of slavery at the next meeting of the Association and WHEREAS a communication has been received from C. A. Warren and 55 others citizens of Warsaw and its vicinity requesting us to abstain from the preaching or discussion of anti Slavery doctrines on the occasion of our Semi Annual meeting Therefore

Resolved

That the Association adopted the resolution referd to from a sense of duty to God and man and can see no sufficient reason to lead them to change their views and furthermore that if they once adopted the principle of concenting [*sic*] to renounce their own principles and inalienable rights out of regard to the feelings of others however respectfully expressed they would frequently have occasion to turn aside from the path of duty or to relinquish those rights Therefore

Resolvd

That we will maintain the privilege of expressing our opinions and will exercise our inalienable rights whenever and wherever in our opinion the case of truth can be promoted

Resolvd, That Brethren Turner and Eelles be a committee to wait on W. H. Roswelt   R. L. Robertson   A. Monroe E. F. Chittenden   L. W. Brown signers of the request and Trustees of the Town of Warsaw and inquire of them if we may expect protection in the exercise of civil rights in this place and in case such protection cannot be enjoyed your committee recommend an adjournment to some place where the association can prosecute its business unmolested

Brother Lucius Parish presented a certificate of appoint-

ment from St Marys Church to attend the association and
took his seat

Brother Reed resigned his seat as Moderator & Brother
Kirby was chosen in his place

Committee on the communication of Brother Sampson
presented their report which was adopted
Wherefore

Resolved, That in consequence of his plea of ignorance of
the Constitution of this body at the time of his reception
that the papers of Rev. Guy C. Sampson be returned to him
and that he be considered as no longer a member of the Congregational Association of Illinois

Committee appointed to wait on the Trustees of the Town
of Warsaw returned with the following communication
To the Congregational association of Ill

We the subscribers Trustees of the Town of Warsaw
cannot promise any protection to said Association from any
disturbance made by the Citizens but feel warranted in saying that there will be no disturbance if the subject of Anti
Slavery is not touched[27]

A MONROE

SAML. W. BROWN

R. L. ROBERTSON

E. F. CHITTENDEN

[27] Excitement over the slavery issue was already high, and conflict between the
two parties had broken out. In 1836 a group in Quincy, Illinois, decided to hold an
antislavery meeting:

"It was noised abroad, and caused a great ferment in the city and country, so
that threats were made that no such meeting should be held. As the appointed day
approached the excitement increased and it became evident that a collision was im-
pending. The place selected was the Congregational Church. Under the raised
platform alluded to elsewhere, was placed such weapons of offense and defence as
were available, shotguns, clubs, hoop poles, etc. The speakers were Rev. Ezra
Fisher of the Baptist Church, Rev. Asa Turner being absent.

"Soon after the speaking began the mob moved up and commenced an assault,
throwing pieces of brick and stone through the windows.

"Under the lead of Joseph T. Holmes who was both deacon and magistrate, the
church arsenal was emptied and an advance movement made on the attacking party.
So vigorous was this assault, and so lively the use of clubs and hoop poles, that the

Articles of the Church at Round prairie receivd and placd on file

Articles of faith of the Church at Denmark receivd and fild

On motion *Resolved*, That Brother Reed be a Delegate to the General assembly of the Presbyterian Church in the United States or its next meeting at Philadelphia

Recess till 8 oclock to meet at Mr. Newburys room

Met pursuant to appointment. On motion *Resolved*, That the Moderator and Clerk be a standing committee to give the necessary certificates to ministers travelling beyond the bounds of the Association.

---

valiant champions of slavery, after two or three had been felled to the earth, ignominiously fled . . . ." (Thomas Pope, "Historical Sketches of the First Half-Century of the First Congregational Church of Quincy, Illinois, Organized December 4, 1830" [unpublished MS in Chicago Theological Seminary Library (1898)], pp. 20–22).

The meeting of the association at Warsaw at this time (April 18, 1839) followed a time of excitement over the slavery issue which cost Rev. Julius A. Reed his pastorate—perhaps because it was known that the antislavery speech was scheduled for the next meeting of the association (it had been decided at the meeting at Griggsville, November 3, 1838, to have such a speech on the program). Rev. A. Hale wrote the society regarding the troubles in Warsaw, under date of February, 1839:

"Since writing the enclosed I have received a letter from Rev. Julius A. Reed, Warsaw. His letter is dated at Jacksonville. He has finished his labors at Warsaw. . . . . He writes as follows, viz, 'one of our members has married a slaveholder—he happens to be proprietor of our meeting house, which he will not permit us to occupy unless we (the church is chiefly antislavery) will promise not to agitate the subject of slavery 'any where' which as I give no pledges, I cannot do. . . . . The Church tried to rent a room, but without success as Warsaw is literally filled.'

"On the subject of the member with a slaveholding wife etc. etc., I have no remarks to make—the works bear testimony for themselves. I have been acquainted with Rev. Reed for years & never knew before that he was at all leaning toward anti slavery principles. He says he has never introduced the subject into the pulpit at Warsaw, & it is very doubtful whether he even would have done it—his crime is that he (& the church more especially) would not promise not to 'agitate' the subject 'any where'—verily we are living in an age when great calmness is deemed necessary on all subjects which have any direct relation to morals & religion!—If the spirit of calmness & fear of innovations & agitation drives Rev. Reed from the pulpit in Warsaw I know not what would become of most of his brethren in this state were they called to that place, as he is one of the most retiring, modest men we have." (Rev. Julius A. Reed had organized the Warsaw church in 1836).

Resolved, That association recommend to the patronage of the churches within our bounds the *Connecticut Observer* & *Christian Journal*.[28]

On motion *Resolved*, That Brethren Kirby & Morris be a Committee to correspond with the Rock River Association.

Resolved, That Brother Turner be associated with the committee of Rock River association in reference to a religious periodical to be printed in this state.

On motion the Clerk was directed to inform the Body from whence Brother Sampson came of the action of the Association in his case. . . . .

April 19th.—. . . .

Voted that the doings of this meeting be published in the Quincy papers

Resolved, That the next annual meeting be holden at Quincy.

Association now proceeded to hear a brief report of the state of religion in the several Churches here represented. . . . .

WILLIAM KIRBY   *Mod*

JNO B. CHITTENDEN   *Clerk*

1839
Nov. 7

The Congregational association of Illinois held its fourth annual meeting in the Congregational meeting house, in Quincy Nov. 7, 1839.

C. A. Warren was chosen Moderator.—Richd. Eells Clerk pro. tem.—. . . . .

---

[28] This journal began publication in 1825 as the *Connecticut Observer* at Hartford, Connecticut, under the editorship of Rev. Horace Hooker. It was the organ of the Domestic Missionary Society of Connecticut and gave much attention to revivals and missions. It was extremely critical of Episcopalians, Catholics, Unitarians, and Universalists, but friendly toward Presbyterians.

Present from the church in Quincy Rufus Brown.—William Keyes, E. B. Kimball, Richd. Eells—delegates—

Church in Jacksonville	A. M. Pearson
Church in Warsaw	C. A. Warren
Church in Payson	Abner Perry

Church at Mission Institute No. II, N. A. Hunt—delegates who after giving satisfactory evidence of their appointment took their seats.

On motion Moses Hunter and William Beardsley Bishop & Br. Herrick, from Mission Institute No. 4 were invited to set as corresponding members

On motion *Resolved*, That a Committee of three be appointed to prepare and bring forward business before the Association—Committee. R. M. Pearson   R. Eells and Revd. Wm. Beardsley— . . . .

Nov 8th. . . . .

A. L. Pennoyer, Bishop and I. A. Collins delegate from the Church in Griggsville

B. F. Morris—Bishop of the Churches in Carthage & Warsaw

William Carter. Bishop of the Presbyterian Chs. in Pittsfield & Atlas—

William Kirby, Bishop and Danl. Bradley—delegate—appeared and—the delegates having presented satisfactory testimonials of their appointment—took their seats.

A communication from Jno. B. Chittenden resigning his office as stated clerk was then read

On motion *Resolved*, That Brother Chittenden's resignation be accepted

On motion *Resolved*, That Brother William Kirby be appointed Stated Clerk of the association

On motion *Resolved*, That the Association tender to Brother Chittenden their cordial thanks, for the faithful and efficient manner in which he has discharged the duties of Stated Clerk—

Richard Eells having resigned his seat in the business Committee, and his resignation having been accepted Revd. Wm. Carter was appointed in his stead.

On motion Moses Hunter, William Kirby and Rufus Brown were appointed a committee to report, on the subject of slavery

The Committee on business reported as follows—

1. Opportunity given for members to propose cases for consultation and advice

2. Report of the State of the Churches—Report accepted.

On motion *Resolved*, That a committee of three be appointed to report on certain difficulties in churches—Brother Carter, Morris, & Collins—Committee.

On motion a recess till 2 o'clock P.M.

After recess, the Moderator being absent Brother R. Brown was called to the chair

Br. Thomas Bray from the church in Mendon appeared with satisfactory testimonials of his appointment and took his seat.

By request the minutes of the proceedings of the semi annual meeting held at Warsaw were read. Moderator resumed his seat

The committee on Church—difficulties reported—which report was accepted and after amendment was adopted and is as follows

Whereas instances have occurred in which individuals, who have received letters of dismission and recommendation from the churches with which they have been connected, have supposed that they were thereby released from their covenant obligations without their uniting with another church.—

Therefore *Resolved*, That it is the solimn and deliberate judgment of the Association, that the selection of church-membership, is not at all affected by a letter of dismission and recommendation untill the individual has been received by some other church; and that it be recommended to churches in our connection to exercise the same watchfulness and discipline over such members, as though no letter had been granted—

That it is the duty of all Christians changing their location to form a speedy connection with some branch of the church in the vicinity and that it be recommended to our churches to use all proper influence to induce such persons to form that connection and that the privilege of occasional communion, in our Church, be limited to a period of one year, except when special reasons exist for extending it

Brother I. T. Holmes from the church in Quincy appeared and took his seat

Thomas Cole Bishop of the Congregational Church in Payson appeared and took his seat.

On motion *Resolved*, That in the opinion of this association no church is justified, in receiving any member, who is not fully established in the belief of the fundamental doctrines of the Gospel.

Recess till after religious service in the evening After recess association met and in the absence of the moderator, Brother Thomas Cole was called to the chair,

Br. Wm. A. Word from Quincy Church appeared and took his seat—

On motion, Brother Kirby, Morris and Pearson were appointed a committee to take minutes and prepare a narrative of the state of religion in the churches—the report of which was made the order of the day for tomorrow morning— Moderator appeared and resumed his seat

Association having been informed by Br. Cole that a Committee of three—of which he himself was one—had been appointed by the Synod of Illinois, to confer with this body on the subject of Christian Union—

On motion *Resolved*, That Brethren Kirby, Carter &

Pennoyer be a committee to confer with the above named Committee

On motion adjourned till tomorrow at 9 o'clock A.M. Prayer by Brother Cole—

Sat. Morn. Met according to adjournment Prayer by Br. Carter—Reports—of the state of religion in the churches Recess till 2 o'clock P.M.

After recess, the Moderator being absent—Br. Morris was called to the chair.

The Church at Mission Institute No. II.—with their Pastor Dr. Nelson unitedly requested a dissolution of the Pastoral relation between them, assigning their reasons for such request—(See letter on file Dated Nov. 9)

On motion *Resolved*, That the Pastoral relation between Brother Nelson & said Church—be dissolved

Moderator resumed his Seat—

The Committee on the subject of Slavery presented their report—which was accepted, and after a protracted & interesting discussion, the vote to accept was reconsidered & the whole recommitted with instructions to report at the next regular meeting—committee Brethren Cole & Kirby

On motion Brother Abner Perry was excused from further attendance

On motion *Resolved*, That the next Semi annual meeting be held at Payson, Adams Co.

On motion Adjourned till tomorrow evening after service Met according to adjournment

By request of Br. Kirby, the Committee on the narrative of the state of religion, were instructed to prepare and publish the same without submitting it to the inspection of the Association

On Motion Brother Pennoyer was excused from further attendance.

On motion *Resolved*, That the stated clerk make out an abstract of the proceedings of the association for publication and forward the same to the N.Y. Evangelist, Connecticut observer & N.Y. Congregationalist—and to the papers published in Quincy

On motion Adjourned to meet at Payson on the third Thursday in April at 9 o'clock A.M. . . . .

C. A. WARREN *Moderator*

RICHARD EELLS, *Clerk, pro. tem.*

Faithfully entered—

Attest WILLIAM KIRBY   *Stated Clerk—*

1840

April 16.—The Congregational Association of Illinois held its fourth Semi-Annual meeting at Payson April 16th 1840, at 9 o'clock A.M.—A. L. Pennoyer was called to the chair—in the absence of the Moderator— . . . . The Association was organized by the appointment of Br. Thomas Cole Moderator and A. L. Pennoyer Clerk pro. tem.

Present from Cong. Ch. at Payson Thos. Cole Minister. David Prince, Fielding delegate Ch. at Griggsville A. L. Pennoyer Minister George Pratt Delegate and Saml. Reynolds

Ch. At. Mendon, William Kirby

Ch. at Jacksonville   E. C. Sturtevant

"   "   "   I. H. Bancroft

" Round Prairie   A. Atkins

The above delegates presented Satisfactory testimonials of their appointment and took their seats.

. . . . Voted to have a recess till half past one P.M.

Association met after recess

Rev. Reuben Gaylord appeared and took his seat Brethren Kirby, Reuben Gaylord & E. C. Sturtevant were appointed a Committee to prepare a docket of business

The Cong. Church of Danville Des Moines Co. Iowa Territory having given it assent to the constitution requested to

be admitted as a member of the association—and on motion
—their request was granted

Richard Ells [Eells]—M.D. a delegate from Quincy Church
appeared and having given satisfactory evidence of his appointment took his seat

Isaih Platt a delegate from the Church at Mendon appeared and having given satisfactory evidence of his appointment took his seat.

Brother A. L. Pennoyer requested to be excused from serving as clerk on act. of ill health and his request was granted—
Br. Reuben Gaylord was appointed in his place.

The Committee appointed to prepare a docket reported in
part & their report was accepted—

The Committee appointed to confer with a committee appointed by Synod Presbyterian—on the subject of Christian
Union—reported progress and on motin—Voted to Continue
the Committee with instructions to the Stated Clerk to inform the Chairman of the Committee of Synods of their appointment

Voted to make the report on the state of the churches—the
order of the day for tomorrow morning

A question having arisen with reference to the admission
of interested persons as witnesses in cases of discipline—and
having been discussed at some length—Brethren Eells &
Kirby were appointed a Committee to draft a paper expressive of the views of the association on the subject—

Adjourned to meet at 8 oclock tomorrow morning— . . . .

Friday

. . . . Brethren Rufus Brown and P. H. Vandoren—delegates from Quincy Church arrived and having presented
satisfactory testimonials of their appointment took their
seats.

On motion Brethren Kirby and Sturtevant were appointed a Committee to draft resolutions—in relation to the practice of cutting timber from non resident lands.

On Motion Brethren Pennoyer and Platt were appointed a Committee to take notes of the reports on the State of the Churches & prepare a narrative

Association then proceeded to hear the reports of the churches

Brother Porter—a member of the Presbytery of Schuyler being present—was invited to sit as corresponding member

Brethren Sturtevant and Bancroft asked leave of absence & gave their reasons for so doing and on motion their request was granted

Voted to have a recess till 2 oclock P.M.

After recess Association resumed business—On motion *Resolved*, That in the opinion of this association, no member of the church is at liberty to absent himself from the table of the Lord for any grievance, real or supposed,—and that any individual by so doing subjects himself to the discipline of the church.

The Committee appointed in relation to the practice of cutting timber on non resident lands reported & their report was accepted and adopted and is as follows.

As the practice of cutting timber without the owners consent from nonresidents' lands is extensively prevalent, in open violation of the law of God—thereby dishonoring God impairing the moral sense of Communities and hindering the progress of the Gospel

Therefore *Resolved*, That in the opinion of this association such a practice is not only inexcusable—but as truly sinful as any other act of trespass

Resolved, That the Churches in connection with this body be earnestly entreated to call offenders in this respect to an account and discipline them as they would for any other gross immorality

The Committee appointed at the last meeting on the sub-

ject of slavery reported a preamble and resolutions & on
motion their report was accepted

The question then being on the adoption of the report

The preamble and resolutions were taken up separately &
adopted—

On motion the preamble and resolutions were adopted as
a whole, and are as follows—

Whereas slavery is a great moral as well as political evil,
not only depriving 3,000,000 of people of their political rights
—but denying to them the attributes of humanity—of moral
beings, whose obligations to Jehovah as their supreme ruler
are paramount to all others—as it denies to them the right
to read the word of God that they may serve & worship him
intelligently—as it compels them to promiscuous concubi-
nage in as much as it denies to them the sacred right of marriage makes female innocence a prey to unbridled lust.—
prohibits parents from training up their own offspring—
multiplies temptations to dishonest & fraud and every vice—
destroys the power of every motive to intellectual & moral
improvement—& makes the Gospel of none effect

Furthermore, as it exerts a deliterious influence upon
Masters themselves—habituating them to the exercise of
insolence and tyranny—inviting to lust blunting the moral
sense—rendering the mind callous to truth and motives to
purity & holiness—thus reducing society to a state of barbar-
ism

And whereas Slavery is directly opposed to the principles
of our free institutions and calculated to submit them—as it
is demonstrably certain that if Slavery is not speedily
abolished our liberties will fall a sacrifice

And inasmuch as the church is the light of the world—as
her influence must be felt in giving tone to public sentiment—
in raising or lowering the standard of morality and religion—
as institutions must stand which receive her sanction or meet

with no rebuke—as those *must* fall against which her power is arrayed,—as communities will advance in virtue and religion no faster than her friends advance,—but rather fall behind.

Therefore as Christians and messengers of the churches, we feel bound to express our utter abhorrence of slavery as a System and in all its parts.—Slavery as it is Sanctioned by law & practice—slavery in its true and legitimate import wherever it is found, and to avow our determination to maintain an uncompromising hostility to it, till it shall be banished from our country and from the world.

Therefore *Resolved*, That in our opinion slave holders have been kept in countenance by the support which the free states and the church have given to the System, and that it is our first duty to labor to effect a resolution in the free states & the Church—both in regard to oppressive laws & the existing prejudice, against the colored race

2. That the subject of Slavery is like any other question of morals a proper subject to be introduced into the pulpit, with a frequency commensurate with its importance

3. That we will rely upon the use of such means as kindness & love, both to the master and slave dictate accompanied by the blessing of God—to effect its removal

4. That we will not knowingly admit slaveholders to our pulpits or Communion tables . . . .

1840
April 18

Brother Saml. H. Fletcher—a delegate from the Carthage Church appeared and presented satisfactory testimonials of his appointment and took his seat

Brother Reynolds asked leave of absence and gave his reasons for so doing—and his request was granted

A resolution on receiving contributions from Slaveholders in aid of the benevolent operations of the day—was after some discussion laid on the table

The Committee appointed to draft resolutions on the admission of interested persons as witnesses in cases of discipline reported & their report was accepted and adopted and is as follows—

Resolved, That it is the duty of any person aggrieved with a brother in the church, to follow the rule laid down in the 18th chap. of Math.—till the case is fully presented to the church. and when thus presented the whole duty of prosecuting the case further devolves on the church.

Resolved, That any person following the rule above referred to—should not be held as a prosecutor but complainant before the church.

Resolved, That as the Scriptures are silent in regard to the rules to be followed in admitting or rejecting testimony on account of interest or consanguinity—these rules must be determined by the common sense and enlightened dictates of the human mind.

On motion *Resolved*, That the next meeting be held at Jacksonville.

Brother Charles Burnham having requested a renewal of his license to preach the Gospel—On motion his request was granted.

On motion voted that the constitution be so amended as to fix the time of the annual meeting upon the first thursday in October.

The delegates from the Quincy church asked to be excused from further attendance and gave their reasons for so doing—and on motion their request was granted.

On motion *Resolved*, That an abstract of our doings be published in the Quincy Whig and the New York Evangelist

Recess till after religious services in the Afternoon.

After recess resumed business—The Committee appointed to take notes & prepare a narrative of the state of religion reported and their report was accepted, and still left in the hands of the Committee

. . . .

THOMAS COLE *Moderator*

REUBEN GAYLORD *Clerk pro tem*

Faithfully entered

Attest WILLIAM KIRBY *Stated Clerk*

At a special meeting of the Congregation Association of Illinois held at Quincy July 9th 1840 at two o'clock P.M. in the Congregational meeting house, Rev. Wm. Kirby was called to the chair in the absence of the moderator, & the meeting opened with prayer. Br. I. T. Holmes was appointed Clerk pro. tem. The Moderator then appeared and took his seat. The following delegates then appeared with satisfactory testimonials of their appointment and took their seats.

From the church at Payson, Thomas Cole, Bishop and M. Gay. delegate

" " Quincy Rufus Brown, & I. H. Ho. mes, Delegates

" " Mendon William Kirby, Bhp. & Henry Baldwin & Edw. H. Fowler

" " Mission Institute No. 1 Br. Fithian, Del.

Rev. William Beardsley presented a letter of dismission and recommendation from the Genusee Association of New York—accompanied by a request to be received as a member of the association

On motion he was unanimously received

The Special object for which the Association had been called together was then stated to be a request in behalf of Br. Daniel Gavin—a missionary among the Sioux, a licentiate of the Evangelical Society of Missions at Lausanne Switzerland,—who now presented himself as a candidate for ordination

On motion Rev. A. Hunter—of Presbytery of Angelica N.Y.—D. Nelson of Presby of Schuyler, Horatio Foote—of Presy. of Champlain N.Y. and Br. Apthorp of Cong. Ass. of Mass. were invited to sit as corresponding members.

On motion the credentials of Br. Gavin were presented and read which on motion were be declared to be satisfactory and the application for ordination received

On motion a Committee was appointed to assign parts in the examination—consisting of Bhps. Foote & Kirby which reported & their report was accepted and adopted and is as follows

On experimental piety & motives for entering the ministry —Bro Apthorp

Natural Theology—Being Attributes of God   Br. Hunter

Evidences of Christianity   Br. Cole

Doctrines, Trinity Moral Govt. purposes of God ⎫ Br. Beardsley

Depravity Atonement— ⎭

Conditions of Salvation, Regeneration Perseverance ⎫ Br. Kirby

Resurrection, Judgment, Final Destiny of Men ⎭

Church History   Br. Nelson

Church Govt. and ordinances   H. Foote

The Moderator was then excused and Br. Beardsley called to the chair

The ass. then proceeded to the examination of Br. Gavin— till its close. Literature & Science having been omitted on act. of the fulness of the testimony of his credentials in this respect

On motion his examination was unanimously sustained and the ordination services appointed for the evening

The Moderator and Clerk were appointed a committee to

assign parts in the ordination service—[see ordination services above].

. . . .

Met at half past seven and proceeded to the ordination of Br. Gavin.

After the close of the services, the Association came to order—the minutes were read and approved. . . . . .

C. A. WARREN   *Moderator*

I. T. HOLMES,   *Clerk pro tem.*

Faithfully entered   attest   WILLIAM KIRBY   *Stated Clerk*

October 1st, 1840. 9 o'clock A.M.

The fifth Annual Meeting of the Congregational Association of Illinois met at Jacksonville on the first Thursday of October A.D. 1840, being the first day of said month.

Association was called to order by Bro. Kirby, and on his motion Bro. Snow was called to the chair in the absence of the last moderator. Present the following ministers and delegates from Churches, to wit:

William Kirby, Bishop ⎫ Mendon Adams
Charles Fisk, Delegate ⎭   County

Willard Keyes Delegate ⎫ Quincy Adams
Henry H. Snow do. ⎭   County

Benj'n. Beckford Delegate ⎫ Griggsville
Aaron Tyler   do. ⎭ Pike County

Asahel Hubbard, Delegate, Round Prairie
            Hancock County.

The said Delegates having presented their certificates of appointment took their seats as members of the association.

The Throne of Grace having been addressed, proceeded to the choice of a moderator; whereupon Bro. William Kirby was duly elected to that office.

On motion

Henry H. Snow was chosen temporary Clerk

Adjourned till 2 oclock P.M. Concluded with prayer.

2 o'clock P.M. . . . .

There being no business before the association, and but few members present, owing to the state of the weather, ...

Friday morning, October 2d. 1840. . . . .

Minutes of last meeting were read and approved. Bro. Robert Blake, Bishop of the Congregational Church of Woodburn, Macoupin County appeared and took his seat.

October 2d. 1840

The following Delegates from Churches appeared and having produced satisfactory evidence of their appointment took their seats, to wit:

> Abner Perry, Payson, Adams County
>
> E. S. Mears ⎫
> Joseph Shaw ⎬ Jacksonville, Morgan County
> Elihu Wolcott ⎭

On motion of Bro. Keyes, Voted that a committee of three be appointed by the Moderator to prepare a Docket of business for the action of the association.

Br. Blake, Keyes, & Mears, were appointed said Committee The committee to prepare a Dockett of business, reported in part, the following items of business, to wit:

Reports of the State of the Churches, applications for advice, applications for License and ordination; which report was accepted.

On motion of Bro. Keyes

Voted that a Committee be appointed by the chair to take minutes of the Reports of the state of the churches, and prepare a narrative of the state of religion: Br. Blake, Wolcott, & Snow were appointed said committee.

The association then proceeded to hear Reports of the state of the churches.

Rev. William T. Allen of the Congregational association of

Ohio being present, was invited to take a seat as a corresponding member.

Voted to take a recess till 2 o'clock P.M.

Friday 2 o'clock P.M.

Association came to order, and resumed and concluded the hearing of Reports of the State of the Churches.

Rev. Luke Lyons of the Presbytery of Illinois being present, was invited to sit as a corresponding member.

Br. Timothy Chamberlain and E. Carter, Delegates from the Church at Jacksonville, appeared and having presented evidence of their appointment took their seats.

Adjourned till 10 o'clock tomorrow morning. . . . .

October 3d, 1840
Saturday Morning October 3d, 1840. . . . . .

Br. William Carter, Bishop of the Presbyterian Church at Pittsfield Pike County, and Reuben Gaylord Bishop of the Cong. Church at Danville Iowa Territory, appeard and took their seats. And being called upon, each gave a report of the State of Religion in their respective churches.

Rev. J. M. Sturtevant of the Presbytery of Illinois being present was invited to take a seat as a corresponding member.

Br. M. M. Reed, Delegate of the Church at Jacksonville and Nathan Burton Delegate of the Church at Round Prairie appeared and having given satisfactory evidence of their appointment, took their seats

A request was presented from Br. Asa Turner and Reuben Gaylord asking for a dismission from this Association, and letters of recommendation, in case it is thought expedient to form an association in Iowa Territory, which request was granted.

Bro. Turner having solicited the appointment of Delegates to attend the formation of an association in Iowa Territory,

Voted to send three Ministers, and one Delegate from each Church represented in the present meeting: Whereupon the following Br. were chosen to wit:

William Kirby ⎫
William Carter ⎬ Ministers
B. F. Morris ⎭

H. H. Snow, Quincy ⎫
Abner Perry, Payson ⎪
Charles Fisk, Mendon ⎪
Nathan Burton, Round Prairie ⎬ Delegates
Joseph Shaw Jacksonville ⎪
Aaron Tyler Griggsville ⎭

A letter was read from Bro. Charles Burnham a Licentiate requesting to be transferred from the watch and care of this association, to the association about to be formed in Iowa Territory; which request was granted and his relation transferred accordingly.

Voted to take a recess till 2 o'clock P.M.

2 o'clock P.M. Association came to order,

Bro. T. M. Post a Delegate from the Church at Jacksonville appeared and having produced evidence of his appointment took his seat.

Bro. Thomas Cole, Bishop of the Church at Payson appeared and took his seat.

Br. Truman M. Post and I. B. Turner appeared before the association and presented a paper containing some views of Christian doctrine and the right to preach the gospel, and also a request for licence. After hearing further statements from the brethren, together with a request that the paper presented by them be spread upon the records of the association, it was

voted that the request for licensure be received, and that the paper presented, as modified by them be entered on the minutes. And that a committee be appointed to draw up an expression of the views of the association on the points contained in the said paper; Br. Wolcott and Burton were appointed said committee

On motion

The following brethren were appointed a committee to assign the parts in the examination of the candidates for licensure to wit Br. Carter and Blake.

The said committee made a report assigning the parts as follows to wit:

On Christian character,	Bro. Blake
Natural Theology	" Kirby
Evidence of revealed religion	" Cole
Doctrines of the Bible	" Sturtevant
Church Ordinances	" Lyons
Ecclesiastical History	" Gaylord

The association then proceeded to the examination of candidates for licensure; and having made some progress therein, ...

After recess the association came to order, and resumed and concluded the examination of candidates for licensure: Whereupon on motion of Br. Carter

Voted that the examination of Br. Post and Turner be sustained.

On Motion of Bro. Reed

Voted that the next semi-annual meeting of the association be held at Carthage in Hancock County.

Br. Gaylord and Burton asked and obtained leave of absence during the remainder of this meeting.

On motion of Bro. Carter, voted that the Third Article of the Constitution be so amended as to read "All those Churches, Associations and Ministers, ordained or licentiate, who adopt this Constitution and articles of faith annexed, may belong to this association.

On motion of Bro. Carter, voted that all licentiates of this association be considered as members in full. . . . .

Monday morning October 5th, 1840 . . . .

Bro. Blake presented the following Resolution to wit:

Resolved, That, being convinced of the need of a Religious Newspaper in this State as an organ of communication on local subjects, and understanding the "Taper," (?) edited by Rev. Thomas Lippincott to be established upon liberal principles, we recommend it to the patronage of the christian public, and pledge ourselves to use our efforts to procure subscribers for it; which was adopted unanimously.

Bro. Beckford obtained leave of absence

The paper presented on Saturday by Br. Post and Turner and which was voted to be spread upon the records is as follows to wit:

It is not with a view of obtaining a right to preach the gospel that we present ourselves to this association for examination. Such a natural right as well as that of administering the ordinances of the Christian religion, being, in our present opinion, in the gift of no man or body of men to bestow or withhold, but derived to all men from the Great Bishop in Heaven. Nevertheless, we do not deem it expedient in the present state of the Christian community to exercise that right, but as peculiar intellectual and moral qualifications are requisite to the usefulness of the public religious teacher, and as consultation and examination previous to the assumption of the sacred office, seem requisite, in order to secure such qualifications in the clerical body, we think a regard to the purity and order and edification of the church, requires in all ordinary cases, the solicitation of such previous examination and counsel. We therefore as Christian brethren, wishing to consult for the order and unity of the Christian Church on earth, as well as to enlarge the sphere of our own usefulness in relation to the salvation of men, request of this association as embracing men of known and approved intelligence and piety, consultation and advice as it regards our attempting to preach the gospel.

October 5th, 1840

The committee appointed to draw up an expression of the views of the association on the points contained in the foregoing paper, made a report which was accepted and adopted, and is as follows to wit:

In spreading this paper on their minutes, the association has been actuated by a desire to gratify the wishes of the brethren presenting it, and not by any apprehension that in the proceeding of examining these brethren, the association has in any respect deviated either from its own usages or from the established principles of Congregational Churches. The only ideas which have ever been conveyed by the word LICENCE as applied to the introduction of candidates for the ministry into Congregational Churches, are two. First a recommendation of the brethren licensed, as, in the judgment of the body licensing, qualified to teach the religion of the Bible; and 2nd a pledge, expressed or implied of the churches represented in the licensing body, not to receive religious teachers who have not been so recommended by some competent ecclesiastical body,

For a statement of the principles of Congregationalism on this point see Bacon's Church Manual pp. 186–9. If an intelligent christian man should find himself cast among pagans with the Bible in his hands, and without any means of intercourse with evangelical countries; and if after a few months residence there he should find himself sufficiently acquainted with the language of those around him, to communicate to some among them in the way of solitary and personal instruction a knowledge of the gospel and if the use of the faculty of teaching should gradually qualify him for the work of public speaking—to him in such circumstances, no ordination, no license, no examination or approval would be necessary as a preliminary to his undertaking the employment of a public preacher of the christian religion.

He would be just as really authorized to proclaim to those

dying sinners the doctrines and invitations of the gospel, praying them in Christs stead "be ye reconciled to God," as if he had been consecrated to that work by the hands of all the prelates and presbyterians in Christendom. And if any of those heathen repenting under his labors and converted to God, should say to him, "see here is water, what doth hinder me to be baptized," he would be authorized to reply, "If thou believest with all thine heart thou mayest." And without fearing any mans prohibition, he might baptize them at once unto the name of the Lord. When his converts had become sufficiently numerous and properly instructed, he might form them into a regular church, teaching them to hold communion not only in prayer & doctrine, but in the breaking of bread; and their eating bread and drinking wine in memory of Christ would be not only as valid, but as regular and orderly as the like ordinance in any church whatever.

In like manner at a proper time he might lead them to the choice of Bishops & Deacons; and the persons thus chosen might be ordained by prayer and the laying on of hands and would need no other consecration to their office. So other churches might be gathered by his labors; and in the course of years, he might find around him a sisterhood of churches rejoicing in the truth and walking in the fellowship of the gospel. All this would be "done decently and in order"; and these churches upon becoming acquainted with other communities of Christians, would have a right to be recognized as churches of Christ; nor would there be any occasion for the rebaptism of their members, or the reordination of their officers.

But from these principles does it follow that it would be orderly and right for any and every man in a Christian community to undertake of his own mere motion the work of a public minister of Jesus Christ. Is it "decent and in order" for him to decide without seeking anybody's advice or approbation, that he is called of God to the business of preaching, and to thrust himself upon the Christian public accordingly? Nay, would not such an unadvised and self confident intrusion into a work so difficult and responsible, prove the man to be exceedingly unfitted for that work? What is plainer than that in order to guard the churches against imposition, and to maintain the purity dignity and efficiency of the ministry, there must be some common understanding as to the manner in which candidates suitable for that work shall be introduced to the notice and confidence of the churches for the trial of their gifts. As to the persons by whom this ceremony (Baptism) was administered, I will say in one word, that this evidently was deemed a matter of little consequence. Paul thought that the ordinance of Baptism was among the least of his duties as a minister of the gospel (1. Cor. 1.14–17) I find nothing in the Bible and nothing in what I have seen of the earliest Christian writers, which implies that it was the peculiar duty or the peculiar honor of this or that officer to administer Baptism.

The Lords Supper was simply eating bread and drinking wine with prayer and thanksgiving in commemoration of the death of Christ. This ordinance seems to have been a part of the Services every Lords day. Where there were church officers then the Bishops presided over this, as over every other part of public worship. To preside over the church at the Lords table belongs to their office as obviously as to preside over the prayers of the church, or over the public reading and expounding of the scriptures, or over the debates of a church meeting for business. But when there were no officers, the organization of the church being, as at Corinth when Paul wrote his Epistles, not yet completed, there is no evidence that this commemoration of Christ was omitted any more than prayer or singing Id. pp. 58–9.

The subject of the duties of Licentiates having been somewhat discussed it was voted that the subject be postponed till the next annual meeting.

On motion voted that the time of the annual meeting be hereafter on the second Thursday of October, and the semi-annual meeting on the second Thursday of April in each year.

The office of Stated Clerk having become vacant by electing Bro. Kirby Moderator,

Henry H. Snow was chosen Stated Clerk of the association.

Voted that the Moderator and Stated Clerk be a committee to publish the proceedings of the present meeting.

Adjourned sine die

(Signed) WILLIAM KIRBY
Moderator

H. H. SNOW

Temporary Clerk. I certify that the foregoing is correctly entered from the minutes of the last annual meeting.

Attest H. H. SNOW *Stated Clerk*

April 8th. 1841

At a semi Annual meeting of the association of Illinois convened at Carthage in Hancock Co. on the second Thursday of April A.D. 1841 being the 8th day of said month: The association was called to order by the Moderator Bro. William Kirby. . . . .

. . . .

Present the following Bishops and Delegates from churches . . . .

On motion

Resolved, That some minister be appointed to preach a discourse on Congregationalism at our next stated meeting: To present its origin, History and general features. Bro. Carter of Pittsfield was appointed to that duty.[29]

. . . .

Adjourned till 8 o'clock tomorrow morning. . . . .

[29] This is an indication of the growing self-consciousness of western Congregationalism.

CHAPTER VII

The Autobiography of Flavel Bascom
1833-40

INTRODUCTION

A STUDY of population movement into early Illinois shows that by 1830 settlement had pushed northward from the Ohio River to about the center of the state. This population had come large-ly from the southern states, but especially from Virginia, North Carolina, and Kentucky. By 1840 the situation had largely changed. Pop-ulation now covered the entire northern strip of the state.[1] In contrast with the population in the southern portion of the state, the people who were fill-ing up the northern sections were largely from the North, with the New Eng-land element predominating. The chief point of entry for these New Eng-land people was the newly established town of Chicago, and settlement was soon spreading farther and farther out from the southwest end of Lake Michigan in a great fan-shaped delta, until it reached the population push-ing up from the Mississippi and the South. The one northern community settled before 1830 was the mining center at Galena[2] in the extreme north-western section of the state. Here a typical bonanza town had grown up before the Indians had left the territory, and it was to this community that Aratus Kent came as a missionary in 1829, probably the first settled Protestant minister in northern Illinois.[3]

The letters of the missionaries of the American Home Missionary Society located in northern Illinois after 1829 contain much information regarding the rapid flow of population into this region. The missionary at Joliet, writing in 1836, states that the year previous Joliet had but thirteen buildings, but within the year the number had grown to from fifty to sixty (J. H. Prentiss to M. Badger, October 1, 1836 [A.H.M.S.

---

[1] See population maps for 1820, 1830, and 1840 in T. C. Pease, *Centennial History of Illinois*, Vol. II: *The Frontier State, 1818-1848* (Chicago: McClurg & Co., 1922), pp. 4, 174, 382.

[2] The early importance of Galena was due to the lead deposits located in the vicinity. It was reported that at this period 5,000,000 pounds of lead were annually mined and the value of the shipments amounted to $200,000. In this region a population of perhaps ten thousand was living in 1828-29.

[3] See Gordon A. Riegler, "Aratus Kent, First Prebyterian Minister in Northern Illinois," *Journal of the Presbyterian Historical Society*, XIII (1928-29), 363-80.

Correspondence]), and within the next year the population had doubled. In 1834 the missionary at Ottawa writes that they cannot get lumber at Ottawa to carry on their building operations.[4] Horatio Newhall, writing to missionary headquarters in 1836, stated that in that year there were twenty thousand inhabitants from the Rock River to the Prairie du Chien including both sides of the Mississippi River and that immigrants were flocking in by the hundreds.[5] Within a year ten new villages had been laid out in lots in this district. The increase in the number of Methodists and Baptists in Illinois was particularly large during the decade from 1830 to 1840. In the former year the Methodists had, in round numbers, about six thousand communicants which had grown to thirty thousand in 1840; the Baptists increased in the same period from thirty-six hundred to more than twelve thousand.[6]

To some of the communities which were being settled in northern Illinois during these years there came a number of organized groups from New England or New York State which had moved west in a body. La Grange in Henry County was settled by a colony from New York and New England that had purchased twenty thousand acres of land.[7] In 1833 fifty-two settlers from Vermont, New Hampshire, and northern New York came to Sangamon County. Another group of settlers from Connecticut founded Rockwell in La Salle County. Weathersfield in Henry County was established by colonists from the town of the same name in Connecticut. In 1836 Galesburg was established by a New York colony, the town receiving its name from a Presbyterian minister George W. Gale, formerly of Adams, New York, who had been largely instrumental in the conversion of Charles G. Finney.[8] Some of the settlements were formed of emigrants already organized into churches, as was the case of Princeton, which was established by emigrants from Northampton, Massachusetts, who had organized a church before setting out for the West. A similar group from Genessee County, New York, settled Hadley, and in 1833 the town of Mendon was settled by New England Congregationalists and was the first Congregational organization actually effected within the state.

At the time of the settlement of northern Illinois the Plan of Union had been in force for nearly a generation and operated there, as everywhere

---

[4] W. H. Hazard to M. Badger, October 8, 1834 (A.H.M.S. Correspondence). Hazard in letters to A. Peters, December 29, 1834; March 12, 1835; September 28, 1836; Hazard to Badger, January 1839, mentions the rapid growth of population in the general region of northern Illinois (*ibid.*).

[5] A.H.M.S. Correspondence, March 7, 1836.   [6] Pease, *op. cit.*, pp. 414–15.

[7] *Ibid.*, pp. 178–79, quoting from the *Sangamo Journal*, June 9, 1837. Pease also states that in 1834 there was a society in Massachusetts called the Old Colony Brotherhood, which was formed to promote emigration to Illinois.

[8] G. F. Wright, *Charles Grandison Finney* (Boston: Houghton, Mifflin Co., 1893), pp. 24–25.

else, to the advantage of the Presbyterians. By 1830, however, a decided denominational consciousness was reawakening among Congregational-ists, which accounts for the formation of several distinctive Congregational churches from 1833 onward. In 1834 there were five Congregational churches in Illinois, and in that year steps were taken to form an associa-tion, the first association of Congregational churches in the Middle West.[9] The church at Quincy had been formed in 1829 as a Presbyterian church, but in 1833 it was reorganized on the Congregational plan, a large number of the first members having moved to other places. After 1836 the num-ber of Congregational churches in northern Illinois increased rapidly. A Plan of Union church was formed that year at Galesburg which later was transformed into a Congregational church, and the same year Knox Col-lege was incorporated. The Congregational church at Naperville was established in 1833 by Nathaniel C. Clark, who during the next several years was responsible for organizing thirty-seven churches in the Fox River Valley.[10]

The foundations of Presbyterianism in Illinois were largely laid by New England men. Illinois College, opened in 1830 at Jacksonville, was the fruit of a dream of a group of Yale Theological Seminary students, known as the "Yale Band," who had pledged themselves to give their lives to the advancement of education in the West.[11] The first Presbyterian minister in northern Illinois, Aratus Kent, had been a Congregational minister in Connecticut and was sent to Galena, Illinois, by the Connecticut Mission-ary Society. Lemuel Foster, who organized the first Presbyterian church at Bloomington, was also of Connecticut Congregational background.[12] Jeremiah Porter, who formed the first Presbyterian church in Chicago, as

[9] "Minutes of a Convention of the Congregational Churches of Illinois, November 28, 1834" (see chap. vi *supra*, pp. 56 ff.). The convention met at the home of Asa Turner at Quincy. The following churches were reported as having been organized in the state: Jacksonville, December 15, 1833, now has about 70 members; the Quincy church had been formed December 4, 1829, with 14 members; in November, 1833, it was reorganized on the Congregational plan; the church at Fairfield was organized in February, 1833, and now has 25 members with 7 to add next communion; the church at Griggsville was organized in the summer of 1834 with 12 members. The convention met the next year at Jacksonville in October. While, strictly speaking, the first Congregational Association in Illinois met November 3, 1836, at Fairfield, Adams County, as a matter of fact there had been three meet-ings previous to the Fairfield meeting (see MS "Minutes" for October 22, 1835 and April 22, 1836).

[10] Pease, *op. cit.*, p. 420.

[11] Charles H. Rammelkamp, *Illinois College: A Centennial History, 1828–1920* (New Haven: Yale University Press, 1928).

[12] See the "Journal of a Pioneer Missionary—the Rev. Lemuel Foster," ed. Matthew Spinka, in *Journal of the Illinois State Historical Society*, XXI (July, 1928), 183–99.

THE AUTOBIOGRAPHY OF

well as numerous other Presbyterian churches in the vicinity, was likewise of New England Congregational stock.

Flavel Bascom, a portion of whose autobiography is here for the first time published, graduated from Yale College in 1828 and in the summer of 1831 was licensed by the New Haven East Association. From 1831 to 1833 he was a tutor at Yale College, and in the latter year he resigned his tutorship to accept a commission from the American Home Missionary Society to preach the gospel in Illinois.

The complete autobiography consists of 278 manuscript pages and was prepared in 1875 while the author was the pastor at Ottawa, Illinois. The autobiography has a special value because it is based on a diary kept contemporaneous with the events described. The part here printed covers the years 1833–40.

CHAP. 6: PIONEER LIFE IN ILLINOIS

Early in my Theological course I had my attention directed to the claims of the West, as a field of Missionary labor. While I had been absent from New Haven, several of my College friends, having entered the Theological department, became particularly interested in Illinois as a field of labor. They sought information. They met frequently for consultation, discussion and prayer. They finally formed themselves into a society, which has since been called the "New Haven Band,"[13] pledging their coöperation in building up a Christian College in this state and in planting christian churches, and in promoting a true christian civilization. When I was informed what they were doing, the object enlisted my sympathies, and their plan commended itself to my

[13] M. K. Whittlesley (ed.), *In Commemoration of the Fiftieth Anniversary of the Organization of the General Congregational Association in Illinois* (Ottawa, Ill., 1894) (hereafter referred to as *Jubilee Papers*), gives the following members of this band together with their dates:

Theron Baldwin	1801–68		Mason Grosvenor	1800–86
J. F. Brooks	1801–88		Romulus Barnes	1800–1846
Elisha Jenney	1803–82		William Carter	1803–71
William Kirby	1805–51		Flavel Bascom	1804–90
Asa Turner	1799–1885	.	Albert Hale	1799–1891
J. M. Sturtevant	1805–86		Lucien Farnham	1799–1874

In 1830 Turner came to Quincy, and in 1833 Brooks was at Collinsville, Jenney at Alton, Kirby at Mendon, Carter at Pittsfield, Hale at Bethel and then at Springfield, Barnes at Clinton, Farnham at Lewiston and then at Princeton, and Bascom in Tazewell County.

judgment. After prayerful consideration, I was persuaded to cast in my lot with them, making it my life work to aid in educating and christianizing, the population of this new and growing State.

I felt a growing interest in the work I had chosen, during the years that I remained in New Haven, and never once wavered in my purpose and preference to occupy my Western field, although eligible openings at the East were from time to time brought before me. In the Spring of 1833 I resigned my Tutorship, and received a Commission from the A.H.M. Society, to preach the Gospel in Illinois, my location to be determined after I should reach the State and should have consultation with their Agent on the grounds.

On the 30th of April I was married to Ellen P. Cleaveland, the daughter of Judge Wm. P. Cleaveland of New London Ct, and after a short wedding journey, and some farewell visits among our relatives we took our departure for what was then regarded as the far West, on the 3rd of June.

It is often interesting to notice how persons are brought together, who are destined for a life long union. It illustrates the text that "it is not in man that walketh to direct his steps," whether or not it proves the maxim, that "matches are made in Heaven." I had looked in another direction, and had formed a different plan of union. But it became unsatisfactory, and after many painful misgivings and struggles, it was relinquished. I was censured by many for so doing, and my own conscience has always been sore and sensitive on the subject. I can justify the course that I pursued only on the ground that it involved the least of two evils to all concerned. I have never ceased to blame myself. But the wrong seems to me to have been rather in forming an unwise plan, too inconsiderately, than in abandoning it when convinced of its unwisdom. My experience has qualified me to give emphatic advice to young people, to postpone all matrimonial engagements, till their education is finished, their tastes formed, their life work chosen, and they are about to enter upon it. My very limited acquaintance with society, up to the time of my entering public life, rendered me very liable to err, and furnished some slight apology for my error.

But in spite of my mistakes, Providence was very kind to me, and gave me a most devoted wife. She was from a prominent family in the City, from a home of refinement of plenty and of luxury, and had a keen relish for all those social enjoyments found in a large circle of kindred & friends. She gave up all these, with a true missionary spirit, and welcomed the privations and self denials of a Pioneer Home Missionaries' family on the Prairies of Illinois. She counted the cost and made the sacrifice cheerfully, & when trials came, she bore them uncomplainingly, and helped to inspire her husband with hope and courage in the darkest hours. Our journey from New London to Albany was by Steamboat. From Albany to Schenectady by Rail Road. These fifteen miles of R.R. were all that were built west of New York City and so far as I was informed, all that were in use in our country, I well remember the little Cart, divided into separate apartments resembling the inside of a Stage Coach, and the diminutive Locomotives trundling on wheels little larger than those of a Wheel Barrow. And arriving at the end of our route we were let down the grade into the village, by a Stationary Engine.

From Schenectady to Buffalo we travelled by Canal Packet Boat. At Lockport we turned aside, making an excursion to Niagara, where we spent a day in viewing the Falls, and arrived at Buffalo in season to spend the Sabbath. From its relation to Canal & Lake navigation, it was supposed that Buffalo would be the largest City west of Albany, But it then was only a frontier Village.

We had expected to find a field of labor in the Southern part of Illinois and had shipped our household goods, to go by Canal to Buffalo, by Steam Boat thence to Cleaveland &

by Canal through the state of Ohio to Portsmouth, & thence by River to St. Louis. But at Buffalo we learned that our goods had gone forward to Chicago, by the Lakes, & finding a Steamer about to leave for Chicago, we concluded to follow our goods to their destination. At that time only two or three Steam Boats were running on the Lakes, and they had no regular routes or times, but made trips as freight and passengers furnished inducements. We embarked Sunday night on the Ben. Franklin bound for Chicago. It was a small and very inferior Boat, in comparison with those which were running a few years later. But we had a quiet time and were beginning to enjoy the Lake, when on Monday P.M. a storm suddenly arose and we encountered a head wind which for some hours almost entirely arrested our progress and made the Boat roll & pitch most uncomfortably, and as we thought alarmingly. Erie Pa. was in sight, but a long struggle against wind and waves to reach it, was ineffectual, and in the evening the Boat was turned about, & ran before the wind back to Dunkirk. There we lay in a quiet harbor till the Lake was calm. Delays at all the ports for delivering & receiving Freights, waiting for fair weather, & encountering head winds proved so great a hindrance, that we did not reach Detroit untill Friday morning. Our experience had more than satisfied us with Lake travel. Finding at Detroit the Schooner; which had our goods on Board, we decided to take our Buggy and harness ashore and to purchase a horse & make the journey from Detroit to Chicago overland. So, Spending Friday in preparation, we set out Saturday morning, behind an Indian Pony, little knowing how it would tax his strength to draw us through the Beech woods & the oak openings of Michigan, and along the sandy shores of the Lake, thro Northern Indiana. We kept the Stage road from Detroit to Niles which varied but little from the route afterwards adopted for the Central Michigan R.R. The road through the woods was more or less miry, and at uncertain intervals deep holes had been worn by the emigrants teams. My light, new buggy, was not made for such roads & needed repairs the first day. Still we reached Tecumseh then a small village 40 miles from Detroit, where we spent our first Sabbath on Home Missionary ground. There was a small Pres. Church in the place. But their regular supply was absent attending the Gen. Assembly at Philadelphia. His place was supplied on that Sabbath by a Home Missionary stationed at Monroe. It was Communion Sabbath. I assisted in the services, and was struck with what I then saw for the first time, though the sight afterward became very familiar viz. glass tumblers instead of metallic goblets, and earthern plates & Pitcher for the Bread and wine of the Sacrament, of the Lord's Supper.

Resuming our journey on Monday morning, we found very few houses along the road except where at intervals of 10 or 12 miles, the nucleus of a little village had been formed by a stage Tavern, and a few houses, with a Store & Black Smith Shop, clustered around it. We did not greatly admire Michigan. Its oak openings, as the people called those lands which were sparsely covered with large Oak trees, were often very beautiful, and the small lakes frequently met in portions of the state, were a very pleasant feature in the landscape. Yet we had no desire to pitch our tent there, although Michigan people assured us that if we went on to Illinois we should probably die of the Ague the first summer, and if not we should freeze the next winter for the want of fuel.

Arriving at Niles late in the week, we decided to remain there over the next Sabbath, as it was too late to reach Chicago, that week, and we could not expect to find a comfortable stopping place any nearer. There was no house of worship or resident Pastor of any denomination in the Village, But arrangements were made for me to preach in a school house in the P.M. and the people were called together by the blast of a Tinhorn.

On Monday we crossed the St. Joseph River, and struck

out into a country almost entirely uninhabited, and the main road was so little travelled as to be sometimes difficult to follow. Niles was then the terminus of public conveyance westward. Hither the Stage Coach came bringing passengers & mails from the East, but no further from Niles to Chicago the Mails were conveyed once a week on horse back. We travelled a part of the first day in company with the Mail carrier who told us that he took two days to make the journey, camping out at night, wherever darkness overtook him, kindling a fire for his comfort and for his protection against wolves.

We had heard of a settlement commenced on Door Prairie, where Laport, Indiana, has since been built, and there, we were advised to spend the first night. But we found only one and that was an unfinished house, in the place & decided to push on several miles further to a Farmer's Cabin, of which we were told. Darkness began to overtake us before any signs of a human habitation met our view, and we began to fear that we must spend the night in the vast solitude of the wilderness. Thrice welcome therefore was the sight of a very humble Cabin, which the twilight indistinctly revealed to us, & in which we found such hospitality as only Pioneers know how to extend to each other. At noon the next day we reached Michigan City, then a little cluster of log Cabins & rude frame dwellings, on the sandy Beach of the Lake, and beside a very high sand hill. We lingered there till the morning, so as to have a whole day in which to travel along the beach to the mouth of the Calumet, River, where was the first stopping place. We took a few biscuit for our dinner, and a few oats for our horse, and set out early, on that most monotonous drive, around the South end of the Lake, keeping near the water's edge & often one wheel in the water because there the sand was compact & the wheel made little or no impression. Looking forward in the morning we could descry a distant point of timber. We would conjecture the distance to it & at what time of day we should reach it. But as we toiled on, hour afrer hour, we seemed to approach no nearer to it, It was ever receding as we advanced. As the day wore away, our Pony grew very weary. We let him stop, but this did not seem to refresh him. Then I walked by his side & thus lightened his load, And still he appeared more & more exhausted. Then we both walked & left him but the empty Buggy for his load. At length he refused to go further. Darkness had now overtaken us, and we knew not how far we were from the only Cabin between us & Chicago. We left our jaded Pony tied to the wheel of the Buggy, and walked on, peering through the darkness, hoping to discover some sign of a human habitation. In about half a mile we heard human voices, and found the log Cabin, kept as a house of entertainment by a Frenchman whose wife was a squaw, and whose style of accommodations was such as might be expected. But it was to us a Palace compared with alternative of lodgings in our Buggy on the desolate shore of the lake.

Finding a resting place for my weary companion, I procured a horse to go back for my Buggy & led my Pony to his night's lodgings. The supper was too unpalatable to be eaten, even by hungry travellers. The night was hot, mosquitos savage, bed dirty, fleas lively, dogs noisy, and sleep very scarce. But morning found Pony rested & ready for the remaining twelve miles that lay between us and Chicago. We were more resigned to a wretched Breakfast, in anticipation of the good fare which we should find, in our Chicago Hotel. Before noon we were guests at Beaubren's Hotel, which had been recommended to us as the best in the place.

In the first appearance of Chicago, we were not a little disappointed.[14] It had no buildings of any architectural pre-

---

[14] An interesting description of Chicago in 1835 is given in Edwin O. Gale, *Reminiscences of Chicago and Vicinity* (New York: Fleming H. Revell Co., 1902). The first chapters describe the experiences of the author when he came to Chicago in 1835. See also Milo M. Quaife, *Chicago and the Old Northwest, 1673–1835: A Study of the Evolution of the Northwestern Frontier, Together with a History of Fort Dearborn* (Chicago, 1913).

tensions. Its business houses were one story unfinished, wooden buildings, and its dwelling houses, were generally very cheap wooden structures. Its best Hotel was originally a log cabin, with sundry additions and extensions of sawed lumber.

The residences and business, extended from Fort Dearborn, along up the Chicago River, as far as the junction of the North & South Branches, and a few dwellings and shops & one Hotel were on the West side of the South Branch. No store or dwelling had ventured so far out upon the Prairie, as Lake Street, on the South Side. The population was estimated at 300, and a large encampment of friendly Indians on the West side, gave the place a frontier aspect.

Our Hotel accommodations[15] were scarcely in advance of our previous nights entertainment, and we determined to hasten our departure into the interior of the State, unless some additional comforts could be found in Chicago. Philo Carpenter & John S. Wright, then young men just commencing business in Chicago, soon called to see us, and interested themselves in finding for us, a more pleasant stopping place. We were soon invited to take our meals at Mr. Rufus

[15] Gale (*op. cit.*, pp. 38–39), gives the following description of hotel conditions which he found in 1835: "The Green Tree having no book for that purpose we were spared the ceremony of registering. Nor was it certain that we could find accommodation until our host had returned from the kitchen wither he had gone to consult his efficient wife, who performed the never ending duties of housekeeper, landlady, meat and pastry cook, scullion, chambermaid, waitress, adviser and personal attendant upon all the ladies and children . . . . while her liege lord filled the many duties of boniface, clerk, bartender, butler, steward, walking encyclopedia and general roustabout.

"The momentous council was at length ended and we were assigned a room adjoining the one we had first entered, which was the bar, reading, smoking and reception room, ladies parlor and general utility place, in one. Our room was about 12 × 12 with two windows 6 × 8, two doors, two beds, two red pictures, two chairs, a carpet worn in two and was altogether too dirty for the comfort of persons unaccustomed to such surroundings. . . . . In the dining room were two tables, the length of the room, covered with green checked oilcloth, loaded with roasted wild ducks, fricassee of prairie chickens, wild pigeon pot pie, tea and coffee, creamless, but sweetened with granulated maple sugar procured from our red brethren. These furnished a banquet that rendered us oblivious to chipped dishes, flies buzzing or tangled in the butter, creeping beetles and the music of the Mosquito Band."

Brown's and for lodgings we occupied the study of Rev. Jeremiah Porter,[16] a young Home Missionary, who had just organized a Pres. Church in Chicago, to which he was ministering, but he was then absent for a few days exploring the adjacent settlements. Mr. Browns family were from Mass. and were then keeping a boarding house in a log cabin, on La Salle Street near the corner of S. Water St. Fort Dearborn stood near the mouth of Chicago River a little north of the Union Depot, and consisted of a quadrangle of houses for officers & Barracks for Soldiers, with Magazine & Commissary's stores &c. Major Wilcox, then in command of the Fort, was an Elder in the Pres. Church. Lieutenant Jamieson & both their Wives were members. Both of those families showed us much kind attention, which has never been forgotten through the long years of varied experiences that have followed.

As Mr. Porter had not returned, I preached for him on Sabbath morning, my first Sermon in Illinois. The congre-

[16] Jeremiah Porter was a graduate of Princeton and during the time when the "Yale Band" was preparing to go into the West, young Porter volunteered and found his first church at Fort Brady which was located at Sault Ste Marie. Here he found a few government officers, soldiers, and traders, together with a motley mixture of Frenchmen and Indians. A Baptist missionary had preceded him, and, after an effort at co-operation between the two groups failed, it was decided to have two separate churches. Porter was very fortunate in having the co-operation of the Indian Agent, Mr. Schoolcraft, who was a fine Christian gentleman who did all he could for the success of the religious work.

Conditions were very bad at the fort, with much drinking besides other forms of amusement which Porter vehemently opposed. Immediately he organized a little Presbyterian church but was able to form a much larger temperance society. This latter organization achieved remarkable results, and soon regulations were passed for prohibiting the landing of liquor on the shores, and it became an unusual thing to find even a drunken Indian. Porter gained the co-operation of the soldiers not only in the temperance work but also in a Bible class, which aroused a large interest among the soldiers, and many of its members joined the little church. Soon Porter opened a weekly service for the French Catholics, attended by from thirty-five to forty.

With the outbreak of the Black Hawk War (1832) many of the troops from Fort Brady were transferred to Fort Dearborn, and the following year (1833) Porter followed and for a number of years was active in the organization churches in Chicago and the vicinity ("Journals of Jeremiah Porter, 1831–32" [photostat copy of MS, Chicago Theological Seminary]).

gation was half citizens & half Soldiers,—the place of meeting was a large room in the Fort, furnished with temporary seats. The Drum was used instead of a Bell to announce the time of meeting, and a Fife was the instrumental accompaniment, to the sacred music.

Little did I then imagine that after a few years of missionary labor in the interior of the State, I should be called to the Pastorate of that church and should spend ten years in the mid-summer of my life in laboring for the interests of religion in that city. But it is not in man that walketh to direct his steps.

The question of my location in the state of Illinois, was to be decided in consultation with Rev. Mr. Hale & Baldwin, both of whom were exploring the new settlements & laboring in the interests of the Home Missionary cause; sometimes in company & sometimes separately. Expecting to meet them in the central part of the State, we resumed our journey in that direction, the following week.

Crossing the South Branch of Chicago River on Lake Street, over a Bridge of poles, we struck out upon the flat Prairie westward. Mr. Carpenter accompanied us on foot nearly a mile from the River and when far out on the Prairie he stopped and turned our attention to an adjacent quarter Section which he had claimed, and to a shanty in which his hired man was living, that he might fulfil the conditions requisite to obtaining a preemption title. After some litigation, and the sacrifice of a considerable portion of his original claim Mr. Carpenter retained enough of it, to lay the foundation of a large estate, from which he has with a wise liberality aided many of our public charities, and ma le himself a prominent benefactor of Society. But as he then intimated, that this piece of flat prairie might make him a fortune when the city should cover it, the idea seemed so visionary to myself & wife that we exchanged glances of amused incredulity at his expense.

No road had been cast up, or even surveyed across that prairie. The beaten track made by travel, was then extremely muddy, although it was mid-summer. We were directed to shun that, and travel on the grass beside it. But in the grass, water was standing, in many places several inches in depth, and to our unpracticed judgment, it seemed miry & impassable. We soon found, however, that the roots of the grass formed a bridge strong enough to support both horse and buggy.

The first house after leaving Chicago, was a log cabin on the Des Pleines, 12 miles distant. The next was 8 miles further, No other habitation was seen till we reached Walker's grove, where Plainfield now stands.[17] From thence 25 miles brought us to Holderman's Grove, the next settlement, Sixteen miles further, without passing any house in sight, and we came to Ottawa.[18] The village here consisted of a dozen houses, and a store & unfinished Hotel, all on the South side of the Illinois River & below the Bluff, not far from the site of the celebrated Mineral spring. Another days journey brought us through some sparse settlements to Union Grove in Putnam Co. where we were kindly welcomed & hospitably

[17] A church was formed in Plainfield in August, 1834. On April 13, 1835, the missionary, A. Greenwood, informs the A.H.M.S. secretary that the church had been organized with the principle of entire abstinence included in their church articles. In November (1835) the missionary reports fifteen Sunday-school members and a temperance society of seventy members. In 1837 the Plainfield church had a membership of twenty, and the town a population of about a thousand (Committee to Peters, November 13, 1837 [A.H.M.S. Correspondence]).

[18] E. H. Hazard to A. Peters, September 4, 1833: "I entered this my present field of labor on the 4th of June and agreeable to the directions of my mission I hasten to give you a succinct report of my labors. . . . . La Salle County being entirely desolate I determined to confine my labors principally to the various settlements in this county. Ottawa and Bailey's Point being the most considerable and central churches I fixed on these as my principle points of operation. . . . . I have assisted in forming a Bible Society. . . . . We are expecting soon to receive a supply of Bibles and Testaments for distribution. . . . . I have circulated a pledge for the promotion of Temperance. . . . . 20 names are now subscribed." Hazard also notes that there is much fear of the Indians. In another letter, dated December 10, 1833, Hazard tells of the organization of a church at Ottawa (A.H.M.S. Correspondence).

entertained by Rev. Mr. Kirby,[19] a former College acquaintance at Yale, and at that time a Home Missionary in charge
of a little Pres. Church. At his house we tarried two weeks,
waiting the arrival of the Home Missionary Agents who were
expected at that place. Mr. Kirby's Meeting House, in which
I preached my second sermon in Illinois, was made of logs,
and consisted of two parts, an old & new part. In the old
part, the seats were made of rough slabs, and in the new part,
there being no floor, the sleepers were used for seats. Men,
women & children in about equal proportions, and a good
supply of dogs, made up the congregation, and the Preacher
and the singers, were not the only ones whose voices were
heard in the assembly. The Pulpit was made by setting too
posts in the ground about four feet apart & on the top of these
nailing a board, for the support of Bible & Hymn Book.
Behind this a seat for the preacher was made, by boring two
holes in one of the logs, in the end of the house, & inserting
two pins horizontally, on which a rough board was placed.
This was a very primitive style of architecture, but the place
was far in advance of many houses, in which I subsequently
preached the Gospel.

Mr. Kirby, & his young wife, both recently from homes of
comfort and refinement in Ct. were living in a new unplas-
tered house of one room, & without chimney or stove, or any
means of cooking food. Their kitchen was the open Prairie,
around the house, on which a fire was kindled, and the meals
were cooked by it, in ways that seemed marvellous to the
uninitiated, & illustrated the Proverb, that "necessity is the
mother of invention." I formed a very pleasant acquaintance

[19] William Kirby was born at Middleton, Conn., in 1805 and graduated from
Yale College in 1827 and from the Yale Divinity School in 1831. He tutored in
Illinois College (1831–33) and preached at Union Grove (1833–34) and Blackstone
Grove (1834–36).

Kirby did not remain long at Union Grove, for in a letter of August 1, 1834, he
says that he has already spent two months at Blackstone Grove. In the same letter
we learn that "the Union Church was organized a year ago."

E. H. Hazard, December 29, 1834, states that J. Porter is serving Chicago and
Union Grove.

in that settlement and was very hospitably entertained in several of the families. The people were quite homogenious, having emigrated from the same settlement in Bond Co. in this state, and previously coming from Southern Ohio, where they had formed a marked religious and anti-Slavery character under the influence of the Dickey's & Rankin's then prominent in the Presbyterian Church of the West.

At Union Grove, and at this time, I met R. W. Patterson, then a Student, prepared to commence his Freshman year at Illinois College in Jacksonville, On the subject of slavery I was a Colonizationist and he was a radical abolitionist—a reader of Garrison's "Liberator," and an Advocate of immediate emancipation. He was unwearied in his effort to convert me to his views, was not a little tried with my conservatism. Little did either of us suppose that we should, in ten years from that time, be the respective Pastors of the 1st & 2nd Pres. Churches of Chicago, and that I should be identified with the radical Anti Slavery sentiment of that period & he with the conservative. Yet such was eventually our change of position.

I had heard much of the "Hampshire Colony,"[20] organized

---

[20] The Hampshire Colony Church has recently published the early documents of their church in a book entitled *The Hampshire Church: Its First Hundred Years, 1831-1931* (Princeton, Ill., 1931) by members of the church. In 1831 a meeting was held at Northampton, Mass., to organize a church from those who anticipated migrating to Illinois. The preamble to the constitution states their purpose as "better providing for themselves and their families, provided the privileges of a social, moral and religious character which they now have and which they highly value, can be made secure to them in their future home." There were members from several churches, including a doctor and his wife. No minister accompanied them. A scout had been sent out the previous year, and he selected a place at Bailey's Point on the Vermillion River and had a cabin ready for the group which arrived later in 1831. The entire group did not come at once, but eventually most of them managed to reach the Illinois settlement. The first entry in the old church record-book reads as follows: "the Hampshire Colony Church of Christ founded at Northampton, Mass., March 23, 1831, settled on the Bureau River, County of Putnam, ... and named the town Greenfield" (pp. 10-11). Rev. T. Baldwin visited the settlement in February, 1834, and a little later Lucius Farnham and William Kirby met here to hold a communion service. A church building was erected in 1835, and Lucius Farnham became the first pastor. At this time the settlement was called Princeton. L. Farnham, in a letter to A. Peters, July 1, 1835, states that he arrived the previous October and found the

in Northampton Mass. two years previously, and located in Bureau Co. 15 miles West of Union Grove. While waiting for advice as to my location, I improved my opportunity to visit that settlement. Borrowing a horse & saddle of Mr. Kirby, I rode over past Hennepin, across the Illinois river, through the timberland beyond which for depth of mud, vividly reminded the traveller of the "Slough of despond," then up the bluff, and along the oak Grove, till suddenly the broad undulating Prairie on which Princeton is now built, opened in prospect. It was a magnificent sight.

But no human habitation or mark of human culture was seen till, I had crossed the Prairie, and approached the Grove on the West side of it. I there found two log Cabins, one oc-cupied by Dr. Nathaniel Chamberlain, and the other by John H. Bryant. The Indian War of the previous year, had in-duced many families belonging to the colony to locate tem-porarily, and some permanently, in other parts of the state less exposed to Indian raids. I enjoyed the christian hospi-tality of Dr. Chamberlain,[21] and called next day on Mr. Bryant, and after learning what I could of the plans and prospects of the colony, I returned little imagining that I should spend twelve years of my ministry in the villages of Princeton & Dover,[22] which should be built on that Prairie.

---

little church awaiting him. He says: "The Bible Class embraces nearly all the Con-gregation." Prayer meeting was held every Wednesday evening, with a female prayer meeting every Saturday afternoon, besides the monthly concert. In April of this year he notes that the land is being entered in order to obtain proper titles, and much hardship is resulting.

Flavel Bascom states in his "Autobiography" that Lucius Farnham came to this church in 1833 and remained for five years. Then followed the long ministry of Owen Lovejoy which extended "with some temporary interruptions until 1856. . . . . Then due to the feelings engendered by the slavery controversy there were five pastors in eight years." Flavel Bascom became pastor in 1864.

[21] Dr. Nathaniel Chamberlain was one of the leaders of the Hampshire Colony and was one of the first to come to Illinois.

[22] Bascom became pastor of Dover in 1857 and remained there until March, 1864 ("Autobiography," pp. 211 ff.). His ministry at Princeton followed that at Dover. He remained five years, during which time "81 were added to the member-ship of the church" (ibid., p. 226).

At length Bro's Hale and Baldwin arrived at Union Grove, and spent a few days in preaching, to the people, who left their work at midday, and came to church although it was mid summer & farm work was pressing.

After due consultation, it was decided that I should locate at Pleasant Grove, Tazewell Co. and look after the religious interests of that place and of all the adjacent villages and settlements. So we "took up our carriages," as the Apostle phrases it, and sought our destination, which was about 50 miles further to the South and West.

At Hollands Grove, where the village of Washington has since grown up, I called on Father Heath a prominent settler and a devout Methodist, In answer to my inquiries, he told me that he did not think there was room for another Preacher in Tazewell Co. Every important point in the County he thought was supplied with preaching, and every Sabbath occupied. But we went forward 12 miles further, where we found the field assigned to us. It was a field whose aspect would have filled us with disappointment and homesickness had we not, by information, gathered by much correspondence with Home Missionaries, been prepared for a day of small things.

The field, instead of being white for the harvest, seemed like the untilled Prairies, requiring to be broken up, & sown and cultivated before sheaves could be gathered.

A few families recently from New England, welcomed us very cordially. Our first call was on Mr. Shurtliffs family. He was originally from Boston, and was a Brother of Dr. Ben. S. of that city, who was a liberal Patron of the Baptist College at Alton, which bears his name.

Mr. S. was not a christian, but was a man of property, and aspired to a controlling influence in the settlement. He had been many years in the West, and had contracted the loose habits of frontier life. He had married a wife who could neither read nor write, and neither of them had any personal

interest in religion. But he was hospitable and made me welcome to his home which was the only frame house in the
settlement. He subscribed liberally toward my support. But
after I had begun to take an active part in behalf of the
Temperance cause, he became alienated, and refused to pay
his subscription. I soon found a boarding place with Mrs.
Brown, from Mass. who with an unmarried daughter and son,
occupied a neighboring Cabin. That family were all christians, and in their kindness to me, were scarcely surpassed by
the family at Bethany, in their affectionate hospitalities to
the Savior. But their means were very limited and their accommodations somewhat meager. Their house contained but
one room.[23] In two corners of the room were bedsteads, each
supported with one leg, after the style then common in log
Cabins. The old lady & daughter occupied one of these, my
wife & I the other, while the son occupied a pallet on the
floor. The floor was made of plank, split, instead of sawed.
There were cracks between them wide enough to admit the
leg of a chair, and I remember once when sitting at the table,
my chair was thus upset, and I was thrown sprawling on the
floor. But these were very "light afflictions" which were
cheerfully borne.

After a few weeks, another family who had a larger Cabin,
rented us one room in which we went to housekeeping for the
winter. In this room was a fire place of sticks covered with
clay. We put two beds into it, our library, bureau and table,
and a ladies work table, and four chairs.

In one of the beds we lodged a lady school Teacher, who
boarded with the other family. Once we had as visitors two
families, consisting of seven persons, whom we entertained for

[23] Rev. Lemuel Foster in his "Journal" says that their first cabin was at a point
on the prairies "20 miles north of Springfield" was "14 feet square, having but one
room, made of unhewed saplings, and the door and the loft overhead were too low for
a six-footer as I happened to be. Still in one place where the puncheons of the floor
were somewhat sunken, I could stand erect, when tired of stooping" (Spinka [ed.],
in *op. cit.*, pp. 188–89).

three days & nights in that same room, and made them pretty comfortable. But during the very cold weather of that winter, it was very difficult to keep warm. While sitting before a blazing fire, as near as possible without scorching, the ink would sometimes freeze in my pen while writing. But we passed the winter with no serious illness.

Having arranged for a temporary boarding place with Mrs. Brown, and secured a room in Mr. Hardings Cabin for housekeeping, when our goods should arrive, I began to inquire when and where I could have stated appointments for preaching.

In the centre of Pleasant Grove, was a log School House, in which preaching was appointed at 12 o'clock on every Sabbath. The Baptists, Methodists and Cumberland Presbyterians filled these appointments in rotation, and if any other denomination wished to be heard, they were permitted to put in a sermon, after the stated Preacher was through & before the meeting broke up. Such was my first appointment at Pleasant Grove. I was to follow a Baptist Preacher from Sangamon County, of Kentucky origin, and uneducated. And having delivered my Message at that place I was to preach late in the P.M. at Pekin 8 miles westward.[24]

[24] Flavel Bascom seems to have sent very few letters to the A.H.M.S. during his first few years in Illinois, so that during the latter part of 1837 Absalom Peters, the secretary of the missionary society, asked him to give an epitome of his work up to that time. The following is a part of Bascom's response: "I came to this country in 1833 and selected a field of labor because of [its] natural advantages. I located in Pleasant Grove a sparse country settlement about the center of the county. Methodists, Baptists, Campbellites, Quakers, Mormons, and Cumberland Presbyterians had the ground before me. Throughout the whole region I was told by an old settler who was a Methodist Father that there were preachers enough here already, no openings, etc. . . . . but relying on your society for temporal supplies and the grace of God to give efficacy for his word I pitched my tent and began to labor as a missionary in Tazewell County. . . . . Thus I labored a year always collecting a cabin full wherever I preached and accumulated something in the way of S.S., Temperance Society, etc. During the year there were only 2 or 3 hopeful conversions . . . . 7/8 of my support was from your society.

"The second year a church was formed at Washington of ten members which I supplied once a year. My labors were also extended to Peoria and a church was formed there during that year. In Pleasant Grove and Sand Prairie which numbers

Before fulfilling this appointment, I returned to Hennepin, to look after my Furniture which was expected to arrive there from Chicago. In returning from that trip, I found myself, on Saturday morning, (the day before my first preaching appointment on my new field) 40 miles from home, with a horse taken suddenly lame & unable to travel. Determined that my first appointment should not prove a failure, I sought in vain to hire a horse, to take me home, that day. I finally gained permission to catch, if I could, a half broken colt on the Prairie, and ride him home, returning him when I should come back for my own. I accordingly caught and saddled the colt, and rode him 8 miles toward home. Then, having dismounted, he would not suffer me to regain my place in the saddle, but rearing & kicking, he threw me from him, upon my back and having regained his liberty, tho saddled & bridled, he left me with almost the fleetness of a bird, taking the direction from which I had just come. I sent word to the owner, of what had happened, by a traveller just then coming up, and I resumed my journey homeward on foot. The Mail Wagon from Chicago to Peoria soon overtook me and carried me a few miles. Then as our roads parted, I resumed my journey on foot & alone. Darkness found me wearied & hungry, seven miles from home, I found a hospitable stopping place at Mr. Philips, where I rested till Sabbath morning's sun was ready to light me across the Prairie to the Cabin where my anxious wife was wondering what had detained me.

---

and strength were gradually increasing about the close of that year. Barnes came to my aid at Washington and Brother Porter at Peoria. Tremont had by that time grown up requiring my attention and next year was given to Tremont and Pleasant Grove; Pekin and Sand Prairie (still deriving half my support from your Society). The next year Pekin and Sand Prairie were left destitute and my whole time was given to Tremont and Pleasant Grove. . . . . At the close of that year my church was divided, the part over which I am now placed claims my whole time and raising my whole salary. The other part has obtained the services of Brother Huntington. The little church which existed in this county in 1833 has increased from 6 members to 3 churches with an aggregate of 100 members . . . ." (Bascom to Peters, January 19, 1838 [A.H.M.S. Correspondence]).

After breakfast I borrowed a horse of Mr. Shurtliff to carry me to my two appointments that day.

I entered upon the public services of that day with some peculiar feelings. I had preached many times during the two preceding years. But my services had been occasional and incidental. But now I was to begin my professional life work.

I had at length reached my own Home Missionary field, away out on the Western frontier. Here I was to have the care of souls, and to test my ability so to preach the Gospel that these pioneer settlers would give heed to it, and be saved; and that all the Institutions of christian civilization would spring up under its influence, on these Prairies.

I began with some trepidation but had the undivided attention of a large audience while I attempted to unfold the truth contained in the text, "Unto you that believe he is precious." This enabled me to strike what I intended should be the key note of my whole Ministry, viz. "Jesus Christ & him crucified."

The impression made upon the audience seemed favorable and I was requested to appoint another time when I would preach at the same place.

Mounting my horse, as soon as my services at the school-house were closed, I rode eight miles to Pekin. Finding a small audience there assembled in the school house, I preached my first sermon to them; without any rest or refreshment. My circumstances were less inspiring than in the former service. I was less satisfied with my effort, and I presume the impression was less favorable. An old gentleman spoke with me after meeting, telling me that he was attracted to hear me by my name, thinking possibly I might be Bishop Bascom whom he had heard & admired in Ohio. Though evidently disappointed, he gave me the compliment of resembling the eloquent Bishop in personal appearance.

Returning homeward I was caught in a hard shower and thoroughly wet. After the shower, night came on, and in the

Grove, through which I must pass before reaching home, I was surrounded with midnight darkness. I let my horse have the reins and trusted to his instinct & superior eye sight to take me through. But he, having eaten nothing since morning, was hungry as his rider, and turned aside into the bushes, and commenced browsing. Dismounting, I felt my way on the ground till I found the path again, and then he carried me through. Reaching home before 9 o'clock I wondered if that days work was a fair specimen of Home Missionary labor. I had walked seven miles through the wet Prairie grass before breakfast, I had travelled twenty miles on horse back, had preached twice and been thoroughly wet in a shower, and had eaten nothing from 8 oclock in the morning till 9 oclock at night. But after a good nights rest, I forgot my fatigue, and was ready for new labors.

In the region round about I found several other preaching places, between which I divided my labors. In Sand Prairie a few miles South of Pekin, I found a Pres. Church of 5 or 6 members, organized by Rev. Calvin W. Babbitt, my predecessor, on this field.[25] There I preached at stated intervals for several years, and the little church was considerably enlarged and strengthened. At Hollands Grove[26] I soon began to make stated appointments for preaching. At Mackinaw[27] Village I bestowed some labor. At Peoria I soon began to preach occasionally. The field was large enough, to give

[25] C. W. Babbitt had considerable difficulty with this church at Sand Prairie owing to the large irreligious population together with the large number of competing denominations. He was also affected considerably by the exodus of population at the time of the Indian uprising in 1833. The agent and Mr. Peters both failed to understand the difficulty of this field and criticized Babbitt. He finally moved to Prince's Grove, where he made a better record. There were many letters written about the problems at Sand Prairie (T. Baldwin to A. Peters, October 20, 1834 [A.H.M.S. Correspondence Letters]).

[26] Holland's Grove became Washington, and Romulus Barnes, one of the Yale Band, became the pastor. This territory was very difficult, and Barnes's letters are filled with notes of discouragement. On September 20, 1838, he says: ". . . . This field is indeed one calculated to try his patience and yours. . . . ."

[27] Mackinaw is always considered as the outpoint of Washington.

full scope to my activity. Ministers of our denomination were then few and far between. The nearest on the North East was Bro Kirby, at Union Grove, Putnam Co. 50 miles distant, Bro Kent[28] at Galena 150 miles to the N. West. Bro. Foster[29] at Bloomington 40 miles East. On the west was none nearer than the Sandwich Islands. On the South Bro. J. G. Bergen[30] at Springfield was nearest in that direction, He was 60 miles distant.

I had been licenced to preach two years previously. But ordination was now desirable, that I might regularly administer the ordinances of the Gospel. A Council of Congregational Churches & Pastors could not be convened for this purpose, for the Hampshire Colony Church in Bureau Co. formed in Northampton in 1831 was the only Cong. Ch. existing in Illinois & that was without a Pastor. I sought ordination therefore by Presbytery. There were three Presbyteries in the State at that time, The one in whose bounds I found myself was Sangamon Pres. which included Bond County on the South and Chicago & Galena on the North. So at the appointed time, I went to Presbytery, meeting with a small country Church in a log meeting house at Athens, Sangamon Co.

Although the territory of the Presbytery was so large the members were few. Only Rev. Mr. Bergen of Springfield, and Ben. B. Spillman of Hillsboro were present the first day. As they did not constitute a quorum, no business could be transacted till Rev. R. Barnes, from Canton arrived the second day. Then Presbytery organized and proceeded to the

[28] Kent did not limit his labors to Galena but extended them all the way to Cassville, Elk Grove, Platteville, Craigs Mills, and other places. In the months of May and June, 1834, he traveled 384 miles (see *Journal of the Presbyterian Historical Society*, Vol. XIII [December, 1929]; also Nahum Gould's "*Diary;*" unpublished MS and letters in the A.H.M.S. collection).

[29] See the "Journal of Lemuel Foster," ed. Spinka, in *op. cit.*

[30] Bergen had been born in New Jersey and educated at Princeton, where he also tutored for some time. After a pastorate at Madison, N.J., he came to Illinois and entered upon his ministry at Springfield in 1828.

examination of Lemuel Foster a College classmate, and myself.[31] Although we were both New School in our Theology
and brought up at the feet of Dr. N. W. Taylor [pro-
fessor of theology at Yale], and a majority of the Presbytery were decidedly Old School no objection was urged
against our ordination. Bro. Fosters trial sermon, I well
remember was from the text "Now then we are Am-
bassaders for Christ" etc. Mine was from the text "Be
ye therefore perfect, as your Father in heaven is perfect."
Then in that humble sanctuary, we were solemnly set apart
to the work of the Gospel ministry, The scenes of that day,
and the feelings with which I looked forward to the work to
which I was thus publicly consecrated, are very distinctly
remembered. I think it was my honest purpose to "make
full proof of my ministry." But how little conception I then
had, as to what, and where, my life work would be! How
different my position then and now! Then I stood at the beginning of my life work. Now at its close. Then it was before me. Now it is behind me, I have well nigh finished my
course. Would that I had a better right to say, "I have
fought a good fight."

All those who took part in my ordination have died, and he
also who stood by my side & was ordained with me, has
finished his work and gone to the better land.

My ordination by Presbytery made me a Presbyterian
minister, and in the circumstances then existing, I saw no
reason to desire a change in my ecclesiastical relations. In the
light of experience, it is natural to regret that the men and
means contributed by N. England, through all those years,
had not been employed in planting Cong. Churches at the
West, instead of Presbyterian. But the plan of Union was

[31] Foster mentions the fact that he and Bascom were ordained together. He also
notes that, inasmuch as there were no Congregational churches in this territory
which could easily ordain them (Hampshire being the only one until 1833), both
these young ministers were examined together. At this time the members of the
presbytery were a little fearful of admitting Congregationalists to their ranks (Foster,
"Journal," ed. Spinka, in *op. cit.*, p. 190).

then in force. The two denominations were cooperative in Home Missionary work, and public sentiment at the East favored our joining Presbytery, rather than causing division by founding churches distinctively Congregational.

From Presbytery I went to a meeting of Synod at Jacksonville. There I had my first sight of the commotion in the Theological and Ecclesiastical elements which in less than five years was destined to rend the Presbyterian Church in twain.[32] Rev. Wm. J. Frazer had been suspended from the ministry, or deposed, for some irregularity,[33] by the Illinois Presbytery, and his appeal to the Synod was the occasion of much heated discussion; and in the decision which approved the action of Presbytery, a strictly party line was drawn, between the Old School & the New. Thence forward till the

[32] Foster's congregation was Presbyterian, and he says that the word "Congregationalism" was fraught with hersey. Accordingly, he preached at Bloomington an entire year without telling his congregation about his own church background (*ibid.*, p. 191).

The letters of the New England ministers in Illinois at this time reveal the emphasis which these ministers placed upon an emotional type of religion. They spoke of "protracted meetings" and judged the success of their work in the light of this emphasis. There were also differences betweeen the two groups in Illinois relative to their position on the question of slavery. The southern territory was the stronghold of proslavery attitudes as well as the theological tenets of the Presbyterian church. The northern groups were largely antislavery. After the split between these two bodies, the Old School invaded the Tazewell County territory and set up rival churches against the New School group.

Theron Baldwin, in a letter dated January 31, 1834, says that the Congregationalists and Presbyterians were suspicious of the management of the A.H.M.S. Each group was suspicious of the other.

[33] In 1833 at the Illinois Presbytery "Rev. William J. Frazer presented a charge of unsound teachings against Ed. Beecher, J. M. Sturtevant and William Kirby. On the other hand, charges of slander were preferred against Wm. J. Frazer for publishing in the 'Illinois Herald' of March 9, 1833 an article highly injurious to the character of Ed. Beecher, J. M. Sturtevant and William Kirby." The charge of unsound doctrine was not sustained, while that of slander against Fraser was sustained. Frazer was suspended from exercising the functions of the ministry (A.T. Norton, *History of the Presbyterian Church in the State of Illinois* [St. Louis, 1879], I, 184).

Frazer made several appeals to higher bodies for redress but lost his case continually and finally joined the Old School church after 1837 and was sent by them to preach at Pleasant Grove, where he was a competitor of the Presbyterian church which had been established there since 1834.

separation, very much of our ecclesiastical business was transacted in that way.

Returning from Presbytery & Synod we commenced house-keeping, as foreshadowed above. Though our home was very humble we enjoyed it. Though our fare was necessarily plain and frugal, we relished it no less than richer dainties are relished in other circumstances.

My accommodations at home, and my labors abroad were very unfavorable to such habits of study as a young minister needs in order to intellectual growth, and to the accumulation of resources for his work. The Books required were not within my reach. The time to use them I could not command, and I had no place for solitary and uninterrupted study. But the customs and tastes of the people did not require written discourses, nor elaborate preparation. The man who could get up and talk with the most freedom and fluency, was listened to with the greatest admiration, without regard to the soundness of his logic or the literary polish of his style. I endeavored to draw sound instruction from the word of God, and present it in my discourses, in a familiar and earnest way, so that I might secure attention, awaken interest, stimulate thought and study, and thus correct the erroneous notions so prevalent around us, and make the way of salvation so plain to my hearers, that they need not err therein. And the result of my preaching was to dispel the mists and fogs, in which ignorant and erroneous preachers[34] had enveloped the

---

[34] The Congregational and Presbyterian missionaries had little respect for the work that had been performed on the frontier by the Methodists and Baptists. They were the "ignorant and erroneous preachers" here referred to. This superiority complex persisted for many years and was the cause of a rising resentment on the part of the Baptists and Methodists against the missionaries of the American Home Missionary Society. The following is Peter Cartwright's estimate of one of these missionaries in northern Illinois:

"The first Presbyterian minister who came to the town, that I have any recollection of, was by the name of ———. He was a well-educated man, and had regularly studied theology in some of the eastern states, where they manufacture young preachers like they do lettuce in hot-houses. He brought with him a number of old manuscript sermons, and read them to the people; but as to common sense, he had

minds of the people and to create a demand for a more thoughtful and less boisterous address from religious teachers.

Although at my coming I was told there was no room for another Preacher, yet in six months, there was room enough and to spare. My predecessors had drawn off & left the ground to me, and to the Cumberland Presbyterians.

But there was a class of early settlers from Kentucky that were not easily reconciled to the change. Their feelings were expressed at one time in my hearing. I had preached at the log school house in Pleasant Grove, on a certain Sabbath, and had been immediately followed by a Preacher of the early Pioneer sort. He commenced by saying that his text was a passage which had come to his mind while the Brother was speaking, viz. "we have this treasure of the Gospel in earthen vessels" &c. This passage, said he, teaches man's impotency to keep the commandments of God. Having thus expounded it, he never referred to it again, but commenced an indiscriminate quotation of passages from the Genesis to Revelations and back again, with apparently no connection between them except that some word in one verse would serve as a catch-word to remind him of another. Thus he went bellowing and blowing through the Bible shedding no more light upon the passages quoted, than the roar of artillery does upon our declaration of independence. But after service, as I was walking toward my horse & Buggy, I heard two women before me discussing the sermons. In reference to the last, one of them said she "allowed that was the greatest sarmon ever preached in that house." "Yes," replied the other, "but I don't like these Yankee Preachers, They are always proving

---

very little, and he was almost totally ignorant of the manners and usages of the world; yet he came here to evangelize and Christianize us poor heathen. . . . . I told him that he must quit reading his old manuscript sermons, and learn to speak extemporaneously; that the western people were born and reared in hard times and were an out-spoken and off-hand people; that if he did not adopt this manner of preaching, the Methodists would set the whole western world on fire before he could light his match" (*Autobiography* [Cincinnati and New York, 1856], pp. 307-8).

things, just like Lawyers." And thus I labored on, trying to teach the people to "prove all things and hold fast that which is good."

The population of our County & of our section of the state, began to increase rapidly about this time by immigration, and my field of labor was continually changing. The village of Washington began to spring up in Hollands Grove, and the little church which I had gathered there, desired a Minister all the time. Bro. R. Barnes,[35] therefore came from Canton and took charge of that congregation. Then a Colony had located south East of Pleasant Grove, and had built the village of Tremont and they wanted preaching. So I removed to Tremont and supplied that place & Pekin & Sand Prairie and Rev. Enoch S. Huntington[36] occupied my place at Pleasant Grove. Peoria had grown also, and had organized a New School Pres. Church, and an Old School Pres. Church, almost simultaneously—the former being regularly organized by a Committee of Presbytery and the latter by a few private individuals without authority, and for the purpose of forestalling the other movement. Rev. Jeremiah Porter having completed two years labor in Chicago, accepted a call to Peoria,[37] and became Pastor of the Main Street N.S. Pres. Church of that city.

In my field of labor, from the first, I had experienced great inconvenience for the want of comfortable places in which to hold meetings. As the settlement on the Prairie North of Pleasant Grove increased, the people desired preaching nearer

[35] Barnes arrived in Illinois in November, 1834, and went to Canton, where he found a church with thirteen members which by January, 1835, had increased to eighty. From November to January he had traveled 500 miles (Barnes to Peters, January 7, 1834 [A.H.M.S. Correspondence]).

[36] Enoch S. Huntington came up from southern Illinois to the northern part of the state at the invitation of Bascom and also because of ill-health (Huntington to Peters, November 8, 1837 [ibid.]).

[37] At the time Porter came to Peoria the church there paid a salary of $1,000 and contributed $1,000 to benevolent objects (Barnes to Peters, January 2, 1837 [ibid.]).

home than the old log school house, So I procured a load of slabs and made seats, and filled my own Cabin, on Sunday morning, with those seats, and the surrounding population would gather there for worship and religious instruction. My first protracted meeting was held under the shade of a little Grove, on Mr. Brown's farm, and there with the aid of Bro. Baldwin, services were held several days and some of the young people commenced a new life. At Sand Prairie also we held Camp Meetings, which drew together greater numbers than we had room for in any house, at our command, and our meetings were blessed to the conversion of some souls. But when the weather was cold we had in some of my preaching places, to meet in private room's, packed densely with people, for whose comfort a large fire must be burning on the hearth and in preaching I was compelled to stand with my back near the fire, and the perspiration rolling down my face as I preached, and then go out and ride in an open buggy 5 or 6 miles against a cold wind to my next appointment.

But gradually with the increase of population, better accommodations for religious meetings were provided, either in better school houses, or in small meeting houses built expressly for religious uses. Such a one was built near my house in 1836.

We introduced S. Schools, as far as practicable in all my preaching places, and one of our earliest S.S. Pupils at Pleasant Grove, was Phebe Scott, who afterward became the wife of Rev. Sanford Richardson, both of whom have long done the Master valuable service as Missionaries of the A.B.C.F. Missions in Turkey.

I endeavored to see that all the families in the region round about were supplied with the Bible, through the aid and instrumentality of the County Bible Society.

In the cause of Temperance, I labored with some success, in all the places where I preached, and organized Societies on the pledge of Total Abstinence from all intoxicating drinks, both distilled and fermented. In no place did I meet with serious opposition except at Washington,[38] in Hollands Grove. There the settlers who came from Kentucky, withstood me vigorously with argument and invective. Even members of the Christian and Baptist churches, saw in the Temperance cause, danger of a Union between Church and State. One family belonging to the Baptist Church, I have heard was excommunicated for joining our Temperance Society in that place. Thus in our new settlements at that time two very different civilizations met, one from the Eastern & the other from the Southern States. Though both gloried in being American, they were not more homogeneous than Yankees & Germans & Irish.

In the meantime, the subject of slavery began to excite much feeling and discussion.[39] Rev. E. P. Lovejoy[40] undertook to publish a religious Paper in St. Louis, and instead of making it subservient to the slave power, he very temperately and judiciously bore testimony against the wrongs of that system as they rose up before him from week to week. He was compelled to move his Press across the River to Alton. There he soon found that public sentiment was little less obsequious to the Slave power, than in Missouri. On the 7th of Nov. 1837, he was shot down while defending his Press

[38] Washington was considered by the missionaries a very hard field. The Baptists there were much under the influence of Daniel Parker, who opposed any outside organizations as well as a paid ministry. One Baptist notes that "Judas was the first preacher to receive pay" (Warren Nichols, Atlas, Ill., to Peters, August 1, 1835 [ibid.]).

[39] Foster has an interesting description of the antislavery feeling in Alton. At one time it was thought that other New England ministers would lose their lives. Another strong outpost of antislavery spirit was at Quincy, Ill. ("Journal," ed. Spinka, in op. cit., pp. 197–98).

[40] For an excellent summary of the career of Elijah Parish Lovejoy see Pease, op. cit., pp. 364–70. Lovejoy was a native of Maine, the son of a Presbyterian minister. He was a graduate of Waterville [now Colby] College and of Princeton Theological Seminary (1833). He began the publication of a religious newspaper, the St. Louis Observer, at St. Louis, which he later moved to Alton, Ill., as a result of a series of difficulties owing to his denunciation of mob violence. He was killed on November 7, 1837, while attempting to defend his press from a mob.

from the Mob who were bent on destroying it a second time. And in his case it was according to the old maxim "the blood of the martyrs is the seed of the church." Like Sampson, he inflicted a heavier blow upon the cause of slavery by his death than in his life.

In the Autumn of 1837 I accepted a proposition from my friends in Pekin[41] to remove to that place, and devote my whole time to that village and the adjoining settlement on Sand Prairie, and was to receive $500. Salary. Scarcely had we become well domesticated in our new home, when it was made utterly desolate by the sudden removal of my loved companion from my side and from all her walks of usefulness on earth. She retired at night in usual health, and rested quitely. In the morning, she had unpleasant symptoms which medical attendance rather aggravated than controlled, & before the next evening, she was not, for God had taken her. It was a stunning blow to me, the full effects of which came to be realized gradually, and were more & more painfully felt in the progress of time.

Mr. & Mrs. Fred W. Sumner, then members of my church, but subsequently of Detroit, moved into my house & kindly cared for me, till the end of the year for which I was hired. Then I was invited to board with Mrs. Mount, who had buried her husband during the preceding summer, and who gave me a pleasant home while I remained in the place. Thus the Lord kindly cared for me.

I labored in Pekin as earnestly as I knew how, But while there was marked improvement in the general aspect of So-

---

[41] Bascom gives the schedule for this parish in a letter to Peters of January 9, 1838: He preached at Tremont at two o'clock and at "candle light. . . . . Next Sabboth I preach at eleven oclock in Sand Prairie and at two oclock and at candle light at Pekin, six miles from Sand Prairie." The church at Pekin presented some difficult problems. There were only twenty-three members, and over half of these were females. While they pledged $500, they were only able to pay $300. Bascom was forced to board with one of the parishoners, and he notes his expenses: "Board and room $4.00 a week, washing .75c–$1.00 a dozen, horse weekly more than $1.00 and clothing was very high" (Bascom to A.H.M.S. December 11, 1838 [A.H.M.S. Correspondence]).

ciety, I had no satisfactory evidence that sinners were saving-
ly converted. There was very little that was inspiring or
cheering in the work. I was prepared therefore to listen favorably to an invitation from the A.H.M.S. in the Spring of
1839, to undertake an Agency in the State, by way of exploring the new settlements & superintending the Home Mission work, of our two denominations on this field.

CHAP. 7: HOME MISSIONARY AGENCY

To superintend the work of Home Missions in Illinois, in
1839, was a very different thing from such a superintendency
in 1895.[42] Then there were no Rail Roads in the State, The
settlements in the Northern half of the state were new, and
wide intervals were between them without any population.
Roads had not been constructed few Bridges had been built.
Public buildings had not been erected except in a few instances, and these were rude & incommodious. Travelling
was slow, wearisome, and in summer exposed one to those
malarious influences, which were productive of fevers & ague,
and in winter to the bleak Prairie winds and driving, storms,
which endangered life as well as health. It was not uncommon in those times, for persons to lose their lives by the cold
in passing from one settlement to another, or to become be-
wildered in a storm on the Prairie's, and perish before they
could find shelter.

In accepting the agency of the A.H.M.S. I therefore stipu-
lated for the privilege of locating at some place, during the
winter months, to supply some vacant church, and thus
relieve the society from paying my salary for that period.

[42] A. Hale, the former superintendent, was to accompany Bascom for a time,
and together on the field they were to work out plans for their labors. Hale had been
laboring for over seven years but was soon to locate at Springfield. Gridley, who had
been touring the state with a huge tent for his meetings, came to Pekin for Bascom
(Peters to Hale, January 17, 1839; Hale to Badger, May 30, 1839 [A.H.M.S. Corre-
spondence]). Hale states that Bascom had been employed as agent at $500 per
year. They planned to begin work with a "protracted" meeting at Beardstown
(Hale to A.H.M.S., May 17, 1839 [*ibid.*]).

My salary was at the rate of $500 a year. I furnished my own horse & Buggy, and charged my necessary travelling expenses to the Society. So hospitable were those pioneer settlers to ministers, and so low were the charges at Hotels, that my expenses all the summer and fall of that year 1839, were only $30, and by donating that amount to the Home Miss. Society I made myself a life member. This expense account covered the whole time from Ap 1st to Dec. 1st. and included Postage, which ranged from 6½ cents to 25 cents each letter, Hotel Bills, Ferriage and horse shoeing.

I had different objects in view in visiting the different parts of my field, In the larger churches I preached on the subject of Home Missions and took collections for the Society. In the missionary churches which were supplied with ministers, I endeavored to ascertain whether the respective congregations were contributing toward this support of their ministers as much as they ought, and whether they were aiming at self support at as early a day as practicable. I sought also, to heal divisions and alienations that might be threatening to unsettle ministers in those churches, and to strengthen their influence with their people, I counselled with vacant churches in regard to procuring Pastors and corresponded with ministers in reference to destitute places. I visited new settlements for the purpose of preparing the way for organizing churches, where materials were found, In many destitute churches I administered the ordinances of the Gospel, I addressed County Bible Societies, delivered Temperance addresses, and aided in protracted meetings when requested, preaching usually three times on the Sabbath, and as many times during the week as I could find audiences. I also attended ecclesiastical meetings, ordinations, Installations and dedications of church edifices whenever it was practicable. In performing such a work on such a territory, I had not much time for rest or idleness. I began the labors of my Agency in Tazewell County where I had been laboring, and extended them to

adjacent Counties, including Peoria, Marshall, McLean, De-
wit, Sangamon, Morgan, Fulton &c. Before the first of December following, I had travelled as far North as Milwaukee,
on the N. West to Galena, on the West to Galesburg, South
as far as Alton & East as far as Bloomington. To have made a
thorough exploration of this vast territory in one season,
with such facilities of travelling as then existed was of course
impossible. But the places which most needed counsel and
supervision were visited and some of them repeatedly. My
visits were every where thankfully received, and they afforded constant opportunities of aiding those early settlers in
devising and excuting plans for promoting the interests of
education, morality and religion in their respective com-
munites.

My first protracted meeting, as Agent, was at Waynesville
De Witt Co. commencing 17 May.[43] In the daytime we met
in the open air an in the evening in private houses. The
attendance was encouraging, and the fruits of the meeting
seemed valuable. In the meeting held in the Grove the morning before I left, all who purposed to follow Christ from that
time forth were requested to manifest it by taking their
places in the circle for prayer, around the stand. Only one
refused the invitation. And while they were coming forward
an old man arose, and appealed to his neighbors to forgive
him for having so long advocated Universal salvation, and
thus as he feared, hindered some of them from becoming chris-

[43] The pastor at Waynesville was Josiah Porter. He was born in South Carolina,
but his parents were from Londonderry, Conn. In 1828 he studied at Centre College and later went to Indiana University and Lane Theological Seminary. Beginning his pastoral activities in Indiana, he soon had trouble because of his "emancipation ideas" and came to Waynesville, Ill., in December, 1838. He labored there
for seven and one-half years (Norton, *op. cit.*, p. 314). During this visit of Bascom
in 1839 he was serving a small church at Mount Hope besides the one at Waynesville. They did not have a church building but commenced one later in 1839. In
another letter he mentions twelve members as being received this year (J. Porter to
M. Badger, September 25, 1839, and March 11, 1840 [A.H.M.S. Correspondence]).

tians. The sermon last evening, said he "knocked my Universalism all to smash," and I am not going to patch it up again. Had he said that the Spirit of God swept away his refuge of lies, it would have described the case more correctly. For the sermon was not eloquent, nor forcible in itself. It was simply a plain illustration and application of the Saviors words "Ye shut up the kingdom of heaven against men. Ye neither enter in yourselves nor suffer them that are entering to go in." It was the Spirit of God that spoke to him as Nathan did to David, "Thou art the man." I think that he & a number of his sons then began a christian life.

My next protracted meeting was at Beardstown,[44] Bro Hale & myself laboring there together. We found a population of 600 or more—one Presbyterian Professor, a Female, A few Methodist Professors but could find no praying man among them. A few German Lutherans, but no preaching. The only stated appointments for preaching were by a Methodist once in four weeks. A distillery and 18 places where Liquor was sold!

The School house in which our meetings were held, was neglected and dilapidated. But attendance was good, and attention solemn, increasingly, to the end—yet no evidence of any saving conversions. The founder of the village & for whom it it was named was a Universalist, and the people that gathered around him, made their material interests their great concern, forgetting that "Godliness is profitable unto all things."

[44] Bascom had visited Beardstown before he became agent and noted that it had a population of six hundred, with the only preacher, a German, leaving for Europe (Bascom to Badger, April 9, 1839 [ibid.]).

Hale mentions that this meeting had aroused more interest than any church service had received for years. Their meetings met a cold response at first, but this wore off by Sunday. He recommended a missionary to come for preaching here and a small place 18 miles away, called Banther's Creek (Hale to Badger, May 30, 1839 [ibid.]). Bascom says, "The American population have no preaching except occasional Methodist rant of the coarsest sort" (Bascom to Badger, April 9, 1939 [ibid.]).

The latter part of June[45] I commenced a tour through the Northern part of the state and into Wisconsin, as far as Milwaukee. Returning the latter part of August, assisted in organizing the 1st Congregational Church in Ottawa, on reaching home, I made the following memorandum.—"absent more than two months—travelled more than 1000 miles—preached more than 30 times and found 13 places where ministers are urgently needed at once."

The next two months were spent in attending protracted meetings with Bro Hale, at Pleasant Grove and at Sand Prairie with a moderate degree of success, and in attending Presbytery & Synod. At the meeting of Presbytery at Farmington, Sangamon Co. I was taken sick with remittent Fever. After being under a Physicians care for a week I rode to Jacksonville to Commencement and Synod.[46] There I suffered a relapse and was confined more than a week under a Physicians care, in the kind family of Judge Lockwood. After a partial recovery, I spent one Sabbath in Waverly, one in Jerseyville, with my former pupil Rev. Joseph Fowler,[47] and then went to Monticello Female Seminary, to visit my old friend Rev. Theron Baldwin, who had become the Principal & the Financial Agent of that institution. I preached in the

[45] Bascom assisted Sturtevant at Springfield between May 18 and May 30 (Hale to Badger, May 30, 1839 [ibid.]). Their plans were to go to Canton and then separate for the summer. "Brother Bascom to take the east and north and myself the west and north including Iowa and the lead mines. The trip is to be made as short as possible and to meet again in Tazewell County, Sept. 1, where we expect to spend three weeks, one at Pleasant Grove, with Bro. Huntington and one with Brother Barnes at Washington" (ibid.). During June, 1839, the Congregational Union on the Fox River was formed (D. Sweet, Big Grove, to A.H.M.S., June 6, 1839 [ibid.]).

[46] The synod of Illinois, N[ew] S[chool], met at Jacksonville, September 19, 1839. Members were present from six presbyteries, and Lyman Beecher was also present (Norton, op. cit., p. 283).

[47] Joseph Fowler was born in Massachusetts in 1809 and when a child moved with his parents to central Ohio. He graduated from Yale in 1834 and from Lane Theological Seminary in 1837. He came to Jerseyville in 1839 but left in 1840 to engage in teaching. In 1845 he returned to Illinois to take the church at Lacon. He died in 1857 (ibid., p. 283).

Chapel of the Seminary Sabbath morning, and in the evening had a return of my fever, which detained me two weeks. In the meantime I experienced much kindness from my host and his good wife, & from Dr. Edwards my Physician, and formed some precious acquaintances. The Seminary at Monticello was built by Capt. Godfrey,[48] and promises to be a source of inestimable blessings, not only to the present, but to coming generations. Would that more men, who have the means had the disposition & wise forethought to erect such a monument, during their life time, as their lasting memorial.

Returning to Pekin with health only partially restored I rested a few days and spent the three succeeding Sabbaths at that place & Sand Prairie, at Farmington Fulton Co. & at Lacon, in the interest of Home Missions.

CHAP. 8: TEMPORARY SUPPLY AT CHICAGO

In view of the difficulty & danger of winter travelling on the Prairies, the Society had consented that I should supply some vacant Pulpit during the three winter months, and thus provide for my own support, during that time. Having received an invitation to preach for the 1st Pres. Ch. in Chicago during the next winter, I left Pekin, Friday Nov 22, in my own Buggy, for that purpose. Saturday evening found me at Peru, in a snow storm. I enjoyed the hospitality of Dr. Seeley over the Sabbath & preached for Bro. N. Gould, who, at that place & in the vicinity had been struggling for two or three

[48] Captain Godfrey was born December 4, 1794, in Chatham, Mass., and when but nine years of age went to sea. He continued a seafaring life until 1826, when he settled at Matamoras, Mexico, as a merchant. Here he amassed a fortune of $200,-000, which was stolen from him when he was on his way to the United States. Until 1832 he was a merchant at New Orleans, and in that year he came to Alton, where he set up his mercantile business. In 1833 he erected the church at that place which was used by the Presbyterians and Baptists for a time, but a little later it was turned over to the seminary. One day, while noticing the power of his wife over the mental development of one of his daughters, he conceived the idea of a "female seminary." It opened its doors in 1838 after Godfrey had erected a building at a cost of $53,000. Theron Baldwin was the head of the seminary at the time Bascom made this visit. Godfrey continued his activities in the school until his death in 1862 (*ibid.*, pp. 701-3).

years, in sickness & privation & discouragement, to build up a Pres. Church & to give to a sparse but rapidly increasing heterogeneous population, the blessings of the gospel.

During that Sunday night the weather suddenly changed and became intensely cold, the thermometer falling lower than at any time during the succeeding winter. On Monday I proceeded only as far as Ottawa, there enjoying the hospitality of Mr. & Mrs. Hollister, Crossing Fox River with my horse & Buggy on the ice, I proceeded on my journey, and reached Chicago, Thursday, 28th Thanksgiving day, being much retarded the last part of the way by muddy roads. Changes of temperature thus sudden & extreme were not uncommon.

Having found a boarding place at Joseph Meekers, I entered at once on my winter's work. Chicago at this time, had 4000 inhabitants & was an incorporated City. It had one Episcopal Church, St. James, on the North side. One Methodist Episcopal on the corner of Clark & Washington Streets. One Baptist, on the corner of La Salle & Washington Streets, one Presbyterian, their house of worship was on Clark Street, corner of Washington, South of the Court House. It had been built about six years, having been located at first a Block and a half further North, on the same street. The increase of business and the growth of the city, had already required the uptown movement of the churches. Originally it had been one half the size, which it had now attained—its length having been doubled at the time of its removal.

Rev. Jeremiah Porter had ministered to the Ch. two years after its organization. For two years subsequently, it had been without a Pastor, depending on Candidates & transient visitors for a supply. Rev. John Blatchford had then been their settled Pastor two years, and had recently been dismissed. The membership of the church was 200, and the congregation could scarcely be accommodated in their long narrow building, about 30×80 feet.

The congregation gave me a kind and cordial reception. I found a good degree of unity, but a very great diversity. There were representatives from all of the New England & Middle States, from several of the Western and Southern, as well as from England, Ireland, Scotland and Wales. In church polity some had been life long Presbyterians and others Congregationalists. In Theology some were extreme old School & some ultra New School. On questions of Reform, they differed in like manner. Some were radically Anti Slavery, and some opposed to all discussion of such questions.

But while all claimed liberty for their own opinions, they were tolerant toward those who differed from them. Accessions to the church by letter were received at the 1st Communion season, and subsequently a few by profession as well as by letter, were expected to unite with the church at every opportunity. Our weekly Prayer meeting, as well as our Sabbath service, was well attended, Our Sunday School was sustained by a good degree of interest & activity, and a union Tract organization was entered into by at least three Evangelical churches, which sent its visitors monthly, with religious Tracts to all the families of the City which were accessable to such efforts. Thus a field for christian activity was provided for those who were willing to enter it, and the direct fruits and reflex benefits of such agency, were not few.

Some of the Brethren soon suggested the appointment of an anti-slavery Prayer meeting the last Monday evening of every Month, in concert with the praying Anti Slavery people throughout the Country. I knew that such a Concert was observed in many places, and it commended itself to my judgment as eminently appropriate, in accordance with the apostolic injunction "to remember them that are in bonds as bound with them." So without forethought of opposition or objection, I appointed the meeting on the last Monday of Jan. 1840, and invited the friends of the Slaves to meet together & pray for their emancipation. Some fifteen or twenty met and spent an hour in prayer and conference on the subject of slavery, and voted to hold such a meeting every month. The next meeting was attended with increased interest. As our petitions were unheeded by the lawmakers & rulers of the nation, it was esteemed a great privilege that we might present them to the Supreme Ruler of Heaven & Earth assured that, we had his sympathy on our side. The outlook on this subject, was very discouraging which ever way we turned, until we looked upward. The legislative, the executive & judicial departments of Government, both state & national, were all proslavery. The religious denominations, were nearly all implicated in the responsibility of lending their sanction to slavery, by their organic connection with the Southern churches. And even the Mission Boards so connected with slaveholding as to commit them to a policy of silence and neutrality. The friends of the oppressed, therefore, seemed shut up to the faith, Every door seemed closed against them except the one into which our Great High Priest hath entered, to intercede for us, and over this it was written "knock & it shall be opened." There we loved to meet and present our cause to him whose Mission it was to proclaim deliverance to the captives and the opening of prison doors to them that are bound.

My senior Deacon was away from the City, the first two Months and knew nothing of the Anti Slavery Prayer meeting, which we had held. But he was present and heard with great surprise, the appointment for that meeting in February. At the close of the morning service, he remained in his Pew, till I was passing down the Aisle, from the Pulpit to the door, He stepped into the aisle before me and arrested my progress, saying as he did so, "by what authority did you appoint an Anti Slavery meeting in this church?" Such was his ability and influence, as a Citizen & as a member & officer of the Church, that I should have hesitated very much to go contrary to his calm & deliberate judgment expressed in private consultation.[49]

But he was now excited, and he assailed me angrily in a public place, when I had no expectation or preparation for such an encounter. I have, however, always been devoutly thankful that it was given me in that trying moment to reply as follows, "If you mean by that question, to deny my right to use this house for an Anti Slavery Prayer Meeting I shall not contend for that. I cheerfully leave that question to the Trustees. If they exclude us, we can meet elsewhere. But if you mean to deny my right as acting Pastor, to appoint and attend such a meeting, I shall continue to do that, on my own responsibility." He replied, "I warn you that if you introduce Abolition into this church, you will break it into a thousand pieces." By this time others had engaged him in debate & I quietly passed on to my study. Without forethought, I had committed myself on the right side of this great question, and was subsequently saved from a thousand temptations to compromise principle.

As Spring approached, the question of calling me to a permanent Pastorate began to be discussed, and, a meeting was called to take action on the subject. The Sabbath before the church meeting was to be held, the Rev. John Cross,[50] a very prominent Anti Slavery Lecturer, called on me in the morning, no doubt, hoping to be invited to preach for me. I had reason to suppose that he would stimulate the zeal of the Anti Slavery members of my congregation, and arouse the

[49] The incident here related illustrates the importance of the slavery issue in the Plan of Union churches. The New England element were largely antislavery, as well as New School in their theology, while the old Presbyterian stock were more likely to be at least antiabolitionist as well as Old School in their theological position.

[50] Cross met a very good response to his message in the settlements where the people were from New England. D. Smith notes that, whereas he was able to raise but $6.00 to be given to the mission to be paid in the future, Cross raised $60.00 to be paid in the very near future (D. Smith, of Lisbon, Ill., March 31, 1840, to M. Badger [A.H.S.M. Correspondence]). In 1844 Cross was in jail for seeking to help runaway slaves to escape (Pease, *op. cit.*, p. 379).

opposition of others, and perhaps thus create a disturbance, which would prevent united action in extending a call to me. My first thought was, that the Adversary had sent him to hinder my settlement, and I must refuse him my pulpit. Then it occurred to me that he might have come Providentially to prevent my settlement, because the Lord did not wish me to settle there. So I determined to do my duty, & dismiss anxiety about consequences. As he was a Congregational Minister in regular standing, I thought it my duty to treat him with ministerial courtesy, and therefore invited him to preach.

In the morning his discourse was so able and unexceptionable that all were satisfied & glad to hear him again in the evening. But in the latter discourse he made a terrific assault on the system of slavery and exposed the sin of aiding or abetting slave holding, by any action in favor of it, in the church or the state, and claimed that even silent acquiescence toward it was criminal. I supposed that my chance for receiving a call had now gone up higher than a kite. But I quietly awaited the result, and to my surprise received a call, for which all the church voted except two young men, who were not prepared to acquiesce in the call till they knew whether I sanctioned the positions taken by Mr. Cross on Sabbath evening.

When the question of accepting the Pastorate in Chicago was thus presented, requiring a decisive answer, I found it more perplexing than I had anticipated. The various elements and diverse sentiments in the church, I was aware would tax the personal influence and prudence of the Pastor, in preserving harmony. The peculiar condition of the city, yet in its infancy, but rapidly developing, with its institutions in process of organization, and its vital connection with a vast interior country which was rapidly emerging from its primitive communities, I knew would require of a Pastor in Chicago many onerous duties, outside of the ordinary labors of a city ministry. Then my relations to the A.H.M. Society, in whose service I had spent the preceding summer, was an argument against accepting the Pastorate. The labors of a Home Missionary Agent were growing continually in importance. My last summers experience had prepared me to do that work in the future more effectively. I had a liking for the work & the Society desired my continuance in it. On the other hand, it was urged that I had united the church, and that there was reason to fear their refusal to unite on another, if I declined their call. I finally decided to compromise these conflicting claims, by accepting the call on the condition that I might prosecute my Agency the next summer and be installed their Pastor the next Autumn, and in the meantime procure a temporary supply for their pulpit.

The church consented to this arrangement, and I accordingly procured Robert W. Patterson, a Student from Lane Seminary, to fill my place for five Months, from the 1st of May till the 1st of October 1840. My first meeting with him I have mentioned on Pages 93 & 94 [p. 246].

Mr. Patterson interested the people as a Preacher, and the congregation prospered under his ministrations. But, to my surprise, he sympathised with the more conservative members, in respect to Anti Slavery sentiment and action, In the progress of events he and I had changed our relative positions, on that subject, and those who disliked to have their Pastor called an Abolitionist, were drawn toward him, as a prudent, cautious, man who was opposed to Slavery, but who could always find some fault with the men and measures, employed against [it].

CHAP. 9: RESUMPTION OF HOME MISSIONARY AGENCY

On the 15th of May, I recommenced the work of my Home Missionary Agency, suspended during the winter.[51]

[51] The financial situation in the East had so reduced the funds of the A.H.M.S. that Bascom was informed to reduce expenses in every way possible; he was also asked to raise as much money in Illinois as possible (Badger to Bascom, April 21, 1840 [A.H.M.S. Correspondence]).

My first trip was into Will County, visiting Thornton, Beebe's Grove, now Crete, Hickory Creek settlement, Goodings Grove, Hadley, Wilmington, Joliet, Lockport, Athens, & Flag Creek, (now Lyonsville.) in all of which places I found small Pres. or Cong. Churches, or scattered members of such churches, desirous of enjoying preaching, and church relations.[52] With these christian people I conferred, & counselled, and preached to them as opportunity offered. Returning to Chicago I prepared for another tour. In Lake County I found a small Church at Mechanics Grove, a few miles West of Libertyville, There I spent a Sabbath preaching and administering the ordinances, and counseling with them in regard to some agitating questions which seemed ominous of

[52] "Beebes Grove is 30 miles south of Chicago. Nearly all the people are Presbyterians but there are a couple Methodist and Episcopal families. The church is newly formed and consists of 20 members. Rev. N. C. Clark assisted in its organization" (Seymour Thompson to C. Hall, March 7, 1840 [ibid.]). Thompson refers to a little church in this vicinity which is called Thorn Grove. It had been recently organized and had preaching occasionally.

A committee from the church at Hadley stated that Hickory Creek was five or six miles south of Gooding's Grove and had a small Baptist church. E. G. Howe became pastor of the church at Gooding's Grove together with the Hickory Church but had considerable trouble because of his attempt to handle a moral problem. Bascom notes that Howe's parisoners criticized his calling because he talked about the stock and crops instead of the condition of their souls (E. G. Howe to A.H.M.S., September, 1840; December 15, 1840 [ibid.]). Howe states that he organized the church at Gooding's Grove with twenty members "most of whom were from Vermont and New York" (Howe to A.H.M.S., July 23, 1839 [ibid.]).

The committee of Hadley, in describing their territory to M. Badger on April 4, 1840, speaks of Lockport as a small town seven miles west of Hickory Creek Church. Later in this year J. D. Porter came to this place as pastor from Naperville.

On an early map dated 1854 Flag Creek Post Office is located near the Des Plaines River, and Lyons Post Office is situated about a mile east. There is no mention of Athens. Probably all these churches were under the care of E. G. Howe, who was the missionary at Gooding's Grove.

Fifteen of the members of the Hadley church organized the church at Gooding's Grove (Farnum to Badger, April 4, 1840 [ibid.]). The Hadley church was organized August 17, 1833, with eight members. The nearest church was in Chicago, thirty miles away. Membership on April 4, 1840, was "about thirty-five" (ibid.).

Howe noted in 1839 that this church was split with dissensions and in a letter from Farnum (November 10, 1840) states that the people are too much interested in politics which has caused the breaking-out of old feuds. Howe in his report for September, 1840, informs the secretary that he holds occasional preaching service at Wilmington in addition to his work at Hickory Creek and Gooding's Grove.

trouble, and in regard to securing stated ministrations of the gospel.

Returning to Chicago, I set out again on the 5th of June, on a distant tour Westward. Stopping at Charleston, now St. Charles,[53] where I found Bro N. C. Clark, who was supplying both that place & Elgin.[54] He came into the state two weeks earlier than I did, and had within the seven intervening years organized a number of churches on the Du Page & Fox Rivers, in villages & settlements whose population was rapidly increasing every year by immigration from the Eastern & middle states. I visited Garden Prairie and Belvidere, preaching and consulting in regard to a Stated Ministry for them. The next week I visited Fox River Union[55] at E. Du Page. This was the first Cong. Association in the state, and was small & feeble. Thence to Aurora,[56] where I prepared the way for Bro C. Cook to locate in charge of the Church at that place. Thence by way of Paw Paw Grove, I went to

[53] On October 22, 1839, Clark writes that St. Charles is a village less than four years old and contains about four hundred inhabitants. "It has the reputation in this country as being quite a moral place." Congregationalists, Baptists, Methodists, and Universalists were all on the ground, and a large proportion of the people were in favor of the latter. Clark reports that he preaches twice at neighboring places during the week (Clark to A.H.M.S. [A.H.M.S. Correspondence]). In this same letter he mentions that a Congregational church was organized at Elgin. Interest had been aroused by the preaching of Gridley, who was touring the state and holding evangelistic services in a large tent.

[54] J. H. Prentiss states that in 1835 there was not a Presbyterian within two miles of Elgin, but in a year's time he had gathered sixteen members. He also reported a Sunday school, two Bible classes, and a temperance society with sixty members. In 1835 there were only thirteen buildings, but a year later there were fifty or sixty. The missionary reports in 1837 one hundred and thirty buildings in the town and fifty professors of religion (Prentiss to A.H.M.S., January 1, 1836[ibid.]).

[55] The Fox River Union will be described in the records of the Naperville church, which was one of the first members. D. Smith in his missionary report of June 6, 1839, mentions the organization of this union as consisting of but three members, but the presbytery of Ottawa was sending a delegate to seek a possible union with them.

[56] H. C. Colton was serving as missionary at Aurora in 1838 and also at Long Grove. Aurora had 120 members in a temperance society (H. C. Colton to A.H.M.S., July 3, 1838 [A.H.M.S. Correspondence]).

Princeton,[57] preaching there in both churches and taking collections for Home Missions. I there found Rev. O. Lovejoy, in charge of the Hampshire Colony Church, now the 1st Congregational. Preached a third service at Dover, where Rev. Mr. Donaldson was supplying. Thence to Lacon, Washington, Pleasant Grove, Springfield, Jacksonville.[58]

In this trip I attended a Convention at Jacksonville, for the promotion of Educational interests, & College Commencement, and returning attended Bro. Hales' Installation at Springfield, by the Sangamon Presbytery.

Returning to Chicago by way of Peoria, I endeavored to confirm the little churches, and encourage the scattered disciples wherever I found them.

I spent a Sabbath with my people in Chicago and enjoyed with them a communion season.

I commenced another tour on the 12th, attending Presbytery at Bristol, where I assisted in the ordination of their young Missionary, Bro. L. C. Gilbert. I visited Rock Creek, an adjoining settlement, in which Bro. G[ilbert] preaches a part of the time,—called on several families and preached in the evening at a private house. The next Sabbath I spent at

---

[57] The Princeton church was originally the "Hampshire Colony." Lucien Farnham was pastor until 1838 and was succeeded by Owen Lovejoy, who remained for eighteen years. Owen Lovejoy, like his brother Elijah P. Lovejoy, was a fearless antislavery man and in 1846 received 3,531 votes for Congress in the fourth Illinois district (Pease, op. cit., p. 372).

The Dover church was organized from a group of members previously connected with the Princeton church. They applied for their letters to form a church at Dover on March 14, 1838, giving as their reason their great distance from the Princeton church (Hampshire Colony Church, op. cit., p. 15). As a result of Bascom's visit to the Dover church, its membership was doubled and improvements were made to the building.

[58] Lacon was located on the edge of Bascom's first circuit in Illinois. There was considerable discouragement among the Presbyterian-Congregational churches in this region at this time owing to the depressed economic conditions and also to the fact that the Old School Presbyterian church was attempting to establish independent churches. For the general religious situation in Jacksonville about this period see Frank J. Heinl, "Jacksonville and Morgan County," *Journal of the Illinois State Historical Society*, XVIII (April, 1925), 5–38.

Sycamore,[59] the County seat of De Kalb Co. where a small church had been formed, but had no stated Ministry. I preached & administered the sacrament, and in the P.M. preached in a settlement three miles distant. The following week I was at Charleston[60] and Big Woods, at Chicago, and the following Sabbath at Naperville,[61] Rev. Jonathan Porter preached his farewell sermon in the morning & I preached on christian Benevolence, endeavoring to call out their liberality in behalf of the cause of Home Missions.

Lake Co. next claimed a visit and I spent a day or two at Indian Creek, thence to Mechanic's Grove,[62] wherewith Rev. O. Lyman by appointment of Presbytery, we inquired into some alledged irregularities, and brought matters to a happy issue. The next Sabbath Aug. 2, I preached in a new log meeting house, to a new congregation six or eight miles further North. The little church which I there organized has had a subsequent history of much interest It enjoyed the faithful ministry for several years, of Father Dodge, and is still ranked among our able and useful country churches. It now is called the church of Millburn.[63]

Thence I returned to Chicago, to accompany Rev. Royal N. Wright, who came there at my request, to Belvidere,[64]

[59] The Congregational church at Sycamore was organized April 11, 1840, in the courthouse (Manual of the Congregational Church, Sycamore).

[60] N. C. Clark was pastor at Charleston besides his work at Elgin. Big Woods Church was organized June 16, 1836, by N. C. Clark. In the beginning the Congregationalists, Methodists, and Baptists worked together (A. E. Bartholomew, "Sketch of Big Woods Church").

[61] See the MS records of the Naperville church.

[62] Mechanic's Grove was near Naperville. O. Lyman lived near Naperville and occasionally supplied that church. For a time he was regular pastor of the E. Du Page church.

[63] The Millburn church was located a few miles northwest of the present town of Gurnee and east of Antioch. It is in operation at the present time.

[64] The church at Belvidere was organized in March, 1839, with twenty-three members. After Wright had been in the community three months, nine new members had been added. Of the total membership, only eleven were males. Besides

where I had prepared the way for him to locate as a Missionary Pastor. He was kindly received & was much pleased with the place as a field of labor. For a few years his prospects of usefulness were realized, But an early death interrupted his plans, and called his people as well as his young family to mourn with a deep sense of bereavement. The next Sabbath at Rockford,[65] preached to an interesting congregation in their new house, and prepared the way for a collection for Home Missions, to be taken by personal solicitation. Preached on the next day at Marcus White's in Garden Prairie, & learned that they soon expect a resident Minister in that place.

At Dundee[66] met Bro. N. C. Clark, and conferred with the people, after preaching, in reference to organizing a church. I encouraged them to go forward and they made an appointment for further consultation and action.

The next Sabbath was spent at Big Woods, where I preached three times and administered the Lords Supper, under the shade of large forest trees, adjoining a school house which proved too small for the congregation. It was a season of tender interest.

From thence I went to Warrenville and delivered a temperance address. Returning I preached again at Bro. Town's

---

preaching twice each Sunday at Belvidere, which was a county seat, he preached once each Sunday at a place five miles distant (R. N. Wright to A.H.M.S., December 1, 1840 [A.H.M.S. Correspondence]). Bascom reports the following information regarding Belvidere (Bascom to Badger, September 10, 1840 [*ibid.*]): The church pays $100 in cash and $150 in produce. Wright is "just from the Seminary at Cincinnati and is thoroughly educated . . . . and is going to New Hamsphire for a wife." In this letter Bascom asks for an appropriation of $200 from the American Home Missionary Society for Belvidere.

[65] The Rockford Congregational Church was organized May 5, 1837, with eight members, and eleven more were added the first year. J. Morrell was the first minister from 1837 to 1838; Wahston succeeded Morrell in 1838 (*Manual of the Rockford Church* [Rockford, 1876]).

[66] Dundee was one of the preaching places which Clark served in addition to his work at Elgin and Charleston.

house & passed on to Plainfield, where I found the church feeble & languishing. Bro. Foster, their former Minister, farming, and preaching, occasionally. He favored the Unionism, advocated by one Merrick and his followers in Western N.Y. whose influence was really adapted to create a new sect, whose distinguishing Article of faith was, that no sect had any right to exist, but that all christians should disband their organizations and be merged in organic unity—in other words, all join the new sect called Unionists. While there was much abstract truth in their creed on this subject, the influence of their preaching & methods was distracting, and enfeebling to the churches. There was therefore much good sense in the remark of an old Deacon, who had sympathised with the doctrine & had favored the aims of the Unionists, but when he saw the practical working of their plans, he drew back, saying "he did not believe in being united all to pieces." 23[rd Aug.] I visited Meacham's Grove,[67] and assisted Bro. Rockwell in organizing a church of 17 members—now the church of Bloomingdale. I preached twice on the Sabbath and administered the Lords Supper in a new Barn. Preached also in a School house on Monday & Tuesday evening, & and attend[ed] the funeral of a child on Wednesday. Much interest seemed manifested in our Meetings, and a salutary impression I trust was made.

On the 2nd of Sept. I attended a meeting of Presbytery at

[67] Meacham's Grove was located in Bloomingdale Township, Du Page County, and in Bascom's time was a country cross-roads with a country store. The church was established there in August 1840 (Rufus Blanchard, *History of Du Page County* [Chicago, 1882], p. 281).

In his report to the A.H.M.S., on September 22, 1840, Bascom states: "I have formed two churches within the last month in very interesting circumstances, one of them in Meacham's Grove, a part of Br. D. Rockwell's field of Elk Grove. The other on Mill Creek in the north part of Lake County. There I found sixteen members and a new log school house full of people who had never before seen a minister of our denomination in their settlement." In February, 1840, the A.H.M.S. granted Rockwell $50 (Badger to Bascom, February, 1840 [A.H.M.S. Correspondence]).

Lockport,[68] and assisted in the installation of Rev. John Porter as Pastor. I preached the Installation sermon and also on the evenings preceding and following.

By way of Big Grove and Ottawa, I went to Lowell[69] to spend a Sabbath, there I found much sickness. Rev. G. W. Elliot & his family were suffering from it. In the morning I preached and administered the Lords Supper, and in the P.M. preach[ed] a funeral discourse,—for two persons whose remains, were before us in the place of worship. Thence I went to Peru, & found the church vacant and almost discouraged. By Homer & Troy Grove,[70] I passed on to Dixon & thence to Buffalo Grove, where I attended a meeting of the Rock River Association, embracing the churches & Ministers as far North as the Wisconsin line and as far South as Princeton. It had in its membership such men as Horatio Foote, John Morrill, Owen Lovejoy &c and rumor had spread a suspicion of their radicalism & unsoundness in regard to doctrine & polity. But my communication with them, in the discussions and fraternal intercourse of that meeting, taught me to confide in their trust worthiness as Ministers and christian Brethren. I remained at Buffalo Grove over the next Sabbath, and supplied

[68] November 5, 1840, Porter to A.H.M.S., states that Lockport was a new town and was filled with worldly people. There were large numbers of Roman Catholics also who "swear, drink, and murder and they will receive few Bibles." In spite of these discouragements he reports, however, that he was starting a church building.

[69] A group of laymen had organized the church at Lowell in 1837 and had expected to obtain a minister at once, but economic conditions prevented. At the time of this visit of Bascom there were eighty members, and all they were able to raise was $300. Differences among the members, the committee states, had hindered the work (Committee to Bascom, Lowell, November 29, 1840 [A.H.M.S. Correspondence]).

[70] "1838 organized a church at Troy Grove. Preached there occasionally the third service—ten miles distant from Rockwell" (unpublished diary of Nahum Gould).
Under the heading January 19–February 14, 1839, Gould says: "The little church organized here last year is in great danger of being swallowed up in this general vortex of infidelity." On July 10, 1841, Gould moved to Troy Grove. He states that he "organized a Presbyterian church at Peru and Rockwell," after his return from general assembly in 1837. He built himself a house and moved there with his wife and four daughters.

their pulpit, and conferred with them in regard to obtaining a Minister.

On the 14th I was at Bloomingville[71] afterward called Byron where I found Rev. Ebenezer Brown recently from Mass. and decided to recommend him for a Commission to the A.H.M.S.

I next passed on to Rockford[72] & Pecatonia, in both of which places sickness was very prevalent. Bro. C. L. Watson of Rockford, very sorely afflicted by the recent death of his fourth wife, accompanied me to Beloit. Rev. Mr. Adams[73] residing on a farm preaches at both Pecatonica & and Beloit. The latter place needed the whole time of a resident Pastor & wished to be so supplied as soon as practicable.

At Winnebago I conferred with Bro. Horatio Foote in regard to filling a larger place, which subject he was willing to consider.

I called at Freeport and urged our friends there to make an effort to obtain stated preaching, promising them Home Missionary aid in making up a Pastors salary.

On the 19th I visited Galena, and spent a Sabbath with Bro. Kent. On Monday had symptoms of Billious fever, &

71 In March, 1840, the missionary at Bloomingville reported sixty-five scholars in the Sunday school, seventy-five members in the temperance society, and twenty-five church members. The church had been organized in 1837 (Ebenezer Brown to Badger, March 23, 1840 [A.H.M.S. Correspondence]).

The following is Bascom's report for Bloomingville, September 15, 1840: "Brother E. Brown and his people wish his commission renewed. They have paid up the old subscription and pledge $200.00 for the coming year. They ask for $125.00. . . . . I hope it will be granted. . . . . It is an interesting community and Br. B. has gained a good foothold here."

72 The Rockford church was organized May 5, 1837, with eight members. The first year it increased to nineteen. G. L. Watson became the minister in 1838 and remained until 1841.

73 Bascom reports that Adams works on his farm during the week and reads his old sermons on the Sabbath. The sermons were prepared for New England and are not suited to his audience. He reports the Beloit people are planning to obtain a full-time minister (Bascom to A.H.M.S., September 15, 1840 [A.H.M.S. Correspondence]).

was too unwell to travel. I called a Physician & took medicine, and was relieved.

On the 24th I was so far recovered as to proceed on Savannah,[74] where I found a few Christians, but no church & no preaching, but some desire for Gospel Institutions, which I endeavored to strengthen. Thence I went to Fulton City,[75] where I found a feeble church and a minister in the midst of a day of small things. I next visited Lyndon[76] & spent a Sabbath with Bro. Hazard & his people, pleasantly & I trust profitably. Thence I passed on to Sharon, Geneseo,[77]

[74] On February 19, 1840, S. S. Lowe sends an appeal from Savannah for a minister. He describes the town as follows: "There are some thirty or thirty-five families with houses, stores, taverns and in the vicinity mills in proportion to the inhabitants." The postmaster also sends a note saying that he thinks they could raise $200 (S. S. Howe to A.H.M.S. February 19, 1840 [A.H.M.S. Correspondence]).

[75] At this time J. H. Prentiss was pastor at Fulton. He had come to Illinois in 1835 and had located at Joliet. Here he had good success, but thought that he would have a better church at Fulton. However, his experience was otherwise. The fevers from the low country ravaged his family to such an extent that at one time they were all sick with the "bilious fever" at the same time. He remained at Fulton from the spring of 1838 until the first part of 1841. He then became the pastor of Naperville. While there were one hundred inhabitants at Fulton, yet he had only one male professor in the town. He held services at Albany, Lyonsville, Union Grove, and Round Grove. In 1839 Fulton paid but $50 on its pastor's salary (Committee to C. Hall, July 1, 1839; April 2, 1838; J. H. Prentiss to C. Hall, July 1, 1839 [A.H.M.S. Correspondence]).

[76] A personal reminiscence of Hazard's coming to Lyndon is given in the *Jubilee Papers*, p. 19: "As my father in 1839 settled at Lyndon on the Rock River, we found there already a Congregational Church three years old, bearing even date with the settlement made in 1836. As the colonists in their mid-week afternoon service were praying for a minister to be sent them, a stranger, who lost his way fell in upon them. He proved to be the "Home Missionary for Ottawa and LaSalle County," Rev. Elisha Hazard. Hazard says the church increased in one year from thirty to seventy-one (Hazard to Badger, January 3, 1840 [A.H.M.S. Correspondence]).

[77] Geneseo was the tenth Congregational church to be organized in the state. It was organized "at the home of Warren Buel in Genesee County, New York." The church decided to emigrate as a body to Illinois and sent an exploring expedition in advance to secure a location. The original church consisted of thirteen members, but they did not all come to Illinois at the same time. In September, 1837, five families started for Illinois, and, when they arrived, they found the exploring group sick and no cabins built. After spending a severe winter, they finally organized the little community known as Geneseo. Wilcox, their pastor in New York, did not arrive until May, 1838, but on his arrival he immediately entered into the growing

Andover, Galesburg,[78] Knoxville,[79] Peoria, & to my first Missionary field, Pleasant Grove, in Tazewell Co. In each of the places just named I tarried a little, and endeavored to gather the facts in regard the circumstances and needs & wishes of those who were Pioneers in laying foundations for christian Society, so that the friends of Home Missions might be enabled to contribute intelligently, in aid them.

At the house of my Bro. Julius in P. Grove, I had a relapse of Billious fever, and was detained a week. Having recovered so far as to proceed on my way, I arrived in Chicago Oct. 24. very thankful that I had fulfilled my Mission as Agent, had completed my wanderings, and was now to enter upon the work of a Pastor, in probably the most interesting & promising field in the State. But my summers work & exposure, had greatly impaired my health, and I was very poorly prepared, physically for the work that was now before me.

---

life of the community and later was instrumental in planting trees for the streets as well as providing for a public square, etc. This church was soon reorganized as Presbyterian (Albert Bushnell, *Semi-centennial of the Organization of the First Congregational Church of Geneseo, Illinois* [Geneseo, 1886] Wilcox to Badger, August 22, 1840, and November 22, 1840 [A.H.M.S. Correspondence]).

At this period Andover was the trading center for Geneseo. A minister from Andover came to Geneseo and administered the sacrament before Wilcox had arrived.

[78] Galesburg was named after G. W. Gale, who was instrumental in organizing the colony. He had come from Oneida, New York, where he was interested in a school for training ministers. Becoming interested in Illinois, the project was transferred to Galesburg, where a church and community developed about the school. Bascom later became pastor of the church and mentions the attempts of some of the members to have the church become Congregational after it had been formed as a Presbyterian (R. W. Gale to G. Hall, December 18, 1840; "Autobiography" of Bascom, pp. 180 ff.).

[79] J. J. Miter was pastor of Knoxville in 1840 and has much to say about a great revival which netted his church over thirty members. He kept closely in touch with the church at Geneseo, and, when Wilcox applied for admission to the Knox Presbytery, Miter made a trip of investigation and reported that they (people of Geneseo) are poor "men of the right stamp." One of his greatest troubles came from the Old School group, who had erected a church in his town worth $4,000 and had removed the temperance regulation from the requirements for admission. This, in addition to the wealth of one of their "elders," was the cause of much dismay in Miter's church (J. J. Miter, Knoxville, Ill., to M. Badger, January 10, 1840; November 26, 1840; July 22, 1840 [A.H.M.S. Correspondence)].

CHAPTER VIII

Early Congregationalism in Michigan
Letters and Reports from Home
Missionaries, 1825-42

THE following letters from some of the early Congregational missionaries in Michigan, selected from the files of the American Home Missionary Society, reveal the diverse problems and difficulties which they faced on the Michigan frontier. They not only disclose the variety and scope of their activities but they also bring to light the principal factors which operated to establish Congregationalism as distinct from Presbyterianism. (See chap. ii.)

PONTIAC, March 18, 1825

DEAR BROTHER,

I hoped to see you at Cherry Valley; but He who doeth all things well did not permit. I was employed by the Cooperstown Agency[1] to labor as a missionary in Michigan Territory, & to be located at Pontiac, Oakland County. . . . .

I set my face towards the Field of my mission about the first of November; & was more than 3 weeks on my journey, passing round the Lake thro Ohio. The friends of Zion in this Territory appeared to be glad that a missionary has been sent among them. They express their gratitude towards those, thro, whose kindness they enjoy the blessing.

The Field, dear Brother, is large, & of our own denomination, I am the only laborer. I know not of any other Presbyterian minister in the Territory except at Mackina. Br. Moore left Detroit last August, but he is expected to return in 2 or 3 months. The people are able & willing to afford him a

[1] An agency of the United Domestic Missionary Society.

support. A chh. was organized at Pontiac, about a year ago, by Br. Goodman, consisting of 13 members.[2] I visited this place in August last, & dispensed the Lord's Supper to them for the first time since they were organized. Four were added at that time, 3 by letter, & 1 by profession. 24 have been added since the first of December; 16 of whom were received from other chhs; & 8 by profession; 4 or 5 of whom have experienced religion recently. Three or 4 are expected to unite next Lord's day, & a number more as soon as it may be convenient. The immigration to this Territory is, at present, rapid;[3] & it is a matter of joy & gratitude that a good proportion are pious or friends to the Redeemer's cause. I think it probable, that, in the course of the year, it will be advisable to organize one or two other churches in this County. I have visited Macomb County, & find that a missionary of our order is needed, & would be welcome there. They wish me to visit them as often as it may be in my power.

I purpose to visit the River Raisin, in Monro Co., as soon as the travelling will admit. There is a chh. there of about 30 members, as I have been informed, & the people desire a minister, & are able & willing, as I understand, to do considerable towards the support of one. The chh at Detroit, I am told, consists of about 30 members. Br. Goodman, who was here a year ago, & who is now in the employment of your Society at Bethany, Pa. would be an acceptable laborer in this Territory. I wish he could be persuaded, & employed, & sent hither.

[2] The Pontiac church embraced the larger portion of Oakland County. Preaching services were held and the Lord's Supper administered at several different locations (George Hornell to A. Peters, Bloomfield, Michigan Territory, April 9, 1829 [A.H.M.S. Correspondence]). This corresponds rather closely to the Methodist circuit. Later, as more churches were organized, the A.H.M.S. missionaries adopted the practice of establishing a circuit of churches, one man serving as many as four or five churches and in addition rendering ministerial service to other settlements when opportunity offered.

[3] The Erie Canal was opened during this year and immediately resulted in a tremendous increase of migration to the frontier area.

. . . . There is one Baptist chh. in this County & an elder who has lately moved his family here. He told me a few weeks since that there had never yet been any one baptised in this Territory, & that this is the only Baptist chh. in the Territory. There are some Methodist & two itinerant preachers in the Territory. Good might be done by Tracts here, & if any can be sent by the Tract Society, they would be gratefully received & used to good advantage. We are about forming a Tract Society which will be auxiliary to that at New York.

Yours in the best of bonds, ISAAC W. RUGGLES[4]

REV. M. BRUEN

PONTIAC, OAKLAND COUNTY MICHIGAN
TERRITORY Augt. 22nd. 1825

REV. & DEAR SIR

. . . . We solicit the continuance of your charity to us still longer. For the support of the Gospel at present, we are able to do but little. It is not seven years since improvements commenced in this county. People in general are poor & came here because they were so. All that we have been able to do for the support of Mr. Ruggles since he has been among us is simply to furnish his *board*. Were he not a man of such self-denial & one whose great object & delight is to promote the glory of God in the salvation of souls, we think he would not have consented to spend a year in the wilderness for the *small* sum of ONE HUNDRED DOLLARS. Some arrangements have

---

[4] Isaac W. Ruggles was born in Brookfield, Conn., July 14, 1783. In 1812, at the age of twenty-nine, he was admitted to the Junior class at Yale, where he studied with President Dwight. Subsequent to his graduation in 1814, he continued his studies with Lyman Beecher at Litchfield, Conn. He was licensed to preach by the Union Association in New York, and then ordained as the pastor of the South Bainbridge Church on February 15, 1820 (biographical sketch in *The American Congregational Year-Book for the Year 1858*, pp. 114-15; George Punchard, *History of Congregationalism* [Boston: Congregational Publishing Co., 1881], V, 305; James H. Hotchkin, *History of the Purchase and Settlement of Western New York*, *etc.* [New York, 1848], pp. 111-12).

been made & by the assistance of your society we hope to retain him longer. . . . . For particulars we refer you to Mr. Ruggles your missionary in whom we have much confidence.

Yours, Sir, with Christian affection
By order of the Church Session

EPHRAIM BURGE   *Clerk*

REV. M. BRUEN   *Cor. Sec. of U.D. Miss. Society*

PONTIAC, Aug. 29—1825

REV. & DEAR SIR:

. . . . My labors have been confined almost entirely to Oakland County. Having no fellow laborer of my own order in the County, I have been constrained to visit & to preach in a large circuit; & owing to the scattered condition of the church, it has been expedient to administer the Lord's Supper in 3 or 4 several places. 41 have been added to the church since the first of December; 22 from other churches, & 19 by profession. 5 or 6 have, we hope, passed from death unto life during the past season. A few days since, we have been called to mourn the loss of one much beloved & esteemed, who was a Deacon & Ruling Elder in this chh. The whole number now in the chh. is 55. Several others will soon be added. I have baptised 21; 7 adults & 14 children; I have dispensed the communion 8 times. I have ordained in this chh. 2 Ruling Elders & 1 Deacon. Pastoral visiting has been my employment almost every day; & in this duty, I have generally, met with a kind reception. The people have often expressed their thanks for my labors of love.

Three Sabbath schools are instituted in the County; 3 concerts of prayer; & 2 Female weekly prayer meetings. A Female Tract Society has been instituted, & a Bible Society is contemplated. Meetings are, in general, well attended.

. . . . The Lord's people are desirous that the same means should be continued, & also that more missionaries of the cross should be sent over to help them. No one, Dear Brother, but those residing in this destitute region, can be adequately sensible of the need there is, that more heralds of salvation should be sent to this part of the Lord's heritage. . . . . Two weeks since, I organized a church in the South part of this County, styled the 2nd. chh. of Oakland County; consisting of 8 members. One was added the Sabbath following. . . . . Here in the wilderness, where 18 months ago, no civilized man resided, the standards of the cross is now erected.[5] . . . .

Brother Foutis, a missionary recently sent out by the General Assembly is now laboring with good success at the River Raisin. Br. Wells who has, the summer past, been preaching at Detroit, is about to be settled there. One or 2 more laborers is needed in Oakland Co. One is needed at Macomb Co., another at Washtenaw County. . . . .

ISAAC W. RUGGLES

REV. M. BRUEN

PONTIAC, Jan. 17—1825[1826][6]

REVEREND & DEAR SIR,

On my return after I saw you, I found occasion to mourn the loss of one very much beloved & esteemed, not only by the church, but by the community; a man by the name of Burge who was a ruling Elder & clerk in the church. In my last I mentioned the death of Deacon Hedges. These mysterious Providences lead us to consider the frailty of man, & to feel more entirely our dependence on God. Such losses ap-

[5] The church at Farmington.

[6] This date should be 1826 for the following reasons: (*a*) Ruggles had just arrived in Michigan about the first of December, 1824. (How, then, could he, a little more than a month later, speak of all these activities, visiting Ann Arbor, etc.?) (*b*) He speaks of the death of Burge, yet Burge signed a letter dated August 22, 1825. (*c*) His letter of August 29, 1825, mentions the death of a "Deacon and Ruling Elder." In this letter Ruggles writes, "In my last I mentioned the death of Deacon Hedges." (*d*) The church at Farmington had not been organized by January 17, 1825. (How, then, could four have been added?) (*e*) It is a common mistake to write the previous year in the date during the first few days of the new year.

pear to be against us; but "in wrath the Lord remembers man." He has sent others who we hope will fill the place of those whom he has taken. The aspect of things at the village of Pontiac is more hopeful than at any time previous.

The people have raised by subscription, a sum which together with 100 dollars from your Society, will make a sufficiency for my support. The church in the South Western part of the County is prospering; 4 have been added since my return. The township is now named Farmington. The people are anxiously hoping that the Rev. Mr. Crawford, whom I mentioned, will be sent to them. I hope it is in the power of your society to grant their request.

I have visited Ann Arbour the County Seat in Washtenaw County which commenced settling about 2 years since. I find the prospect of building up a church here very flattering. The influencial characters are professors of religion; & almost without exception, are of our own profession. There are about 20 in & near the village who are professors in the Presbyterian Church, & contemplate being organized soon.

Yours in the best of bonds,

ISAAC W. RUGGLES

REV. M. BRUEN

PONTIAC, June 17—1826

REVEREND & DEAR SIR,

Since my last Report, spiritual affairs have continued much as they were then, in a low state. . . . . Within the last 3 months, 6 have united with the church at Pontiac; 5 of them by letter, & one by profession. . . . .

No fellow servant yet, comes over to help me; duty therefore, constrains me to visit & to preach in a kind of circuit throughout the county. A Baptist Brother who moved into the Territory before I did, preaches at Pontiac one half the time. He is a good man & a helper. Methodist Circuit riders pass thro the County once in 2 or 3 weeks & I hope are doing some good. We are all harmonious, & endeavor so to arrange our appointments that we may not interfere, but accommodate the people with preaching as well as we are able.[7]

Yours Affectionately

I. W. RUGGLES

REV. A. PETERS[8]

PONTIAC, Sept. 15—1826

To the Secretary of the American Home Missionary Society.

VERY DEAR SIR

The Presbyterian Church of Pontiac Oakland County, Michigan Terr. acknowledges with livliest gratitude the aid received from your Society in sending a Pastor to this distant and feeble Church. . . . . We are constrained to solicit a continuance of support, that this people may not sink into that darkness which envelopes the savages who roam in their forests.

Yours most affectionately

STEPHEN T. R. TROWBRIDGE

Clerk of the Session

PONTIAC, March 6—1827.

REV. & DEAR SIR.

. . . . You wish to obtain some knowledge of our Aux. M. Society.

The sum specified in my commission is raised by our Soc. More might be obtained, were it not for the extreme scarcity

---

[7] This co-operative spirit is in marked contrast to the more orthodox Presbyterians who considered any field "destitute" that did not enjoy the ministrations of a Presbyterian minister. Such a co-operative spirit, however, is typically shown by most of the frontier documents.

[8] The American Home Missionary Society had replaced the United Domestic Missionary Society earlier in the year.

of money. Produce abounds here; but of money, there is little or none.[9] The officers of our Soc. are Rev. I. W. Ruggles, Pres.—Dea. Jacob Vorhiis V. Pres.—Stephen V. Trowbridge Sec.—Dea. Om. Chamberlin Treas. . . . .

If you think proper, you will please to retain in your Treasury, $25 out of the $100 which may be due me, & I will receive the $25 raised by our Society.

Yours in the best of bonds—

I. W. RUGGLES

REV. A. PETERS

PONTIAC, Sept. 12—1827

REVEREND & DEAR SIR,

Since my last the affairs of Zion have continued much as they were. . . . . I have recently organized a church consisting of 9 members, at Rochester, about 10 miles to the east of Pontiac.[10] 12 or 15 more are expected to unite with them as soon as convenient. Rochester is a village now in its infancy; but has excellent water privileges, & will probably, in time, become a place of some importance. It stands on the river Clinton, the same river on which Pontiac is situated.

A Presbytery has been organized for the Territory. Only 3 ministers now belong to it, but 2 or three others will unite; & we hope others also will come over & help us.

. . . .

The people have showed me much kindness, & appear willing to afford me support. They have aided me, the sum-

---

[9] The scarcity of money on the frontier constituted one of the major factors necessitating continued missionary support. The settlers had spent their money to purchase their lands, and markets were not available for the sale of their produce. As late as 1839 E. P. Hastings wrote that "the opinion is prevalent that there is not money enough in circulation in the State to pay the taxes now in the process of collection" (E. P. Hastings, Detroit, December 25, 1839 [A.H.M.S. Correspondence]).

[10] This is usually credited with being the first Congregational church formed in Michigan (Punchard, op. cit., V, 307). Ruggles, however, had already formed a Congregational church at Farmington which later became Presbyterian.

mer past, in building a house at Pontiac. It has been done principally by donations. . . . .

　　　With much affection & esteem, I subscribe myself your fellow servant, & your brother in the best of bonds.

　　　　　　　　　　　　　　　　　　I. W. RUGGLES

REV. A. PETERS

REV. & DEAR SIR

We the Presbyterian Society of Pontiac in the County of Oakland . . . . consider the Rev. Mr. Ruggles a faithful servant of the Lord— He is the man of our choice; & we desire to retain him as our minister. We wish to afford him an adequate support, but the scarcity of money renders us unable to do all that we wish to do.

We therefore respectfully solicit a continuance of your charity. We make our request as a society & not as a church by reason of our peculiar circumstances. There are no male members of the church in Pontiac, & only five or six within six miles. As we are anxious that Mr. Ruggles should labor more constantly at Pontiac than hitherto, we are willing to make all reasonable efforts for the purpose.[11] . . . .

We wish you prosperity

　　　　　　　　　Yours respectfully

　　　　　　　　　G. O. WHITTEMORE
　　　　　　　　　　　　　　　Secretary

REV. ABSALOM PETERS,
PONTIAC Feby 16th 1828
　By order of the Society
OLMSTEAD CHAMBERLAIN
　　Chairman

[11] About a year prior to this a dispute had arisen between Ruggles and the session of the Pontiac church. The session wished to remove Ruggles, and the society which was subsequently formed rallied to his support. There was much correspondence on the subject, but it is difficult to reconstruct the true situation. The session admitted that Ruggles was a good man but said that he was a poor preacher whom the people were unwilling to support. Yet immediately thereafter the people of Pontiac

Office of the American Home Miss. Soc.

144 NASSAU ST., NEW YORK   April 1, 1828

Rev. Isaac W. Ruggles,

DEAR SIR,

An application has reached us from the Presbyterian Society of Pontiac, asking for continued aid in support of yourself as their minister which was laid before the Executive Committee of the Society at our last meeting. This application is signed by O. Chamberlin, Chairman, & G. O. Whittemore, Secy., & is not in behalf of the Church but of the Society, & from what has been several times intimated to us, we feel a reluctance to act in the case. We have understood from sources worthy of credit, that while your ministry there has been useful, & while you are regarded by all as a faithful labourer in the vineyard, there is yet a want of unanimity in the church & Society in desiring you to continue as their minister; also that you have, yourself, expressed a willingness, if not a desire, to leave them, that they may obtain a minister in whom they may be more united. We are informed also that some of the people, even since this application was sent to us, have held correspondence with a Candidate for the

---

erected a house for him (Ruggles to Peters, September 12, 1827 [A.H.M.S. Correspondence]) and pledged him their support.

The members of the session lived at centers outside the village of Pontiac, to one of which centers the Presbyterian church was later removed. Further, the members were staunch Presbyterians, and it may be that they disliked the strong Congregational tendencies of their pastor.

By 1831 Ruggles had ceased to preach in Pontiac and was centering his activities about Bloomfield and Auburn. The Pontiac church called George Hornell to be its pastor, whereupon Ruggles organized a Congregational church in the village, at the house of Samuel Brent. This church received members from the Presbyterian church over the protest of Hornell and the Presbyterian session. On July 2, 1831, the church was reorganized in a more orderly way, at the court house, with the help of Hornell (Hornell to Peters, Auburn Village, M.T., July 26, 1831 [*History of Oakland County, Michigan* (Philadelphia: L. H. Everts & Co., 1877)]).

Lending color to the hypothesis of a controversy over the form of church polity is the fact that Aaron Williams found these members of the Congreational church to be uncompromising in their devotion to Congregational principles (A. Williams to A. Peters, Pontiac, M.T., July 2, 1835 [A.H.M.S. Correspondence]).

Ministry inviting him to visit them with a view to a settlement. These things render it improper for the Committee to act in the case until the state of feeling can be more fully explained, & we can know, better than we now do, what the desire of the church & people is as to your continuance. I am induced therefore to write to you; & state these things, in confidence that you may make such use of them as you deem judicious, rather than to state them to the people, by which your feelings might be injured, & perhaps your usefulness impaired. If the church & Society are not united in desiring you to stay, it may be best for you to leave the place open for another, in which case this Committee will be disposed to do for them what may seem to be duty.

I shall not reply to the application now before us until I hear from you, which I hope will be soon, as they request an early answer. With high respect & affectionate regard,

I am your Friend & Br.

ABSALOM PETERS

Cor. Sec. A.H.M.S.

PONTIAC, April 22—1828

REVEREND & DEAR SIR,

Yours of the 1st Inst. I have just read; & I thank you for your kindness towards me. On the subject attended to, in your letter, I feel reluctant to say anything; but my duty to you demands it. A communication was made from the elders to me in January or February of last year, stating that it was thought expedient that my labors here should discontinue with the expiration of my mission for that year. The reason then given, was, that the people of Pontiac were unwilling to do anything for my support. I told them that I ever stood ready to leave the place to another, when the prosperity of the Redeemer's cause required me so to do. I told them, likewise, that I would use my influence to procure another minister. The people of Pontiac hearing that I contemplated leaving them enquired the reason; & being told, unanimously averred that it was not so. They said they were entirely willing to support me; but they had never been solicited. Measures were immediately taken by the people for my support & encouragement. The elders opposed these measures, &, by some imprudence excited an animosity which, I fear, will not be easily allayed. I made a proposition to the elders of what I supposed requisite to preserve unanimity, but they regarded it not. From the commencement of these movements, I have "Endeavored to keep the unity of the Spirit in the bond of peace." I should have given you some information on the subject before us, when I gave my last report; but at that time I was sick with the Ague; & beside this, I was expecting every day, that a missionary would arrive here. The elders told me they were expecting one. I thought such a one could communicate intelligence on this subject better than I. About 2 months since, a member of the Society inquired whether my mission had been renewed. I told him that it had not; neither did I expect it to be done. He said the Society should make an application. I told him this would be unavailing, unless made thro the medium of the church.

As for myself, I feel willing to go or stay, as may appear to be my duty. It is my happiness to be active in the service of my divine Master. . . . . I ask your prayers. I hope you will shortly send over a faithful brother to labor in the Lord's vineyard here. Be assured, dear Brother, that from no one here will a faithful missionary meet with a more cordial welcome than from me. When such a one shall arrive & obtain knowledge of circumstances, he will be able to judge; & I shall thankfully receive advice from him & you with respect to my duty. . . . .

With high respect, I am yours in the best of bonds—

I. W. RUGGLES

REVEREND A. PETERS

A. Peters *Ex. Cor. Sec. A.H.M.*

Herewith I transmit the proceedings of our society meeting in conformity with your letter of 5 June last. I humbly beg your aid in supporting the Rev. I. W. Ruggles as our Minister at Pontiac

very respectfully yours,

O. Chamberlain, P.M.

At a meeting of the first Presbyterian society of Pontiac held at the village of Pontiac on the 12th day of July 1828, Deacon Jacob N. Voorhis was called to the Chair and Wm. F. Moseley was chosen Secretary.

By order of the Meeting a Letter was read from the Cor. Sec. of the American H. Miss. Society in New York to O. Chamberlain Esq dated June 5th 1828.

On Motion it was ordered that the following Article be adopted (viz) "We the subscribers hereby wish to be considered as members of the first Presbyterian Society in Pontiac and to progress in such course as shall best conduce to its advancement."

On Motion ordered that a committee of three be appointed to circulate the foregoing Article and the following persons to wit Jacob N. Voorhis   Isaac Voorhis & Judah Church were appointed.

On Motion ordered that said committee notify the members of the Society of the time & place of the next meeting—

Meeting adjourned to Saturday the 19th Insty. 4 O.C. p.m.

Saturday July 19th 1828

Society met according to adj't. Comittee returned the names of forty two persons who have signed the foregoing article.

On Motion ordered that the votes be taken by division of the house. It was moved and seconded that Rev. Isaac W.

Ruggles be the Minister to said Society for the ensuing year. Motion carried in the affirmative.

On Motion ordered that this meeting be adjourned till the 30th day of August next.

[*Signed*]

JACOB N. VOORHIS, *Chairman*
WM. G. MOSELEY, *Sec.*

FARMINGTON, July 28, 1828

DEAR SIR,

. . . . Two of the Elders of Pontiac church have requested me to mention to you that they are in great want of a minister. I am well acquainted with Brother Ruggles who resides at Pontiac. He is I think, a good man & one who has done much good in the Territory. He has conversed with me, freely, respecting his connection with Pontiac church. I have no doubt, but what it is his desire, that another minister should come there, he would receive one most cordially, & do every thing in his power, to make him useful to the people. There has been, I believe, a kind of hardnes on the part of the church towards Brother R. thinking that he ought to leave, for, so long as he continued there, they could not get another minister. The church are now becoming convinced that Mr. R. wishes for them spiritual good. . . . .

Yours affectionately ERIE PRINCE[12]

REV. A. PETERS.

In Session July 31 1828
BLOOMFIELD. OAKLAND CY.

Rev. Absalom Peters

DEAR SIR

The Session of the Presbyterian Church of Pontiac, deem it expedient to address to you this joint letter in reference to the

---

[12] Erie Prince came to Michigan from Rush, Monroe County, N.Y. (Ruggles to Peters, Pontiac, September 15, 1826 [A.H.M.S. Correspondence]).

state of this church and the destitute situation on a/c of a Pastor and the present differences existing between the Church and Rev. Mr. Ruggles.

The Church was organized by the Rev. Eldad Goodman in 1823 and soon after was visited by Rev. Mr. Ruggles, After Mr. Ruggle's return to the east a meeting was held for the purpose of determining whether to give him a call and it was determined in the negative. Mr. Ruggles was informed of the result but returned and commenced labouring and red'd the aid and approbation of the church generally but the fears of many were realized. (Viz) That he was not an able, efficient, and argumentative preacher, that few if any save the members of the Church would attend his preaching and finally that he has suspended entirely his labours in the Church.

The section of Country within the bounds of this Church includes three large townships and about 3/4 of the County which is 30 miles square and Mr. Ruggles has ceased preaching regularly as we believe. He has not attended the meetings of the Session and we verily believe is not calculated to combat the strong grounds of Infidelity and irrelition which prevail here to an alarming extent.

We have been informed that applications for aid in support of Mr. Ruggles have been made to you by persons who make no pretensions to religion. If so we would caution you on this subject.

We feel willing to bear testimony to the piety and exemplary conduct of Mr. Ruggles but when we regard him in the light of a Pastor, we feel bound to say that he does not possess those requisite qualifications which are absolutely important.

The Church is in fact destitute of a leader and in a County composed of 3500 souls we think it important something should be done.

We want an able, humble, devoted and talented man and there is no doubt but such a one would receive a full support after the first year.

We have used all exertion to obtain such a person, but so long as Mr. Ruggles continues no other one will come upon the ground—

Yours in Christian fellowship

Decm 21st.[13] We wish to add that Rev. Mr. Hornell is now with us, and the church have unitedly engaged to employ him for one year and from the destitute situation of the church generally we would renew our application for aid. . . . .

Yours in the bonds of Christian fellowship

V. R. TROWBRIDGE
ELIJAH S. FISH   *Elders*
JACOB N. VOORHEIS

BLOOMFIELD Aug. 23, 1828

Rev. Absalom Peters

DEAR SIR

The Session of the Presbyterian Church of Pontiac feel it their duty to address to you this letter on the subject of the destitute situation of this church respecting a minister. . . . . The Elders of the Church in Session this afternoon have concluded to obligate themselves to raise 200 dollars in produce for the support of a missionary for one year and now most earnestly look to you to select the individual and send him amongst us. . . . .

Yours in Christian Fellowship

I. W. RUGGLES
V. R. TROWBRIDGE
WM. CHAMBERLAIN
ELIJAH S. FISH
JACOB N. VOORHEIS.

[13] It is to be noted by the date of the postscript, that, before this letter was sent, Ruggles had united with the session in asking that a new minister be sent to the church.

Rev. Absalom Peters.—   PONTIAC, Ap. 17—1830
DEAR SIR,—

   . . . . I suppose the field in which I labor is large enough for
2 or 3 laborers. The places where I preach alternately, are,
you recollect Washington (Hoxis), Rochester, Munson's Settlement, & Wing Lake. . . . .[14]

I. W. RUGGLES

    REV. A. PETERS.

Rev. Absalom Peters   PONTIAC Nov. 3, 1830
DEAR SIR

   The Session of this church again wish to apply to you for
aid in support of its pastor. Mr. Hornell is still with us and
we feel confident of his increasing usefulness. . . . .

In the bonds of the Gospel
We are affectionately

S. V. R. TROWBRIDGE } *Members of*
ELIJAH S. FISH   } *Session*

RE. & DEAR SIR;   DETROIT, Nov. 6, 1830

   . . . . On the subject of the foregoing application from Oakland we have to express our concurrence—and regret that
little or nothing is contributed out of the church for the support of Mr. Hornell. The opposition is however subsiding &
we have no doubt it will soon be entirely allayed. . . . .

Yours in the best of bonds,

E. P. HASTINGS

I concur in the above

NOAH M. WELLS

---

   [14] After stepping aside in the Pontiac situation, Ruggles turned his attention
to some of the other settlements where he had previously ministered when opportunity offered.

PONTIAC APRIL 25—1831

REVEREND & DEAR SIR,

Since the time I rendered my last report I have been laboring in a new field. I will state the reason. Brother Shaw visited me in the winter. We conversed on the circumstances of the people where he was then laboring, & also of those in this part of the Territory. We concluded that there was more need for him in this part, than where he then labored. For accommodation, & by the consent & direction of the Committee Messrs Wells & Hastings, he has entered the field formerly occupied by me, & I have entered a new one. The field where I now labor lies to the West & N. West of Pontiac. . . . . The place where this settlement is, is called Grand Blanc. . . . .

Your humble servant

ISAAC W. RUGGLES

REV. A. PETERS

DETROIT, August 27, 1831

DEAR SIR,

. . . . Mr. Ruggles has selected four places, viz Grand Blanc, 30 miles N. W. of Pontiac, Silver Lake, 4 mi. West. Pine Lake 4 m. S. W. and Tuckers Settlement[15] 4 m. North of the same place, and desires a renewal of his Commission for another year. We have heretofore expressed our views respecting his qualifications and will here only say that we believe he will be useful in visiting and organizing Churches— perhaps more so than any who could be selected. The people in those neighborhoods have requested his services and we hope the request will be granted. . . . .

Yours sincerely,

E. P. HASTINGS

[15] Later known as "West Pontiac" (Ruggles to Peters, October 22, 1832 [A.H.M.S. Correspondence]).

AUBURN VILLAGE OAKLAND Co. M.T.

REV. & DEAR SIR   July 26, 1831

.... With the assistance of brother Ruggles, I have formed a Congregational Church at Pontiac; consisting of 12 members; partly members before belonging to the Presb. church,& partly of those who had not united with any Church since they came into this country. . . . .

GEORGE HORNELL

REV. ABSALOM PETERS.

PONTIAC, April 16, 1832

To the Rev. Absalom Peters—

DEAR SIR,

On account of the scattered condition of the people in the field of my labors, and other unfavorable circumstances I have little to say in my reports which might seem encouraging. . . . .

Since Br. Hornell left preaching at Pontiac, which is about 3 months ago, it was thought my duty, on request of the people, to spend some part of my time with them. I have done so. A Congregational church was organized at Pontiac in June last, of 8 members; 12 have been added since by letter, and 6 by profession. About half of these are from the settlements in the vicinity of Pontiac where I labor. There has been of late some unusual attention to religion at Pontiac; 7 or 8 have hopefully passed from death unto life. We have in contemplation a protracted meeting at Pontiac. . . . .

Yours in the best of bonds—

ISAAC W. RUGGLES

REV. A. PETERS.

REVEREND & DEAR SIR,—   PONTIAC, Oct. 22—1832

I had conversation with your committee, Mssrs. Wells & Hastings about the time at which my commission closed; they told me to continue my labors, my commission would be renewed. I have done as they directed, but no commission has come. I saw Mr. Hastings a few days since; he said he had forgotten at what time my commission expired, he supposed it was not until this fall; he therefore had given you no directions on the subject. He directs me to discontinue laboring at Grand Blanc and Silver Lake, and to confine my labors to West Pontiac, (formerly Tucker's Settlement), and to Pine Lake and Orchard Lake, which two lakes are included in one settlement. . . . .

Yours affectionately
Isaac W. Ruggles

Reverend Absalom Peters.

Detroit Nov. 24, 1832

Dear Sir,

Yours of the 14th inst. communicating an extract from W. Ruggles' letter was received this afternoon. Mr. Ruggles is mistaken in saying we told him *his commission would be renewed.* As our duty is only *to advise* we simply said we would do so, *with the conditions named to him* at the time.

We have been at a loss *what* advice to give under the existing state of things in that region and have concluded to give you a detail of the difficulties which have existed, with our opinion as to the best means of settling them and leave it to the wisdom of your Committee to decide.

Mr. Peters I believe is already possessed of some of the facts—but in his absence it may be proper to give you the whole in connexion—

About two years after the appointment of Mr. R. to labor at Pontiac the Church—which then embraced the whole County—unanimously requested Mr. Ruggles to retire with a view of finding a man of more talents. He, with several of the members of the Society took exception to the proceedings and an excitement was produced which has unhappily existed to the present time. He however consented to yield to the wishes of the Church and promised to select another field. Upon the introduction of Mr. Hornell into his place, he applied for a Commission to labor at Rochester and Romeo and promised to abandon entirely the ground occupied by Mr. H. He was advised by your Committee to take his family to one of those villages for the purpose of allaying the excitement which existed at Pontiac in consequence of the introduction of Mr. H. He however continued to reside at Pontiac and to receive from the people something towards his support. During this period he organized a Congregational Church at Pontiac and received some of the members of the Presbyterian Ch. over wh— Mr. H. labored contrary to the wishes of the Session of that church.

Upon complaint being made to us the writer visited Mr. R. and his Deacons and succeeded in satisfying them that the proceedings were improper and in obtaining their consent to return again into the Presbyterian Church and to proceed in an orderly manner to constitute a new Church if one was desired. This course was approved by Mr. Hornell and his Session and peace was restored. The Congregational Church however refused to comply and they have considered Mr. R. their Pastor ever since.[16]

Upon Mr. Ruggles' application for a reappointment in 1831 we objected to the course he had pursued particularly in organizing a Ch. within the bounds of M. Hornells after having agreed to give up the field—and also to his remaining with his Family at Pontiac while he labored in other places knowing that his presence kept the people from uniting in the support of Mr. H.[17] He satisfied us of the impracticability of his leaving at the time—but he agreed to withdraw wholly from

[16] A new Congregational church had been organized in Pontiac in June, 1831, with the assistance of Mr. Hornell. His account of the organization is contained in his letter of July 26, 1831, and Mr. Ruggles' account in his letter of April 16, 1832.

[17] Ruggles to Peters, April 16, 1832 (A.H.M.S. Correspondence).

both Churches and labor in Grand Blanc, Silver Lake, etc. Soon after his reappointment we received a unanimous call from the Society at Pontiac and at the same time a letter from one of the Deacons desiring him to be appointed exclusively for that Village.[18] We consented to recommend this change provided they would agree to support him and be satisfied with his continuance for the term of one year. This they declined as they desired a man of more talents. We of course refused to recommend a change and stated our reasons to Mr. Peters which were approved by him. Upon Mr. Ruggles application last Spring I renewed the objection again to his residence and stated further that in my opinion there was no immediate prospect of raising up Congregations at either of the places—but advised him to remain there—being under the impression at the time that his commission did not expire until autumn.[19] He proposed to take the places named in his letter to you[20] and I consented to apply in his behalf *provided it was the wish of the people and there was a prospect of building up Churches.*

Upon his application in Oct. I stated I had not written in his behalf because I had not heard from the people at those places. He returned in a few days with written applications and received for reply *that as soon as M. Wells returned I would consult with him and write.* I may have added that he would probably be reappointed.

Soon after the return of Mr. Wells we ascertained that M. Hornell had found it necessary to leave his station and we have been at a loss how to decide respecting the numerous and conflicting applications from the people embraced in this field.[21]

[18] Above, pp. 297–98.

[19] Ruggles to Peters, October 22, 1832.

[20] See Ruggles' letter to Peters, April 17, 1830, and Hastings' letter to Peters, August 27, 1831.

[21] According to Ruggles, Hornell left Pontiac in January or February of 1832, whereupon he (Ruggles) returned to preaching there (Ruggles to Peters, April 16, 1832).

Much of the difficulty has arisen from the agency of Mr. Ruggles in forming Congregational Churches. He has been charged with exerting his influence against the Presbyterian form of Govt. and producing divisions among the people. This however he denies and we are ignorant in some measure of the facts. It has been the wish of our Presbytery (and your Committee have always advocated the course) to leave the people to adopt either form uninfluenced by the Missionaries. But as your Committee are *Presbyterians* it has been difficult to satisfy Mr. R. that their designs are not to build up Presbyterianism. We are happy to state that these jealousies are giving way to a better state of feeling and that there is a prospect that peace will be restored especially should Mr. Ruggles be continued until the Churches are supplied.[22]

We have heretofore stated that Mr. R. was deficient in talents and was not very acceptable as a preacher. He is active as a Pastor and is useful in visiting from House to house and raising up congregations. The probability is he will never find a people who will consent to settle him as a permanent laborer—but he will prepare the way for the settlement of others and be willing to remove to a new field.

We think it will have a tendency under all the circumstances to restore harmony to reappoint Mr. Ruggles for one year. We will endeavor so to divide the field and locate him as to prevent any future difficulty—and if in the opinion of your Board he should not be hereafter continued we will tell him so. Mr. Hornell has received a call to Adrian. . . . .

Yours respectfully[23]

N. M. WELLS
E. P. HASTINGS

[22] Complaint against the supposed Presbyterian bias of the A.H.M.S. was common.

[23] The letter was addressed to B. H. Rice, associate secretary of the A.H.M.S.

ROMEO, MACOMB COUNTY[24]
MICHIGAN TERRITORY, JUNE 10, 1831

To the Cor. Sec. of the A.H.M. Society,
144 Nassau St. N.Y.
REV. AND DEAR SIR;

I have delayed writing you longer than I thought. . . . .
Since my last report, things continue here much as they were.
There has been a religious Society formed and measures taken
to support the gospel in part at least.

A site has been selected for a Meeting House and a Grave-
yard; and it is now in contemplation to build next season.
Our School is filled to overflowing on the Sabbath. Some go
away because they can [not] be accommodated, or rather because they can not get in. This is, on the whole, the most
moral, industrious and hospitable Settlement I have found in
the Territory. . . . .

A "Conference of the Churches" has been recently established in this vicinity. We have had but one. It was a season
of deep interest. Members of different denominations of
Christians attended & many of them resolved to spend a few
minutes every day between sun down & dark, to pray for the
prosperity of religion in the Territory. . . . .

Yours etc.

LUTHER SHAW[25]

---

[24] According to Punchard (*op. cit.*, V, 308), the church at Romeo was the second
Congregational church organized in Michigan, being organized by Isaac W. Ruggles
on August 16, 1828. Romeo at that time was an isolated settlement, accessible only
by foot trails, and known as "Indian Village."

[25] Luther Shaw was born in Rutland, Vt., in 1800, graduated from Middlebury
College in 1826 and from Auburn Theological Seminary in 1830, and was ordained
that year by the Congregational Church of Henrietta, N.Y. (*The Congregational
Year-Book for the Year 1889*, p. 37). He became an active leader in the General
Association after it was organized.

Romeo, Macomb County Michigan
Feb. 15, 1833

To the Cor. Sec. A.H.M.S.

Rev. and beloved br.

This date closes the year of my missionary services in Romeo & Rochester. I rec'd a commission dated "Feb. 15, 1832" & post marked "July 30" on the 15 Jan'y 1833. I was informed as early as the 15 Augt. that you had forwarded it to Mr. Hastings.

There is a difference between his & my statements as to what the good people of Romeo & Rochester would subscribe for my services. I wrote you in Apl. that the amount which could be raised in both places would be about $250 for the year. Mr. Hastings wrote you in June that he thought it would be upwards of $300. This, I find, is the reason assigned why the Commission was forwarded to him rather than to myself. He was authorized to fill the blank with any sum not exceeding $100.

For the two years which I have spent in Romeo & Rochester I have rec'd from the two congregations the following sums

From Romeo	1. year	$100 ($10 of which cash)—	$100
" "	2. "	$110 subscribed not pd.	110
From Rochester	1 year	77 ($25 cash)	77
" "	2 "	60 ($1 cash)	60
			$347

I may receive the $110 subscribed in Romeo and $20 perhaps $30—more than what I have already rec'd. from Rochester.[26] I make this statement, not to find fault, but to let you know the facts in the case. . . . .

We had a Protracted Meeting in Romeo which resulted in great good. The members of the Church have generally been

---

[26] This tabulation indicates the difficulty of securing cash support for the ministry so long as the inhabitants had no market for their produce.

more active since. There have been nine added, one death &
one suspension during the year. Six or eight more, we expect,
will ere long join us in Church fellowship. This Church now
numbers 33.

Six have been added to the Church in Rochester & three
have been dismissed. This Church has now 18 members.
When I came two years ago there were only 9 members.
Twelve have been added. The church in Romeo had only 17
members two years ago; 19 have been added. . . . .

Yours Sincerely,

LUTHER SHAW

REV. ABSALOM PETERS
  Cor. Sec. & C.

—————,   ROMEO March 23rd, 1833

The Rev. Mr. Shaw is now in this place; he expects to
preach here 3/4 of the time and in Ray, the Town adjoining,
1/4 of the time. This soc. have felt for some time that the
occasional services of a minister, was of but little avail, and
being impressed with the importance of having the *regular*
and *constant* ministration of the word of God, they have made
an effort to raise $250, which, it is thought will be done, and
being much attached to their pastor, (Mr. Shaw) they are
desirous to retain him, hoping to see the work of the Lord go
forward in this place. This place will, in about 3 or 4 yrs.
be able to support a minister without any assistance from
your soc. but not short of that time. It is expected that an
Academy will be erected here the present season, the second
story to be reserved and finished off for the accommodation
of the Congregational soc.[27] There was a protracted meeting

———————————

[27] Here, as elsewhere, both the Congregationalists and the Presbyterians were
active in the cause of education. Ruggles and his wife kept a classical or select school
in their home in Pontiac for a number of years before the academy was founded. A
large share of the stock in this Pontiac academy was owned by the trustees of the
First Presbyterian Church of that village (*History of Oakland County, Michigan*,
p. 92). McEwen speaks of the Congregational church raising money for its com-

in this place in Nov. last which resulted as we then hoped in the conversion of about 20 souls, but there was no shepherd and the lambs are scattered (we had a minister 1 day out of 14 only)*

Yours in the Lord

SYMAN W. GILBERT

REV. ABSALOM PETERS
Cor. Sec'y the A.H.M.S.
N. York

* I then resided at Rochester 15 miles distant from Romeo.

L. SHAW

DEAR BR.   ROMEO March 27, 1833

Through the politeness of Rev. Mr. Shaw I am allowed to address you a few lines in regard to our prospects, wants, etc. as a moral and religious community. I came to this place about 4 years ago. There was then here no Church save a Methodist, but by great exertion on the part of the friends of the cause of Christ—assisted by the Home Missionary Society—they have been able to do much—but much remains to be done. The enemies of the cause are active, and shall we slumber? A few of us are ready to answer no: but we must be hindered in our work unless we continue to receive assistance from the H.M. Society. We shall raise here & in Ray $250 this year, which is twice as much as has been raised in one year before, we have full confidence therefore in the belief that if the benevolence of the Society is extended to us 3 or 4 years more, we shall then not only be able to support the gospel among us, but contribute our mite toward sending it to other portions of our destitute country.

Respectfully yours,

N. T. TAYLOR—*Trustee of Romeo Con. Soc.*

REV. A. PETERS
N. York

---

pletion (McEwen to Peters, Pontiac, October 8, 1833 [A.H.M.S. Correspondence]). John D. Pierce, of Marshall, was the first superintendent of public instruction in Michigan.

ROMEO MACOMB COUNTY
MICHIGAN June 28, 1833

Rev. A. Peters Cor. Sec. etc.

DEAR BR.

. . . . Next week I am invited to go to St. Clair to assist br. Worthington in organizing a chh. & to administer the Sac. of the Lord's Supper. The week following I am requested to go to Lapeer Centre for the same purpose; next week after, to go to Grand Blanc for the same object; & soon after to go to Bruce, this Co. to organize another. I shall have to travel in all near 190 miles.

I am your friend and br. in the Lord.

LUTHER SHAW
Miss. in Romeo & Ray, M.T.

ROMEO MACOMB CO.
MICHIGAN Aug't. 30, 1833

To the Cor. Sec. of A.H.M.So.
150 Nassau St. New York

REV'D. AND DR. SIR,

. . . . A union meeting of two day's continuance was held in Ray last week. There [were] present ministers of four different denominations who took a part in conducting the religious solemnities; & such was the love, harmony & good feeling among them that the enemy could not help acknowledging "These Christians do love one another."

. . . . Opposition to the truth, in this region, is bold and exceedingly bitter. Those calling themselves Universalists, generally if not all, are Socinians. They believe Jesus Christ to be a mere man; raised up only to set us an example of virtuous conduct. They are making vigorous efforts against the truth in the circulation of periodicals of such a stamp as they

like etc. I was told a few days since, that they were attempting to form a Soc. whose principal object was "*to watch the clergy.*" One man, I understood, said he would give a year's labor if it could not be set on foot without: & 2 or 3 others say they will give their farms!! But God will confound them.
. . . .

> In the bonds of Christian fellowship
>   I am yours in the Lord
>   LUTHER SHAW
>   *Miss. Romeo & Ray M.T.*

ROMEO MACOMB COUNTY
MICHIGAN Feb. 15, 1834

Cor. Sec. of the A.H.M.S.
No 150 Nassau St. N.Y.

REV'D AND DEAR BR.

. . . . Ten have been added to our feeble chh. during the year—seven by letter and three on profession of their faith. Seven within the field of my labor, have hopefully passed from death unto life, who have not yet united with any Christian chh.

The cause of Temperance in this place is gaining ground. The society now numbers upwards of 100. . . . .

The little chh. & Society in Romeo are making an effort to erect a small meeting house. We need one very much. We have now only a small School House in which all denominations have equal right. All the hewn timber is on the ground and arrangements are making to have the edifice put up and completed as soon as may be.

At a late annual meeting of the Macomb Co B. Soc. held in this place a resolution was passed to re-examine the Co. & supply all the destitute with the Word of God. The work is nearly completed.

We now have four S. Schools which we consider as connected with us. They contain about 130 or 140 scholars—and all are flourishing. The school in Romeo has assisted Schools in the settlements around us by loaning them books till the inhabitants should become interested & be thus induced to purchase for themselves.

. . . . In regard to my remaining here another year, I know not what to say. The little chh are anxious to have me remain; but they are weak. One or two from whom considerable sums have been rec'd to support your Missionary, have failed in business—& 6 or 8 members of the chh have moved away. They are trying to build a Meeting House, & the expense devolves on a few. And this few have to support me. I intend to make a statement of facts to Mssrs. Wells & Hastings soon & they may make any communication to you that they may think best. . . . .

Yours in the bonds

LUTHER SHAW

ROMEO, MACOMB COUNTY
MICHIGAN Augt 22, 1835

To the Revd. Levi Pratt
Sec. of the H.M. Soc.

REVD. & DEAR SIR

. . . . In that time which I have spent in the Terr'y. there have been 15 or 20 hopeful conversions in the places where I have labored; I have assisted wholly or in part in organizing 5 chhs.; I have helped to form 5 different Temperance Socs.; have circulated many thousands of pages of Religious Tracts & have aided in forming quite a no. of Sabbath Schools. From 80 to 100 members have been added to the different chhs. where I have preached—statedly or occasionally. This Co. has been explored & supplied twice with bibles since I came here. . . . .

The current of Infidelity is strong in the Terr'y. Unwearied pains are taken to disseminate error. Infidel Publications are extensively circulated. About 20 or 25 copies come to the P.O. of our Villages every week; these are not all however taken in the Village. Several copies go into the surrounding settlements. Universalism & Deism are the most common and popular errors. The maj. of the community, however, do not care what they believe provided it is in opposition to the *"Orthodox"* as they term Presbyterians.

The chh. of this place numbers about 45—scattered over considerable extent of territory. They are generally in moderate circumstances & of course can not give much to support your Miss. Most of the wealth in the Terr'y. is in the hands of wicked men. . . . . If pious families possessing some wealth could be induced to emigrate west & settle down in feeble congregations & assist in sustaining Sabbath Schools & the Miss'es. who are already in the field they w'd. do more good than in almost any other way. What we need in this place is that about 6 or 8 families sh'd settle among us. There are a no. of excellent farms for sale—now owned by Universalists or Deists who wish to sell & go farther into the woods—as one of them said a few days since—that he might be where he c'd. hunt on the Sabbath & not disturb his neighbors. . . . .

Yours in peculiar & affecting bonds

LUTHER SHAW

REVD. LEVI PRATT *Sec &c*

ROMEO MACOMB COUNTY
MICHIGAN Nov. 15, 1835

REVD. & DEAR SIR

. . . . I have it in contemplation to form a sort of colony next season & have already some encouragement from 15 or 20 families from Vermont & New York— Some few have selected the location & made purchases. The place is entirely new—about 40 miles from Detroit in Lapeer Co. on the Belle River.

We hope that we shall form a Settlement of good people who will be decided in the cause of religion & virtue. All who know much of the state of new countries as they are generally settled, are well aware how difficult it is to sustain religious institutions & schools even, not so much for want of funds, as for want of interest & union. We do not intend to exclude all who do not profess religion by any means, but we want those who are decidedly in favor of all good institutions religious, moral, literary & political, & who will readily contribute by example & otherwise to build up a good Society.

As this is my plan at present, of course, I do not expect to be in the employ of your soc. during the winter. If spared, I purpose to return in the Spring.[28] . . . .

Yours in Christian affection

LUTHER SHAW

REVD. ABSALOM PETERS
Cor. Sec etc.
142 Nassau St. N.Y.

PONTIAC, MICHIGAN TER. Oct. 8, 1833

Rev. Absalom Peters,

DEAR SIR,

I arrived here on the 5th of July, having been directed hither by the committee of your Soc. for this section. . . . . When I arrived, there was no preaching, or means of any kind enjoyed, except occasionally, from one of our Baptist or Methodist brethren. There was a Sab. School in operation, and a Bible class. These were thinly attended, by children and adults of all denominations. I waited on some of the members of the Cong. Church in this place, and stated my object in coming, and proposed to preach the Gospel, if a

---

[28] Shaw did return with his colony and became the minister of their church at Armanda, Mich.

place of assembly could be provided. The Court room, it seems, had been used for such purposes by all denominations, as they could get the opportunity; and would be unoccupied on the ensuing Sab. in the afternoon. I accordingly commenced my labors, as a preacher on the Sab. immediately after my arrival. At my request, the church met, during the following week, and made arrangements to procure a place for regular worship and preaching. They hired a backroom for the winter, and there I have preached twice a day every sabbath since, save one, when I failed half of the day on account of its ——(?).

In addition to these labors I have been the Superintendent of the Sab. School, and Bible class in the Village, and of another Bible Class three miles out of the place. The Sab. S. I attend in the morning; the Bible Class, after service in the afternoon. The other Bible Class I visited on Thursday P.M. each week. I have occasionally established a weekly meeting of the S. S. teachers in the village, attending it always myself. I have endeavored to create an interest in the Monthly Concert for Prayer, and have so far succeeded, as to make it a regular thing and secure a respectable attendance. After much ado, I have induced the church to contribute for foreign missions, a thing never known among them before. I have also held a weekly prayer meeting, and this on the Sabbath, for the accommodation of all the population, the church especially being scattered. I have also visited the members of the church, and those generally, who I found were attending on my ministrations, or in any way accessible. . . . .

As to support, I have only to state, that the contributions of the people have been rather in provision, than in money. They have helped me some and will continue to do so increasingly. The next year, if I remain, they hope to be able to support a minister. At present they feel embarrassed in regard to the payment of money; for they are building a meeting-house, to cost $2000, are finishing an academy, worth

$1200, and have had their staple, the wheat crop, in some cases wholly, for the most part, partially, cut off by the insect. . . . .

Yours in the Lord   R. McEwen[29]

DETROIT 20 Jan'y 1834

D. SIR,

. . . . Mr. McEwen found the church in Pontiac in a divided state. They are now erecting a neat church which is nearly finished & he has not thought it prudent to present the subject of a salary to the people. They have however promised me to take up the subject and think they can raise 200 Dolls. I have said to them "they must raise 250$ and would recommend an appropriation of 150. In the mean time Mr. McE. will draw as little as possible until the question is settled. From present appearances I should judge that harmony would be restored and the So. will soon be able to sustain themselves. It is however a corrupt place. . . . .

Sincerely yours

E. P. HASTINGS

PONTIAC April 14th, 1834

DEAR BROTHER;

. . . . The attendance on the means of grace is enough to make any one who has known this place of old ask, who are these? Well attended prayer meetings—not only professors but impenitent men taking their seats, are wonders also to be seen here. And to see our little band of Christians after all their coldness, & division, flowing together with full hearts, &

---

[29] Robert McEwen, the son of the well-known Congregational preacher, Rev. Dr. Abel McEwen, was born in New London, Conn., in 1808. He graduated from Yale College in 1827 and from the Yale Divinity School in 1833. He came to Pontiac immediately following graduation but remained only a short time, being compelled to return to New England on account of his wife's health (*The Congregational Year-Book for the Year 1884*, p. 30).

speaking often one to another, is truly in Pontiac, to see the bow of promise after the storm and flood.

. . . .

Other circumstances encourage us to hope that the institutions of the Gospel are to be permanently established and *appreciated* among this people. Week before last a religious society was organised in connection with the church to which I minister, under the name of "First Congregational Society of Pontiac." The meetinghouse is to be dedicated in May. They have also given me a call to become their pastor, & I am to be installed the first of June.

This leads me to speak of my connection with the A.H.M.S. With present prospects, we shall not need to draw on your funds any longer, certainly not for this year.

I remain yours, in the Gospel

R. McEwen

Rev. A. Peters

Pontiac, June 14, 1834

Dear Sir,

. . . . We have had our separate place for meeting & our attendance has been overflowing—often recently many were compelled to stand without the doors, though our room is large & well seated. . . . .

Yours in the Lord

Robert McEwen

Rev. Absalom peters

Detroit, 17 Dec. 1834

Rev. and Dear Sir,

. . . .

Pontiac, one of our most important villages, which we supposed was well manned by Mr. McEwen, was left destitute by Mr. McE's determination not to return. A few weeks since

I met with a young clergyman from Pittsburg[30] on his way to the neighborhood of Chicago. In one hour, I had him on a horse, started for Pontiac, and in ten days more, he had an unanimous call from the church & society, & has gone to Pittsburg after his family. . . . .

                                                     Yrs,
                                        JOHN P. CLEAVELAND

                              PONTIAC, M.T. April 1st, 1835
Rev. Absalom Peters, Cor. Sec. etc.
DEAR SIR,

Agreeably to instructions contained in my commission, I now present my first quarterly and annual reports together. My regular ministrations here commenced on the *last Sabbath* (28th) *of December*, ult. so that my first quarter has just expired.

Any general information concerning this place which may be desirable, you have doubtless previously rec'd from my predecessor, br. McEwen. His labors here have been very manifestly blessed, and I feel it a privilege to reap where he has sown. When I arrived here (in Nov. last) the hearts of the people were just bleeding afresh, from the intelligence that their late minister, Rev. Mr. McEwen, could not return to them, as he had expected to do when he left. Through his labors he had been instrumental in redeeming Pontiac, in a great measure, from its "bad preminence" as being one of the "*hardest places*" in the Territory. The church was increased in members, and greatly quickened in its graces, and the *world* has been brought to respect religion and to unite cheerfully in sustaining its institutions. . . . .

. . . . I had never *heard* of such a place as *Pontiac*, until I arrived at Detroit on my way to the St. Joseph Country, about the middle of last Nov. At the request of Mr. Cleave-

---

[30] Aaron Williams (see following letters).

land, I came to P. to spend the Sabbath, previous to proceeding on my journey westward; & at the earnest solicitation of
the people I consented to delay my journey another week. I
preached to them the second Sabbath—accepted a unanimous invitation to become their minister,—abandoned all
my previous arrangements—and set out on Monday home-
wards, for my family. . . . .

The great mass of the male heads of families in the village
are irreligious, a majority of them Universalists or Skeptics.
Nearly all of the old inhabitants are of this character. They
are, however, friendly to religion for its *temporal benefits;* and
most of them occasionally attend my preaching. . . . .

I spent last Sab. week at Grand Blanc, a little church in the
wilderness about 30 miles N. W. of this. I administered the
Lord's Supper to them in one of their small log cabins. . . . .
On Monday I visited the "Mt. Morris Settlement" . . . .
They are a most interesting people, as are also those at
Grand Blanc. They came fresh from the N. York revivals, &
still retain much of the spirit. Both churches hold "reading
meetings" on the Sabbath. They are now reading Finney's
"Lectures on Revivals," and it might be gratifying to Mr. F.
to know that his thrilling appeals are heard & felt with little
less interest away here in the wilds of Michigan, than in
Chatham St. Chapel itself. . . . .

. . . . Congregational Church of "Pontiac, M.T." . . . .

Yours in the gospel,

AARON WILLIAMS

PONTIAC, M.T. 2nd. July 1835

Rev. A. Peters, Cor. Sec. etc.

DEAR SIR, ...

. . . . My instructions call for a report of "difficulties" as
well as of successes. I could give no small catalogue of these.

One of the most discouraging is the apathy of some of the leading members of the church. One man, holding important public office,—a Trustee, & one of the most influential members of the church, made so much opposition to the introduction of the *Temperance* test of membership in the church that the proposition was abandoned. He is also a clamorous opposer of the cause of missions, etc.; and although the majority of the church feel very differently, yet—by throwing in his influence with the people of the world who think with him, & who chiefly own the house of worship, & without whose cooperation the *church* can do but little to support a minister—he manages to clog our operations very much. . . . .

I have concluded that it is not my duty to remain here during the full year for which I have been appointed. The principal reason is the feeble state of my wife's health. Her constitution requires a warmer climate. . . . . Other circumstances also have weight in leading one to the determination to leave this—as the general unhealthiness of this place (fever & ague abounds)—the entire deficiency of pecuniary support; —and my unwillingness to be installed over a purely *congregational* church, with no prospect of peacable change to Presbyterian.[31] . . . .

Respectfully submitted by your missionary

A. WILLIAMS

PONTIAC Aug. 4th 1835

Rev. A. Peters Cor Sec, etc.

DEAR SIR,

When I last wrote I expected as I informed you, to remain here until the first of October; but on further reflection I have concluded that it will be best, upon the whole, both for the church and myself, that I should leave sooner. . . . . I have made arrangements to leave in *two weeks* from this time. . . . .

[31] Hornell to Peters, July 26, 1831.

I have to lament that so little has been effected by my efforts;
—still there has been something to encourage. The attendance upon the means of grace, is good (for Pontiac) & some I
trust have not heard the word in vain. . . . . On Saturday
last I (with br. Ruggles) organized a Presbyterian church of
10 members at White Lake, 16 miles N. W. of this place. . . . .

I bid you adieu

yours etc

A. WILLIAMS

PONTIAC, April 15—1833

REVEREND & DEAR SIR,

Soon after my last report[32] I organized a church at Orchard
Lake of 9 members; 4 have been added since, by letter. They
held the Concert of Prayer. They have made a request that I
may continue to preach for them. In the vicinity of Pine &
Orchard Lakes there are two places where I preach; in the
Forenoon at one place, & in the afternoon at the other. There
is a good & an increasing attention on the dispensation of the
gospel. They have a Sabbath School of about 30 scholars.
They have requested that I should continue preaching there.
At Silver Lake there is a S. School of about 25. At Springfield, on the Saginaw road, about 12 miles from Pontiac, I
preach occasionally. At which place there are 7 professors of
our order, and a prospect of more.

At Grand Blanc there is a good attention on preaching. In
the course of the next month they contemplate having a
church instituted. There has recently a pious physician come
to reside with them, of our persuasion; a very active man in
religious matters, such a one as they need for an officer in the
church; and there is now a fair prospect of being built up in
the order of the gospel, and of having a Concert & a S.

---

[32] Ruggles to Peters, October 22, 1832.

School. They express an anxiety that I should continue preaching with them, and this they have expressed to your Committee.

. . . . I was first sent to this Territory by your Society; (in the Fall of 1824) & there was then no other preacher of our order in the Territory except Br. Ferry at Mackinac. Ever since I have been here, it has seemed to be my duty to serve as a pioneer. As fast as other Missionaries have come, I have given place to them, and have myself, gone farther back, into places more recently settled. . . . .

Yours in the bonds of the gospel

ISAAC W. RUGGLES

REV. A. PETERS

PONTIAC, Sept. 20—1833

REVEREND & DEAR SIR,

Since I wrote, which was at the close of the year for which I was commissioned, I have continued to labor in the same field.

In July I organized a church at Grand Blanc of 13 members. They have 2 men among them of good abilities, zealous, & men of influence, who were deacons of churches at the East, and were again chosen to the same office. This church seems to be in a fair way to be built up; but they desire and greatly need a pastor; & I hope they will not be forgotten by your Society.

Since that time Br. Shaw & I together, organized a church at La Pier,[33] of 9 members. More are expected soon to come among them, & be added to their number.

They also desire to be remembered by your Society in its benevolent efforts. La Pier is the County seat of La Pier County about 16 miles to the east of Grand Blanc, & the

[33] Or "Lapeer Centre" (see Shaw's letter of June 28, 1833).

settlement has recently commenced. You are already informed that a church was organized at Orchard Lake last February. Three have been received by letter since.

They have petitioned your Committee, Mssrs. Wells and Hastings, that I may minister to them constantly as their pastor, and that they may continue to receive the aid of your Society in my support. . . . .

Yours in the bonds of the Gospel—

ISAAC W. RUGGLES

REV. A. PETERS

Office of the A.H.M.S. 150 Nassau St.
NEW YORK, Dec. 11, 1833

Revd Isaac W. Ruggles
Bloomfield, M.T.
D SIR,

The Executive Com. of the A.H.M.S. have formerly felt some reluctance to grant aid in your support owing to your want of a center of operations, or more properly to the too wide distribution of your labors. They are now happy to learn that you expect to confine your efforts to a single congregation, & confidently hope for more important success. . . . .

Your Fellow Labourer,

CHAS. HALE.

PONTIAC, Jan. 7—1834

REVEREND & DEAR SIR,—

My commission has not yet come to hand, but my reappointment appears in the Home Missionary; I therefore suppose it my duty to send another report.

There are now in the church at Orchard Lake 20 members, 10 males & 10 females. . . . . 13 of this church are Scotch, 1 Englishman & the others of our own country. A woman has recently come to Orchard Lake from the family of Rev. Phinney [Charles G. Finney] of your city. She is the wife of Mr. Andrews who is the brother of Mrs. Phinney. Mr. Andrews is a devoted man & a member of Orchard Lake church. His wife also is a devoted woman, & will connect herself with the church soon. . . . . There is a Sunday School & bible class. The concert of prayer is attended.

There is a Temperance Society in West Bloomfield, which includes O. Lake, of about 50 or 60 members. The Society is prospering & so are all the T. Societies in our Territory.

My family reside at Pontiac, for the present, as a matter of convenience. I contemplate moving them to O. Lake the ensuing Spring. . . . .

. . . . You may be assured, dear Brother, I feel for the people in Canida when I read what you have recently published of their needs; & while we were reading, my wife & I were almost moved to go over to help them. But upon second thought, we have more than we can do where we are. The church at Grand Blanc, the church at La Pier, the church at Paint Creek, & the church at Wing Lake are repeating their requests that I would visit them & break to them the bread of life. . . . .

Yours in the bonds of the Gospel—

I. W. RUGGLES

REV. A. PETERS.

ORCHARD LAKE, Ap. 16—1833[1834][34]

REVEREND & DEAR SIR,

. . . . Religion is in a very low state; & I hardly know what means to use in order to a better state of things. The people

---

[34] This date should be 1834 for the following reasons: (1) there is another letter written by Ruggles to the A.H.M.S. on April 15, 1833, and he would not have written two reports on two successive days; (2) the content of this letter fits the situation of 1834; (3) the last two numerals in the year on the original letter look as if the ink had faded and the numerals been filled in by another, probably by someone in the A.H.M.S. office.

are, for the most part, directly from Scotland; & have brought
with them their peculiarities. They have bibles & read them;
& in this they do well. But they are extremely tenacious of
their old modes of faith & practice. They are very apprehen-
sive of new measures & are unwilling that any extraordinary
means should be used, lest it should appear Pharisaical. It
seems, therefore, almost impossible to produce an excitement
among them. . . . .

The concert of prayer is generally attended by the praying
ones; but I am sorry to say we have not yet any weekly
prayer meeting. They excuse themselves by saying "We live
so far apart, & we have so much to do." I tell them; they are
condemned out of their own mouths. It is a proof that they
are too much actuated by a worldly spirit.

There is a female prayer meeting lately commenced in a
neighborhood where there are no Scotch. A very active woman has recently come among them from the Rev. Mr. Phinney's [Charles G. Finney] family.

. . . .

You do not suppose that I have sought my own ease in taking so large a circuit of labor. It has seemed expedient to me
& to others who were acquainted with the circumstances of
the people. The people in every place where I have labored,
I believe, have expressed their wishes that I could stay with
them. But had I settled down & confined myself to one place,
it seems that my usefulness would have been limited, tho my
labors would have been much less abundant. I have labored
where no other minister would have done; for there has been
none here that could do it. Churches have been instituted &
public worship practiced when it would not be had I not done
as I have. People have expressed anxiety that I should visit
them; & I have been constrained, by compassion for them.[35]

[35] There had long been some feeling on the part of those in the home office that
Ruggles ought to confine himself to one field of labor (N. M. Wells and E. P. Hastings to B. H. Rice, November 24, 1832.

I have not designedly violated the rules of the A.H.M. Society. It has seemed needful that some one in this part of the Territory, should labor as an evangelist; & with the knowledge of what is so much needed, I have willingly subjected myself to extraordinary labors, in some measure to supply what was lacking. . . . .

Yours in the bonds of the Gospel

I. W. RUGGLES

ORCHARD LAKE, July 16—1834

REVEREND & DEAR SIR—

. . . . The people give good attendance on the Sabbath; but it is not so easy a matter to bring them together at other times as I should wish. They have excuses. They live so far from each other; they have to be constantly engaged at work in order to get a living, etc.

It is true they have just commenced on land entirely wild and uncultivated, & therefore, diligence is indispensable. But it is a lamentable fact, they are far too worldly minded. Instead of living above the world as they ought, I tell them then, they appear to love & serve the creation more than the Creator; & give men occasion to say, 'what do ye more.' Coming into this new country with money sufficient only to purchase their lands, they do indeed find hard times; but there is a prospect of that they will yet become a wealthy people.

We have a temperance Society within the bounds of my charge which is increasing in numbers & interest. Our Scotch brethren tho' not intemperate, are extremely tenacious of their privileges, & are not easily persuaded to sign the pledge of total abstinence. They seem averse to hearing or reading anything on the subject. One of them, however, who,

three months ago, was as far from it as any of them has subscribed the pledge, & is endeavoring to persuade his brethren. . . . .

Your unworthy servant,

I. W. RUGGLES

REV. A. PETERS.

ORCHARD LAKE, Oct. 16, 1834.

REVEREND & DEAR SIR,

. . . . There are 22 in the church. About one third of these
give evidence that they are what they profess to be; the
others we have reason to fear, have a name to live which they
are dead to. . . . .

These came recently with letters from churches in Scotland, & for this reason I am the more disappointed with respect to their conduct. I expected to find them a peculiar
people; more punctual in their attendance on religious ordinances than others. But it is not so. I have been unable to
get them together, except a few, once a month at a prayer
meeting. The Bible class has not succeeded as it ought. Only
one of the *Scotchmen* has been persuaded to subscribe the
temperance pledge. They, indeed, openly oppose Temperance Societies. I know not that any one of them has been
found intoxicated; but they want the liberty to drink when
they have a mind to do so.

I have endeavored to exercise prudence, & at the same
time to be faithful. But it seems like laboring on a Barren
soil, without any prospect of fruit. They express an unwillingness to be left without a minister. But I think it expedient
to leave them, & to turn to some of the destitute fields by
which I am surrounded, & where there is a prospect of doing
more good.

There is indeed, Dear Sir, great need of more ministers in

this part of the Territory. Br. McEwen, a devoted servant of the Lord, & just such a one as we need here, has been constrained to leave Pontiac, & return to Connecticut, by reason of the ill health of his wife. There is no prospect of his returning.[36]

No less than 8 churches in this region are destitute of preaching. Pontiac, Wing Lake, Bloomfield, Rochester, Paint Creek, La Pier, Grand Blanc, and Flink River. I am often requested by these churches to visit them. It seems to me of no small importance that some one should visit them as an evangelist, until a sufficient number of ministers can be sent to settle with them. . . . . I wish to do nothing inconsistent with the rules of your Society, & therefore wish not to be commissioned; but considering the destitute condition of the people, seems to be duty to labor in a less circumscribed field than during the past year. Duty, I think calls me to volunteer in the service of my Master.[37]

Commissioned by the U.D.M. Society, recommended by the Cooperstown agency, I came to this Territory in the Fall of 1824, at a time when immigration had but just commenced. There was not at that time, another minister of our order on

---

[36] Williams to Peters, April 1, 1835.

[37] Thus Ruggles ended his connection with the A.H.M.S., whose officials in the home office could not understand his itinerant work among the people of the new settlements, rather than give up his work to which he thought God and duty called him. He seems to have carried out his intention of acting as a shepherd to the numerous destitute churches in that part of Michigan. At intervals he wrote to the A.H.M.S., soliciting aid for various churches and recommending men for commissions. Evidently, he again supplied the pulpit of the Pontiac church for a time in 1838 (*Michigan Pioneer and Historical Collections* [Lansing: Robert Smith Printing Co., 1908], XXVIII [1897–98], 404).

Ruggles ceased active work in the ministry in 1845 and retired to a small farm near Pontiac (*History of Oakland County, Michigan*, p. 102), but as late as May, 1848, he helped to organize the Oakwood Congregational Church (*ibid.*, p. 156). He died at Owasso, Mich., while attending a meeting of the Congregational General Association, on May 28, 1857, at the age of seventy-three (*American Congregational Year-Book for the Year 1858*, pp. 114–15).

the whole peninsula of Michigan. Br. Ferry was at Mackina; & Br. Wells came to Detroit in May or June after. I have labored here 10 years, 8 years under commission of your society, & 2 years without commission. I have continued to labor in a large field until the last year. Since I have been here, I suppose I have travelled more than twice the distance that any other Missionary has done, & have performed all my journeys on foot. . . . .

Yours in the bonds of the Gospel

I. W. RUGGLES.

MARSHALL MAY 20th 1835

REV. & DEAR SIR,

The letter of the Assist. Secy. of the 17th ult. came to hand a week last Saturday, and how much soever I might have had occasion to be surprised at the result of our application for aid, I should have bowed in silence to the decision had it not been founded on what I consider to be a total misapprehension of the facts in the case . . . . and . . . . no man should be condemned without having an opportunity of meeting the accusers face to face. The power of the Com. is immense— & when brought to bear on an individual may do him an essential injury. I am aware of some of the influences that have operated in the present case. My course as a minister has not given satisfaction to all. I am myself a Congregationalist in sentiment, & these churches are established on the Congregational plan of church government, & this is the sentiment of nearly every member. I state these facts to show why we have not united with the Presbytery. I have uniformly opposed what are called new measures. I did all I could to discountenance them while in N. Y. & I have done all I could to prevent their being introduced among this people, & I have ever advocated & preached the doctrines of grace as taught in general by such men as Calvin, Hopkins, Edwards, Bellamy, West, Mills, Strong, Austin, Cattin & Emmons. . . . .

I am your fellow servant

JOHN D. PIERCE[38]

MARSHALL NOV 10, 1835

REV. & DEAR SIR,

As I did not receive your commission until I had entered upon the fourth quarter of the year, I thought it would not be expected that I should report before its termination. I perfectly agree with the Ex. Com. that it is neither proper nor consistent for Missionaries to be engaged & involved in worldly business and responsibilities and here I beg leave to say that if such had been my circumstances, no application on my behalf would have been suffered to be made. While the Com. believed what was represented to them, their decision was perfectly correct. While they believed me to be "a tavern keeper, a high political party-man, a great land speculator, the keeper of the Post-office, all over engaged in the world, and by the ears with my neighbors"—I see not how they could have decided otherwise. For a time after I came here I

---

[38] John D. Pierce was born at Chesterfield, N.H., in 1797. He graduated from Brown University in 1822 and was a student for one year at Princeton Theological Seminary. He was ordained at Sangerfield, N.Y., in 1825 by the Oneida Association, serving the church there until 1829. We have been able to discover no record of this church ever having affiliated itself with a presbytery (*Congregational Year-Book for the Year 1883*, p. 28).

When Pierce arrived in Detroit in June, 1831, as a missionary of the A.H.M.S., he says he was informed that "it was best for me, and that it was expected, that I should join the Presbytery," and, furthermore, that "it would not be either desirable or wise to organize any Congregational churches." He answered that he had examined "the question of Church order and government, and was satisfied that Congregationalism was the Scriptural mode; and if it was adapted to primitive times, and to New England in its infancy, it would not be less so to the new settlements of the west" (*Congregational Quarterly*, II [1890], 192). He refused to join a presbytery, and he did organize Congregational churches. Although after a few years he gave his major attention to educational matters, he maintained an active interest and participation in Congregational affairs. He died at Ypsilanti in 1882.

did as others have been obliged to do, admit persons to my dwelling to prevent their lodging in the open air, but no longer than was absolutely necessary. This is the amount of my tavern-keeping. I have occasionally voted & sometimes in my own house expressed an opinion on political matters. It is true also that I own three or four hundred acres of land & also for a time was to some extent engaged in secular affairs, *but while thus engaged I neither asked nor would I receive any compensation for my services as a minister*, though several times offered. At the request of the Post Master the office was once kept at my house a few months. And as to my being by the ears with my neighbors there is no truth in it farther than this. I have had some difficulty or misunderstanding with two or three individuals, concerning one of whom the Methodist clergyman declared that he was "the most accomplished scoundrel he ever knew," the second is notoriously a Sabbath breaker, as is also the third. But these are the men who have declared that they would have me put down if they could, that I should neither receive aid nor preach if they could prevent it. I have every reason to believe that such are not the feelings of the great body of people, and I have thought it due in justice to myself to make this further statement on a subject to me extremely painful. . . . . .

The doings of the church here in respect to the coming year will be made known to you by the Committee appointed for that purpose. Mr. Clark who was commissioned for the county will probably take up his residence at Homer. We need more preachers. Our population is nothing short of 4000 and immigration is pouring in upon us. Before the arrival of Mr. Clark there was no minister of our order who could be called upon to perform any ministerial duties besides myself. Though restricted to the towns of Homer and Marshall, yet I have not felt at liberty to decline any service when called upon from other quarters. Hence I have found at times my labours so great as to impair my health. Imagine yourself in the midst of a population of 4 or 5000 souls scattered over a whole County & yourself the only one who could be called upon to perform any ministerial duty, with the care of two churches 12 miles apart resting upon you, & you may form some just conception of the amount of labor that would be required.

I am yours in the gospel,

JOHN D. PIERCE

REV. ABSALOM PETERS D.D.
Cor. Sec. of the A.H.M.S.

MARSHALL May 8, 1837

REV. & DEAR SIR—

I write not this on my own account, but at the urgent solicitation of the members of "the Michigan Association," and I do it with reluctance because I shall be obliged to state some things, which must be unpleasant to you, as they are painful to me. The Mich. Asso. was formed sometime last winter and consists of four ministers and ten or twelve chhs— with a fair prospect of a large addition of both ministers and chhs at its next meeting in Sept. Upon an interchange of sentiment, at its late session in April, it was found that the several ministers had the same causes of complaint and grievance, as have existed in regard to myself, and which I have heretofore communicated to you. I know of no Congregational minister in the state who has not had the same difficulties to encounter. The most slanderous stories and reports put in circulation, and all for what? shall I say that these things have been done with a view to prevent their receiving any aid from the A.H.M.S.? and to put down Congregationalism? Facts, which have come to my knowledge, and letters, which I know to be in existence, oblige me to say—, I believe such to be the case. Suppose yourself, poor and pennyless, to be laboring in a remote section of the west, and with a people prefering the Cong. mode of govt and sup-

pose you should receive a letter from a leading member of
the Presbytery to this effect—You must not organize a chh
there on that plan—if you do you can have no reason to
expect any further support? What would be your conclusion?
Knowing at the same time that if aid is received from the
A.H.M.S. it must come through committees and agencies
belonging to that connection!—I was not present when the
Asso. was formed, but was present at its meeting in April,
when the question was seriously entertained of making an
expose of grievances, and appealing directly to the N. E. chhs
for help. I observed to them that I had no doubt the circumstances would justify such a course.—but suggested
whether it would not be best to apply to the H.M.S. first
as I believed the fault rested not with the Ex. Com. but with
their agents here—that some plan might be adopted that
would afford them all the relief they could reasonably ask. It
was this suggestion which led them to urge me to write to you
on the subject. It has occurred to me that the appointment
of a Committee of our Cong. brethren, through whom applications for aid of these chhs. and ministers may be made to
your Society would be satisfactory. It is important that
something be done. It will be found in the sequel that the
Congregational interest has taken deep root in this State; and
all that is wanting to cause its influence to be felt, is a concentration of its strength, and that concentration has already
commenced. Such is their want of confidence in the present
organs of communication with your society that, however
great their need, they can hardly be induced to make further
application through them. They know well that a large proportion of the funds of your So. come from Cong. chhs, and
they believe that if those chhs knew how their Cong. brethren
of the west were treated in these matters, they would so
direct their contributions, as to afford them ample relief. . . . .
All the Cong ministers and chhs can ask, or desire, is to be
put on an equal footing with the Presbyterians. But while all

the Coms and agencies are of that connection, they cannot be said to be on that footing. . . . . I scarcely know of a Cong. minister, who has not been, for some cause or other, proscribed. . . . .

JOHN D. PIERCE

VERMONTVILLE EATON CO. MICHIGAN
Sept. 28, 1838

To the Cor. Secy. of the A.H.M.S.

DEAR SIR

The Petition of the Congregational Church and Society of Vermontville in the County of Easton and State of Michigan humbly showeth, that the Church and Society here, although located in the wilderness, are very desirous, and anxious to enjoy the stated ordinances of the Gospel, but as we are an infant settlement located in a timbered country, and as our means were limited when we emigrated, and as we have not as yet been enabled to raise the means of Support for our families, it is impossible for us to sustain a Minister without some foreign aid. . . . .

Perhaps a short history of our place will not be uninteresting. It will at least exhibit our present & future prospects. In the winter of 1836 several individuals from different towns in Vermont organized themselves into a Colony for the purpose of emigrating to some of the western States—They sent their agents in the Spring of the same year and purchased 5760 acres of Govt. land. this was divided into 34 shares. One article of their compact was, that they should endeavour to carry with them the religious privileges, which they had enjoyed in Vermont. But in making so large a purchase in one body, free from unbroken land, the agents were obliged to retire about 15 miles from any inhabitants, which has subjected the colony to much expense, and privation—A village was laid out as nearly the center as conveniently [could] be done, into lots of ten acres each, so that each colonist might from the beginning enjoy the privilege of school and meeting— A fund of $900 was secured toward the building of a Meeting House when we got ready to build one—A lot of 60 acres was reserved for a Parsonage, & this adjoined the village—This we calculate will do much toward supporting the Gospel in a few years. Most of our colonists are on the ground, and we are progressing as fast as our means and the difficulties & privations we have had to encounter, will permit—

The region which was an unbroken wilderness when we came in, from 15 to 40 miles around us is now settling quite fast, and we find many professors scattered up and down, who need looking after, & we consider it an important field for a missionary—Our Church is the only one of the Congregational or Presbyterian order in the County who have enjoyed the Stated labours of a Minister.

We therefore pray you if your funds will permit to grant us the aforesaid sum, to enable us to sustain our Minister for the year to come.[39]

By order of the church

S.——. Church

VERMONTVILLE EATON CO. MICHIGAN
Sept. 28, 1838.

JACKSON, March 7, 1842

Rev. Milton Badger

DEAR SIR

Having been unusually pressed with labors in the feeble churches & surrounding districts in the vicinity, during week days, I have almost unconsciously omited the second quarterly report of labor until now. . . . .

[39] Sylvester Cochran, who had been instrumental in organizing this colony in Vermont, and who became the minister of this church in Michigan, joined a presbytery in 1844 and became the minister of the Presbyterian church in Northville. He died in Northville in 1860 (*Congregational Quarterly*, II [1860], 344).

My appointments for the present week are this evening (Monday) at the county poor house, 4 miles N West of this, Tuesday in the village, Wednesday at Leoni 8 miles east, Thursday at Hanover 14 miles South west, & Friday in the village. I regularly preach every evening except Saturday & my health has been uniformly such as to endure it without inconvenience.

A brief history of the church under my care may not be uninteresting. Five years ago the first of May I preached my first sermon in this village, & as I was informed the third sermon by a presbyterian ever preached here.

The same season, June 9th 1837 I organized a presbyterian church of 13 members. They consented to this organization, though mostly congregationalists from New England, some of them more recently from New York.

They have remained quiet until last spring, when a case of discipline, in the decision of which, the Session & Presbytery unanimously concured, was revers'd by synod. After which my church was fixed in the purpose to be congregational in its form of government.

A number were presbyterian & wished to retain their organization, the church then consisting of about 100 members.

Accordingly a congregational church was formed of 85 members to whom letters had been voted for the purpose, including the entire board of elders with the exception of the excinded member. A number more of them have since united with us, & a few more are still purposed to do so. The remaining few have a house of worship 20 feet by 30, which they have now rented to the Freewill baptists.

There has been since the organization of the congregational church, not the least collision between the two.

Of the nine churches in,—& partially in this county, five are congregational & two others have passed resolutions to become so.

Of the four ministers now in the county two are congregational & one about to become so.

Since my last report I have thought it my duty to present
my certificate from Marshall presbytery & unite with the
eastern Association of Michigan because almost entirely surrounded with congregationalists & retaining still my New
England feeling. . . . .

In bonds of christian love I remain your br in the Lord

MARCUS HARRISON[40]

JACKSON, MICHIGAN.

[40] The obituary of Marcus Harrison does not appear in either the *Congregational
Year-Book* or the *Quarterly*, and it seems probable that he was removed from the
Congregational scene, perhaps by death, before the publication of these works was
begun.

CHAPTER IX

Congregational Indian Missions: Letters and Reports from Missionaries to the American Board of Commissioners for Foreign Missions, 1831-38

THE Indian Missions of the Congregationalists were carried on under the direction of the American Board of Commissioners for Foreign Missions and the documents in this chapter have been chosen from the great collection of manuscripts in the possession of that Society. All that is attempted here is to make available typical letters and reports for the years in which Congregational Indian Missions were carried on most extensively.

DOCUMENTS

1. A Letter from Rev. Sherman Hall to the American Board of Commissioners for Foreign Missions Relative to a Visit to the Chippewa, August 2, 1831
2. A Letter from Rev. William Montgomery to the Board, August 27, 1832, Describing the Situation among the Osage Indians in and around Union Mission, in What Is Now the State of Oklahoma
3. A Letter from Rev. Cutting Marsh, Green Bay, Michigan Territory, Dated November 5, 1833, Discussing the Policy To Be Pursued among the Stockbridge Indians
4. Traveling Expenses of an Exploring Tour among the Indians of the Upper Mississippi Made by Dr. Thomas S. Williamson in 1834
5. A Letter from Henry H. Copeland, the Government Schoolteacher in the Choctaw Nation, Commenting on the Work of the American Board, November 11, 1836
6. A Letter from Rev. J. D. Stevens Written at Lake Harriet, a Mission Station among the Dakota Indians near Fort Snelling (Minn.), September 13, 1838

1. A LETTER FROM REV. SHERMAN HALL TO THE AMERICAN BOARD OF COMMISSIONERS FOR FOREIGN MISSIONS RELATIVE TO A VISIT TO THE CHIPPEWA, AUGUST 2, 1831

Rev. Sherman Hall (1800–1879), the writer of this letter, was a graduate of Dartmouth College and Andover Theological Seminary. In 1831 he was

sent by the American Board of Commissioners for Foreign Missions to open
a mission among the Chippewa on the south shore of Lake Superior. He
established a mission at La Pointe, a fur-trading post on Madeline Island.
Here he remained until 1852. He was very successful, especially in his
conduct of several Indian schools, learned the difficult Chippewa language
and translated or supervised the translation of textbooks, hymns, and the
New Testament into that tongue (*Dictionary of American Biography*, VIII,
144). The mission at Mackinaw, of which the La Pointe mission was an
extension, had been taken over by the American Board from the United
Foreign Missionary Society in 1826. This letter contains Hall's report
relative to the establishment of the Chippewa mission.

MACKINAW, M.T., August 2, 1831

Mr. David Green
Assist. Sec. of the A.B.C.F.M.

DEAR SIR:

You may perhaps have expected us to write before this
time; but as nothing occurred on our way which required it,
and as it seemed to us on our arrival that some little alteration in the plan of our mission to Lake Superior, for that proposed by the Committee, was required, we chose to wait till
some plan should be fixed upon.

We reached this place on the morning of the 13th of July,
just one month from the time we left Boston. Our boxes did
not arrive at Providence in season for the boat the day we
left, in consequence of which Mr. Boutwell[1] remained their
[*sic*] till the next day. His delay together with some irregularity in the boats detained me at New York two days. Mr.
B. was also detained at Buffalo from Thursday till the following Monday on account of our goods. He went to the Seneca
station and preached on the Sabbath. It was thought best
that myself and wife take passage in the first boat for Detroit,
in order to make provision for a passage to this place with as
little delay as possible. We reached Detroit early on Sabbath morning, 13 days from Boston. We were unable to leave

---

[1] William T. Boutwell was Hall's traveling companion and a fellow-missionary to
the Chippewa.

Detroit, however, till the Saturday following. I delivered our letters of introduction to Messrs. Hastings and Davis on Monday morning. Mr. D. took us to his own house where we were very hospitably entertained during our detention, free of expense. On Mr. Boutwell's arrival he was invited by Mr. Bingham to his . . . . house. Mr. Hastings treated us very kindly, but said it was not convenient to entertain at his house on account of his family being unwell.

We were eleven days in making our passage from Detroit to Mackinaw, owing to calms and head winds. We encountered a heavy blow on Lake Huron, which lasted two days, during which we suffered considerable from sea sickness. On our arrival we were very cordially received by the mission family, who have been expecting us for several days. We found them in usual health.

Most of the traders had arrived from the interior. Mr. Ayer had returned from Le Point. He commenced a school soon after his arrival at Le Point, and succeeded in collecting into it about 27 different scholars. He was not able, however, to sustain it during the year on account of his health. His health is now much better than when he left Mackinaw last year.

He has paid some attention to learning the Chippewa language during his absence. It is the opinion that very little can be done for the Indians around Lake Superior without a school. Mr. Ferry, Mr. Warren and others are of the same opinion.[2] It is not easy to convince an Indian by argument or big promises. He must be convinced by his senses, if at all. If a school is commenced at all, it ought to be continued without interruption.

From the best information which we can obtain, it is the opinion so far as I know, that Le Point is the best place to commence the mission. That place is easy of access, and is a place through which more people pass during the year than

[2] William M. Ferry was the missionary and superintendent of the Mackinaw mission. Mr. Warren was the principal trader at La Pointe.

any other in that section of the country. There are about as many Indian families residing there as at any of the trading posts. It is said that more Indians reside near Leech Lake than any place known through that vast tract of country south and west of Lake Superior. But that place which is 600 or 700 miles west or n. west of Le Point is too distant and to[o] difficult of access to be thought of as a mission post at present. The post which Mr. Dingly has occupied is spoken of as next to Le Point in importance for a mission station. On some accounts it is perhaps preferable to the latter. It is possible that the committee may fix upon that place for the principle station. Whatever we do in the way of maintaining a school, we shall take upon ourselves no responsibility of furnishing food or clothing to the scholars.[3]

We have thought it proper to depart a little from the letter, though I think not from the spirit of the instructions which the committee gave us, as to the plan of operation in this mission, since we arrived here. In doing this we have acted not only according to our judgment, but also according to the opinion of Mr. Ferry, Mr. Stewart, Mr. Warren and others. We are aware that we are taking upon ourselves great responsibilities in departing at all from the instructions of the committie, but it appeared to us that the case required it.

The plan we have adopted is this: that Mr. Boutwell remain at Mackinaw till next year, and Mr. Ayer, myself and wife, and Mrs. Campbell go immediately to Le Point.[4] The reasons for adopting this plan are the following:

1. Mr. Ayer has spent one year in the country, and has become acquainted to some extent with the Indians there,

---

[3] Among the instructions given by the Prudential Committee to Hall and Boutwell was a caution against boarding schools because of their great expense. They state that "they have doubtless done much good . . . . but to think of boarding school so far in the interior, and in a climate so unfavorable to agricultural pursuits, is out of the question" (see A.B.C.F.M., *Report, 1832*, Appen., p. 164).

[4] The traders at Le Pointe were kindly disposed toward missions. During their annual visits to Mackinaw they attended the mission services regularly, and four of their number, for example, joined the mission church in the summer of 1830. They insisted upon having a station established at their own trading post. Con-

their habits, modes of thinking, prejudices, etc. He will be a
great assistance to a missionary who is unacquainted with
the Indian character.

2. One of the first objects to which the committee would
have us direct our attention is the acquaintance of the Chippeway language. Mr. Ferry and Mr. Warren are decidedly of
the opinion that Mackinaw affords more facilities for its
acquisition to a person just commencing the study of it, than
the interior country. Our opinion is the same. The reasons
for this opinion are: (1) The want of suitable interpreters in
the Indian country. (2) Many of the girls in the school here,
speak Chippeway language, and would make good interpreters for a person residing here, but are not suitable persons
to send into the interior in that capacity. (3) Dr. James of
the U.S. Army, who resides at Sault St. Mary [sic], has made
very considerable acquaintance in that language, and offers
any assistance which he can afford toward acquiring it. He
has several manuscripts which he will lend to the one who
shall remain here. He is willing also to give instructions oral-
ly, if he can have opportunity. He has invited Mr. Boutwell
to spend some time with him. He will probably go to the
Sault and spend two or three weeks in the course of the year.

3. If one of us should remain here, he would be able to
assist Mr. Ferry in his public religious exercises, while nothing will be lost towards accomplishing the ultimate objects of
the Board in regard to our mission. Such assistance Mr. F.
very much needs. He will also learn many things in regard to

---

sequently, "when they were at that place [Mackinaw] the preceeding year, they
were encouraged to expect that a missionary would be ready to accompany them
to their trading posts." Since no suitable missionary could be found and rather than
disappoint them, Mr. Ayer, a teacher at Mackinaw, and one of his pupils, acting as
interpreter were allowed to return with them for a year. One of the traders sent a
boat expressly for their conveyance, hence there was little expense to the mission.

Mr. and Mrs. Campbell were of mixed Indian descent. After serving as helpers
at Mackinaw for a number of years, they removed to Le Pointe where the former
served as mechanic and the latter as interpreter (ibid., 1830, p. 95; ibid., 1883,
p. 124).

conducting missions which may be of very great service to him. The expense of living here will not be greater than in the Indian country.

4. It is expected that Mr. Ayer, with the assistance which Mrs. Hall can render him, will be able to sustain the school, without calling me from other labours to engage in the business of teaching. It is the opinion of Messrs. Ferry and Warren, in which also we concur, that one can do as much towards giving religious instruction to the Indians and exploring the country the present year, as both could, were we to go. For the want of good interpreters we shall be in a great measure shut out from the means of usefulness in preaching the gospel to the Indians till we are able to communicate with them in own language. This renders it vastly important that we acquire the language as soon as possible.

5. On many accounts it is advisable that a missionary should have a family with him in the Indian Country. There are many unpleasant things in living in the family of one [of] the traders, both to them and to the missionary. Aside from this, the wife of a missionary can find many opportunities of doing good to the Indians, which are less accessible to a man. There is no reason to apprehend any difficulty on account of a missionary's having a family with him, from any prejudices of the Indians, or of the traders. It will rather serve to confirm them in the belief that a missionary has come to stay with them and do them good. There are no difficulties in the way of taking a family into the Indian country now, which will not exist two or three years hence. Mr. Warren has comfortable buildings with which he will furnish us for the present free of expense. He will not feel that we are under any obligation to remain at his post, if the committee should fix on some other place as more eligible for a permanent mission station. The expense of living in a family by ourselves will not be greater than that of living with the traders.

Mr. Ayer thinks that should sufficient help go out this

summer, much might be done next fall and spring towards raising a large part of the provisions necessary for the support of the mission family another year. In the present arrangement, such provision is made. This may be done at very little expense with the assistance which Mr. Warren will afford us. He has cultivated more land for two years past than formerly, and finds the soil at his post more productive the more he works it. Mr. Warren has a considerable stock of cattle, farming utensils, etc. He takes with him some pigs this year. He says the Indians will not object to our residing there and cultivating [the] land.

Mrs. Campbell goes with us as [an] interpreter. There is no one now in the school, who would answer our purpose in that capacity, and who could be spared. When Mrs. C. learnt [sic] that we were not able to obtain an interpreter she came forward and voluntarily offered her services. She leaves her family here except her babe, 10 or 12 months old, which she takes with her. She will be a valuable helper. She understands the French and Indian languages and can interpret from both of these into English, and vice versa. She has been employed much by Mr. Ferry and his wife in interpreting religious instruction to the Indians.

I attended the examination of the Schools which took place after our arrival. I was very much gratified with the appearance of the scholars, and the promptness with which they answered questions on the subjects to which they had been attending. I believe all who were present at the examination were satisfied with improvement, which the scholars made.

Dr. James has been here since our arrival, and we have had several interviews with him. He is very friendly to our object, and will give us some small manuscripts which he has made in the Chippeway language, to take along with us. He has considerable part of the necessary materials for an Indian grammar collected. I believe he does not design to publish anything of the kind at present. He will furnish Mr. Boutwell with what he has written on that subject in MS. He has the materials all prepared for a small spelling book in the Chippeway language. He has been accostomed [sic] to make use of the English alphabet in writing in Chippeway. Mr. Loomis has been to visit him and confer with him in regard to adopting in the main the anthography recommended by Mr. Pickering.[5] He has concluded to adopt it in the little work which he is about to publish. It is found that that anthography can be introduced with great advantages in writing the Indian language. The Chippeway spelling book is to consist of 12 pages, I believe. Certainly besides spelling lessons, a few lessons in reading. It will go to press very soon.

As to Dr. James' competency to translate the Scriptures correctly into the Indian language, I am not able to decide. I have some doubts whether he is the proper person to employ for that purpose.

I hope you will write us as soon as convenient and tell us whether the committee approve the plan which we have adopted. Mr. Ferry will write you, and give you all the information respecting the traders. We regret that Mr. Dingley has left the Indian country. His post is to be under the controul [sic] of Mr. Warren at present.

I have paid to Mr. Ferry thirty dollars of money which is the property of Mrs. Hall and which she chooses to retain at present. Mr. F. will direct you or Mr. Hill to charge him with that sum. I wish that amount to be paid to Mr. Aaron Hall of Weathersfield, Vt., when he shall order it. It was not convenient for us to agree upon the price of our passage from

[5] "Mr. Loomis who was engaged temporarily as a teacher, left Mackinaw with his family in June, after having remained there about a year and a half" (*ibid., 1832*, p. 116; there seems to be no other information about him in the *Reports*).

"In writing the [Chippewa] language, they will expect you to use Mr. Pickering's orthography as a basis. This is used by the missionaries at the Sandwich and Society Islands, and among the Choctaws, Ottawas, Senecas and Abernaquois" (*ibid., 1832*, "Instructions to Missionaries," Appen., p. 165).

John Pickering prepared for the press a Cherokee grammar to be published at the expense of the board (*ibid., 1824*, p. 94).

Detroit to this place, on account of the absence of the owner of the vessel at the time we left D. Mr. Hastings was to settle it. He will forward to the Board his account which Mr. Hill will charge to us.

Yours very truly,

S. HALL

Mr. D. GREEN, *Asst. Sec.*
of the *A.B.C.F.M.*

2. A LETTER FROM REV. WILLIAM MONTGOMERY TO THE BOARD, AUGUST 27, 1832, DESCRIBING THE SITUATION AMONG THE OSAGE INDIANS IN AND AROUND UNION MISSION, IN WHAT IS NOW THE STATE OF OKLAHOMA

Union Mission had been established by the United Foreign Missionary Society and was taken over by the American Board in 1826. The church at Union Mission had been established in 1821, though in 1832 it had but one Osage member. There was a school at the mission with 154 children and youths in attendance, including 54 Creeks, 29 Cherokees, and 71 Osages. The writer of this letter, William B. Montgomery, was one of the two missionaries in charge of Union Mission, the other being Rev. William F. Vaill. Abraham Redfield was the farmer and mechanic. The missionaries had a poor opinion of the Osages generally, stating that they had manifested "little or no desire to hear the gospel" (*Report, 1833,* pp. 115–20).

The other Osage mission stations at this time were Hopefield, Boudinott, and Harmony. Clermore's band, to which reference is made in this letter, was a large Osage village some twenty-five miles from Union Mission, containing some two thousand souls. It was named from Chief Clarmore, who toured the country at public expense during Jefferson's administration (*ibid., 1832,* p. 113; *ibid., 1829,* p. 90).

UNION MISSION, Aug. 27, 1832

DEAR SIR:

The removal of Clermore's band to the reservation, which you are aware has been long in agitation, it is now generally expected will take place next spring. They will then be situated far beyond the sphere of this mission; and it will be for the committee to make such arrangements as their new circumstances may require. Before the subject comes up for decision, I have thought it would be my duty and not unaccept-

able to the committee to express briefly my views in regard to
the sort of aid which their case demands, and which would be
consistent with the interests of the Board to afford. On this
question we enjoy a great advantage over the Society by
which the missions were first established. It had nothing but
the unmeaning promises of the Indians from which to form a
judgment. We have eleven years' experience of their character and especially of their dispositions in regard to the
privileges which we have to offer them. And certainly whatever obscurity rested on this subject eleven years ago has long
since been removed by the history of these missions. Very few
children were ever received into this school from the large
town, and none of them were suffered to remain till any benefit was realized, and there is not now a single family who have
any disposition to put a child to school. All the children who
have continued long enough to realize any benefit either came
from the settlement, or were of the mixed race. The Osages
are as yet absolutely destitute of the motives which have ever
been found necessary to inspire a people with any regard for
letters. Still bound in chains of darkness, they have no religious objects to accomplish by a knowledge of the art of
reading. Neither have they the motives which arise from
business, and from prospects of improvement in their circumstances. Any part of our attainments which they at all
value is our skill in farming and in making cloth (and also our
practice of medicine), and it appears that they will have to
experience something of the benefits arising from these pri-
mary arts before they will set any store by privileges of
schools.

Such is the state of their feelings at present, and whether
their expected removal will be productive of any change for
the better is very uncertain. Unless measures be taken which
shall effectually improve their condition, their temper towards the Americans will certainly be soured, and their
prejudices encreased [sic]. But however beneficial the con-

templated measures may prove to be, it is by no means likely
that their utility will be soon acknowledged by the Indians.
In these circumstances there is certainly no encouragement to
continue to them the privileges of a boarding school. Nor
would the securing of the stipulation in the treaty in regard to
compensation to the Osages for the loss of the establishment
at this place be any adequate inducement for maintaining
such an institution. The possession of ten or twelve thousand
dollars' worth of buildings not really applicable to the purposes of the Board among the Osages would be dearly obtained at the annual expence [sic] of one of our large mission
families. But it maybe alleged that the opening of the school
might be delayed till the disposition of the people shall become more favorble. To this I would reply that before this
change can be rationally expected, the Osages will be living in
a stationary manner, and it may be hoped will be willing to
board their own children and do something toward the support of teachers, as the Creek people are now engaging to do
to the Methodist Missionaries.[6] And until this shall be the
case, the other fields of the American Board will furnish much
more productive employment for its benevolent exertions
than the cultivation of reluctant Osages at an expense of
three or four hundred dollars per head. The boarding of children must ever be an expensive business in an Indian country
where wages are so high and hands so slack.

The erection of buildings, conducting a large farm, and the
domestic concerns constitutes a business of very considerable
extent, presenting too many occasions of error and waste to
be encountered without the most evident necessity by the
conductors of missions.

In regard to preaching, it is cheering to reflect that not

[6] The Creeks, before their removal, had been strongly influenced by Baptist and
Methodist missionaries. John Davis, a Creek youth and a graduate of the Union
Mission school, was appointed, shortly before this time by the Baptist Board of
Foreign Missions, to serve his people as catechist. At least three Baptist stations
were located in or near the Creek reservation. Two or three small schools were
carried on among the Creeks by the Baptists and Methodists (*A.B.C.F.M., Report,
1831*, p. 88; *ibid., 1834*, p. 117).

only the broad ground of encouragement from the Saviour's command still remains, but that better facilities for communicating than formerly are now within our power. This has in fact always been the real point of difficulty with us. There is now good reason to hope that Charles Mogsin [?], a young man educated at the expense of the Board, will prove all that could be expected in an interpreter. Hoping that I may enjoy a portion of his time as may be arranged with Br. Dodge,[7] I feel sensibly encouraged both in my hopes of preaching and translating, and of acquiring more of the language myself. Should the committee think it advisable that I for one should remove with the Indians, I should prefer leaving the subject of location entirely open at present, as it will certainly be some time before the affairs of the district [will] be sufficiently shaped for that purpose. To vacate a couple of cabins or any change in the settlements or other circumstances would be of no great matter. After some pains in making an estimate, I think my small family could ordinarily be provided for at $120 or $150 per annum. Should I be obliged to keep a hired man through the year, it would add one hundred doll[ar]s to the bill. I would, of course, expect to be fitted out with a few cows, a yoke of oxen, perhaps two yoke of oxen, and a waggon [sic] or cart. The pay of an interpreter would also be additional. A settler's claim to which I am entitled will bring me 275 or 300 doll[ar]s. This money I would request the privilege of using in the hire of an interpreter and translator. An interesting marriage took place here, Aug. 14. Peter Kenouse to Rebecca Williams, Osages formerly of the school at Harmony—he has built a house and made a field near Mr. Dodge's. She was educated at the expense of young ladies in New York 1st Presb. church.

Yours,
Wm. MONTGOMERY.

[7] Nathaniel B. Dodge, a native of Vermont, had been a missionary among the Indians since 1821, having been previously connected with the United Foreign Missionary Society. He began his connection with the American Board in 1827. His connection with the board was severed in 1836 (*ibid.*, *1836*, p. 96).

3. A LETTER FROM CUTTING MARSH, GREEN BAY
MICHIGAN TERRITORY, NOVEMBER 5, 1833

Cutting Marsh was born in Danville, Vermont, July 20, 1800. Educated at Andover Academy, Dartmouth College, and Andover Theological Seminary, he was licensed to preach by the Andover Association, April 22, 1829, and in September was ordained for missionary work under the American Board of Commissioners for Foreign Missions. The following year he departed for his field of work among the Stockbridge Indians at Green Bay, Wisconsin. Here he remained until 1848, when the board ceased its work with the tribe. For years Mr. Marsh made reports both to the American Board and to the Society for Propagating Christian Knowledge of Edinburgh, as both were giving aid to the mission. Marsh succeeded Rev. Jesse Miner, who had died in 1829. After his withdrawal from the mission, Marsh served as a home missionary in northern Wisconsin for three years, when he located at Waupaca on the Indian reservation. Here he lived until his death in 1873.

The Marsh papers constitute a voluminous collection of reports, letters, journals, and miscellaneous documents, now in the archives of the Wisconsin Historical Society. Some of the papers have been published by the society (see *Wisconsin Historical Society Collections*, Vols. II, IV, VIII, XII, XIV, XV, X).

Statesburg was the name of the old Stockbridge village and the seat of the mission. In 1834–35 the tribe was removed to a new site some twenty miles distant, and the new town was called Stockbridge. The tribe was constantly harassed by frequent removals, by the gross intemperance of Menominees, who were located near them, and by their own internal dissentions. The following letter reveals some of the problems faced by Cutting Marsh (see Paul G. Dibble, "Christian Influence among the Stockbridge Indians" [University of Chicago thesis, 1930]).

STATESBURG, NEAR GREEN BAY, M.T., Nov. 5th, 1833

To Rev. David Greene,
Boston

DEAR SIR:

I wrote you in much haste on the *2d.* inst. but had not time to mention some additional particulars which I wish to in this. As important changes are contemplated in this mission and must necessarily take place in consequence of removal, I wish to express my mind more fully than I have. As I refered [*sic*] in my last [letter] to a plan of future operation which Mr. L. will lay before the Board, perhaps before this reaches you, the thought has occurred to me, that the Board might think me in fact opposed to it, altho my name was appended to it. But as it respects the plan itself so far as the Board approve of it, I am willing that it should be tried.

The Board have often stated that they intend this to be a small station, and as the above-mentioned plan recommends a Supt. and mechanic, I have thought it possible they might feel that the mechanic might be Supt. also, and under present circumstances I see nothing to prevent it. The Indians have a good deal of jealousy respecting the introduction of white families amongst them for almost any cause, because they fear that by and by when their children shall grow up, these assistant missionaries will say to them, "we have brought up our children amongst you and have been all the while laboring for your good; give us a little land for them." Altho this may be regarded as merely a surmise, still such sentiments have actually been expressed to me by one who stands at the head of the [Indian] nation.

I do not think under circumstances that it will be advisable to undertake building a framed mission-house, barn and meeting-house under two or three years. At present it appears probable that a considerable of a number will plant here next spring and so will not remove before another fall, and in addition I very much dislike the manner in which they have laid out their settlement for according to their present plan they will be scattered far more than they now are. If possible I shall induce them to make some alteration, but I feel it will not be done; I wish therefore to wait in order to see where the centre of population is going to be before the mission buildings are erected.

Whilst they are settling, a pious, *judicious* mechanic would [be] very serviceable and, I doubt not, do much good in assisting them about erecting mills and houses, in the meantime he might supt. the mission.

As the Indians here agreed to pay over their school fund to the A.B.C. I am very anxious that the school should take a higher stand as I have before mentioned to you than it ever has before. I have assured the Indians that it shall; they are expecting it; and I am fully persuaded it may be done. But the teacher must devote his whole attention to instruction; not merely teaching children a few hours in a day, and then dismissing them to see or think perhaps no more of them until the hour of school again calls him to his task. Whilst in the interval his time and attention have been occupied about something else. A teacher will do but little good amongst these Indians unless he visits often the parents and especially delinquent scholars, for discipline in most of the families is very imperfect, and the children are under little restraint, consequently their attendance at school whenever there is any want of inclination is not insisted upon, neither is there that vigilance that there ought to be in searching and finding out where or what their children are about, when out of sight. I have talked much in private and preached much on the subject, and I hope they are beginning to feel it a little; and I wish for a Teacher who will co-operate with me in this highly important particular.

P.S.   I stated in my letter of the 5th inst. that I had given my consent to Mr. L. to have him return again provided the Indians invited or wished him to, and the Board thought it expedient. Last Spring Mr. L. stated that if the Indians did not request him to return when he left, he should not. This as I have observed was one part of the agreement between us (Mr. L. and myself), and a few weeks before he left he says to me, "If you wish, the question may be put to the Indians whether they wish me to return." I replied of course I expect that it will be done. I conclude however it was never put; for the most, after a long struggle, that could be obtained was the consent of the Indians to recommend the plan which he had drawn up to the Board and their letter expressing in general terms their approbation of the mission. Such were the findings at that time elicited toward Mr. L.; feelings indeed which I did not at the time anticipate, that I was upon the point of advising him to withdraw his plan and say nothing further to the Indians about it; still fearing that I should be charged with interference, etc., I did not.

I was at the last surprised that he should suppose or say that the Indians had left it wholly with the Board to decide whether he should return, etc.

But in one word—it is my opinion that Mr. L. would be more useful some where else than he would amongst the Stockbridge Indians.

Yours, etc.

C. MARSH

P.S.   The above together with the enclosed I have intended for you personally, still you can make such a use of it with the *committee* as you think proper.

4. TRAVELING EXPENSES OF AN EXPLORING TOUR AMONG THE INDIANS OF THE UPPER MISSISSIPPI MADE BY DR. THOMAS S. WILLIAMSON IN 1834

Dr. Thomas S. Williamson was born in South Carolina in 1800, was graduated from Jefferson College in 1820, and had graduated in medicine at Yale College. He practiced medicine in Adams County, Ohio, for nine years before entering the ministry. He began the study of theology in 1833 and was licensed to preach the following year by his local presbytery and the same year made the journey to the Upper Mississippi described in this document. It was doubtless on the strength of this report that the American Board appointed him a missionary to the Dakota Indians after his return. He was ordained in September, 1834, and began his mission among the Dakotas in July, 1835. He began his work at Lac qui Parle, where his medical knowledge and his common sense, together with his intense and simple piety, gained him a favorable reputation among the Indians (Winifred W. Barton, *John P. Williamson: A Brother to the Sioux* [New York, 1919]; S. R. Riggs, *Mary and I; or Forty Years among the Sioux* [Boston, 1879].

Dr. Williamson started on this tour the first of May, proceeding up the Mississippi as far as Fort Snelling. He had letters of recommendation from the secretary of war, asking Indian agents and military officers to give him every facility for carrying out his inquiries. The agent at Fort Snelling arranged interviews with Indians in the vicinity. Williamson descended the Mississippi to Prairie du Chien, where was located another Sioux agency and where he learned that the Indians were friendly to missionary labors among them. At Rock Island, the seat of the agency of the Sac and Fox Indians, he met Cutting Marsh of the Green Bay Mission, and before his departure from Rock Island both Cyrus Kingsbury and Cyrus Byington arrived and aided in obtaining information and forming plans for missionary work in the region (A.B.C.F.M., *Report, 1834*, pp. 122-22).

(AUGUST 23, 1832[1834])

TREASURER OF A.B.C.F.M. [American Board of Commissioners for Foreign Missions (Congregational)] IN ACCOUNT WITH THO. S. WILLIAMS[ON] DR.

To travelling expenses on a exploring tour among the Indians of the Upper Mississippi [in] 1832 [1834] viz:

April 25th:	Passage on St[eam] Boat from Ripley to Cincinnati	1.75
26 and 28th:	Expenses in Cincinnati and sundries for [my] Journey	3.18-3/4
29th	Passage from Cincinnati to Lousville	4.00
May 2	Do from Lousville to St. Louis	10.56-1/4
3 to 7th	Boarding at St. Louis	2.00
8	Water biscuit and other provisions for [the] Journey	5.00
	Washing, stationary, medicines, etc.	3.25
15	Passage to Prairie du Chien	15.00
15-22	Sundries at Prairie du Chien	2.18-3/4
26	Passage from Prairie du Chien to Fort Snelling	3.00
26-June 2	Sundries at Fort Snelling	1.50
June 2d.	Blanket for travelling	6.00
5th.	Passage from F. L. to Prairie du Chien	1.25
5th to 19th.	Sundries at Prairie du Chien	1.18-3/4
19-21st	Stage from P. D. Ch. to Galena	10.00
	Meals and lodgings in this trip	.87-1/2
25th	Sundries at Galena	.50
	Passage from Galena to Rock Island	3.00
26th	Washing at Rock Island and Sundries	.87-1/2
27	Passage from Rock Island to Yellow Banks	2.00
27-July 5th	At. S. S. Phelps Lower Yellow Banks	.06-1/4

6th–19th	Expenses of visit to Appinoos Village	42.87–1/2
19th to August 2	Expense of returning home from the Commerce at the head of the Des Moines Rapids	25.00
	[Total]	$147.06–1/4
Tr. A.B.C.F.M., Cr.	]	
	[.................	200.00
April 28th by Cash of Rev. A. Bullan]		
Still in my hands		52.93–3/4

New Ripley, Ohio, August 23, 1832 [1834]

Henry Hill, Tr., A.B.C.F.M.

Dear Sir:

On the preceding page is an acct. of my expenses while travelling in the service of the Board, not including anything for clothing. A few remarks may be necessary by way of explanation.

Expenses at Cincinnati and sundries there and elsewhere were for stationary, books, washing, taking care of my baggage from surrays and other like expenses.

The provisions purchased in St. Louis were useful and indeed necessary in my travels down the river in a canoe, and in our visit to the village of Apinoos, where we were one week dependant on the provisions we carried with us.

The medicines I purchased because the cholera was prevailing on the river and it seemed probable I might need them. But through the goodness of God, I was preserved in health and gave most of the medicine to brother Marsh when I was about starting home.

The blanket was necessary in consequence of having to sleep on the ground in the open air when coming from Fort Snelling to Prairie du Chien.

In the 42.87–½ expenses of visit to Apinoos is just the amount of money which I paid out from leaving Mr. S. S.

Phelp's till I started home from the Mississippi river in Hancock County, Illinois. Of this $17.00 was for the hire of a guide and interpreter and $18.00 for the hire of horses for myself and Mr. Marsh.[8] Mr. Marsh supposed that I paid towards the expenses of this journey $2.71, which was properly charged to him and gave me a receipt for that amount. The cause of my paying this was Mr. M. was apprehensive he would be scarce of funds to take him again to his home and I supposed that I had more than sufficient for that purpose. 25 dollars is about what I suppose it would have cost him to return home in steamboats which is the usual way of travelling. For reasons elsewhere given I came by land. If I could sell my horse for what he cost me, I would save several dollars by coming by land, but it is probable I shall lose something in the price of the horse. If the committee prefer having the exact amount expended in this as I have given it in every other part of my journey, inform me so and when my horse is sold I will make out my account in that form.

I have put down nothing for clothing, though my expenses in this as well as several other respects were greater (travelling, as I did to collect information from strangers) than they would have been if I had been living at home, or travelling on my ordinary business. As [there was] my family . . . . to support as well as clothes to purchase for myself, I think I may justly claim something for my time, and services in this tour, but if we are sent out this fall and funds furnished us to purchase sufficient outfit, I do not know that I shall claim any more than is charged in the bill above. If we should not go till spring, I shall be under the necessity of claiming something for the services rendered towards supporting my family this winter. I have already been one year on expense and making nothing. Even if I should not have this till Spring,

[8] While at Rock Island Williamson met Cutting Marsh of the Green Bay Mission, who had been instructed to accompany a band of Stockbridge Indians from the latter place on a visit to the Sacs and Foxes, "with whom they claim affinity, and for whose spiritual welfare they felt solicitous" (A.B.C.F.M., *Report, 1834*, p. 121).

the season will be too far advanced by the time I shall know this for me to look out a place and engage in any business by which to support my family. Whilst waiting for instructions from the Board of course I can do nothing in this way.

As respects outfit, I observe that I have reserved and provided with my own funds such bedding as I suppose we will need for a year or two, also considerable clothing, and some articles of furniture, such as will be suitable for us to take with us. But going to a colder climate we will need stoves and some other articles of furniture, and some clothing which we have not. I will also need a small stock of medicines to take with me. What these will cost I cannot say, but I will endeavour to be strictly economical and hope the Board will allow me to purchase whatever may be necessary and furnish the funds to pay for it.

I shall thankfully receive and attend to any suggestions from you on this subject, but as I consider my time precious I will not think it right to be long hindered from the grand object in view by want of funds. When I know when I am to go, I will endeavour to make out and forward a more particular estimate of what will be necessary.

I have delayed writing this letter that I might see Mr. Higgins and a number of the members of the Philadelphia Presbytery. Owing to the situation of Mr. H.'s family it is doubtful whether it will be advisable for him to go out this fall and though on several accounts it seems desirable to have him with us, I do not know but he may do more for the cause by staying and procuring and bringing on such supplies as we may need in the Spring. I hope the Board will have this matter to be arranged as shall to us seem best.

This presbytery meets near Chillicothe on the 17th of September, and between that and the 20th, I expect to be ordained as a missionary to the Heathen. If the Board informs me of my destination and provides the necessary funds in time, I suppose I can be at Cincinnati on my way out by the 1st of October.

I hope your committee will bear in mind that the Mississippi is liable to freeze in November and that I may lose a whole winter from the study of the language, and making other important arrangements for the mission by being detained a single week waiting either for my instructions or for funds.

Affectionately yours,

Tho. S. Williamson

[Addressed to Mr. Henry Hill, Treasurer of the American Board of Commissioners for Foreign Missions, Missionary Rooms, 28 Cornhill, Boston, Mass.]

5. A LETTER FROM HENRY H. COPELAND, A GOVERNMENT SCHOOLTEACHER IN THE CHOCTAW NATION, COMMENTING ON THE WORK OF THE AMERICAN BOARD, NOVEMBER 11, 1836

Eagle Town was founded by Rev. Loring S. Williams in 1832. He gave it the name of Bethabara because of its nearness to the chief fording-place of a fork of the Little River. It was located twenty-five miles north of Wheelock, the principal mission station in what is now McCurtain, the southeastern county of the present state of Oklahoma. There was a large settlement of Indians near the station, at least a thousand within a radius of five miles (A.B.C.F.M., *Report, 1833*, p. 112).

Some three years after the writing of this letter, its writer became mechanic and farmer at the Cherokee station called Dwight. In 1843 the principal Indians at the Choctaw station of Wheelock requested that he reside among them. With the approbation of the board, he took up the work at Wheelock, finally becoming assistant missionary. Owing to the ill-health of Mrs. Copeland, he withdrew from the mission in 1856 (*ibid., 1856*, p. 193.)

Eagel Town, Choctaw Nation

Nov. 11th, 1836

Dear Sir:

You will doubtless recollect a draft which I have [drawn payable to] Mr. Joseph Bennett, of Montgomery's Point,

Ark. Ter., bearing date of Nov. 13th, 1835, for the sum of one hundred dollars, payable at sight. Probably you might infer from the note I wrote under the same that I was in some way connected with the Miss[ion] in this country and in some respects I am, but not as too [sic] my support. I do not receive my support from the A.B.C.F.M., but I trust my heart is in close connection with the cause of Missionary opperation [sic] among this degraded, ignorant people, and the cause of Miss[ions] generally.

I am one of those who receive their support from funds appropriated by the United States, by Treaty, for the support of schools among the Choctaws. I should therefore feel myself highly culpable, if I did not refund to the Society the money for which I gave the draft on you, for (with interest if required) I could not have accomplished my journey to this place without the money, which I received from Mr. Bennett. I feel much obliged to him, for the same, and I am now ready to refund the same to any person you may designate, perhaps you wish me to pay it over to someone of the brethren here. (Brethren, I say! for I feel that they are and I esteem them as such, with them I have taken sweet . . . . council.), and with them (if the Lord spares our lives) I hope to have more pleasant and profitable interviews; I also feel the importance of dedicating my all to the service of my Saviour. I did not expect from what Br. Byington told me, when in Ohio, that I should be able to save anything from my salary, but as the Lord has blessed me, and my companion, with health since we have been here, I have been able to meet all my expences, for the last year, and a little left, you will therefore add $10. to the draft which you may give on me to Br. Byington, if you please.

The schools in the vicinity at the present time are in a flourishing state, more so than they were some months past. I think the miss. schools are conducted on much the best plan, the pupils are taught Choctaw first and then English, if they remain in school, but most of them do not remain in school long, after they can read their own language. The Government schools are English altogether, but they will not be of much benefit to the Nation. Some of my pupils who commenced with the A. B. C.[s] now spell very readily words of four syllables, and read in easy lessons, but they know not what they read; it is to be lamented very much that these schools are conducted on the plan which they are. I had thought for several years past, that if I possessed the requisite qualifications I would have offered myself to the Board to be employed in some Mission, but when I thought of the importance of having well-qualified teachers, I shrunk from the idea of offering myself, lest I should be a burden, instead of a help to the cause, but since I have been here, and see how much the heathen need instruction, I have felt that I would willingly relinquish all the enjoyment and privileges of Cristian [sic] society and dwell among any people, where I could be of any benefit to them, in bringing them to the knowledge of the Saviour, or of assisting any of the missionaries so that they might have more time to devote to the spiritual wants of the Heathen.

Last. Jan. I had Br. Williams and Br. Byington[9] send to Orleans for goods and groceries for me, and I paid them the money for the same, cost and charges. I intended to have Br. Byington send to Boston for some things for me this year, but I learned since I began to write this, that he had made out his bill and sent it on. I wish therefore when you make

[9] Cyrus Byington, a graduate of Andover Theological Seminary in 1819, set out the following year, with a company of some twenty recruits under appointment by the American Board, as missionaries to the Choctaw Indian nation. Byington was placed in charge of the company. Almost at once Byington set to work on a Choctaw grammar and dictionary and later translated portions of both the Old and the New Testaments into the Choctaw tongue. His dictionary contains some fifteen thousand words and was published in 1915 as *Bulletin 46* of the Bureau of American Ethnology. His Choctaw grammar was published in 1871 in the *Proceedings of the American Philosophical Society* (XII, 317–67). Byington's work is highly regarded by philologists (*Dictionary of American Biography*, III, 380–81).

out Br. B.['s] bill you would put up some few articles for me, and I will pay over the money to him for the same. I wish for 3 prs. women shoes, no 3-½ or 4, high qua[lity] of good firm calf-skin; 1 pr. calf skin boots for women's ware [*sic*], then Jane or satinette, 9 y[a]r[d]s for pantaloons; Blue 12 yds. Irish shirting, two patterns for vest, for summer ware [*sic*], dark collor [*sic*]. Br. Byington told me I had better send to Boston for such articles as I wanted, and have them come on with his, directed to him, and I could pay him for them. If you will therefore forward the above articles with Br. Byington, you will very much Oblige yours,

Most ob't. Servant,

HENRY H. COPELAND.

MR. HENRY HILL

P.S.   To the above I would add 6 lb. Sal Eratus, one bottle of Soda, one of acid, 2 Lb. of Ginger, 2 lb. pepper, 1 lb. allspice.

6. A LETTER FROM REV. J. D. STEVENS, WRITTEN AT LAKE HARRIET, A MISSION STATION AMONG THE DAKOTA INDIANS, NEAR FORT SNELLING (MINN.), SEPTEMBER 13, 1838

Lake Harriet was located about seven miles from Fort Snelling and was established as a mission station in 1835. Jedediah D. Stevens, after teaching some three years in the Stockbridge mission at Green Bay, where he was associated with Cutting Marsh, and after spending some time studying theology, was licensed to preach by a New York presbytery and appointed by the American Board to the Dakota mission (A.B.C.F.M., *Report, 1834*, p. 122). He proved to be more or less a failure, either being unable to learn the Indian language or refusing to do so, and was a stormy petrel among his brethren. In 1839 he accepted the offer of the post of farmer among the Dakotas which he accepted. The board willingly dismissed him from their service (*ibid., 1839*, p. 145).

The annual *Reports* of the American Board cast light upon the Indian depredations described in this letter. That for 1839 states: "During the past summer a murderous disposition of some of the [Sioux] bands, awakened and irritated in part by disappointment in regard to the reception of their annuity from the government of the U.S., broke forth with more fatal success upon their Ojibwa neighbors, resulting in the murder of more than a hundred of their enemies, principally women and children, and in a loss of about fifty of their own number" (p. 111).

LAKE HARRIET, Sept. 13th, 1838

Henry Hill, Esq.
Mission Rooms, Boston
SIR:

From the 1st [of] June up to the 1st [of] August the expenditures of this station, including labour, mer[chandise] . . . . postage, and other incidental expenses are $43.97. For 9 cop[ies] Ch[urc]h Psalmody furnished the garrison, I recd. $7.12–½, sub[tracted from the above amount leaves a balance of] 36.84–[½]. This amount, according to the arrangement in the circular, if I mistake not, may be still drawn from the Treasury for the year ending with [the] 1st [of] Aug[ust]. If what is due from traders for Board and location of their children is promptly paid, I hope I shall not be under the necessity of making a draft on the treas. for the above, and still be able to replace the amount ($80) I have expended from private funds [during] the past year for labour.

On the 21st [of] June I made a draft for $100 in favor of G. W. Fuller, Galena, for supplies for this station. The 11th inst. another of the same amount for the same purpose. These two drafts with the $80 included in my last returns are for supplies for the present year.

When at Peterboro, N. Y., in Oct. last a few of the friends of missions there made a donation to this mission of a carriage and harness for one horse, which, with a horse I had left there three years before, I brot with me to this station. The carriage and harness I believe was purchased (at a public auction) for $50. or thereabout. The horse I valued there at $75, I suppose could not be purchased for less [than] $100 [here]. This horse I have charged to the account of the mission. I may hereafter make a donation of the same. The two horses purchased for the use of the mission at the commencement of the station, I have found to[o] [light] and imperfect to be of much service, and as the expense of keeping them is about the same as those far more serviceable, I thot best to dispose of them. One I sold for $50. last winter as already reported. The other I shall probably sell for $40. the present autumn unless Bro. Pond thinks best to retain him for traveling among the Indians. I don't wish to have any more stock of any kind at the station than is absolutely needed. Two good horses, a yoke of oxen, and a horse seem to be indispensable for the use of the station, asside [*sic*] from rendering assistance to the Indians, such as cultivating ground. For this we trust [the] Govt. will soon make provision.

Several of our cattle have been killed by the Indians [during] the present season. In all 4, 3 young creatures and a large ox. They were probably worth to the mission $100. If it had been possible to have obtained labourers so as to have made a sufficient enclosure, protecting them from straying away from the station, they would in all probability have not been killed.

The U.S. Indian Agent at this post has furnished us with a yoke of young oxen (unaccustomed to the yoke) to supply the place of our team which was broken up by the depredations [mentioned] above. Whether he intends these as pay for the cattle killed in whole or part, I have not made any enquiry. The proposition was entirely from himself and doubtless intended for our convenience, altho it only added to our labour and care. The cattle must be broken before they can be used and it occasions much trouble to keep them from straying away.

The Indians about us for several months past have manifested dissatisfaction and restlessness, occasioned principally by a delay in carrying into effect the Treaty made with them last fall. [They] have committed many depredations as above [mentioned] about the Fort and vicinity, and have seemed bent on doing mischief. Several Ojibway Indians came to this post a few weeks ago to visit the agent on business. The evening after their arrival, just at twilight, near the Fort, and within a few yards of several of the officers and soldiers and others, they were fired upon by a young man of this Band of Sioux Indians who had [just] come themselves. One Ojibway Indian fell dead upon the spot and another [was] severely wounded. One of the young men, as above, sprung from his place of concealment to take the scalp from his fallen enemy and while in the very act was shot thro the shoulder and jaw by one of the Ojibways. He fell, but soon sprung upon his feet and ran a distance, fell again, and again recovered so as to reach the lodges t[w]o miles or more distant.

For a week or more his recovery was thot impossible, but is now able to walk about. The Indians were urged by the agent and commanding officer here to deliver up the other two young men to the whites, which they did without any hesitation and they were confined in the guard house.

After holding several councils with the chiefs on the subject, they were delivered up again to them to be punished according to the mode of their own prescribing, (by beating or flogging). All fighting between the different bands of tribes on the reservations is positively prohibited by the Govt. on pain of severe punishment of the aggressor. There are some palliating circumstances for this barbarous act on the part of the Sioux. The principle man of this party was the leader of the party who so treacherously and inhumanly massacred those three lodges of Sioux near Lac qui Parle last spring. Many of them were the near relatives of these Indians. It was . . . . [this man] they were bent on destroying at all hazards. He being aware of this, he exchanged clothes with one of his men and escaped the death he justly no doubt deserved; the man, with whom he exchanged clothes [and who] was killed, is said to be one of the worst in oppression[?] and killing[?] in the country. This affair occurred the latter part of July. Since then the Indians have appeared more quiet. But "destruction and misery" .... "is in there [sic] ways and the way of Peace they have not" and it is to be feared most of them never will know.

Yours with truly Christian esteem,

[Signed] J. D. STEVENS

CHAPTER X

Documents Relating to the Congregational and Presbyterian Convention of Wisconsin, 1840-47

THE activity of early Congregationalists in Wisconsin centered in the Presbyterian and Congregational Convention of Wisconsin, formed in 1840, and in the labors of Stephen Peet, the agent for Wisconsin of the American Home Missionary Society to 1848. These documents, therefore, have been selected with these two main agencies in mind.

Congregationalism in Wisconsin had a relationship to Presbyterianism different from that in any of the regions in which the Plan of Union principle operated. Here there was no amalgamation of the two bodies. The individual churches remained either Presbyterian or Congregational, while the convention for the Presbyterians was a presbytery and that for the Congregationalists was an association. Nor in Wisconsin did the Presbyterians tend to dominate the situation as in most other places where the two bodies worked together. This was due to the fact that not only was denominational consciousness among the Congregationalists on the increase during the years of early Wisconsin settlement but that also immigration from New England and New York prevailed over that from other regions.[1]

DOCUMENTS

1. The Call for the Congregational Convention To Be Held in Troy, Welworth County, October 6, 1840
2. J. U. Parsons, Missionary, to Messers. Badger and Hall, A.H.M.S. Scribners, Southport, Wisconsin Territory, November 3, 1840
3. Jeremiah Porter to Milton Badger, Green Bay, Wisconsin Territory, October 24, 1840
4. D. A. Sherman, Missionary, to Milton Badger, Troy, Wisconsin Territory, December 17, 1840
5. D. A. Sherman to Milton Badger, East Troy, Wisconsin, December 9, 1841

[1] [Richard Day Leonard, "The Presbyterian and Congregational Convention of Wisconsin" (University of Chicago thesis [1938]).]

6. P. W. Nicholas, Missionary at Prairie du Sac, to Milton Badger, May 1, 1843
7. Nathaniel Kingsbury to Milton Badger, South Prairieville, June 28, 1843
8. Lemuel Hall to the Secretary of the A.H.M.S., Geneva, March 23, 1843
9. D. Clary, Minister at Beloit, to the Secretaries of the A.H.M.S, Beloit, Wisconsin Territory, September 7, 1843
10. Stephen Peet to Milton Badger, Milwaukee, March 30, 1844
11. Milton Wells, to Charles Hall, Burlington, August 20, 1844
12. O. P. Clinton, Missionary at Lake Mills, to Milton Badger, March 26, 1845
13. Stephen Peet to Milton Badger, Beloit, May 20, 1846
14. B. F. Parsons to Milton Badger, Watertown, November 2, 1846
15. M. Montague to Charles Hall, Fort Atkinson, June 9, 1847

1. THE CALL FOR THE CONGREGATIONAL CONVENTION TO BE HELD IN TROY, WELWORTH COUNTY, OCTOBER 6, 1840

A Convention of Congregational ministers and churches will be held in Troy, Welworth county, on Tuesday the 6th of October next, at 2 o'clock P.M., to consider the plan of union proposed by the Presbytery of Milwaukee, or to adopt such other form of organization as will best subserve the interests of religion in the Territory; and also to deliberate on whatever questions may incidentally arise, affecting the cause of Christ. All Congregational churches are requested to send their delegates and Congregational ministers and brethren throughout the Territory are invited to attend. It is understood that the meeting of the Presbytery, which was appointed at this time, will be postponed until the deliberations of the Convention are closed. Extensive consultation has been had with the churches and ministers on the subject, and it is believed that this arrangement will meet the feelings of all concerned, and best subserve the objects contemplated.

The following are the only articles in the plan of union proposed, which are of particular interest to Congregationalists.   OTIS F. CURTIS

ARTICLE 4.—The licensing of candidates, the ordination of ministers and their installation over churches and dismission from churches belonging to this body, shall be by the Presbytery.

ART. 10.—When any minister proposes to join this Presbytery it shall be the duty of the Presbytery to satisfy themselves respecting his religious sentiments and conduct, and reject or admit him as they shall deem expedient. The Presbytery shall also satisfy themselves respecting the religious sentiments and christian practice of any church before admitting it to this body.

ART. 11.—Every minister connected with this Presbytery who shall organize a church within its bounds shall report the same at the next stated meeting, together with a copy of the confession of Faith and Covenant adopted by such church.

ART. 12.—Members of this Presbytery, before organizing a church, shall instruct those wishing to be so organized, respecting the regulations of this body and urge upon them the importance of being connected with the Presbytery.

ART. 13.—*Individual ministers or churches, belonging to this Presbytery, may adopt either the Presbyterian or Congregational mode of church government, and each church shall be represented at the meetings of the Presbytery by one delegate.*

ART. 16.—Appeals, complaints, protests, etc. may come up to the Presbytery from those churches which are, in their internal structure Congregational, in the same manner as from those that are Presbyterian; or the decisions of the church shall be final, as shall be decided upon by the church.

ART. 17.—The Presbytery shall be the standing council of the churches under their care, to whom it is expected all cases of difficulty in which council [sic] or advice is desired, will be referred.

ART. 21.—Each church shall, at the stated meeting in January, exhibit their records to the Presbytery for examination, and present a satisfactory statistical report.

ART. 22.—All alterations of these regulations shall be proposed at a stated meeting previous to the one at which they are adopted, and shall require the concurrance of two-thirds of the members present. *But the thirteenth article shall never be affected by any alterations which these regulations may receive.*

The above is a true copy of articles agreed upon in convention and adopted by the Presbytery of Milwaukee in February last, as a part of the Constitution of that body. These articles, as is believed, embrace all the provisions of the plan of union, which in any way affect the rights or privileges of Congregationalists. The remaining articles contain provisions relative to Presbyterian churches, and principles and rules of business common to all ecclesiastical bodies. The whole will be present at the Convention.

The Presbytery will of course meet according to appointment on the 6th of October, but will doubtless immediately adjourn to give opportunity for the Convention to assemble and transact their business. It is expected that Congregational churches will send, each, one delegate to the meeting of the Presbytery. Thus, to some extent, at least the same individuals will be members of both bodies, and it is hoped that the important subject of our ecclesiastical organization will be brought to a final issue, and a permanent and happy union be consummated.

STEPHEN PEET
Stated Clerk of Presbytery

MILWAUKEE, August 8, 1840.

P.S.—Churches to whom this circular is sent will please regard this as a sufficient notice of the meeting of Presbytery.[2]

2. EXTRACT OF A LETTER OF J. U. PARSONS, SOUTHPORT REGARDING THE MEETING OF THE CONVENTION AT TROY, OCTOBER 6, 1840

SOUTHPORT (W.T.) Nov. 3, 1840

Messers Badger & Hall

DEAR BRETHREN

[The first page and one-third of the second of this letter deal with personal matters, mostly regarding his illness.]

. . . . I was able once to go out & form a church in a fine settlement 15 miles from here, & also to attend the convention & Presb. at Troy. That was a very solemn, interesting & important meeting. Brethren were present from every ex-

[2] A copy of the printed call was found inserted between pp. 44 and 45 of the MSS minutes.

tremity of the Territory, Porter from Green Bay, Chaffy [Chaffee] from Plattville [*sic*], Adams from Beloit &c. It was found there are already eleven Cong. & seven Presb. churches in the Territory, many of which are stretching out their hands for pastors. After a very affecting discussion of the question of union, an eccl. body was formed called the "Presb. & Cong Convention of Wisconsin", in lieu of the Presbytery. Br. Peet & myself were appointed a Com. to prepare the proceedings for publication & submit them to the next meeting of [the] Convention, in Feb. when they will be forwarded to you, to lay before the churches.

[Then follow more personal matters.]

Yours

. J. U. Parsons

3. EXTRACT FROM A LETTER OF JEREMIAH PORTER, GREEN BAY, DESCRIBING THE MEETING OF THE CONVENTION OCTOBER 6, 1840, AND HIS JOURNEY

GREEN BAY WIS. TER.
Oct. 27th 1840

Rev Milton Badger
DEAR BROTHER

[The first page and a half deals with personal matters and affairs of his parish, which was very large and involved much traveling in the wilderness. He begins the description of a journey south toward Fond du Lac and then continues:]

. . . . My principal object in this journey was to attend Presbytery & a Convention called by the Pres. & Congregational churches of the Territory. My distance from the place of meeting, about 175 miles, made it necessary for me to be absent over two sabbaths. After traveling five days on horseback, in company with a delegate from this church, during four of which days it rained a considerable part of each, I reached Milwaukie, & was happy to find Brother Peet in so inviting a field, & to preach to his interesting congregation three times on the following day, the Sabbath. On Tuesday the 6ᵗʰ of Oct. I met the Convention at Troy a days ride south west of Milwaukie. There I saw much to delight me & to inspire high hopes for the religious prosperity of this new land. There were present twelve Presbyterian & Congregational ministers, four fifths of all now residing in the territory, & delegates from more than that number of churches who had come together, praying for the peace of Jerusalem. The object of the Convention was to see if these two denominations could cause the prayer of our Savior to be answered so far as it related to us. . . . . Many of us deemed it highly important that in laying the foundation in this region so lately redeemed from the heathen, there should "be no division among us." For this we prayed very earnestly, & a union was consummated after two days candid deliberation, & after a touching, melting season of social prayer (having suspended the business of Convention for such a season of intercession), & many, if not all the brethren present, thought it was brought about as an immediate answer to prayer. God seemed evidently in that place by his Spirit, moving upon the hearts of his ministers & . . . . drawing them together, as kindred drops soon mingling into one. The two denominations have become one ecclesiastical body,—(tho. individual churches are not deprived of any of their rights & retain their previous government as far as they choose,)—to be known by the name of "The Presbyterian & Congregational Convention of Wisconsin." This body is to be subdivided & make minor District Conventions when the number of ministers shall make it necessary;— This will then be the General Convention of the Territory— of State, as it may then be. Many brethren felt they had received "an unction from the Holy One" at this meeting, & that a blessing would follow them to their people. One lay brother remarked to me: "I believe God will pour down great blessings upon Wisconsin this winter.". . . .

[The paragraph closes with similar pious remarks, mention of the journey home, and further about his parish work.]

With sincere love your bro. in the Lord

JEREMIAH PORTER

4. EXTRACT FROM A LETTER OF D. A. SHERMAN
EAST TROY, DESCRIBING THE FORMATION
OF THE UNION CONVENTION

TROY (WISCONS.) Dec. 17. 1840

REV.ᵈ & DEAR SIR

[The first part of the letter deals with his activities in his parish: his participation in "an ordination which so far as I am informed, is the first which has taken place in the Territory."]

Perhaps the most important event which has taken place within the Territory, since its settlement, is the union of the Presbyterian and Congregational churches in what is styled "The Presbyterian and Congregational Convention of Wisconsin." This desireable event was not accomplished without some difficulty. A convention of the Congregational churches, was summoned to meet at this place. There is reason to believe that prayer was prospectively made, in reference to the meeting. The Congregationalists, in general, seem to have come to the meeting, with their minds made up against a Union. On the assembling of the Congregational Convention, the Presbyterian brethren were invited to sit and take part in the exercises. As the discussion progressed, the prospect of a union between the two denominations, seemed very unpromising, and a committee appointed to report on the subject,—brought in resolutions entirely adverse to the plan. These resolutions were warmly debated, and intense interest was excited as to the result. At this crisis, at the suggestion of a beloved brother, further proceedings were suspended, to give opportunity for a season of prayer. It was a melting scene; and when the proceedings of the Convention were resumed, the effects were immediately visible. Views that had seemed to some, entirely visionary, began to appear quite practical; and obstacles were easily got over, that had appeared insurmountable. The result was, that the Union was unanimously agreed to, each denomination retaining its peculiar usages slightly modified. This issue seems to give general satisfaction, so far as I have heard, to the Presbyterian and Congregational churches throughout the Territory. The event seems the more important, as a Union on similar ground is contemplated in the adjoining State of Illinois and perhaps in other western regions.

[The rest of the letter gives his reflections and observations on temperance, and especially common-school education (Sherman was once a college president), and closes with personal remarks.]

I am respectfully,

your friend & brother

D. A. SHERMAN

REV.ᵈ MILTON BADGER
Sec. A.H.M.S.—

5. A LETTER FROM REV. D. A. SHERMAN OF EAST TROY GIVING THE PROCEEDINGS OF A CONVENTION ON OCTOBER 5, 1841

E. TROY Dec. 9. 1841

REV.ᵈ & DEAR SIR

Early in October, the Presbt. & Cong. Convention of Wisconsin, held an extra meeting at Beloit a flourishing village on Rock River, adjacent to the State of Illinois. The object of the meeting was, to attend to Reports of committees appointed at the last semi-annual Convention, to present the claims of the several benevolent objects of the day. Some of these committees did not report inform. [-ation?] The Convention, however, was addressed on the subject of Sabbath

Schools, the Education Society, and Temperance. An evening meeting was devoted to the consideration of revivals and a full audience was addressed with much feeling and intelligence, by the several brethren designated to that service. An epidemic was prevailing in the place, and the sitting of the Convention was suspended for most of one afternoon, to give place to a funeral discourse pronounced by the Presbyt. pastor of the place, at the previous request of the deceased a Methodist brother, there being, at the time, no Methodist minister in the vicinity.

The subject of slavery, was discussed with much spirit, and seemed to awaken great interest among the inhabitants, as well as in the Convention. The debate arose on the adoption of a resolution excluding slave-holders and their abettors, from the pulpit and the communion-table. The resolution passed, by a great majority; but as I was informed, the decision did not accord with the views of a large portion of the inhabitants, many of whom attended the discussion. Being convinced that the hostile feeling towards the South, prevailing on this subject so extensively in the N.W., among the churches, is dangerous to the Union of the States, and rises in a great degree, from a misconception of the character of our Southern brethren, and from want of correct information respecting the state of things among them, I considered it my duty to oppose the passage of the resolution.

In accordance with a recommendation of the Convention, a day of fasting and prayer was, so far as I am informed, observed by the churches connected with the Convention.

The meeting of the Convention, was well attended, on the part of the brethren; and several ministers from N. Illinois were admitted as sitting members. A number of newly formed churches united with the Convention; and some others will probably be added at the next meeting. A young gentleman who had commenced the practice of Law, was licensed to preach the Gospel. Last winter, another young man was licensed, and he is now preaching with much acceptance, at South Port.

In connection with our Methodist brethren, I attended a series of evening meetings preceding and following a Quarterly meeting at our central district, about the beginning of November. No very important results are apparent from these efforts; tho a seriousness on the minds of some, is said to exist. Within the district where I reside, two or three cases of hopeful conversion, have lately come to my knowledge. Two of them seem to have been occasioned by the death of a relative, which took place some months since.

The Sabbath School in the central district, is still continued, and a box of books has come to hand, contributed partly by the church at Suffield, Conn., and partly by benevolent individuals at the East. The donation has given a fresh impulse to the children of the school and to those engaged in its instruction. The Bible Class in the district where I reside, is continued; that at the centre, is at present, suspended, tho I am not without hope of its revival under a more interesting and useful form.

In the N° district where I reside, we have been compelled to meet for worship, hitherto, in a private house. A new & commodious school house designed, also, as a place of worship, has just been completed, and we met in it, for the first time, on the last Sabbath.

Besides the usual service on the Sabbath, I have attended weekly religious meetings in various parts of the town; and I have occasionally preached in contiguous or neighboring towns, on the Sabbath, having provided, on these occasions, for the supply of my own pulpit. Thro' the blessing of Divine Providence, I have not, so far as I recollect, been prevented by ill health, from fulfilling any appointment, since I have been your missionary.

Nothing effectual has recently been done in the Territory,

so far as I can learn, on the subject of Temperance. The enemy, however, has not been idle. It was the boast of temperance men, a year ago, that but one distillery disgraced the Territory. But another has been established; and there is a prospect that an additional one will be set on foot, on a scale still more extensive. Intemperance has evidently advanced among us, during the past year, and is doing great mischief. The church has not escaped the evil, as some sad falls in our own vicinity, evince. The editor of the only Temperance Journal in the Territory, a young lawyer of great promise, and an elder in the Presbyterian church at Milwaukee, was lost on board the Erie. The annual meeting of the Territorial Temperance Society, is however at hand and some measures are in train, for arresting the evils. But it is evident that the enemy will not leave us quiet in our new abode; and that the most energetic measures will be necessary here, as well as in other regions, to prevent his gaining the ascendancy. As long as intoxicating liquors can be sold, there will be men unprincipled enough to furnish it. We are not, however, without much to encourage us in our struggle with the adversary. There is, not far from us, a rising town in which intoxicating liquor has never been sold as a beverage. It bears the name of *Delavan*, in the county of *Walworth*. Two gentlemen by the name of Phoenix, of the Baptist denomination, were its early proprietors; and they took effectual means for preventing the disgraceful traffic from being introduced.

The boxes of clothing for the ministers of this Territory, have come safely to hand, and their arrival is hailed with much gratitude, especially by the brethren who have families.

With much respect

I am your brother in the Gospel

D. A. Sherman.

6. CORRESPONDENCE, SOMEWHAT ABRIDGED, SHOWING IN FULL DETAIL THE PROCEDURE OF APPLYING FOR AID TO THE HOME MISSIONARY SOCIETY

PRAIRIE DU SAC May 1st 1843

Rev Mr M Badger

DEAR SIR

The Rev Mr P. W. Nichols Ministerial Services for the last year ended the first of last month & the church feeling satisfied with his services, wish to retain him another year.

[Here follows a description of the church, its small size, and the difficulty of raising money.]

We feel greatful [*sic*] unto God for the assistance we have received from the H.M.S. for the last year, & in order to retain the Rev. Mr. N. for another year, we wish $150. more may be sent to him from the H.M. Society for his support. . . . .

Respectfully Yours

[signed by two deacons whose names cannot be deciphered]

[Next follows a note by the pastor, P. W. Nichols]

REV AND DEAR SIR

We feel greatfull [*sic*] to your Society for past favors and sympathies shown us in these ends of the Earth while we are trying to build up the Redeemer's Kingdom—we ask that we may be aided another year by your liberality

P. W. NICHOLS { *Missionary*
Prairie du Sac
Wisconsin

[The letter was sent to Stephen Peet, the agent at Milwaukee, by the postmaster at Prairie du Sac as free mail. In order to do this, he added a note to Peet requesting some hymnbooks for the Sunday school. The rest of the sheet is filled by Peet with one of his characteristic judgments of the man and recommendations:]

MILWAUKEE   May 11. 1843

Rev M. Badger,

DEAR BROTHER—

The above bears *internal evidence* of *its genuineness*—The place is increasing in population and it is important that the station be occupied. It is the only foothold we have on the north side of the Wisconsin River. The region around is filling up rapidly. No other Denomination is on the ground at present, I believe, and we have no other minister within 25 miles—Mr Nichols proves to be all we anticipated. He exerts a good influence by his admirable and consistent deportment, and is on the whole edifying and useful in his preaching; though [he] has not the talent or force of character requisite to turn the world upside down at once. I should think he was preparing the way for a good, steady, permanent society & church. I regard him as worthy your patronage and the church as needing your aid. They say nothing about the amount.[3] I presume the amount granted last year (which I think was $125.00) will be satisfactory.

Yours &c   STEPHEN PEET

7. THE LAST REPORT OF NATHANIEL KINGSBURY

SOUTH PRAIRIEVILLE   June 28th 1843

REV M. BADGER—

Your are now to receive in a few words the last report I shall ever make of South Prairieville church. Perhaps there is as much harmony of feeling in the church, as can be expected in any church in the western country. The pecuniary means of the church are so extremely limited that it has seemed as though it must suspend its operations for the present. But there are some praying Souls that seem to have such power with God that the church cannot be given up.

---

[3] Peet was wrong about the amount not being stated, as the application asks for $150.

There can be no doubt—there is some of the salt of the earth in this church. I can do nothing more for the church than to commend it to the care and blessing of the Great Shepherd and Bishop of Souls. I must now take my leave of the Missionary Society. The Lord has now made it manifest that my services are not needed any more. I am in the last stages of the consumption. If you should see fit to send me a draft for the closing term, I should hope it would help my family to adjust some unsettled concerns, and to bury me without public expense.

N. Kingsbury[4]

8. THE ANTI-CATHOLIC MOTIVE IS ILLUSTRATED IN THE FOLLOWING LETTER

Geneva.   March 23 1843   Walworth Co.

W. Territory

To the Sec. of the A.H.M. Society.

Rev. Dear Sir.

[The bulk of this letter deals with the missionary's efforts in his parish and statistics, but the following paragraph is significant.]

. . . . My attention has been arrested by the accounts of the great immigration of Roman Catholics into our country, and to the consequent danger connected with large bodies of these fanatics being controlled by a few, or by a single hand. I have consequently been looking over McHenry, & have endeavored to ascertain the number of families of this

---

[4] Rev. Nathaniel Kingsbury, the second Wisconsin minister to die on the field (the first being William M. Adams, March 12, 1842), was a native of New Hampshire and an Amherst College graduate. He came to Danville, Illinois, in 1835, and to Racine, Wisconsin, in 1840 and began ministering at South Prairieville in April, 1841. His health began to fail in the spring of 1843, and he died July 12, 1843, at the age of forty-six. The foregoing letter is written in another hand, evidently dictated. The draft requested was promptly sent, although he had done no work for some months (indicated in the letter). This letter is a fine illustration of the spirit of the frontier missionaries. (The facts of Kingsbury's life are taken from Peet's *History*, p. 83.)

The South Prairieville church was disbanded in March, 1847, and its members joined with the churches at Genesee and Waukesha.

caste within its bounds. According to the best authority I can obtain there are about 200 families, which probably would constitute one fifth of the whole number of inhabitants. They have located themselves apparently with the expectation of having many to settle around them. The ignorance of these Romanists is such, that this apparent design must have originated with some one who had more design about it than they. They have a church and a priest. I fear that in the coming year we shall see armies of these Romanists rushing in to occupy the still vacant lands of our country.....

There are many Roman families around Geneva W. T. and they are about erecting a church in this village. The numbers of Roman families in Walworth Co is less than in McHenry.....

LEMUEL HALL.

9. A LETTER REGARDING FRONTIER EDUCATION

BELOIT WIS. TER. Sept. 7. 1843

Messrs Hall & Badger

BRETHREN

As I know not who else to address I take the liberty of writing to you on the subject of "Education at the West"—. I have noticed the formation of a society in New York for the promotion of this object, and I wish to lay before that Society the state of thing in that department, as they exist in this place and vicinity, that they may see whether it would be consistent with their general plan of operations to extend their action here——

This place is on the Rock River—central east and west in the Ter.—the Village has 6. or 700 inhabitants. The Congregational Church, of which I am pastor, has over 100 members & by *quite an effort* are able to get along in my support without calling on the H.M. Soc. for aid.—We are surrounded by a *beautiful* and *excellent* country which is rapidly settling—We have a meeting house nearly finished—and a High School under the direction of Trustees .... just commencing its operations—having secured a male & female teacher of the *first* character & qualifications, & we hope to have a permanent school, worthy of the name *"High School."* Our wants of course will *not* be *few* and our expenses are already considerable in proportion to our means—— If therefore your Society—I mean the Society above alluded to, shall see it consistent to aid us .... it will be very timely at this stage in our affairs..... [Mr. Fisher, a member of the Trustees,] goes East tomorrow by way of Milwaukie and if Brother Peet is at home he will say what he thinks proper in confirmation of my statements—or in *addition* to them, if he should be absent he will write you I presume as soon as he shall learn that Mr. Fisher has gone East—for he is much interested in the subject of Education *generally* and also *particularly* in this place.....

The Young Gentleman engaged to conduct the school[5] is from Mass. a recent graduate of Dartmouth College, highly recommended by the Pres.[t] and Professors—He is decidedly pious—& will co-operate with the friends of this Institution in their efforts to have it one of the *first character* for *morals* as well as literature.

Our present wants are some things which would be the *beginning* of an apparatus—e.g.—

1. A globe or pair of globes—terrestrial & celestial—
2. An air pump,—one of small size would answer
3. An Orrery—also a cheap one
4. A Magic Lanthern
5. A Camera Obscura—or *glasses for* one & it could be made here—

We will not *name* any thing else—but should your means allow of it you can add what you think would be useful—a small Electrifying Machine w[d] be of great service.

[5] The "school" was Beloit Academy, precursor to Beloit College, and the "Young Gentleman" was Sareno T. Merrill.

This School is designed to meet the wants of an extensive region around about and to grow with the growth of the country—and *perhaps some* day be a college. . . . .

> I am very respectfully and truly
> Yours—
> D. Clary
> *Pastor of the Congregational*
> *Church in this place*

10. A LETTER TYPICAL OF A REPORT TO THE A.H.M.S. BY STEPHEN PEET

Milwaukie March 30, 1844

Rev M. Badger

Dear Brother

I propose to furnish you with some *materials* from which you can make out an article to suit yourself for your Annual Report, instead of giving a very *elaborate* & *extended* report of my own.

During the past year large accessions have been made to our churches by means of immigration and the revivals of religion which have been enjoyed among us, and *Ten* new churches have been organized. The whole number of churches connected with our General Convention is *Sixty One*, of which Fifty Three are in Wisconsin, Seven in adjacent Counties in Illinois and one in Iowa Territory.*

The population of the Territory has increased the past year at an astonishing rate. The tide of immigration has been greater than in any former season. It is estimated by many intelligent men that our population has doubled during the year. (It was previously about 45,000.) This estimate may be too high; but the increase, I think, has been not less than 30,000.—Some of these have settled in our villages and

---

* Twenty Three are Pres. and Thirty Eight Cong. All those formed the past year are Cong. and *two* have changed from Pres. to Cong.

places where religious privileges are enjoyed; but the largest portion have gone among our scattered settlements, and made their way into portions of country beyond the limits to which former immigration had reached, and have spread far and wide over our fair and fertile Territory. By this means the fields already occupied have been much enlarged, the labour and responsibilities of those who occupy them increased, and the range of missionary operations greatly extended:—Not less than Fifteen new fields have been opened which ought to be immediately occupied. Let the friends of Missions and of the West think of this. THIRTY THOUSAND *have been added to the population of Wisconsin and* FIFTEEN NEW MISSIONARY *fields opened in one year.* It requires more than horse speed to keep up with the tide of immigration. The calls for ministers and for the visits of your Agent to organize churches and advise and assist in securing religious privileges have been more numerous and pressing than at any former period. These calls come from every part of the Territory.—from the interesting and favored region bordering in Lake Michigan,—from the beautiful and fertile valley of the Rock River,—from the borders of the Missisippi [*sic*] and the "Mining region," where "the harvest is great and the labourers few,"—[*sic*] from the Fox Lake country and around Winebago at the North, and from beyond the Wisconsin river and far up that river to "the Pineries," where is a large population destitute of a preached gospel. Never have I had my feelings more deeply affected than when listening to these calls and could find none to go and preach the gospel to them, and in many instances, could not even afford them the meagre benefit of a single visit.

It is of immense importance that this tide of immigration be followed up, and that these opening fields be speedily supplied with efficient and devoted ministers. The multitudes that are now rushing to our Territory will no less need religious privileges than did the earlier settlers of the country. The principle which was so happily adopted and has been so successfully acted upon of an early & thorough occupancy of this ground, ought to continue to be *carried out* as the floods of immigration swell the amount of our population. But while the work on our hands has been thus increased, and new fields have opened around us, the number of labourers has not been enlarged. True, we have had the pleasure of welcoming to our Territory a number of excellent brethren from Eastern Seminaries and elsewhere, but at the same time an equal number have, from various causes, ceased their labours among us.—Some from ill health, some called to other fields in the west—one returned to New England,—one has been appointed chaplain in the U.S.A. at Fort Winebago, and one dear brother, Rev D. A. Sherman, has gone to receive his reward. But his work was done and his Lord when he came found him at his post "watching" and ready. May the event serve to make us who remain more diligent and zealous in our Master's work.

The history of the "rise and progress" of religious institutions in Wisconsin is without a parallell [*sic*] in respect to their early establishment, their rapid advancement, and the harmony and success which has characterized the plans and labours of those who have been called to occupy this interesting field. When I made my first tour through the Territory in 1839, I found only six churches and *three* ministers. Now we have a general Convention and Three District Conventions which embrace *Sixty one* churches and over *Forty* ministers. But it will be seen, from the preceeding statements, that a great work is still to be done: and let me say, there is no time to be lost, and there should be no relaxation of efforts. The enemy is not asleep. Errorists of various names are rallying, and although heretofore their forces have not been as great, nor their movements as efficient as in some portions of the west, still a foothold has been obtained in several places, and these are indications that a more desperate effort will be made to establish themselves here and scatter the seeds of mischief and death among our increasing population. The ground should be immediately occupied by good men and true, and the "good seed" of the kingdom should be sown broadcast over the Territory.

More has been done the past year in erecting houses for public worship than in any previous year since the settlement of the country. *Three* large and elegant churches have been completed, and dedicated to Jehovah,—Two at Milwaukie and one at Beloit, and another is in progress at South Port. Several neat and commodious houses, of smaller dimensions, have also been built, and are occupied from sabbath to sabbath with interesting assemblies. Several ministers have been *installed* during the year, and there is an increasing interest among our churches in regard to *settled pastors.* The prominent example of the churches in Milwaukie and Beloit in this respect, will have an important influence, and will be extensively imitated where it is practicable and expedient. Besides these installations *six* young men who came among us as licentiates from eastern ecclesiastical bodies, *have been ordained* to the work of the gospel ministry.

The number of ministers within the Territory, who are employed by the churches, or are under the patronage of the A.H.M.S. is *Thirty.* Five others connected with us are labouring among our churches in Illinois and at Dubuque—making only 30 *working men* in the Territory and 35 of the same character who belong to the Convention. There are several ministers in the country who are not labouring among our churches and ought not to be considered as a supply (among these is Clark at Ft. W. Dr Arms, Parsons, Ordway, Hubbard, D. Smith and Case.)

I here give you an extract from the Narrative of religion adopted at the last meeting of the General Convention, which will show the views of the whole Convention in regard to our plan of union—It was not written by myself. I hope you will use it in your report, and recognize it as coming *officially* from that body.—It is as follows.

"The past year is full of encouragement to the friends of Zion in this Territory. While it has served to develope [*sic*] more fully the vast importance of this new field of Christian enterprize; and has swelled the tide of imigration [*sic*] which is pouring in upon us, and of course increased the necessity for vigorous and enlarged efforts to supply our teeming population with the means of grace; it has also demonstrated more fully than ever, the wisdom of our plan of ecclesiastical organization, and furnished abundant evidence of the Divine approbation in the success which has attended its practical operation, designed to unite in one common bond, brethren who so nearly agree in all essential points as do Presbyterians and Congregationalists, but who have hitherto been too often divided, both in feeling and effort, it is cause for devout gratitude that our plan of union has succeeded beyond the most sanguine expectations of its warmest friends. It has secured, hitherto, the most perfect harmony among both ministers and churches, and served to combine, in a remarkable degree, their efforts in urging on to a glorious triumph, the principles of our common religion among us. Sufficient time has now elapsed to warrant us in congratulating ourselves that *the principles of our Convention are permanently established.* Every ground of jealousy and contention is removed, and no distinction is known or manifested between churches which adopt either form of government, or between ministers or private members who are connected with them. Presbyterians and Congregationalists are here emphatically *one* denomination, and we hope and believe ever will form but one great, united, harmonious and active brotherhood, within our bounds. Zealous only for the glory of God and the promotion of his cause.

"With this heaven inspired union, with numerous revivals to animate us and strengthen our numbers, and past success to stimulate us, and God's spirit to aid us, we may well be encouraged to persevere in our efforts untill [*sic*] this whole Territory shall become the garden of the Lord, and its people as fruitful in all good works as is its rich soil in all the productions of nature."

I have finally written so much of a report that my first paragraph may as well be stricken out. If you use any portion of this you will amend, correct or expunge at your pleasure. I have felt an aversion to making loud public appeals lest it should bring a flood of useless ministers among us. Still that cannot be helped, the facts must be told and then we must do the best we can.

Things are generally posperous [*sic*] in the Territory, but there has been fewer revivals the past winter than common. The state of the roads & the season has had some effect. I hope the Lord will be with you at your anniversary as well as all other times. The Home Mission cause must move on, and with increased power or our country will come well nigh to ruin. I am glad to learn that it is increasing in favor & in means.

Yours. STEPHEN PEET.

COLLECTIONS TO APRIL 1, 1844

S. Prairieville. Coll	$ 6.32
Plattville Mon. Con	5.70
East Troy. Pres. church	4.20
Madison Cong. church	10.00
Beloit S.T.C. avails of needle—	5.0
" Mrs. B. Brown	2.00
South Port Mon. Con	7.00
Mineral Point bal of subs	5.00
Pike Grove balance	1.00
Rev D. A Sherman	3.00

You will charge to my account Forty Nine 22/100 Dollars, the amount of the above collections—($49.22)

11. A LETTER SHOWING THE SOCIAL CONDITIONS AMONG THE FOREIGN-BORN IMMIGRANTS TO WISCONSIN AT THIS PERIOD

BURLINGTON, WIS. TER. August 20, 1844

Rev. Chs. Hall
Secy, A.H.M.S.

DEAR BRO,

.... This settlement occupies a space of country commencing about 5 miles above the village of Rochester on the Fox River, and extends up that river about 10 miles, with a breadth of several miles. The number of inhabitants I am not able to give. It is thickly settled however. The majority of them know nothing of the English Language and from so far as I learn, care nothing for it. An English school has been taught among them one or two winters by means of which a few of the children have acquired some knowledge of our language. Many of the Parents, however reject the opportunity, and with ignorant self-conceit, say they have no need of English. A few of them posses abundance of pecuniary means have neat and comfortable dwellings and live well. But the great majority of them, and especially those who emigrated from the barren high land regions of Norway, are poor and miserable, and know little of the arts of husbandry whereby to gain a livilihood, consequently they have been wasted by famine and disease to a fearful extent. The amount of wretchedness and suffering which prevailed among them last winter, was such as absolutely to mock all description. One family I visited in which I found every individual, eight in number, prostrated with disease two of them, the father and a daughter of some 16 years of age, were then shaking violently with a fit of the ague. The daughter shoeless, & both nearly destitute of all clothing stood hovering over a few live coals, by the side of which stood an old filthy looking copper tea kettle, from the spout of which they would take their turns in drinking. The others were huddled together into bunks filled with prairie hay with nothing over them to shelter them from the rigorous cold of a December day, save of few sheep skins sewed together. Aside from the tea kettle we saw but one article of furniture, and that a wooden bowl partly filled with what I took to be short neaded & prepared for baking. This, as near as I could learn, was all they had in the house with which to support life.

In another family which Mrs. W. visited in connection with the physician, she found the *sick mother* in bed with her *dying husband*, with no one to administer to their necessities, or even to speak a word of consolation to them save two little girls of some seven and nine years of age. Before the fire stood a little naked child reduced to a perfect skeleton, and having every appearance of being literally starved, for so far as could be judged no disease was preying upon it. At another hut where the physician called he found a dead man lying upon a bench out of doors and ten sick ones, some of whom were dying in doors. These are by no means isolated cases. They are just what might have been witnessed almost any day during the last winter. One hundred deaths are reported to have occured among them. These startling disclosures might seem at at first to astonish one, considering that they are in a country distinguished for its abundance as well as Christian benevolence. Whether that vigilent charity which is ever on the alert to seek out the abodes of want existed in due degree we will not undertake to assert. We fear not. Many palliating considerations may however be offered in extenuation; among which, I may state that a foreign language & withall jealous of every thing American, also wrapped up in ignorant self-conceit may be supposed not to enjoy much intercourse with our Citizens. Consequently their condition must remain hid from observation till it becomes so insupportable that the convulsive heaving of starvation and death, no longer able to endure the shameful and inhuman barrier of National prejudice rolls their tale of woe on the diffusive winds of Heaven in a language not to be misunderstood by common humanity. It must be farther observed that a large portion of these suffer[ers]s consisted of emigrants who had just arrived from Europe in the last days of lake navigation and without any means of self-support, the frosts of a sterile winter closed upon them and no alternative remained, but to force themselves by scores into the poorly provided habitation of their countrymen. Herded together, as they were, in narrow abodes, by the combined influence of famine and personal impurity, they soon became victims to fell disease. In their distress they were not altogether neglected. The wakeful and sympathetic ear of Samaritan kindness was at length arrested by the sad tale of misery, and forth sped the messengers of mercy without stint or grudging. Barrels of flour and meat were dispatched with praiseworthy promptness and sorr[ow]ing to Elijah's God. Many of their children were taken into by the Americans; so that now it is very common to find a Norwigien boy or girl in almost every family. This people have a minister settled among them. They call themselves Lutherans. There is one family among them who have been in America for several years and have become hopefully pious. They speak and read English. They have very little intercourse with the others, owing as they say to the Enmity existing against them on account of their religion. They regard them but little better than the Catholics. . . . .

[MILTON WELLS]

12. A SUMMARY OF CONDITIONS FROM A MISSIONARY POINT OF VIEW

LAKE MILLS JEFFERSON CO WIS TER March 26 1845

DEAR BROTHER BADGER

I sit down to give you an expression of my views of the state of religious matters generally in this Territory in wh the H.M.S. are particularly interested—I am aware that rumors have gone abroad calculated to excite suspicions of our soundness & prudence & wh if not corrected may embarrass the minds of your Committee while carrying out the plans of the Society—I came to this country with such fears of the tendency of things, as have kept me on the lookout for these cisms [sic], those dangerous breakers, upon wh our Zion has been so often wrecked for the last few years—I think you are not entirely ignorant of the high esteem in wh I formerly held the old Puritan Land marks, the value & importance of wh have not in the least degree lessened while labouring to contribute something towards setting them up in this great valley—In importance they have rather mangified before the mind in view of the foundations to be laid here— And in this state of mind nothing could I have dreaded more than unsoundness in the ministery, or disorganizing innovations among the churches—And I have studied to be a careful observer of the tendency of things—And I have by no means been alone in these feelings—So far as I am able to judge the Missionaries in this Territory, are those who watch for souls as those who are to give account—We have from time to time thanked God & took courage when you have been sending us men furnished for their work, & ready to sustain the great principles which have made New England an example to the world—And although (as in many older & orthodox bodies at the east) there may be a few restless spirits among us, or some undesireable occurances, yet in the main I believe our churches & the ministry stand fast in the faith of the gospel as held by their fathers, & are ready to contend earnestly for it—

THEOLOGY

I think the Theology held & taught by the ministry here bears in the main the New England stamp—There may be, & doubtless are metiphysical differences such as exists in the

Evangelical ministry elsewhere. Still I am not aware of a tendency to heterodoxy, or a leaning toward heresy—N. England Theology has emigrated with its ministers & I see not but it has stood as erect in this pleasant valley as among the granate hills—Nothing like Oberlinism has been indorsed or to any extent found sympathy among us—A little has sailed in but the landing of the freight has been so exceedingly difficult, that it has either floated off with down sails, or stood off in perpetual quarantine—There may be a few private members in some of our churches a little spiced with that *ism*, but to no considerable extent—The Milwaukee Convention I think has refused to receive a man of that stamp, & others have been kept off by wise individual influence—One man is laboring in the bounds of the Beloit Conv. who somewhat tinctured with those sentiments, but is not disposed to raise the flag—He appears to be a spiritual working man, willing to deny himself for the good of souls—He pledges himself not to introduce anything calculated to mar the peace of our Zion. He knows ful[l] well, if he starts out on that track, such is the state of thing[s] among us he will be immediately headed[?]—And he appears to have little or no feeling upon the subject—Individual influence had kept him out of the Convention that he may be fully tried—Farther than this I know not as we have any of this cism. . . . .

MEASURES

I see no prevailing tendency to wild & ultry [*sic*] measures —The ministers here are mostly working men, & labour to produce immediate effects, yet there is an almost universal desire to lay foundations broad & deep—With rare exceptions when special efforts are made or in other words the ordinary means of grace multiplied, the exercises are conducted with solemnity & prudence—No Evangelists are employed among us & the revivals with wh we have been favored have been worked with the presence & power of the spirit of God without the discount of modern human extravagancies. The idea of getting up religious excitements . . . . has been to no considerable extent encouraged. But there has been a prevailing disposition to preach the truth faithfully, mark the leading of the spirit, & take advantage of the same. . . . .

SLAVERY

Although most of our ministers are Abolitionists, yet I am not aware that there is a tendency to wildness or disorganization—True there are strong feelings upon the subject, & yet many of our ministers take the N.Y. Observer & none ask them why do ye so—And were I to look for exclusiveness in this matter I doubt whether it would be found to exist with greater, if in as great degree in any one brother as in Rev A. Crane your Agent in N.Y. . . . . We cannot subscribe to slavery & can but abomonate it, for wh I think the benevolent will not cast us off—

CHURCH GOVERNMENT

When I came to this country I was suspicious that there was a strong tendency to give preference & advantage to Presbyterianism, & if so I was determined not to go into the organization—But I found it to be otherwise, & I see not the least ground of fear upon the subject—The organization works admirably—A general satisfaction & harmony prevails, & our Conventional meetings are becoming more & more interesting—

YOUR AGENCY & AGENT

I consider this agency as highly adventageous to the religious interests of this Country—It is adapted to break ground & prepare the way of the Lord—It keeps things in shape, & effects chh organizations with more safety than they could otherwise be affected—And further you have made choice in my estimation of the right man—

1. Because he is evidently sound in the faith & a man of God—
2. He exercises great wisdom & prudence in organizing churches—
3. He is a wise counsellor in our Ecclesiastical matters—
4. He exercises well directed zeal & moral courage in breaking ground—

[Then follows a polite conclusion]

Yours in great esteem O P CLINTON

13. A LETTER FROM STEPHEN PEET ILLUSTRATING THE CHANGING RELIGIOUS SCENE IN WISCONSIN AND HIS TROUBLES WITH THE OLD SCHOOL PRESBYTERIANS AND THE ULTRA-CONGREGATIONALISTS

BELOIT May 20, 1846

Rev M. Badger

DEAR BROTHER.

The Old School are determined to make a push in the Territory. They have already cast in the leaven in some places. The main ingredient which gives it any power is *money*. They hold forth encouragement of liberal aid in support of their missionaries and tell about their "church extension" plan, and thus lead the people to expect assistance in building churches. Rev M. A. Fox who was commissioned by your Society last fall has resigned his commission, and, as I suppose, has received one from the O.S. Board. He wrote us before he came to the Ter. and said he had examined our Constitution & Confession of Faith, and heartily approved of them, said he should join our body & cooperate with us. He came strongly recommended by *Doctor* Aikin of Cleveland, as a safe man for us to encourage. We gave him a place in one of our fields, and now he will turn & fight us.

There is a little uneasiness at Madison, and things are rather critical there. They are ready to make a pitch there if they get a chance. I go there to-morrow at their urgent request to see a little to this thing, but especially to advise with them about building their church. They have decided to build this season. At Prairieville also and at Elkhorn the O.S. folks have been at work among some disciplined & disaffected members; and their missionary went to Washington just before he left and engaged to come there as their minister or send a man. This is an important point on the Lake between Milwaukie and Shebayan [sic]. I was there last fall and promised to visit them again & form a church, and send them a minister this spring. It is wholly our ground. But they were in want of some preaching.

Now, I want you to do what you can to send us several more ministers this spring. We want 4 or 5 *immediately, very much.* Several places have been destitute so long that they are ready to seize the first man that comes. If we could place a few men at some particular important points *now,* I think it would materially check their movements, and would assist us very much in keeping our ground without coming in direct collision with them. I want advise [sic] on this subject. We have never had to meet this thing before, and it is important in the outset to adopt a wise course. The *ground is clearly ours.* Their movements are an *intrusion* & *interference,* & are calculated, if not designed, to make division among us.

My views on the subject are that [it] is best to treat them kindly, but maintain firmly our ground. The difficulty is in carrying out these principles—whether it is best to speak out and inform the churches respecting their designs and advise them not to employ or encourage them and also whether, if they crowd in upon our ground where we are not organized, or have no minister at the time, it will be expedient for us to go on the same ground, claim our rights &c &c, or to let *them alone.*

I want information on a few points connected with this matter which I presume you can readily furnish.

1. What course is generally pursued by the New School

& Congregationalists in regard to fellowship with the O.S.? Do they invite them to sit as corresponding members in their Eccl. meetings? Do they generally invite them into their pulpits, exchange &c? or do they let them alone? What course do your missionaries generally pursue on this subject?

2. What is the true state of the case in respect to their "church extension" scheme? Have they done much? Have they any funds? Is the plan likely to succeed?

3. How are they doing in their Home Missionary operations? Do they interfere with you or infringe upon your ground? Have they funds, and are they liberal in their appropriations?

Communicate any thing else that I need to know in order to pursue a wise course and meet the pretences made, or the measures they shall pursue. I am not for fighting. But it is sometimes well "in peace to prepare for war." I shall aim to avoid difficulty, and "as far as in me lies to live peaceably" [sic] with them. But in order to do this & to properly take care of our own interests, I need to know their plans, policy, means & general characteristics. We have got to meet it and I trust God will enable us to do it in a right spirit. I am not alarmed nor disturbed, but wish to be awake to the interests of our churches & of the A.H.M.S. in the Ter. and to do what these interests require at my hand.

You may have thought I was too sensitive in regard to the interference of the Puritan and the obvious intention to crowd ultra Congregationalism into our Ter. But I felt on that subject as on this. I deprecate the introduction of extremes and things that will produce division & distraction; and wish to do what I can consistently to prevent these evils. But I know what the tendency of the age is, and what spirit is at work in the churches or rather among ministers who stir up the churches in the matter; and I have no expectation of keeping things always quiet as they have been in the Territory. I never supposed the Devil would let us alone. I should be glad to see things remain in their present shape, because we have enjoyed peace & been greatly prospered, and the arrangement has served to unit God's people and lead them to regard ecclesiastical order as of minor consequence and devotion to spiritual matters of first importance. But if the folks at Boston or Philadelphia will bring in their ultra & sectarian influences & measures; and divisions must come—and these evils cannot be diverted—why, then we shall follow the advise [sic] of Dr Bellamy to his students, and "when it rains, let it rain"—But as an Agent of the A.H.M.S. occupying this new and rising field I wish to lay foundations right, and as far as I can, preserve them when they are laid. This has been my desire & my aim, & I mean it shall be still. I need wisdom from on high & try to seek it—and I shall be glad of advice from those who have knowledge or experience in these matters.

OTHER SUBJECTS

At the last meeting of our Board at Milwaukie an application was made from the people in McHenry Ill. for Missionary aid in support of Rev Spencer Baker. The church as such had nothing to do with it. But a meeting of the *citizens* was called and resolution passed in favor of Mr Baker and requesting the aid of the A.H.M.S. in his behalf. It was stated that there was no church now in existence, but that the people who were friendly to religious institutions had felt the importance of having preaching and made this movement, having themselves raised a respectable amount towards Mr Baker's support.

The Board declined recommending the case & have informed the people accordingly. Our reasons were, That the field was out of our Territorial limits and its circumstances & wants unknown to us except so far as communicated in the application, That Mr Baker had been absent from us some length of time, and had, as we understood, made application to be received to an Eccl. body in that region, but was not received. (The reason & the merits of the case we do not know.) That there were Missionary committees in that region through whom they could apply—That we had once had some difficulty in a case from that same place on account of not understaning [sic] the matter, and thought it better that they should come to you through the channels opened in the state—We did not pretend to judge of the merits of the case at all, but purposely left it unburdened with a refusal from us. Still from what we know of the case, we suppose it will need to be well inquired into before an appropriation is made. I have my fears that Baker is like his predecessor, Kellogg, rather wanting in stern and strait forward principles.

Rev Mr Kidder of Attica N.Y. formerly of W. Brattleborough Vt. wrote me some time since for a field of labour. I told him we had some vacant fields but they were all on the missionary list & he must obtain your sanction or a Commission, before he should come. I saw him last year. He is a sort of a tolerable, pretty fair kind of a moderate, good New England minister. All well enough, only not quite the thing for the west. Do what you please. We can set him to work, but should rather have a man with more "go off" to him.

I received a letter some time since from Mr John Gerish of Bangor Theo. Semy. making inquires [sic] about Wisconsin—I want you to send those Bangor students here. They are probably the right men for us, though nothing superior. But from what I have learned respecting them I would as soon try them as the Andover or N. Haven men.

We must have more men. Mr Hart I understand is to leave South Port. I dont know where he intends going. Br Warner of Potosi has not been able to preach for some months. It is feared he will go into a "decline"—and soon close up his work. Br Gaston's health has failed & he is laid aside. Rood & Hurd who have filled some small places are out of the account, and we have non[e] to fill these places of all these brethren, besides the numerous new fields which are calling loudly for ministers.

I start to-morrow morning for Madison & several other places—am to be at Washington on the Lake 95 miles from here on Sab. the 31st instant—at home to meet a student of Auburn who is coming to reconnoiter the Territory on the 4th of June—and then go up north and then immediately to the mining region.

Yours &c STEPHEN PEET—

14. HOW ONE MISSIONARY BEGAN HIS WORK

WATERTOWN, November 2, 1846

Rev M. Badger

DEAR BROTHER:

On reaching Watertown I found a small church; formed a year since; in a cold & lifeless state, scarcely realizing they had ever been united into one body; composed of 9 members 6 Females, 3 Males. They had not been visited since their formation; had not even been called together;—& few in no- as they were they could not inform me who those few were. Had it not been that Mr Peet had given me their names, should have found it somewhat difficult to have discovered them. My first business then was to look after this feebly band. The Deacon lived some 6 miles from Town & could give me no assistance detained as he was by a sick family; the other 2 Male Members were not in circumstances to render me any aid. Adopting therefore the true *Yankee Method*, with the list of names on a card, I coursed my way through the town & by dint of perseverance found out the members & through inquiries of them & others, succeeded in discovering some 12 or 15 others, who were members of Cong- & Presby- churches East; stated to them my object & the probability that I might remain should it seem desireable. Some, surrounded with such evil influences as prevail here manifested little interest in having the regularly sustained ministry of the Gospel among them. Dark & discouraging indeed did it look to see *Christians* manifest so little feeling. The warm hearts of a few Christians, who had recently come here & the deep interest of many who were not professors however greatly encouraged me. The next Sab P.M. I preached to an audience of some 35—; in the evening nearly a hundred were present—attentive & deeply solemn.

B. F. Parsons

15. AN ESTIMATE OF STEPHEN PEET BY ONE OF HIS CONTEMPORARIES

Fort Atkinson   June 9. 1847

Rev & dear Sir;

[The first part of the letter is irrelevant.]

You wish me to explain a little in regard to a sentence in a former letter of mine, touching Mr. Peet. This I shall most frankly do. I shall state my own convictions and state them too as I would to Mr. P. did my years allow it, with no intention to do him in any way injury. Mr. Peet has ever from some reason been to me apparently a warm friend, a brother & consellor [*sic*]. But the *fact* in the first place—"he is held in little respect" and in the next place the *reasons*. The *fact*. I mean this relatively of course. As a man of good sense—of energy—of christian character he is respected. but so far as pertains to his work. his influence is greatly diminished in the churches. With many prominent men in the chh and I think I speak not at random when I say with some of the missionaries also. Such I think is the fact from what I have observed for a year or more past and from frequent remarks which have been made to me directly. It will I am aware apply to some places more than to others. For instance, where there is no stated ministry and where there is no one to preach to them an occasional sermon but Mr. Peet—

in such places he is I am confident held in high respect. But the fact is true more emphatically in the churches which have been organised [*sic*] some time and in which he is seen in connection with a stated ministry.

But the *reasons*. Mr. Peet has been most wofully [*sic*] abused in a good many things. The attacks which have been made upon him in the Puritan I can have no sympathy for. Mr. P. has often been charged . . . . of being partial—partial to chh. partial to missionaries—partial to church gov^{nt} &c.—partial in the distribution of clothing from missionary boxes and in his recommendation of missionary aid. In regard to these complaints which are in deed quite common and kindred other ones, I am inclined to think, are unjust & unfounded. If a church or a missionary gets an idea of *favoritism*, it is because they take only one point of observation and that is self. Much of this supposed partiality has its origin here. The whole field is not surveyed, nor can be so well, as by the agent where he is *intent upon* his *business*. Many churches get this idea or speak of partiality from the principle mentioned in your letter. The agent speaks of their ability and urges them to depend more on their own recouses [*sic*]. The agent is not to blame in so doing. That Mr. Peet is partial to one form of ch govt I disbelieve entirely since the charge comes as often from Congregationalists as from Presbyterians and do vica versa. Mr. P. is placed here in a difficult position and I would be ready to make proper allowance. But the head and front of Mr. P.s offending does not lie in any of these things which I have mentioned: That is, these things may be and are believed, but there is something else which lies at the bottom more essential and that is his *dictatorial spirit* or I might qualify it by saying his dictatorial *manner*, as it is difficult to judge of the disposition. There are in Mr. P. a good many qualities which eminently qualify him for his station. But here is wanting one most essential element and in the lack of which he sometimes greatly injures his own influence and the best interests of the H.M

Society. He does not possess or exhibit a mild, winning & affectionate manner. His words have the tone of command, not of counsel, both to churches & individuals and I may say sometimes too to conventions. His language is this, "you ought to do this—you can do it, you must do it." rather than this—"Can you not do much? and in this way." I do not wish to bring the charge "the would be Bishop," which is so often heard, but his general manner of speaking will often imply both in private & public "*pro auctoriati mihi commissa.*" Many a severe word has fallen from him which has made a wound not [able?] to be cured. . . . . Some young ministers & feeble chh who have been toiling hard and praying fervently have been cut to the quick by such a remark as this. "What have you been about all this time that you have not got a revival befor now?" A remark like this I am told sunk [*sic*] deep into the soul of our beloved & lamented Br Pitkin and how much it had to do in the consumation [*sic*] his melancoly end I cannot say.

I have given you but an imperfect outline of my idea. I hope in this respect we may see Mr. Peet change a little or otherwise I think he has seen his most useful days in the Ter. Would he lay aside his habit of scheming and planning—his habit of arbitrary dictation he would still continue a blessing to our chu[r]ches. I hope the Beloit college will be put in operation this year that he may another year have more time to attend to his appropriate business.

You may make what use your wisdom dictates of this letter. I will write you more fully on some one point should you desire it. In stating what I have stated I have had in view I think no . . . . [illegible] injury. I ought not perhaps to have dropped the remark I did in the first place. As I did, such are my convictions.

Yours truly & affct

M MONTAGUE

REV CHAS HALL   *N. York.*

BIBLIOGRAPHY

BIBLIOGRAPHY

MANUSCRIPTS

AMERICAN HOME MISSIONARY SOCIETY CORRESPONDENCE. Chicago Theological Seminary, Chicago, Ill. This collection consists of some 100,000 letters from missionaries on the field together with 150 volumes of "press" copies of letters written by officials of the society to the missionaries. The years covered are from 1825 on.

AMERICAN BOARD OF COMMISSIONERS FOR FOREIGN MISSIONS CORRESPONDENCE. The major portion of this large collection of manuscripts is housed in the Andover-Harvard Theological Library, Cambridge, Mass. As all the Indian missions were conducted under the auspices of this society, the extensive correspondence relating to that work will be found here.

Transcripts of the A.B.C.F.M. Correspondence relating to Indian missions are to be found in the Newberry Library in Chicago. These consist of nearly three thousand letters besides Journals and Reports.

MISSIONARY SOCIETY OF CONNECTICUT PAPERS located in Memorial Hall, 426 Asylum Street, Hartford, Conn. These consist of the Records of the Connecticut Missionary Society. Here also are found records of county missionary societies.

OBERLIN COLLEGE LIBRARY houses the papers of the Ohio Church History Society containing Records of numerous Ohio Congregational churches and associations.

ILLINOIS COLLEGE MANUSCRIPTS (Jacksonville, Ill.). Consisting of Baldwin-Sturtevant correspondence, the Jonathan Baldwin Turner Letters, and miscellaneous papers.

BELOIT COLLEGE MANUSCRIPTS. Papers relating to the founding of the college and early Wisconsin Congregationalism.

See also the manuscript collections listed in the Bibliography of *Religion on the American Frontier*, Vol. II: *The Presbyterians*, pp. 888–89.

CONGREGATIONAL PERIODICALS

The Adviser or Vermont Evangelical Magazine. 7 vols. Middlebury, Vt., 1809–15.

Christian Mirror. 77 vols. Portland, Me., 1822–99.

Concord Observer. 4 vols. Concord, N.H., 1819–22. (Changed to *New Hampshire Repository and Observer*, 1822–27; changed to the *New Hampshire Observer*, 1828–35; became the *Christian Panoply*, 1836–40.)

Connecticut Evangelical Magazine. 15 vols. Hartford, Conn., 1800–1814.

Connecticut Observer. 16 vols. Hartford, Conn., 1825–40.

Hopkinsian Magazine. 9 vols. Providence, R.I., 1824–32.

Iowa News Letter. 6 vols. Dubuque, Iowa, 1861–67.

Massachusetts Missionary Magazine. 5 vols. Salem, Mass., 1803–4; Boston, 1804–8. (United with the *Panoplist* in 1808.)

The Panoplist or Christian's Armory. Boston, 1805–8. (From 1808 to 1818 the *Panoplist and Missionary Magazine;* 1818–20, *Panoplist and Missionary Herald;* since 1820, the *Missionary Herald.*)

The Religious Intelligencer, Vol. I. New Haven, Conn., 1816.

Spirit of the Pilgrims. 4 vols. Boston, 1828–32.

Vermont Chronicle. 48 vols. Bellows Falls, Vt., 1826; 1827–28, Windsor, Vt.; 1828–74, Montpelier, Vt.

PRINTED MATERIALS

ABBOTT, LYMAN. *Reminiscences.* Boston and New York: Houghton Mifflin Co., 1915.

ADAMS, EPHRAIM. *The Iowa Band.* Boston: Congregational Publishing Society, 1870.

AMERICAN HOME MISSIONARY SOCIETY. *Reports, 1827–1850.*

———. *The First Report of the American Home Missionary Society Presented by the Executive Committee, at the Anniversary Meeting, May 9, 1827, with an Appendix Containing an Address to the Christian Public, Forms of Constitutions for Auxiliary Societies, etc.* New York, 1827.

ANONYMOUS. *The Prairie Missionary.* Philadelphia: American Sunday School Union, 1853.

AVERY, REV. FREDERICK D. *Historical Address of Rev. Frederick D. Avery, at the Centennial of the Tolland Association, Held at Tolland, Connecticut, June 11, 1889.* Rockville: Journal Press and Bindery, 1889. (Also in Congregational Society of Church History for the Middle West, *Documents.*)

BACON, LEONARD. "Historical Discourse," in *Contributions to the Ecclesiastical History of Connecticut,* pp. 2–81. New Haven, 1861.

———. "David Bacon," *Congregational Quarterly,* XVIII (1876), 1–19, 260–82, 387–417, 562–91.

———. *The Story of the Churches: The Congregationalists.* New York: Baker & Taylor Co., 1904.

BACON, THEODORE D. *Leonard Bacon: A Statesman in the Church.* Edited by BENJAMIN W. BACON. New Haven: Yale University Press, 1931.

BALDWIN, REV. THERON. "Absorption of Congregationalism," *Congregational Quarterly,* XII (January, 1870), 19–24.

BARTON, WILLIAM E. "Early Ecclesiastical History of the Western Reserve," *Ohio Church History Society Papers,* I (1890), 14–42.

———. "History of the First Congregational Church of Wellington," *ibid.,* III (1892), 21–55.

———. *The Law of Congregational Usage.* Chicago: Advance Publishing Co., 1916.

BASCOM, REV. FLAVEL. "The Beginning and Progress of Congregational-ism in Illinois." (A paper read before the Congregational Club of Chi-cago, March 20, 1883.) Chicago: Chicago Theological Seminary Li-brary. (Typewritten.)
——. *A Historical Discourse . . . . Settlement of Galesburg, Illinois, 22 June, 1866.* Galesburg, Ill., 1866. (Reviewed in *Congregational Quar-terly*, IX, 287.)
——. "Past and Future of Congregationalism in Illinois," *Illinois So-ciety of Church History, Congregational, Papers*, I (1895), 78–85.
BEARD, REV. A. F. "The Days of Old and Our Own": A Thanksgiving Sermon Preached in the First Congregational Church of Norwalk, Conn., Thanksgiving Day, November 30, 1882. Syracuse, N.Y.: Mas-ters & Stone, 1882. (Also in Congregational Society of Church History for the Middle West, *Documents.*)
BRACKETT, W. O. "The Rise and Development of the New School in the Presbyterian Church in the U.S.A.," *Journal of the Presbyterian Histori-cal Society*, XIII (1928–29), 117–40, 145–74.
BROWN, MRS. ABRAM. "History of the First Congregational Church of Columbus," *Ohio Church History Society Papers*, VIII (1897), 45–61.
BROWN, F. J. "Congregationalism in Illinois." Chicago: Chicago The-ological Seminary Library. (Typewritten.)
BROWN, W. F. *The Past Made Present.* Beloit, Wis., 1900.
BURT, REV. D. "Congregationalism in Minnesota," *Congregational Quar-terly*, II (1860), 67–72.
BUSHNELL, HORACE. "An Historical Estimate of Connecticut," pp. 167–226, in *Work and Play*. New York: Charles Scribner's Sons, 1903.
CALHOUN COUNTY, MICHIGAN. *History of Calhoun County, Michigan.* Philadelphia: L. H. Everts & Co., 1877.
CALKINS, ERNEST ELMO. *They Broke the Prairie: Being Some Accounts of the Settlement of the Upper Mississippi Valley by Religious and Educa-tional Pioneers, Told in Terms of One City, Galesburg, and of One College, Knox.* New York: Charles Scribner's Sons, 1937.
Cambridge Platform: A Platform of Church Discipline Gathered out of the Word of God; and Agreed upon by the Elders and Messengers of the Churches Assembled in the Synod at Cambridge, in New England; To Be Presented to the Churches and General Court, for Their Consideration and Acceptance in the Lord, the Eighth Month, Anno 1648. Boston, 1808.
CHAPIN, AARON L. "Dexter Clary," *Congregational Quarterly*, XVIII (July, 1876), 357–66.
——. "Puritan Pioneering in New England, as Compared with Puritan Pioneering at the West," in *Contributions to the Ecclesiastical History of Connecticut*, pp. 111–17.
CHAPIN, JOHN E. "Sketch of Cutting Marsh," *Wisconsin Historical So-ciety Collections*, XV (1900), 25–39.
CHICAGO, FIRST CONGREGATIONAL CHURCH. *The Quarter-Centennial of the*

First Church of Chicago, May 21st and 22d, 1876. Chicago: Culver, Page, Hoyne & Co., 1876. (Sermon by Rev. E. P. Goodwin, D.D.; Address by Rev. W. W. Patton, D.D.; Address by Hon. W. W. Farwell; Address by Rev. J. E. Roy, D.D.; A Statistical Statement by the Clerk. In Congregational Society of Church History for the Middle West, *Documents.*)

"Chronological List of the Congregational Churches of Ohio, 1797–1898," *Ohio Church History Society Papers,* IX (1898), 68–77.

CLARK, JOSEPH S. *A Historical Sketch of the Congregational Churches in Massachusetts from 1620 to 1858.* Boston: Congregational Board of Publication, 1858.

———. "A Lesson from the Past: Early Methods of Church Extension," *Congregational Quarterly,* I (1859), 53–59.

———. "New England in the West: Congregational Church Polity as Administered in N.E. at the West," *ibid.,* III (1861), 20–28.

COMSTOCK, JOHN M. *The Congregational Churches of Vermont and Their Ministry, 1762–1914, Historical and Statistical.* St. Johnsbury, Vt.: Caledonian Co., 1915.

CONCORD, NEW HAMPSHIRE, FIRST CONGREGATIONAL CHURCH. *Historical Addresses Delivered on the One Hundred and Fiftieth Anniversary of the First Congregational Church, Concord, N.H. November 18th, 1880. Published by Vote of the Church.* Concord, N.H.: Office of the Granite Monthly, 1881. (Also in Congregational Society of Church History for the Middle West, *Documents.*)

Congregational Catechism, The. New Haven, 1844.

Congregational Churches of Michigan for the First Fifty Years, The Addresses Delivered, Papers Read, and Reports Made at the Jubilee Meeting at Jackson, May 19–22, 1892. Jackson, Mich., 1892.

"Congregational Necrology," *Congregational Quarterly,* I (1859), 96: Rev. Jos. Bloomer, died McGregor, Clayton County, Iowa; *ibid.,* p. 98: Rev. Luther R. White, d. Iowa; *ibid.,* p. 445: Samuel Austin Worcester, d. among Cherokees; *ibid.,* III (1861), 68: Rev. John Lewis, d. Platteville, Wis.; *ibid.,* p. 212: Rev. Henry H. Snow, d. Quincy, Ill.; *ibid.,* p. 306: Rev. James Kimball, d. St. Louis, Mo.; *ibid.,* p. 378: Rev. John Hough, d. Fort Wayne, Iowa; *ibid.,* p. 379, Rev. Dana Lamb, d. Springvale, Wis.; *ibid.,* IV (1862), 306: Henry Hutchins, d. Prairie du Sac, Sauk County, Wis.; *ibid.,* V (1863), 265: James Tisdale, d. Tonica, Ill.; *ibid.,* p. 349: Albert Smith, d. Monticello, Ill.; *ibid.,* VI (1864), 115: Elkanah Whitney, d. Oxford, Oakland County, Mich.; *ibid.,* VII (1865), 422: William Fowler Vaill, d. Weathersfield, Ill.; *ibid.,* p. 425: William T. Clapp, d. Edinburgh, Portage County, Ohio; *ibid.,* VIII (1866), 212: Moses Robinson, d. Steamboat, Iowa; *ibid.,* p. 302: Charles E. Blood, d. Galesburg, Ill.; *ibid.,* p. 392: Garry C. Fox, d. Victor, Mich.; *ibid.,* IX (1867), 205: Alvan D. French, d. Denmark, Iowa; *ibid.,* 206: Warren Bigelow, d. Mazeppa, Minn.; *ibid,* X (1868), 43: Parshall Terry, d. Troy, Geauga County, Ohio; *ibid.,* p. 47: Simeon

Brown, d. Ottumwa, Iowa; *ibid.*, p. 215: Benjamin A. Spaulding, d. Ottumwa, Iowa; *ibid.*, p. 288: Samuel D. Bowker, d. Topeka, Kan.; *ibid.*, XI (1869), 65: Richard C. Dunn, d. Oneida, Ill.; *ibid.*, p. 289, Lucius Parker, d. Larimer Mills, Neb.; *ibid.*, p. 298: Horace Smith, d. Richfield, Ohio.; *ibid.*, p. 427: Abram Frowein, d. La Grange, Lewis County, Mo.; *ibid.*, XII (1870), 55: James Loughead, d. Morris, Ill.; *ibid.*, p. 405: Christopher C. Cadwell, d. Lamar, Mo.; *ibid.*, XIV (1872), 565: John C. Hart, d. Ravenna, Ohio; *ibid.*, p. 568: Lucius H. Parker, d. Galesburg, Ill.; *ibid.*, p. 578: Lemuel Foster, d. Chicago, Ill.; *ibid.*, XV (1873), 577: Nathaniel C. Clark, d. Elgin, Ill.; *ibid.*, XVI (1874), 69: Darius Gore, d. LaHarpe, Ill.; *ibid.*, XX (1878), 619: Joel Goodell, d. Tabor, Iowa.

CORDLEY, RICHARD. "Congregationalism in Kansas," *Congregational Quarterly*, XVIII (1876), 367–86.

COWLES, HENRY. "Ohio Congregationalism," *Congregational Quarterly*, V (1863), 132–43.

CRISTY, A. B. (ed.). *Cleveland Congregationalists: Historical Sketches of Our Twenty-Five Churches and Missions.* Cleveland, Ohio, 1896.

CROMWELL (CONN.) CONGREGATIONAL CHURCH. *Record of the Services at the Semi-centennial Anniversary of the Dedication of the Cromwell Congregational Church, January 6, 1891.* Middletown, Conn.: J. S. Stewart, 1891. (Also in Congregational Society of Church History for the Middle West, *Documents*.)

CUNNINGHAM, HAZEL D. "Presbyterian and Congregational Activity in Early Wisconsin." University of Wisconsin thesis, 1936. (Typewritten.)

DEXTER, FRANK N. (ed.). *A Hundred Years of Congregational History in Wisconsin.* Madison: Wisconsin Congregational Conference, 1933.

DEXTER, H. M. "Meeting Houses: Considered Historically and Suggestively," *Congregational Quarterly*, I (1859), 186–214.

DICKINSON, C. E. "The History of the First Religious Society of Marietta," *Ohio Church History Society Papers*, I (1890), 78–97.

———. "The Come-Outer Movement," *ibid.*, IX (1898), 57–67.

———. "Rev. Joseph Badger, Pioneer Missionary of the Western Reserve," *ibid.*, XI (1900), 5–22.

DILL, REV. JAMES H. "Congregationalism in Western New York," *Congregational Quarterly*, I (April, 1859), 151–58.

DOUGLAS, TRUMAN O. "Builders of a Commonwealth (Iowa)": Vol. I, "The Patriarchs and Their Associates" (short biographies of William P. Apthorp, Asa Turner, Reuben Gaylord, Zeriah Kent Hawley, Thomas P. Emerson, Julius A. Reed, Allen B. Hitchcock, Charles Burnham, Oliver Emerson, J. C. Holbrook, Aaron Dutton, Charles Granger, Israel Holmes, Thomas Dutton); Vol. II, "The Iowa Band" (short biographies of Harvey Adams, E. B. Turner, Daniel Lane, Erastur Ripley, James J. Hill, Ephraim Adams, Ebenezer Alden, William Salter). (Typewritten.)

———. *The Pilgrims of Iowa.* Boston and Chicago: Pilgrim Press, 1911.

DRURY, CLIFFORD MERRILL. *Henry Harmon Spalding, Pioneer of Old Oregon.* Caldwell, Idaho: Caxton Printers, 1936.

————. *Marcus Whitman, M.D., Pioneer and Martyr.* Caldwell, Idaho: Caxton Printers, 1937.

DUDLEY, REV. M. S. *History of Cromwell: A Sketch.* Middletown, Conn.: Constitution Office, 1880. (Also in Congregational Society of Church History for the Middle West, *Documents.*)

DUNNING, ALBERT E. *Congregationalists in America.* New York: J. A. Hill & Co., 1894.

DWINNELL, REV. S. A. *Wisconsin: As It Was and as It Is.* Milwaukee, 1867. (Reviewed in *Cong. Quart.,* IX, 288.)

ELLIS, FRANKLIN. *History of Genesee County, Michigan.* Philadelphia: Everts & Abbott, 1879.

EMERSON, JOSEPH. "The Work and the Man: A Memorial of Rev. Stephen Peet," *Congregational Review,* X (1870), 415–25.

FAIRFIELD, J. H. "John Keep," *Congregational Quarterly,* XIII (April, 1871), 209–24.

FIRE LANDS HISTORICAL SOCIETY. *The Fire Lands Pioneer,* VIII (June), 1867.

FLANDRAU, C. E. "The Ink-pa-du-ta Massacre of 1856," *Minnesota Historical Society Collections,* III, 386–452.

FOLWELL, WILLIAM WATTS. *A History of Minnesota.* 4 vols. St. Paul: Minnesota Historical Society, 1921.

FOSTER, FRANK H. "The Oberlin Objiway Mission," *Ohio Church History Society Papers,* II (1891), 1–25.

FRARY, R. B. "Paper Read at the Semi-centennial Anniversary of the Organization of the Lamoille, Ill., Congregational Church," *Illinois Society of Church History, Congregational, Papers,* I (1895), 120–23.

FRASER, J. G. "A Century of Congregationalism in Cleveland," *Ohio Church History Society Papers,* VIII (1897), 1–44.

————. "Reproduction of the Records of the Ecclesiastical Convention of New Connecticut: Commentary on the Above," *Ohio Church History Society Papers,* IX (1898), 1–31.

————. "An Ohio 'News-Letter' of 1817," *ibid.,* XII (1901), 1–11.

FULLER, Mrs. A. O. "History of the Austinburg Church, 1801–1899," *Ohio Church History Society Papers,* X (1899), 63–79.

GAMBRELL, MARY LATIMER. *Ministerial Training in Eighteenth-Century New England.* ("Studies in History, Economics and Public Law," No. 428; edited by the Faculty of Political Science of Columbia University). New York: Columbia University Press, 1937.

GENERAL CONGREGATIONAL ASSOCIATION OF ILLINOIS. *A Memorial of the Congregational Ministers and Churches of the Illinois Association, on Completing a Quarter of a Century of Its History, Consisting of a Commemorative Discourse by Rev. William Carter, of Pittsfield, an Original Member, Delivered at Quincy, Oct. 26, 1860; and an Historical Appendix, Compiled by Rev. S. Hopkins Emery.* Quincy, Ill.: Whig and Republican

Steam Power Press, 1863. (Also in Congregational Society of Church History for the Middle West, *Documents*.)

———. *Fiftieth Anniversary of the Organization of the General Congregational Association of Illinois. (Jubilee Papers.)* Ottawa, Ill.: General Congregational Association of Illinois, 1894.

GLEASON, C. A. "History of Paddy's Run (Congregational) Church, 1803–1899," *Ohio Church History Society Papers*, X (1899), 80–100.

HADDEN, ARCHIBALD. *Congregationalism in Minnesota, 1851–1891.* Minneapolis: Beard-Hudson Printing Co., 1891.

HARRISON, ELLA WARREN, et al. *The Hampshire Colony Congregational Church—Its First Hundred Years, 1831–1931: A Record Assembled by the Historical Committee, March, 1931.* Princeton, Ill., 1931.

HART, REV. JOHN C. "Congregationalism in Portage and Summit Counties, Ohio," *Congregational Quarterly*, II (1860), 269–72, 386–90; *ibid.* III (1861), 149–53, 285–87, 329–31; *ibid.*, IV (1862), 36–37, 176–78, 239–40, 332–35.

HAZEN, HENRY A. *The Congregational and Presbyterian Ministry of New Hampshire,* Part I: *Towns, Churches, and Pastors;* Part II: *Alphabetical Catalogue of Ministers.* Boston: Alfred Mudge & Son, 1875. Reprinted from *Congregational Quarterly*, October, 1875, and April, 1876.

HEINL, FRANK J. "Jacksonville and Morgan County: An Historical Review," *Journal of the Illinois State Historical Society*, XVIII (1925), 5–38.

HOBART, C. "Religious Movements in Minnesota," *Minnesota Historical Society Collection*, I, 84–88.

HOMER, NEW YORK. *Seventy-fifth Anniversary of the Organization of the Congregational Church, of Homer, N.Y., October, 11th and 12th, 1876.* Homer, N.Y.: Wm. O. Bunn, 1876.

HOOKER, HORACE. "Congregational Home Missions in Connecticut," in *Contributions to the Ecclesiastical History of Connecticut*, pp. 163–79.

HOTCHKIN, JAMES H. *A History of the Purchase and Settlement of Western New York and of the Rise, Progress, and Present State of the Presbyterian Church in That Section.* New York: M. W. Dodd, Brick Church Chapel, 1848.

HOUGH, REV. J. W. *Fifty Years of My Life: A Sermon Preached to the First Congregational Church of Jackson, Mich., by Its Pastor on the Fiftieth Anniversary of His Birth, Nov., 26, 1882.* Jackson, Mich.: Daily Citizen Press House, 1882. (Also in Congregational Society of Church History for the Middle West, *Documents*.)

ILLINOIS SOCIETY OF CHURCH HISTORY (CONGREGATIONAL). *Historical Statement and Papers*, Vol. I: *Congregationalism in Illinois.* Chicago, 1895.

JACKSONVILLE, ILLINOIS. *The Congregational Church, Manual of.* Jacksonville, 1891.

JENKINS, FRANK E. *Anglo-Saxon Congregationalism in the South.* Atlanta, Ga., 1908.

JOHNSON, REV. SAMUEL. "History of the Susquehanna Association (New York)," *Congregational Quarterly*, XVII (April, 1875), 296–99.

JOHNSON, THOMAS S. "Moses Ordway, Pioneer Presbyterian Missionary," *Wisconsin Magazine of History*, II (March, 1919), 266–74.

Jubilee Memorial of the Congregational Convention of Wisconsin, 1840–1890. Madison, 1891.

KITCHEL, REV. H. D. "The New England Zone," *Congregational Quarterly*, III (October, 1861), 341–48.

LEONARD, REV. DELAVAN L. *A Century of Congregationalism in Ohio, 1796–1896. Prepared by Request of the Executive Committee of the Ohio Home Missionary Society.* Oberlin, Ohio, 1896.

———. "Early Annals of the Oberlin Church," *Ohio Church History Society Papers*, VIII (1897), 8–109.

———. "A Century of Congregationalism in the Upper Ohio Valley," *ibid.*, XII (1901), 12–32.

LEONARD, RICHARD Day. "The Presbyterian and Congregational Convention of Wisconsin, 1840–1850." University of Chicago dissertation, 1938. (Typewritten.)

LONG, BYRON E. "Joseph Badger, the First Missionary to the Western Reserve," *Ohio Archaeological and Historical Publications*, XXVI (1917), 1–42.

MAGOUN, G. M. *Asa Turner, a Home Missionary, and His Times.* 1889.

Manual of the Congregational Church, in Burlington, Iowa. Burlington, 1878.

MATHEWS, LOIS KIMBALL. *The Expansion of New England: The Spread of New England Settlement and Institutions to the Mississippi River, 1620–1865.* Boston & New York: Houghton Mifflin Co., 1909.

———. "Some Activities of the Congregational Church West of the Mississippi," pp. 3–34 in *Essays in American History Dedicated to Frederick Jackson Turner.* New York: Henry Holt & Co., 1910.

Michigan, History of Oakland County. Philadelphia: L. H. Everts & Co., 1877.

Michigan Pioneer and Historical Collections, Vol. XXVIII (1897–98). Lansing: Robert Smith Printing Co., 1900.

"Mortuary Statistics of the Theological Seminary, Andover, during the Fifty Years (the Number Dead, according to States)," *Congregational Quarterly*, I (October, 1859), 357–58.

MURPHY, LAURENCE E. "Education and Religion on the Frontier: A Life of Stephen Peet." (Typewritten.)

NEILL, E. D. "Dakota Land and Dakota Life." *Minnesota Historical Society Collections*, I, 254–94.

NICHOLS, REV. W. A. "Pioneer Enterprise in Chicago, from 1853 to 1864," *Illinois Society of Church History, Congregational, Papers*, I (1895), 97–114.

NOBLE, REV. FREDERICK A. *Ten Years of Ministry in Chicago. An Anniversary Sermon Preached to the Union Park Congregational Church, Chi-*

cago, Ill., by the Pastor, Rev. Frederick A. Noble, D.D., Sunday Morning April 21, 1889. Chicago, 1890. (Also in Congregational Society of Church History for the Middle West, *Documents.*)

NORTON, A. T. *History of the Presbyterian Church in the State of Illinois.* St. Louis: W. S. Bryan, 1879.

NOYES, DANIEL P. "Methods of Missionary Labor at the West," *Congregational Quarterly,* II (1860), 223–25.

Ohio Church History Society Papers, Vols. I–XII. Oberlin, Ohio, 1890–1901.

OSTRANDER, EVAH IRENE. *The American Home Missionary Society in Oregon, 1849–1870.* University of Chicago dissertation, 1932; typewritten.

PARRISH, GEORGE R. *History of the Congregational Association of Southern Illinois.* Chicago: Congregational Association of Southern Illinois, 1892.

PATTERSON, REV. D. WILLIAMS. "First 'Susquehannah Association'" (New York), *Congregational Quarterly,* XVI (April, 1874), 285–90.

PATTON, REV. WILLIAM W. *The Last Century of Congregationalism: Or, The Influence on Church and State of the Faith and Polity of the Pilgrim Fathers.* Washington, D.C.: W. M. Stuart, 1878. Reprinted from the *New Englander* for October, 1876. (Also in Congregational Society of Church History for the Middle West, *Documents.*)

PEASE, THEODORE CALVIN. *History of Illinois,* Vol. II: *The Frontier State, 1818–1848.* Springfield, Ill.: Illinois Centennial Commission, 1918.

PEET, STEPHEN D. *A History of Early Missions in Wisconsin.* Madison, 1886.

PIERCE, REV. JOHN D. "Congregationalism in Michigan," *Congregational Quarterly,* II (1860), 190–97.

POND, S. W., JR. *Two Volunteer Missionaries among the Dakotas: Or the Story of the Labors of Samuel W. and Gideon H. Pond.* Boston & Chicago: Congregational Sunday School and Publishing Society, 1893.

POPE, THOMAS. "Historical Sketches of the First Half Century of the First Congregational Church of Quincy, Illinois, Organized December 4, 1830." Unpublished MS in the Chicago Theological Seminary Library, 1898.

POST, T. M. "The Mission of Congregationalism at the West," in *Contributions to the Ecclesiastical History of Connecticut,* pp. 93–102. New Haven, 1861.

PRUDDEN, REV. THEODORE P. *Twenty Years of the History of Plymouth Church, Lansing, Michigan: A Sermon by the Pastor, April 27, 1884.* Lansing: W. S. George, 1884. (Also in Congregational Society of Church History, *Documents.*)

PUNCHARD, GEORGE. *A View of Congregationalism, Its Principles and Doctrines; the Testimony of Ecclesiastical History in Its Favor, Its Prac-*

tice, and Its Advantages. Boston: Congregational Board of Publication, 1856.

――――. *History of Congregationalism*. 5 vols. Boston: Congregational Publishing Society, 1881.

QUINT, A. H. "Statistics of the American Orthodox Congregational Churches, as Collected in 1859," *Congregational Quarterly*, II (1860), 97–140.

――――. "Statistics of the American Orthodox Congregational Churches, as Collected in 1860," *ibid.*, III (1861), 73–130.

RAMMELKAMP, CHARLES HENRY. *Illinois College: A Centennial History, 1828–1920*. New Haven: Yale University Press, 1928.

REED, ANDREW, AND MATHESON, JAMES. *A Narrative of the Visit to the American Churches by the Deputation from the Congregational Union of England and Wales*. 2 vols. New York: Harper & Bros., 1835.

REED, JULIUS A. *Reminiscences of Early Congregationalism in Iowa*. Grinnell, Iowa: Herald Office, 1885. (Also in Congregational Society of Church History for the Middle West, *Documents*.)

RICH, REV. A. B. "Collegiate and Theological Education at the West," *Congregational Quarterly*, XI (1869), 543–57.

RIGGS, STEPHEN R. *Mary and I, or Forty Years among the Sioux*. Boston: Congregational Publication Society, 1879.

――――. "Dakota Portraits," *Minnesota History Bulletin*, Vol. II, No. 8 (November, 1918).

――――. "Protestant Missions in the Northwest," *Minnesota Historical Society Collections*, VI, 117–88.

RODMAN, REV. SAMUEL JOHNSON. "Black River Association, New York," *Congregational Quarterly*, XX (1878), 577–90.

ROSS, A. HASTINGS. *The Church-Kingdom, Lectures on Congregationalism, etc.* Boston and Chicago: Congregational Publication Society, 1887.

ROY, JOSEPH E. *A Half Century of Home Missions in Illinois—1876*. Illinois Home Missionary Society, n.d. (Also in Congregational Society of Church History for the Middle West, *Documents*.)

――――. "History of Congregationalism in Illinois," *Illinois Society of Church History, Congregational, Papers*, I (Chicago, 1895), 24–66.

――――. *Quarter-Centennial of the First Congregational Church of Chicago*. Chicago, 1876.

SANDERSON, JOHN P. *Outstanding Personalities and Eras in Michigan Congregationalism. An Address Delivered at the Diamond Anniversary of the Michigan Congregational Conference in Jackson, Michigan, May 17, 1917*. Jackson, Mich., 1917.

SARGENT, REV. ROGER M. "Historical Sketch of Congregational Church in Dover, Illinois," *Illinois Society of Church History, Congregational, Papers*, I (1895), 115–16.

――――. "Sketch of Woodburn (Macoupin Co.), Illinois, Church," *ibid.*, pp. 117–19.

SAVAGE, REV. G. S. F. "A Chapter of the Early History of the Chicago Theological Seminary," *Illinois Society of Church History, Congregational, Papers*, I (1895), 11–23.

———. "Reminiscences of Early Congregational Ministers and Churches in the Fox River Valley," *Third Annual Report of the Fox River Congregational Club, Together with Constitution and By-Laws, List of Members, etc., 1890–1891*. Elgin, Ill.: Elgin Courier Print. (Also in *Illinois Society of Church History, Congregational, Papers*, I [1895], 67–77; and in Congregational Society of Church History for the Middle West, *Documents*.)

SCHAFER, JOSEPH. "Congregational Beginnings in Wisconsin." Madison, Wis.: Wisconsin Historical Society. (Typewritten.)

SCOTT, FRANKLIN D. (ed.). "Minutes of the Session of the First Presbyterian Church in Morgan County, 1827–1830," *Illinois State Historical Society Journal*, XVIII (1925), 142–58.

SEVERANCE, H. O. *Michigan Trailmakers*. Ann Arbor, Mich.: George Waler, 1930.

SEWARD, JOHN W. "The History of the Puritan Conference," *Ohio Church History Society Papers*, VIII (1897), 62–69.

SHORTRIDGE, W. P. "The Transition of a Typical Frontier with Illustrations from the Life of Henry Hastings Sibley, etc." University of Minnesota Dissertation, 1910.

SMALL, C. H. "History of the Congregational Church of Hudson," *Ohio Church History Society Papers*, IX (1898), 32–40.

SPINKA, MATTHEW. *Fifty Years of the Congregational Club of Chicago*. Chicago, 1933. (Pamphlet.)

STRONG, WILLIAM E. *The Story of the American Board: An Account of the First Hundred Years of the American Board of Commissioners for Foreign Missions*. Boston: Pilgrim Press, 1910.

STURTEVANT, JULIAN M. "William Carter," *Congregational Quarterly*, XIII (1871), 497–513.

———. "Theron Baldwin," *ibid.*, XVII (1875), 213–37, 395–419.

STURTEVANT, J. M., JR. (ed.). *Julian Sturtevant: An Autobiography*. New York, 1896.

SWEET, WILLIAM W. *Religion on the American Frontier*, Vol. II: *The Presbyterians*. New York: Harper & Bros., 1936.

SWING, ALBERT TEMPLE. *James Harris Fairchild, or Sixty-eight Years with a Christian College*. New York: Fleming H. Revell Co., 1907.

TAYLOR, ELLA HUME. "History of the Congregational Church and Society, Genessee, Illinois," founded in Beagen, *Genessee County, New York*. Typewritten copy in Congregational Theological Seminary Library, dated September 13, 1836.

TAYLOR, REV. LATHROP. "History of Central Association," *Illinois Society of Church History, Congregational, Papers*, I (1895), 91–96.

TENNEY, H. M. "The History of the First Congregational Church of Cleveland," *Ohio Historical Society Papers*, II (1892), 26–44.

THALHEIMER, M. E. "History of the Vine Street Congregational Church of Cincinnati," *Ohio Church History Society Papers*, IX (1898), 41–56.

THAYER, LUCIUS HARRISON. *Congregationalism in New Hampshire during the Nineteenth Century, Including a Sketch of the General Association for One Hundred Years. An Address Delivered at the Centennial Anniversary of the General Association of the Congregational Churches of New Hampshire, at Boscawen, May 19, 1909, by Lucius Harrison Thayer, Minister of the North Church, Portsmouth.*

THOMPSON, REV. JOSEPH P. "Congregationalism in Eastern New York," *Congregational Quarterly*, II (1860), 33–42.

THRIFT, CHARLES T., JR. *The American Home Missionary Society in the South, 1826–1861.* University of Chicago dissertation, 1936. (Typewritten.)

WHITEWATER, WISCONSIN, CONGREGATIONAL CHURCH. *Exercises at the Semi-centennial Anniversary of the Congregational Church in Whitewater, Wis., June 28 and 29, 1890, 1840–1890.* Whitewater, Wis.: Register Print, 1890. (Also in Congregational Society of Church History for the Middle West, *Documents*.)

WILLIAMS, REV. JOHN M. "History of the Chicago Congregational Association during Its First Quarter Century," *Illinois Society of Church History, Congregational, Papers*, I (1895), 86–90.

WILLIAMSON, T. S. "Napehshneedoota, the First Male Dakota Convert to Christianity," *Minnesota Historical Society Collections*, III, 188–91.

WINN, E. H. "The Activities of Stephen Peet in Wisconsin from 1837 to 1845." Chicago Theological Seminary thesis, 1929. (Typewritten.)

WOODSTOCK, VERMONT, CONGREGATIONAL CHURCH. *Rededication June 5, 1890, of the Reconstructed Old White Meeting House, Woodstock, Vermont. Peter McMillan, Pastor.* Woodstock, Vt., 1890. (Also in Congregational Society of Church History for the Middle West, *Documents*.)

ZORBAUGH, C. L. "The Plan of Union in Ohio," *Church History*, VI (1937), 145–64.

INDEX

INDEX

Accommodation Plan, 17

Adams, Rev. Mr., minister at Beloit, Wisconsin, 282, 372

Adrian, Michigan, church at, 307

Alabama, 55

Allegheny Mountains, states west of the, 46

Allen, Ethan, 6

Allen, William T., 222

Alton, Illinois, 196; church of, 234, 268

Alton Mob, 26

Alton Observer, 134

American Board of Commissioners for Foreign Missions, 34, 42, 51, 352, 355, 361, 362; Indian missions of, in 1830, 54; *Annual Report* for 1846, 57; letters and reports to, 340; Chippewa missions of, 341; instructions of, 343

American Home Missionary Society (A.H.M.S.), 36, 48, 68, 105, 398, 399; aid to Swedish missionary, 26; auxiliaries to, 48; and Plan of Union, 49; summary of its work, 1826–50, 50; affiliated with Missionary Society of Connecticut, 99, 105; funds of, 180; letters to, 231; resentment against by Baptists and Methodists, 257; funds of reduced, 274; circuit of churches and, 286, 327; auxiliary society of, 291; complaint against Presbyterian bias of, 307, 311; rules of, 328

Anderson, Paul, 26

Andover, Illinois, church of, 284

Andover Theological Seminary, 41, 54, 340, 362, 400

Andreen, A., 26

Andrewson, Ole, 26

Antislavery, 29, 157, 205, 265, 270, 271, 272, 274; conflict in Alton and Quincy, Illinois, 206, 261

Apthorp, Rev. Mr., of Congregational Association of Massachusetts, 220

Arkansas, 56

Armanda, Michigan, church at, 316

Articles of faith, 130, 159

Association of the Western District of New Haven, Connecticut, 196

Athens, Illinois, church of, 275

Atlas, Illinois, church in, 166, 171, 187, 209

Auburn, Michigan, church of, 294, 303

Auburn Theological Seminary, 36, 38, 308

Augusta, Illinois, 176

Aurora, Illinois, church of, 276

Babbit, Calvin W., 116, 120, 253

Bacon, David, 88, 89, 92

Bacon's *Church Manual*, 227

Badger, Joseph, 68, 88, 92, 111, 112, 113, 115; letter from, describing conditions in Western Reserve, 77–81

Badger, Milton, secretary, A.H.M.S., 231, 337, 368, 369, 371, 372, 375, 379, 380, 382, 384, 392, 396

Bailey's Point, Illinois, church of, 244

Baker, Spencer, 399

Baldwin, Theron, 25, 133, 158, 175, 234, 243, 246, 248, 268; letter of, to A.H.M.S., 167; principal of Monticello Seminary, 267

Bangor Seminary, 36

Baptists, 74, 126, 174, 203, 206, 250, 275, 277, 287, 316; and Jeffersonian party, 10; and opposition to compulsory support of Congregational clergy, 10; wide distribution of, 11; and paid missionaries, 166; in Illinois, increase in number of, 232; college of, at Alton, Illinois, 248; and temperance, 378

Barnes, Romulus, 234, 251, 253, 254, 259, 267

Barr, Thomas, 111, 112, 113, 115

Bascom, Flavel: autobiography of, 231–84; pastor at Ottawa, Illinois, 234 commission from A.H.M.S., 235; journey of, to the West, 236; first sermon of, in Illinois, 242; support of, by A.H.M.S., 250; ordained by Sangamon Presbytery, 255; agent for A.H.M.S. 263; temporary supply at Chicago, 268

Beardsley, William, 219

Beardstown, Illinois, church of, 266

Beebe's Grove, Illinois, church of, 275

Beecher, Edward, 28, 156; heresy trial of, 158; slander against, 256, 267

Beecher, Lyman, 6, 287; sermons of, on intemperance, 166

Bellamy, Dr. Joseph, quoted, 199

Beloit, Wisconsin, church of, 282, 387, 389, 394, 396, 404

Beloit College, 39, 369, 372, 375, 382

Belvidere, Illinois, church of, 276, 278

Benedict, Joel T., 46

Bergeron, J. G., 254

Bethany, Pennsylvania, 286

Bethel, Illinois, church of, 234

Bible class, 166, 242, 191, 377

Bible societies, 244, 260, 264, 313, 316, 317, 326, 329

Bibles, distribution of, 166

Big Grove, Illinois, church at, 128, 165, 190

Blackhawk Purchase, 39

Blackhawk War, 232

Blackstone Grove, Illinois, 245

Blake, Robert, 195, 200, 225

Blanchard, Jonathan, president of Knox College, 29

Blatchford, John, 269

Bloomfield, Michigan, church of, 294

Bloomingdale, Illinois, church of, 280

Bloomington, Illinois, Presbyterian church of, 233, 254

Bloomingville, Illinois, church of, 282

Boutwell, William T., 54, 341, 343, 344, 346

Boyd, James, 94

Brainerd, first missionary station, Choctaw mission, 51

Brick Presbyterian Church of New York, 49

Bristol, Illinois; see Long Grove, Illinois

Brooks, J. F., 234

Brown, Ebenezer, 282

Bruce, Michigan, church of, 312

Bruen, M., 287, 288, 289, 290

Buffalo, New York, a frontier village, 236

Burge, Ephraim, 288

Burlington, Wisconsin, 369, 390

Burnam, Charles, 200

Bushnell, Jedidiah, 87, 89

Butler, Dr. Elizur, 56

Byington, Cyrus, 356, 361; his knowledge of Choctaw language, 362, 363

Calhoun, John C., 14

California, 62

Campbellites, 164, 174, 250

Cannonsburgh, Pennsylvania, 98

Canton, Illinois, church of, 254, 259

Carter, William, 28, 158, 162, 163, 200, 210, 223, 224, 234

Carthage, Illinois, church of, 176, 186, 191, 202, 209

Cartwright, Peter, quoted, estimate of missionaries, 257

Cazanovia, New York, 134

Centre College, Kentucky, 265

Chamberlain, Dr. Nathaniel, 247

Chamberlain, William, 292, 294, 297, 300

Channing, William Ellery, 5

Chapman, Ezekiel J., 68, 88; ordination and commissioning of, to New Connecticut, 82–85

Cherokee Indians, 51, 55, 348, 360; mission to, in Arkansas, 54; forceful removal of, 56

Cherry Valley, Michigan, 285

Chicago, Illinois, 123; First Presbyterian Church of, 25, 233, 242, 246, 268, 275; appearance of, in 1835, 240; Second Presbyterian Church of, 246; churches of, in 1839, 269

Chicago Theological Seminary, 39

Chickasaw Indians, 51, 55; mission to, in South Carolina and Georgia, 54; mission to, closed in 1835, 57

Children, education of, 94

Chippewa Indians, 88, 340–48; language of, translated, 341, 344, 346, 347

Choctaw Indians, 51, 53, 360–63; mission to, in 1830, 54; removal of the, 55; language of, translated, 362

Cholera, 122

Christian church, 261; *see also* Campbellites

Christian Indians, 55, 62

Church government, 121–395; adoption of congregational mode, 120; change from Presbyterian to Congregational, 125

Church membership, 151; rules for, 210–11

Church polity, controversy over, 294, 307

Church records, 106–55

Church of Scotland, 124

Church union: rare in the nineteenth century, 167; between Baptists and Methodists, 278

Churches: small membership in, 174; distribution of, 183; Congregational planted instead of Presbyterian, 255

Civil War, the, 62

Clark, Jonas, of Lexington, 4

Clark, Nathaniel C., 27, 106, 116, 120, 122, 124, 125, 126, 127, 132, 133, 146, 233, 275, 276, 278, 279

Clary, D., letter of, to A.H.M.S., 382–84

Clayton, Illinois, church of, 187

Cleaveland, John P., 320

Clinton, Illinois, church of, 234

Clinton, O. P., letter of, 293–96

Cochran, Sylvester, 337

Cohler, D., missionary of Evangelical Lutheran Synod of Pennsylvania, 186

Cole, Thomas, 186–87, 200; letter of, to A.H.M.S., 187

Coleton, H. C., 276

Collinsville, Illinois, church of, 234

Colonization societies, 101

Colton, Herman S., 175

Columbus, Illinois, church of, 185

Communion set, presented, 134

Confession of faith: of Congregational church of Madison, Ohio, 108–10; of Congregational church of Du Page, Illinois, 144–45.

Congregational Association of Illinois, 28; minutes of the, 1835–40, 161–230; constitution of, 167; names of ministers and churches of, 200

Congregational Association of Iowa, 41

Congregational Association of Massachusetts, 220

Congregational Association of New York, 193

Congregational Association of Ohio, 222

Congregational church, 316; home missions of, 43–50; county missionary societies of, 44; in Connecticut, 73; disestablishment of, in Connecticut, 74; ministers of, in Illinois, 164

Congregational churches: at the close of the Revolution, 9; in counties east of Hudson River, 9; in Massachusetts, Connecticut, and New Hampshire, 10; on the Western Reserve, 19; in Illinois in 1826, 28; in Wisconsin, 1839, 34; in New England and New

York, delegation to, 163; ministry of, 227

Congregational home missions, 43–50

Congregational Indian missions, 51–63

Congregational mode of government, 123

Congregational organizations, west of the Hudson River, 10

Congregational and Presbyterian Convention of Wisconsin; see Wisconsin, Presbyterian and Congregational Convention of

Congregational principles, devotion to, 294

Congregational renaissance, 42

Congregational union, 130

Congregational Union of Fox River: constitution of, 139–44; confession of faith of, 144–45

Congregationalism, 285; handicap to the national expansion of, 11; absorption of, by Presbyterians, 16; principles of, 227–28; and baptism, 229; and the Lord's Supper, 229; self-consciousness of, 230; doctrine of grace of, 332; polity of, opposed, 335, preferred, 331–32

Congregationalists, 167, 174, 270, 276; as Federalists, 10; claim of, in propagating Christianity, 26; and slavery issue, 29; resolutions of, against slavery, 177; denominational consciousness of, 233, 368; from New England and New York, 338; Indian missions of, 340; against union, 374

Connecticut, 60, 73; Congregational churches in, at close of Revolution, 9; Congregationalism of, 12, 14, 16; natives of, 14; settlers from, 232

Connecticut Evangelical Magazine, 45, 90

Connecticut Missionary Society, 19, 22, 67–105, 233; formation of, 44; appropriations of, in 1814, 46

Connecticut Observer and New York Congregationalist, 213; recommended, 208

Connecticut Reserve; see Western Reserve

Connecticut River, 198

Consociation, 12

Constitution, the, 130

Convention of Congregational churches, 127

Convention of the Congregational churches of Illinois: minutes of the, 157–61; articles of faith of, 169; organization of, 233

Convention of New Connecticut, 19

Cook, C., 276

Cooke, Noah, 37

Copeland, Henry H., letter of, 360–63

Covenant, 119, 130

Cowles, Giles H., 113

Crane, A., 395

Creek Indians, 51, 348; mission to, closed in 1837, 57; Baptist and Methodist missions to, 350

Cross, John, 272, 273

Cumberland Presbyterians, 174, 250, 258

Curtis, Otis F., 369

Cutler, Manasseh, 71

Dakota Indians, 42, 59, 355, 363–67; mission to, 58–63; language of, 61; insurrection of, 62; Nebraska removals of, 63

Danville, Iowa, 40, 213, 223

Dartmouth College, 340, 383

Davenport, Iowa, 41

Davis, John, Indian catechist, 350

Day, Jeremiah, president of Yale, 171

Day of fasting and prayer, 376

Deism, 6, 315

Denmark, Iowa, church of, 40, 204, 207

Derrow, Nathan B., 22

Detroit, Michigan, 31, 342; church of, 286, 301, 318, 331

"Dickey's and Rankin's," 246

Dill, James H., quoted, 17

Discipline: principles of, 141–44; cases of, 188, 218; report on, 189

Documents, listed, 340, 368–69

Dodge, Nathaniel B., 351

Domestic and foreign missionary boards, support of, 179

Domestic Missionary Society of Connecticut, 99, 105, 208; committee to correspond with, 183, 188

Domestic Missionary Society of Massachusetts, 100

Douglas, Truman O., quoted, 40

Dover, Illinois, church of, 247, 277

Dubuque, Iowa, 41

Dundee, Illinois, church of, 279

Dunning, A. E., Congregational historian, quoted, 48

Du Page, Illinois: church of, 27, 106, 165; church record of, 116; and articles of faith of, 117–19; controversy over location of church of, 147–49

Du Page River, Illinois, churches on, 276

Dwight, Arkansas, mission at, 53

Dwight, Oklahoma, Indian mission, 360

Dwight, Timothy, 6, 7, 8, 13, 287

Eagle Town, Oklahoma, 360

Eastern states, the: immigrants from, 276; sectarian influences of, 399

East Troy, Wisconsin, 369, 374, 375; church of, 389

Ecclesiastical Convention of New Connecticut, 18

Ecclesiastical Society of New Connecticut, 99

Education, Congregational and Presbyterian activities in, 310; see Schools

Education society, 376, 382, 383

Edwards, Jonathan, 175

Elcorn, Wisconsin, church of, 397

Elders, election of, 120

Elgin, Illinois, church of, 276, 278

Eliot, Choctaw mission, 52

Eliot, John, 43

Elliot, G. W., 281

Emancipation Proclamation, 27

Emmons, Nathanael, opposes centralization of Congregationalism, 11–12

Episcopalians, 74, 208; and Jeffersonian party, 10

Erie Canal, 34, 38, 179, 286

Erie Presbytery, 94, 113

Esbjorn, L. P., 26

Euclid, Ohio, church of, 38

Evangelical Association of Illinois, 161

Evangelical Association of the Wabash Valley, 22

Evangelical churches, 270; services of, in tent, 276

Evangelical doctrine: hostility to, 164; accepted by Congregationalists, 169

Evangelical Magazine, 45

Evangelical Society of Missions, 219

Fairchild, President J. H., 18, 20

Fairfield, Illinois, church of, 158, 159, 160, 165, 187, 193, 195, 202, 233; articles of the Congregational Association of Illinois adopted by, 171

Farmington, Michigan, church at, 31, 292, 298

Farnham, Lucien, 26, 234, 246, 247, 277; letter of, to A.H.M.S., 179

Fellowship, 159; evangelicals admitted to, 160

Ferry, William M., 324, 342, 344, 345

Finances, disagreement over, 187

Finney, Charles G., 19, 232; Lectures on Revivals, 321

Fish, Elijah S., 300, 301

Fisher, Ezra, 206

Flint, Abel, 83, 84, 85, 90

Folwell, W. W., quoted, 62

Foot, Hiram, 146

Foote, Horatio, 281, 282

Foreign missions, 197, 317

Fort, H., 146

Fort Atkinson, Wisconsin, 369, 402

Fort Snelling, Minnesota, 59, 62, 63, 340, 355

Foster, Isaac, 133, 146; letter of, to A.H.M.S., 183

Foster, Lemuel, 25, 233, 249, 254, 255, 256, 280

Fowler, Joseph, 267

Fox, M. A., 396

Fox Indians, 355, 358

Fox River, Illinois, Congregational Union of, 28, 132, 162, 165, 267, 276; presbytery of, 6, 31

Fox River Valley, churches in, 27, 233, 276

Franklin, Illinois, 176

Frazer, William J., suspension of, from ministry, 256

Free Baptists, 11

Freewill Baptists, 338

French Catholics, 242

French mania, 5

French Revolution, influence of, 5

Frontier, the, 179, 252; difficulties of, 155, 285; dissensions on, 165; denominational consciousness on, 167; illness on, 191, 238, 281, 282, 376, 390; communion Sabbath on, 238; church on, described, 245; cabin on, described, 249, 252; conflict of southern and eastern civilizations on, 261; migration to, 286; scarcity of money on, 292; rudeness of, 390–91; plight of immigrants on, 391–92

Fulton, Illinois, church of, 283

Gale, George W., 232, 284

Galena, Illinois, 25, 34, 39; growth of, 231; church of, 233, 254, 282

Galesburg, Illinois, 29; church of, 233, 284

Garden Prairie, Illinois, church of, 276

Gavin, Daniel, among the Sioux, 219

Gaylord, Reuben, 40, 195, 200, 223, 225

General Assembly, 7

General Assembly of Philadelphia, 238

General Assembly of the Presbyterian Church, 113; Illinois delegate to, 207

General Association of Connecticut, 44, 68, 113, 181; and adoption of Plan of Union, 15; 1830 meeting of, 105

Genesee, Wisconsin, church of, 381

Genesee Association of New York, 219

Genesee County, New York, settlers from, in Hadley, Illinois, 232

Geneseo, Illinois, church of, 283

Geneva, Wisconsin, 369, 382

Georgia, defiance of United States Supreme Court by, 56

Gerish, John, 400

Gilbert, L. C., 277

Gilbert, Syman W., 311

Godfrey, Captain, 268

Gooding's Grove, Illinois, church of, 275

Goodman, Eldad, 286, 299

Gould, Nahum, 268; diary of, quoted, 281

Grand Blanc, Michigan, church of, 302, 304–6, 312, 321, 323, 324, 326

Grand River Presbytery, 113, 115

Granville, Massachusetts, 21

Granville, Ohio, church of, 21

Green, David, 341, 352

Green Bay, Michigan Territory, mission at, 352, 358, 363, 368, 372

Greenwood, Alfred, 131, 162, 244; letter of, to A.H.M.S., 165

Griggsville, Illinois, church of, 158, 159, 160, 164, 171, 172, 195, 209, 221, 224, 233

Grosvenor, Mason, 234

Gumble, J. M., 189

Hadley, Illinois, church of, 275

Hale, Albert, 234, 243, 248, 263, 267, 277; letters of, to A.H.M.S., 184, 207

Hale, Charles, 325

Hall, Charles, 369, 390

Hall, Lemuel, 371; letter of, to A.H.M.S., 381–82

Hall, Sherman, 54, 368, 369; letter of, to A.B.C.F.M., 340–48

Hampshire Colony, 246; church of, 254, 277

Hampshire Missionary Society, 100

Hanover, Michigan, church of, 338

Hardy, Solomon, 27, 159

Harmony Association of New Hampshire, 203

Harrison, Marcus, 33, 339

Hart, Levi, 83, 84, 400

Hartford, Connecticut, 76, 82, 113

Hartford Presbytery, 19, 113

Hasselquist, T. N., 26

Hastings, E. P., 292, 301, 307, 309, 314, 318, 325, 327, 342, 348

Hawes, Joel, 7

Hawley, L. K., 202; letters of, to A.H.M.S., 174, 203

Hazard, E. H., letter of, to A.H.M.S., 244, 283

Herndon, William H., 29

Hill, Henry, 357, 360, 364

Hobart, Leander Smith, 33

Holmes, Joseph T., 206

Home Missionary Magazine, 38, 175

Home Missionary Society, aid of, solicited, 155

Home missions, Congregational, 43–50

Homer, Michigan, church of, 32

Hooker, Horace, 104, 208

Hopkins, Samuel, 47

Hornell, George, 286, 294, 300, 303, 305, 306

Howe, E. G., 275

Howe, S. S., letter of, to A.H.M.S., 283

Hoyt, A. P., 33

Hudson River, 11, 34

Hunter, A., 220, 225

Hunter, Moses, 193

Huntington, Enoch, 251, 259

Illinois, 14, 22, 56, 375, 376; Swedish Lutherans in, 26; Congregational movement in, 156; northern, first settled minister in, 231; in 1830, 231; in 1840, 231–32; Congregational churches in, 233; Presbyterianism in, 233; A.H.M.S. in, 234; without railroads in 1839, 263

"Illinois Association," 23

Illinois College, 25, 28, 29, 40, 156, 245, 246; established, 23; opened, 233

Immigration, tide of, 183; into Illinois, 183; into Michigan, 286; into Wisconsin, 380, 381–82, 385

Immorality, 37, 95

Indian lands, greed of whites for, 55

Indian policies of federal government in 1820, 52

Indiana, 14, 21, 46; Congregational churches in, 22

Indiana University, 265

Indians, 241; within the United States, 51; Congregational missions to, 51–63; missions to, by all American churches, 52, 340; removal of, 55; customs of, 61; education of, 342, 348, 350, 354, 361; character of, 349; sentiment of, toward whites, 349, 353; school fund of, 361; depredations of, 363, 366; fighting among, on reservation, 366–67

Infant baptism, 129

Intemperance, 378

Interpreters, 344

Iowa, territory of, 14; Congregationalism in, 39–42; Congregational Association in, 223–24

"Iowa Band," 41

Irreligion, 299; publications of, 315

Jackson, Michigan, 33; church of, 339

Jacksonville, Illinois, 26, 157, 167; church of, 27, 127, 161, 171, 173, 180, 185, 207, 209, 233, 277; synod at, 256

James, Dr., 344; knowledge of Chippewa language of, 346

Jefferson College, 107
Jenney, Elisha, 234
Jewett, Merrick A., 22
Joliet, Illinois: growth of, 231; church of, 275

Kalamazoo, Michigan, 33
Kennedy, W. S., *The Plan of Union*, quoted, 17
Kenosha, Wisconsin, 35
Kent, Aratus, 25, 34, 231, 233, 254, 282
Kentucky, 56; population from, 231, 258, 261
Kingsbury, Cyrus, 51, 356
Kingsbury, Nathaniel, letter of, 380–81
Kirby, William, 27, 28, 39, 176, 195, 200, 204, 219, 224, 225, 234, 245, 254, 256; antislavery sermon by, 205
Knox College, 29, 233
Knoxville, Illinois, church of, 284

Lacon, Illinois, church of, 267, 268, 277
Lac qui Parle, Minnesota, 355, 366
LaHarp, Illinois, church in, 174, 202
Lake County, Illinois, churches of, 278
Lake Harriet, Minnesota, mission at, 363, 364
Lake Michigan: an entry for population, 231; Indians, on 343; region of, 385
Lake Mills, Wisconsin, 369, 392
Lake Superior: Indians on, 341, 342; mission to, 341
Lancaster Presbytery, 21
Lane Theological Seminary, 265, 267
Lapeer Centre, Michigan, church of, 312, 316, 324, 326
LaPointe, Michigan: church of, 341; school at, 342, 343
Lausanne, Switzerland, 219
Lawlessness, 179
Lawton, John, letter of, to A.H.M.S., 176
Lee, Jason, Methodist missionary, 57

Leoni, Michigan, church of, 338
Leslie, Jonathan, 93, 97, 107, 111, 112, 113, 115; licensing of, 90–92
Lewiston, Illinois, church of, 234
Liberator, Garrison's, 246
Library, 165, 191
Lincoln, Abraham, 26
Lincoln, General, 4
Lippincott, Thomas, 226
Lockport, Illinois, church of, 152, 275
Long Grove, Illinois, church of, 165, 175; letter by trustees of, to A.H.M.S., 175
Louisiana, 46
Lovejoy, Elijah P., 26, 261; "martyrdom" of, 178; shot, 261, 277; and slavery, 261
Lovejoy, Owen, 26, 277, 281
Lowell, Illinois, church of, 281
Lutherans, 266
Lutheran Synod of Pennsylvania, 186
Lyman, O., 278
Lyons, Iowa, 41
Lyons, Luke, 223
Lyonsville, Illinois, church of, 275

McCoy, Isaac, Baptist missionary, 55
McCurtain, Oklahoma, 360
McEwen, Abel, 311, 318, 319, 320, 330
McHenry, Illinois, church of, 399
Mackinac, Michigan, church of, 324, 331
Mackinaw, Michigan, mission at, 341, 343, 344, 347
McMillan, John 68, 98, 107; letter of, 90–92
Macomb County, Michigan, 286; conference of churches in, 308, 313
Madison, Ohio, church of, 106; formation of, 106–15, covenant of, 110, regulations of, 113–15, ministers of, 115
Madison, Wisconsin, church of, 389, 396
Mahan, Asa, 19

Maine, 13, 46, 47; Congregational churches of, in 1800, 9; Congregational associations in, adopt Plan of Union, 16; conference of Congregational churches in, 171

Maine Missionary Society, 45, 46, 47, 100

Marietta, Ohio, 68; church of, 20, 21, 71

Marsh, Cutting, 34, 54, 340, 356, 358, 363; letter of, to A.B.C.F.M., 352–55

Marshall, Michigan, church at, 32, 332; presbytery of, 339

Massachusetts, 46; adoption of the federal Constitution by, 4; Congregational churches of, 8; Congregational associations of, adopt Plan of Union, 16; Indians of, 43

Massachusetts Missionary Magazine, 45

Massachusetts Missionary Society, 45, 100; little influence of, in the West, 47

Maumee Indians, Ohio mission to, 55; given up in 1835, 57

Mayhews, the, 43

Mazakootamane, Paul, 62

Mendon, Illinois, church of, 26–27, 210, 214, 221, 234

Menominee Indians, intemperance of, 352

Merrill, Sareno T., 383

Methodists, 11, 39, 74, 167, 174, 250, 258, 266, 277, 311, 316, 333, 376, 377; and compulsory support of Congregational clergy, 10; and Jeffersonian party, 10; increase in numbers of, in Illinois, 232; circuit of, 286, 287; missionaries of, to Creeks, 350

Michigan, 14, 88, 340; Congregationalism in, 29–33; General Association of, 33; Congregational churches in, 33, early Congregationalism in, 285; immigration to, 286, 330; presbytery of, 292; education in, 310, 311, 313; destitute churches in, 330; Association of Congregational Churches, 334, 339

Michigan City, Indiana, 22, 28; church at, 165

Middlebury College, 27, 308

Middle States, the, immigrants from, 270, 276

Military District, the, 187

Millburn (Mechanic's Grove), Illinois, church of 275, 278

Mills, Samuel J., 22

Milwaukee, 379, 373, 379, 384; presbytery of, 34; churches of 387, 399

Mineral Point, Wisconsin, church at, 37, 389

Ministers, 191, 394; ordination of, 161, 168; letter of, to A.H.M.S., 175; examination of, 197, 220, 225; licensing of, 370; clothing for, 378; calls for, 385, 397

Minnesota, 59, 62; Congregational pioneers in, 42; movement of population into, 62

Minor, Jesse, 352

Mission family, expenses of, 351, 358-59

Mission Institute: No. 1, church at, 186, 188, 189, 193; No. 4, 209; No. 11, 209, 212

Missionaries: support of, 36, 47, 124, 174, 187, 203, 259, by A.H.M.S., 175; sacrifices of, 36; ordaining and commissioning of, 82–85; busy life of, 176; the early, 179; supply of, 183; on the frontier, 183, 190; difficulties of, 190, 191; labor of, 198; letters of, 231, 340; little respect for Baptist and Methodist by Congregational and Presbyterian, 257; scarcity of, 263–64, 329, 333; frontier hospitality to, 264, 285; radicalism of, 281; letters and reports from, 1825–42, 285; little cash for, 309; as evangelists, 328; work of wives of, 345; orthodoxy of, 394

Missionary Herald, 45; circulation of, 197

Missionary magazines, 45

Missionary Society of Connecticut, 77; organization of, 67; trustees of, 68, 83, request permission to raise funds for work in new settlements, 74–76, and permission granted, 76–77; report of, to June, 1802, 86–90

Missions: foreign and domestic, 135; plan of operation of, 343; expenses of, 364–65; anti-Catholic motive in, 381–82

Mississippi River, 198; population from region of, 231

Missouri, 48, 56; slave power in, 261

Miter, J. J., 284

Monmouth, Illinois, church of, 186

Montague, M., letter of, 402–4

Montgomery, William, letter of, to A.B.C.F.M., 348–51

Monticello Female Seminary, 25, 267

Moral decline, throughout New England, 8

Morals, laxity in, 5

Morgan County, Illinois, 157

Mormonism: spread of, 190; opposition to, 191

Mormons, 164, 174, 250; departure of, from Missouri, 190

Morris, B. F., 200, 224; letter of, to A.H.M.S., 191

Munson's Settlement, church of, 301

Murdock, C. E., 200; letter of, to A.H.M.S., 198

Muskingum Association, 21

Naperville, Illinois, 132, 147; church of, 154, 233, 275, 278; see also Du Page, Illinois

Nelson, David, 188, 189, 193, 212, 220

New Connecticut. See Western Reserve

New England, 104, 202; Baptists in, 3; Congregationalism in, 3, 14; Episcopalian parishes in, 3; Quakers in, 3; population of, at close of Revolution, 3; clergy of, influence in winning independence, 4; churches of, impoverished by the war, 5; communities of, state of religion in average, 7; population of, 9; expansion of, and contribution to other states, 13; immigrants from, in Ohio, 18; life of, poured into the West, 23; immigrants from, in Michigan, 33, 35, in Wiscon-

sin, 38; organized groups from, in Mendon, Illinois, 232, 246; population from, 270, 368, predominant, 231

New Haven, 7; Western Association of, 171; East Association of, 234

New London, Iowa, 40

New Ripley, Ohio, 357

New School party, 156

New School Presbyterian churches, 63

New settlements, address to the inhabitants of, 68–71

New York City, First Presbyterian Church of, 351

New York Evangelist, 213, 218

New York State, 14, 45, 46, 86, 104; increase of population in, 1790–1820, 13; migration of New England people to, 13; Plan of Union in, 16; Indian mission in, 55; organized groups from, 232, 315; immigration from, 368

Newhall, Horatio, 232

Newton, Illinois, church of, 187

Nichols, P. W., letter of, 379–80

Nichols, R. H., on Plan of Union, 16

Nichols, Warren, 162; letter of, to A.H.M.S., 166, 190

North Carolina, population from, 231

Northampton, Massachusetts, settlers from, in Princeton, Illinois, 232

Norton, A. G., letter of, to A.H.M.S., 174

Norway, immigrants from, 391

Oakwood, Michigan, church of, 330

Oberlin College, 18; and the Congregational-Presbyterian situation, 19

Oberlin Seminary, 36; in bad repute with both Congregationalists and Presbyterians, 20; strongly antislavery, 20; theology of, 36

Objibewa Indians, 364, 366; mission to, 54

Ohio, 14, 22, 45, 285, 355; Congregationalism in, 20, 21; presbytery of, 80, 97, 98; population from, 246

Ohio Company, 20

Old School Presbyterians, 36; churches of, 63, 156

Oklahoma, 340, 348

Orange Association, Illinois, 195

Orchard Lake, Michigan, church of, 304, 323, 325, 328, 329

Ordway, Moses, 34

Oregon Indians, mission to, 57; closed, 58

Osage Indians, 348–51; missions to, in Arkansas and Missouri, 54; mission to, abandoned, 56

Otherday, John, 62

Ottawa, Illinois: growth of, 232; church of, 234, 244, 267; presbytery of, 276

Paine, Thomas, *Age of Reason*, published, 6

Paint Creek, Michigan, church at, 326

Panoplist, 45

Parker, Daniel, 261

Parsons, B. F., letter of, 401–2

Parsons, J. U., letter of, to A.H.M.S., 371–72

Patterson, R. W., 236, 274

Paw Paw Grove, Illinois, church of, 276

Payson, Illinois, church of, 186, 194, 198, 209, 211, 224

Peet, Leister, 116

Peet, Stephen, 36, 371, 372, 373, 379, 380; outstanding in Wisconsin Congregational history, 37–39; letters of, 384–89, 396–401; estimate of, 402–4

Pekin, Illinois, church of, 262

Pennoyer, A. L., 188, 200; letter of, to A.H.M.S., 165

Pennsylvania, 14, 45, 46, 86

Peoria, Illinois, church of, 251, 259, 277, 284

Perfectionism, 20

Perkins, Nathan, 7

Peru, Illinois, church of, 281

Peterboro, New York, mission donation from, 364

Peters, Absalom, 104, 250, 286, 291, 292, 294, 295, 301, 303, 306, 312, 316, 319, 320, 323, 324

Pickering, John, originator of orthography for Chippewa, 347

Pierce, John D., 31, 311, 332, 334, 336

Pike Grove, Wisconsin, church of, 389

Pilgrim Fathers, 42

Pine Lake, Michigan, church of, 302, 304

Pittsfield, Illinois, church of, 209, 223, 234

Plainfield, Illinois, church of, 244, 280

Plan of Union, 22, 34, 35, 106, 113, 156, 255; adopted, 15; provisions of, 15; in New York, 16; in Western Reserve of Ohio, 17; and A.H.M.S., 49; advantageous to Presbyterians, 232–33; churches of, importance of slavery issue in, 272, discouragement in, 277; operation of, 368; as proposed by presbytery of Milwaukee, 369, 375

Platteville, Wisconsin, church of, 389

Pleasant Grove, Illinois, church of, 248, 250, 259, 267, 277, 284

Pond, Samuel, 60; and Gideon, 59, 62

Pontiac, Michigan, church of, 31, 285; Presbyterian church of, 291, 293, 294, 297, 300, 318, 319; Congregational church of, 294, 296, 298, 303, 305, 320, 322, dispute with Ruggles, 293

Population: movement of, from New England into New York, 9, 13; movement of, into Illinois, 231; immigrants in, 232

Porter, Amasa, 84

Porter, Jeremiah, 25, 116, 127, 150, 233, 242, 245, 251, 259, 269, 275; letter of, 372–74

Porter, John, letter of, to A.H.M.S., 281

Porter, Jonathan, 278

Porter, Josiah, 265

Post, Truman M., 224

Potosi, Wisconsin, 37

Prairie du Chien, Wisconsin, 356

Prairie du Sac, Wisconsin, 369, 379

Prairieville, Wisconsin, 397

Pratt, Levi, 314, 315

Prayer meetings, 122, 166

Prentiss, J. H., 154, 155, 231, 276, 283

"Presbygational," 18

Presbyterian church, 104, 106, 187; General Assembly of, adopts Plan of Union, 15; division in, in 1837, 34; in Wisconsin in 1839, 34

Presbyterian and Congregational Convention of Wisconsin: formation of in 1840, 35; change of, to Congregational and Presbyterian Convention in 1874, 36

Presbyterian polity, 32

Presbyterianism, 14, 270, 285; on Western Reserve, 18; controversy within, 32; foundations of, in Illinois, 233; antiabolitionist, 272; Old School, found independent churches, 277; orthodox, not co-operative, 291; opposition to orthodox, 315; Old School, support of missionaries, 396; New School, fellowship with Congregationaliss, 398

Presbyterians, 167, 208; wide distribution of, 11; increase of, in the Western Reserve, 19

Presbytery: of Ottawa, 171; of Schuyler, 171, 172, 215, 220; of Orange, N.B., 172; of Cincinnati, 188; of Buffalo, 189; of Angelica, New York, 193, 220; of Missouri, 193; of Champlain, New York, 220; of Illinois, 223; of Philadelphia, 359

President and Society for the Propagation of the Gospell in New England, 43

Prince, Erie, 298

Princeton, Illinois, church of, 234, 247, 277, 281

Princeton Theological Seminary, 38

Profanity, 95

Protracted meeting, 131, 303, 309

Putnam, Rufus, 68, 71

Quakers, 74, 250

Quincy, Illinois, 39; church of, 25, 166, 171, 173, 184, 189, 193, 195, 202, 208, 213, 221, 224; antislavery conflict in, 206

Rawson, Andrew, 112

Ray, Michigan, church of, 310, 312

Reason the Only Oracle of Man, by Ethan Allen, first real anti-Christian work in America, 6

Reed, Julius A., 39, 40, 200; letter of, to A.H.M.S., 173, 191; loss of pastorate by, over slavery issue, 207

Religion: decline of, throughout New England, 5; narrative of the state of, 181, 190; neglect of, 190, 191; state of, 212; apathy for, 322; low state of, 326; prosperous state of, in Wisconsin, 373

Religious experience, relation of, required for church membership, 129

Religious periodical, 192, 196, 208; need of, in Illinois, 226

Religious Repository, 45

Religious tracts, 121, 123, 314

Revivalism, 321; emphasized in Illinois, 256; in protracted meetings, 260, 265, 266, 267

Revivals, 388, 389, 404

Revolution, the, 3

Rhode Island, 46; Congregational churches in, in 1790, 9

Rhode Island Missionary Society, 45, 47

Rice, B. H., 307

Richardson, Sanford, 260

Riggs, Stephen R., 60, 62

Rochester, Michigan, church of, 31, 292, 301, 305, 309, 311

Rochester, Wisconsin, 390

Rock Creek, Illinois, church of, 277

Rock Island, Illinois, 356, 358

Rock River Association, Illinois, 188, 196, 202, 281

Rockford, Illinois, church of, 279

Rockwell, D., 280

Roman Catholics, 174, 208

Romeo, Michigan, church of, 31, 305, 308, 309, 311, 312, 313, 314

Round Prairie, Illinois, church of, 171, 172, 181, 185, 195, 198, 202, 207, 221, 224

Ruggles, Isaac, 29, 31, 287, 289, 290, 291, 292, 293, 294, 296, 297, 299, 300, 301, 302, 303, 305, 306, 307, 308, 323, 325, 326, 327, 328, 329, 330, 331

Sabbath, the, 164, 165, 174; decline of Puritan, 7; breaking of, 95; observance of, 96; resolution for observance of, 178

Sabbath schools, 165–66, 191, 197, 198, 260, 270, 282, 314, 315, 316, 317, 323, 326, 376, 377; hymnbooks for, 121, 379; committee on, 200

Sac Indians, 355, 358

St. Clair, Michigan, church of, 311

St. Louis Observer, 164

Saint Mary's, Illinois, church in, 174, 176, 181, 185, 198, 206

Sampson, Guy C., 181, 200, 204; ejected by Congregational Association of Illinois, 206

Sand Prairie, Illinois, church of, 253, 262, 267

Sangamon County, Illinois, presbytery of, 267, 277

Sault Ste Marie, church in, 242, 344

Saybrook Platform, 12

Schools, 94, 250, 266, 310–13; Indian, 343, 346, 350, 354

Scotland, letters from churches of, 329

Scott, Abraham, 68; report of, 92–99

Separation of church and state, 10

Shaw, Luther, 308, 309, 310, 311, 312, 313, 314, 315, 316, 324

Sherman, D. A., 386, 389; letters of, 374–79

Shiloh Prairie, Illinois, 176

Silver Lake, Michigan, church of, 302, 304, 306

Singing school, 166, 190

Sioux Indians, 219

Skepticism, tendency toward, 5

Slavery, 177–78, 196, 198, 210; resolutions of Illinois Association on, 216–17, 246, 261, 271, 273, 274, 376, 395; committee on, majority and minority reports of, 201

Smith, David, 190, 272

Smith, Joseph, 190

Society, improvement in, 262

Society for Promotion of Collegiate and Theological Education at the West, 25

Society for Propagating Christian Knowledge of Edinburgh, 352

Socinians, 312

South, the, population from, 231

South Carolina, 355

South Port, Wisconsin, 368, 371; church of, 389

South Prairieville, Wisconsin, 369, 380; church of, 381, 389

Southern states, the, 104

Spalding, H. H., 57

Spillman, Benjamin B., 254

Spring, Gardiner, minister of the Brick Presbyterian Church in New York, 49

Springfield, Illinois, church of, 234, 254, 277

Springfield, Michigan, church of, 323

Statesburg, Michigan, 352

Stephens, Jedediah, 340; letter of, to A.B.C.F.M., 363–67

Stiles, Ezra, 3, 6

Stockbridge Indians, 34, 352–55, 358; mission to, 54; school fund of, 354

Story, Daniel, 21, 71

Strong, Cyprian, 84

Strong, Eliphalet, 133, 135, 145, 146

Strong, Nathan, 90

Sturtevant, J. M., 28, 157, 158, 223, 234, 256

Superior, Michigan, 88

Swedish Lutherans, letters from ministers of, to A.H.M.S., 26

Synod: of Western Reserve, 20; of Wisconsin, 36; of Pittsburgh, 92, 113, 119; of Illinois, committee of, on Christian Union, 211, 214

Taper, the, recommended, 226

Taylor, N. T., 311

Taylor, Nathaniel W., influence of, in theology, 255

Tazewell County, Illinois, churches of, 234

Tecumseh, Illinois, church of, 238

Temperance, 192, 244, 249, 260, 264, 279, 313, 322, 376, 378; report on, 199

Temperance Herald, 199

Temperance societies, 165, 191, 242, 244, 314, 326, 329, 378; delegates from, 192, 203; opposed by Baptists and Christians, 261, 282

Tennessee, 46, 56; Presbytery of the Western District of, 176

Terre Haute, Indiana, 22

Terrysville, Illinois, ecclesiastical council at, 195

Theology, 175; Hopkinsian, 80; New School and Old School, 255, 270, 272; relation to slavery views, 256

Thompson, Seymour, 275

Thornton, Illinois, church of, 275

Towner, James, 134

Tract Society, 175, 287; Female Tract Society, 288, 314

Traders, relations of, with missionaries, 343, 347

Treadwell, John, 71

Trowbridge, Stephen P. R., 291, 292, 300, 301

Troy Grove, Illinois, church of, 281

Troy, Wisconsin, 35; Congregational Convention in, 368, 369, 371, 373

Turner, Asa, 25, 27, 39, 40, 158, 159, 162, 163, 183, 185, 193, 200, 204, 206, 223, 225, 233, 234; agent for Iowa, 41; delegate to ecclesiastical council at the East, 174; opposed as pastor, 194

Turner, J. B., 224

Union Grove, Illinois, church of, 245, 246, 254

Union meeting, 312

Union Mission, Oklahoma, church at, 348

Union Seminary, 36

Unionists, 280

Unitarians, 174, 208

United Domestic Missionary Society, 31, 49, 285, 291

United Foreign Missionary Society, 341; establishment of Union Mission by, 348

United States, the, in 1815, 51

United States government: treaty of, with Indians, 55; annuity of, to Indians, 363; Indian agent of, 365

Universalists, 164, 174, 209, 266, 276, 312, 315, 321

Upper Mississippi, Indians of the, 355–60

Vaill, William S., 348

Vermont, 6, 13, 27, 37, 45, 46, 87, 89, 90, 106; Congregational church in, at close of Revolution, 9; Congregational associations in, adopt Plan of Union, 15; settlers from, 232; organized groups from, 315, 336

Vermont Missionary Society, 45, 47

Vermontville, Michigan, church of, 336

Virginia, 46; population from, 231

Vorhiis, Jacob, 292, 297, 298, 300

Walker's Grove, church of, 165

Walworth County, Wisconsin, 381, 382

Warner, Calvin, 37, 400

Warsaw, Illinois, church of, 39, 173, 174, 180, 187, 193, 195, 202, 204, 205, 207, 209, 210

Washington, George, 4

Washington, Illinois, church of, 251, 259, 261, 277

Washington, Michigan, church of, 301

Watertown, Wisconsin, 369; church of, 401

Watson, Cyrus L., 39, 282

Waukesha, Wisconsin, 35, 37, 381

Waynesville, Illinois, church of, 265

Wells, Milton, letter of, 390–92

Wells, Noah N., 289, 301, 306, 307, 314, 325, 327

West, the, education in, 233; Presbyterian church of, 246

West Pontiac, Michigan, church of, 302, 304

Western Reserve, the, 68, 73, 77, 98, 106, 113

Wheelock, Oklahoma, 360

White Lake, Michigan, church of, 323

Whitman, Marcus, 57; murder of, 58

Whittemore, George, 293, 294

Whittlesey, William, 181, 184, 185, 200

Wick, William, 80

Wickedness, 164

Will County, Illinois, churches of, 275

Williams, Aaron, 294, 320, 321, 322, 323

Williams, Loring S., Cherokee missionary, 51, 360, 362

Williams, Nathan, 83

Williamson, Thomas S., 60, 62, 63, 340; traveling expenses of Indian tour, 355–60

Williston, Seth, 86, 89

Wilmington, Illinois, church of, 275

Winchester, Illinois, church of, 195

Wing Lake, Michigan, church of, 301, 326

Wisconsin, 14, 267; Congregationalists in, 33–38, 368, 369, 371; Congregational and Presbyterian churches in, in 1839, 34, 35; Congregational churches organized in, in 1840, 34; Waupace reservation in, 352; Presbyterian and Congregational Convention of, 368, 372, 373, 374, 375, 376, 387; churches in, 372; ministers in, 373, 387; intemperance in, 378; temperance journal in, 378; articles of union proposed by Presbyterians in, 379; Roman Catholics in, 381–82; increased population of, 385; progress of religious institutions in, in 1839, 386, in 1844, 386–87; state of religion in, 392–96, 396–401

Wisconsin River, 380

Woodburne, Illinois, church of, 195, 222

Wood Lake, battle of, 62

Woodville, Illinois, church of, 186

Woodward, James W., 86, 87, 88

Worcester, S. A., 56

Wright, Royal N., 278; letter of, to A.H.M.S., 279

Wyandot Indians, 88

"Yale Band," 23, 25, 26, 27, 159, 233; members of, 234, 242

Yale College, 8, 14, 37, 39, 40, 234, 244, 267, 287, 318, 355, 400

Yale Divinity School, 33, 36, 39, 40, 233, 245, 318

"Yankee method," 401

Youngstown, Ohio, 80, 81

Ypsilanti, Michigan, church at, in 1829, 31

Zorbaugh, Charles L., quoted, 17